Judging Insanity, Punishing Difference

The Cultural Lives of Law

Edited by Austin Sarat

Judging Insanity, Punishing Difference

A History of Mental Illness in the Criminal Court

Chloé Deambrogio

Stanford University Press

Stanford, California

Stanford University Press
Stanford, California

Printed in the United States of America on acid-free, archival-quality paper

Library of Congress Cataloging-in-Publication Data
Names: Deambrogio, Chloé, author.
Title: Judging insanity, punishing difference : a history of mental illness in the criminal court / Chloé Deambrogio.
Other titles: Cultural lives of law.
Description: Stanford, California : Stanford University Press, 2023. | Series: The cultural lives of law | Based on author's thesis (doctoral - University of Oxford, 2020) issued under title: The mind on trial : mental illness and capital punishment in America's highest execution state. | Includes bibliographical references and index.
Identifiers: LCCN 2023006427 (print) | LCCN 2023006428 (ebook) | ISBN 9781503630321 (cloth) | ISBN 9781503637368 (ebook)
Subjects: LCSH: Insanity (Law)—Texas—History—20th century. | Criminal liability—Texas—History—20th century. | Insanity defense—Texas—History—20th century. | Forensic psychiatry—Texas—History—20th century. | Capital punishment—Texas—History—20th century.
Classification: LCC KFT1766.6 .D43 2023 (print) | LCC KFT1766.6 (ebook) | DDC 345.764/04—dc23/eng/20230713
LC record available at https://lccn.loc.gov/2023006427
LC ebook record available at https://lccn.loc.gov/2023006428

Cover design: Daniel Benneworth-Gray
Cover art: William Kieckhofel, *Balance Scales*, 1940, The National Gallery of Art. Digitally enhanced by RawPixel.
Typeset by Elliott Beard in Adobe Garamond Pro 11/14.5

For Scott, Julian, and Angelica
with love

Contents

Tables

Acknowledgments

Judging Insanity, Punishing Difference is the culmination of years of meticulous archival research, started during my time as a doctoral student at the University of Oxford's Centre for Criminology. It has followed me through many wonderful, yet challenging, stages of my life, including the birth of my two young children, three international relocations, and my first professional experiences as an early career researcher. Its publication represents, in many senses, the end of an era for me.

As with many works of this kind, this book would not have been possible without the advice and support of many inspiring individuals, to whom I wish to express my gratitude. A deeply felt thank-you goes to my incredible husband, Scott, for discussing every detail of this project with me, reading and commenting on uncountable drafts, and encouraging me to never give up, even under the most difficult circumstances. My darling, I could not have completed this book without your loving support and personal sacrifices, and for this I will be eternally grateful. A special thank-you also goes to our wonderful children, Julian and Angelica, for their unconditional love throughout this long and demanding process. Thank you, little ones, for inspiring me, completing me, and grounding me in time and place.

My deepest gratitude also goes to my family and friends for their unwavering support during this intellectual journey. I am especially grateful to my sister, Bianca, my mother, Jessica, my father, Nanni, and my grandmothers, Anita and Floriana, for always offering a listening ear and firmly believing in my vision at every stage of this project. A warm thank-you also goes to my dear friends Jasmina Arnež, Annalisa Betella, Sophie Evekink, Larisa Lara, Pablo Cogis, Viviana Perego, Ranu Sinha, César Giraldo Herrera, and Haris Krijestorac for the stimulating discussions, mutual support, and moments of joy we have shared over the years. While lands and oceans separate us, you are always close to my heart.

I have been extremely fortunate to be able to complete this book in the wonderful academic environment provided by Merton College, Oxford. A special thank-you goes to the former warden of the college, Professor Irene Tracey, for believing in my project and offering me the opportunity to bring it to fruition among Merton's inspiring community of scholars. Further thanks go to my mentor, Professor Jennifer Payne, for her helpful professional advice and ongoing encouragement as I revised this manuscript over the past year.

I am also grateful to the inspiring academics from the University of Oxford's Centre for Criminology, who encouraged me to develop my ideas, push my boundaries, and cultivate my voice as an author. A special thank-you goes to my supervisor, Professor Carolyn Hoyle, for her insightful feedback and intellectual guidance as I completed the ambitious research project on which this book is based. Further thanks go to my thesis examiners, Professors Lucia Zedner, Nicola Lacey, and Mary Bosworth, for helping me clarify my theoretical approach and methodology through their constructive criticisms and thought-provoking suggestions.

Finally, I wish to thank all the dedicated professionals who have helped me bring this project to life. In particular, I wish to thank the archivists of the Texas State Library and Archives Commission and the clerks of the Texas Court of Criminal Appeals for helping me identify and locate the archival sources used in this book; my editor at Stanford University Press, Marcela Maxfield, for believing in this project and supporting me through the various stages leading to its publication; the anonymous peer reviewers for helping me improve the manuscript through their insightful feedback and comments; and my copyeditor, Mimi Braverman, for helping me refine my writing style with her meticulous edits.

My thoughts and compassion go to the victims and families affected by the violent crimes discussed in this book and to the mentally ill defendants who suffered violence at the hands of the state.

Introduction

> The study of man from the physiologic standpoint has an undoubted tendency to make him, in the eyes of his investigator, a creature of forces beyond its control. Man in this aspect ceases to be a free agent in the eyes of the student. . . . It will hardly be denied that the tendency of psycho-physical study of man must be towards a denial of spirit. Law, on the other hand, stands pre-eminently for the freedom of the will. Without this as a foundation-stone juridic science has no existence, for the very test of juridic responsibility is man's power of choice. To this the juridic philosopher brings the sentiment of humanity, the teachings of metaphysics and the experience of history, which are repugnant to the physical measurement of the soul; he contends that after you have taken man's brains to pieces you have not yet found his mind; that molecular interaction may be demonstrated as the physical counterpart of thought, but it is no thought.[1]
>
> —GINO SPERANZA

Gino Speranza, a little-known lawyer from the state of New York, was ahead of his time when, in 1901, he started advocating for an alliance between the behavioral sciences of his day and the criminal law. His hope was that by joining forces, forensic psychiatrists, judges, and attorneys could reach a fuller understanding of the human mind and offer a solution to the problem of criminal behavior that was concerning American citizens. At the time of his writing, legal professionals in the United States were gradually recognizing the breakthroughs made in the behavioral sciences and were hoping that their principles and insights "would lead to the rehabilitation of those criminals who were not biologically, or otherwise, beyond salvation."[2] However, legal commentators were unwilling to accept the fundamental premise of the new "rehabilitative penology," namely, that all behavior has an organic cause and that humans, especially if afflicted by a mental health condition, are not responsible for their conduct. The cultural traditions of common law lawyers prevented them from embracing the deterministic assumptions that informed much scientific writing in fin de siècle America, hindering the full assimilation of psychiatric principles into legal doctrines of criminal responsibility.

In this book I explore how the rise of the new behavioral sciences embraced by Speranza in 1901 shaped American courts' assessments of defendants' mental health and criminal responsibility over the twentieth century. During this period, research into the pathological roots of criminal behavior, along with legal discussions about the relevance of such inquiries for courts' evaluations of offenders' moral blameworthiness, underwent a series of paradigmatic shifts that warrant close scholarly attention. New psychiatric notions of the mind and its readability, legal doctrines of insanity and diminished culpability, and cultural stereotypes about race and gender shaped the ways in which legal professionals, mental health experts, and lay witnesses approached mental disability evidence, especially in cases carrying the death penalty. Using Texas as a case study, I examine how these medical, legal, and cultural trends informed psycho-legal debates in state criminal courts, while shedding light on the ways in which experts and lay actors' interpretations of "pathological" mental states influenced trial verdicts in capital cases. I show that, despite mounting pressures from advocates of the "new" rehabilitative penology, Texas courts maintained a punitive approach toward defendants allegedly affected by severe mental disabilities, while allowing for moralized views about personalities, habits, and lifestyle to influence psycho-legal assessments, in potentially prejudicial ways.

A New Look at an Old Debate

Texas has historically played a central role in the American death penalty debate, both for its high execution rates and for its punitive approach to mentally disabled capital defendants. Recent reports suggest that the state has executed about 30 individuals with long histories of paranoid schizophrenia and other severe mental illnesses since resuming executions in 1982, and that 15–20% of Texas's death row inmates receive ongoing psychiatric treatment.[3] Similarly, current estimates show that the Texas Court of Criminal Appeals (TCCA) has overturned at least 19 death sentences imposed on individuals affected by intellectual disabilities since the

U.S. Supreme Court ruled in *Atkins v. Virginia* that the execution of such individuals was unconstitutional.[4] These numbers are especially concerning if one considers that Texas has consistently ranked first for number of death sentences and executions in the modern era of capital punishment, taking 573 prisoners to the death chamber as of 2022.[5]

Forensic psychiatrists and legal scholars argue that the reason for Texas's punitive approach to mentally ill defendants is that the state's courts tend to rely on outdated clinical criteria and stereotypes without scientific foundation in their mental incapacity evaluations. For example, scholars have taken issue with the state's reliance on a modified version of the English *M'Naghten* rules, a narrow test of legal insanity that requires defendants seeking criminal exculpation to prove that, at the time of the charged offense, they did not know that their conduct was wrong because of a mental disease or defect.[6] According to critics, although the "right and wrong" test is generally problematic because of its exclusive focus on the defendant's cognitive capacities,[7] Texas's version of the rules is even more troubling because it limits the legal protection to those who, at the time of the alleged offense, did not understand that their act was "legally" rather than just "morally" wrong—a significantly higher threshold.[8]

Scholars have similarly criticized Texas's capital sentencing statute of 1976 for asking jurors to base their sentencing decision on an assessment of the defendant's future dangerousness, while failing to provide a procedural mechanism that would allow them to give effect to the mitigating evidence presented by the defense.[9] As argued by the U.S. Supreme Court in *Penry v. Lynaugh*, this sentencing structure forces jurors to ask whether a defendant's mental health problems increases his or her likelihood to engage in future violent conduct, rather than whether it should prompt a more compassionate legal response based on a consideration of the defendant's medical history.[10] Given people's tendency to falsely perceive the mentally ill as more violent and unpredictable and therefore more dangerous than the healthy population, Texas's capital sentencing scheme has turned mental health evidence into a "two-edged sword" that increases rather than decreases a defendant's likelihood to receive a death sentence.[11] Although the Texas legislature amended its capital sentencing scheme to include a special mitigation instruction in 1991,[12] until the early 2000s Texas courts continued to either deny a defendant's right to such instruction or allow jurors to consider the defendant's mitigating evidence as an aggravating factor at sentencing.[13]

Psychiatrists and criminal lawyers have importantly highlighted the contradictions and pitfalls of current insanity doctrines and capital sentencing frameworks, both in Texas and elsewhere. Taking a normative approach to the issue, they have advocated different interpretations or changes to the *M'Naghten* rules,[14] argued for reforms to states' capital sentencing laws,[15] and proposed an extension of the constitutional exemption from capital punishment to severely mentally ill defendants.[16] Although these normative approaches shed light on the ethical, constitutional, and medical issues involved in the psycho-legal dispute, they are problematic insofar as they take for granted the underlying assumptions on which dominant notions of mental illness and criminal responsibility are based. In *Judging Insanity, Punishing Difference* I challenge this general trend and provide an original viewpoint from which to analyze the mental incapacity debate. Rather than taking a normative position in the discussion, in line with existing literature, I seek to deconstruct the wider processes that allowed such normativity to establish itself in the first place. Specifically, starting from a detailed sociological and historical analysis of American psycho-legal theory and Texas courtroom interactions, I strive to identify the deeper dynamics that underpinned the formation of specific understandings of mental illness and criminal responsibility over the twentieth century, and the ways in which these understandings in turn influenced the process of legal adjudication in capital cases.

Inspired by the postmodern challenge to Western Enlightenment philosophy,[17] I argue that rather than taking the dominant psycho-legal framework as the ultimate authority on issues of subjectivity, agency, and criminal accountability, one should see it as a subjective and partial interpretation of reality, which has acquired meaning and acceptance as it resonated with specific cultural codes shared by particular social groups.[18] To advance this claim, I embark on a fascinating historical journey through the archives of American forensic psychiatric publications, courtroom documents related to the trials of male capital defendants who raised mental incapacity claims (i.e., insanity and diminished responsibility), and social and cultural histories of forensic psychiatry and psychology and

U.S. penal practices. The aim of the historical investigation is to provide a counternarrative to the one that can be elicited from the exclusive reading of trial court records and appellate opinions, which draw a decontextualized picture of the lives of capital defendants and of the psycho-legal paradigms used to interpret their mental state for the establishment of criminal liability. The purpose of this counternarrative is to reveal the influences of political interests and cultural values on the ways in which defendants' mental health conditions were diagnosed, classified, and represented in twentieth-century death penalty trials, and to highlight the crucial role played by linguistic exchanges in constructing different interpretations of such conditions, regardless of their empirical reality.

Central Claims

In *Judging Insanity, Punishing Difference* I advance two central arguments. First, I show that even though the twentieth century has witnessed dramatic psychiatric and legal developments aimed at enhancing courts' understanding of defendants' mental health conditions and criminal behaviors, in Texas proceedings these changes have not led to more "scientific" assessments of defendants' mental health or to more "objective" evaluations of their criminal responsibility. On the contrary, I propose that despite their claims to scientific objectivity and legal neutrality, over the course of the twentieth century American psycho-legal theorists and Texas expert witnesses, defense attorneys, prosecutors, and appellate courts have consistently provided morally charged descriptions of mentally ill offenders that reveal a far from dispassionate approach. Second, I show that, although progressive medico-legal scholars have tried to advance more compassionate legal responses tailored to offenders' individual characteristics, in Texas courts these attempts have been consistently frustrated by a set of practical, tactical, and cultural obstacles that undermined the exculpatory or mitigating potential of the mental health evidence presented by the defense. In this section I summarize some of these obstacles and show that, rather than encouraging sympathetic legal responses, Texas trial actors helped to overshadow the human suffering that lay behind the criminal offenses, to increase the perception of dangerousness historically attached to the mentally ill, and to stigmatize the different and disenfranchised through stereotypical descriptions and diagnostic labels.

Let us begin with the practical level. As we will see, over the twentieth century defendants trying to advance insanity defenses and diminished culpability arguments in Texas courts faced two fundamental challenges. The first one concerns psychiatrists' epistemological and methodological limitations when dealing with individual cases. As the cases analyzed in this book will show, psychiatrists testifying in Texas proceedings often lacked the medical knowledge and/or professional skills to conduct thorough mental health evaluations and present evidence that went beyond superficial descriptions of symptoms and diagnostic labels. This descriptive approach significantly undermined their ability to advance convincing insanity and diminished culpability claims that required, or at least would have benefited from, an explanation of the mechanisms connecting defendants' mental "impairments" with their criminal conduct.[19] Moreover, even when defense experts tried to trace the complex mechanisms linking defendants' criminal acts to biological "defects" or childhood "traumas," their arguments tended to advance a defense of "irresistible impulse" rather than of "cognitive deficit," falling short of the rationalistic criteria established by Texas's "right and wrong" test.[20]

The second obstacle refers to the poor levels of legal representation typically offered to indigent capital defendants in this jurisdiction. As we will see, because of financial restrictions and low professional standards, court-appointed defense attorneys generally failed to investigate defendants' medical and social histories and to hire expert witnesses who could do justice to the mix of biological, social, and psychological factors that led to the criminal event.[21] Moreover, even when defense lawyers had the resources to call several expert witnesses to the stand, they tended to ask formulaic questions that failed to elicit explanatory accounts that could have supported the defendants' insanity claims and/or humanized them in the eyes of the jury. Finally, in several cases the defense attorneys presented expert witnesses who, by diagnosing the defendants with personality disorders associated with antisocial tendencies (rather than with a recognized medical pathology), reinforced the image of dangerousness and incorrigibility advanced by the prosecution, while undermining the defense's insanity and diminished culpability claims in the eyes of the jury.[22]

These problems were exacerbated by the trial tactics developed by the defense and the prosecution in cases involving mentally ill defendants. As we will see, throughout the twentieth century Texas attorneys used a series of strategies that, wittingly or unwittingly, essentialized capital defendants as inherently sick or evil, reinforcing the ontological assumptions that inclined jurors to impose death sentences. For example, Texas defense experts tended to link defendants' mental health problems and criminal acts to biological and psychological "defects" internal to the individual and to deemphasize the role of broader environmental influences (such as a history of racial oppression, socioeconomic disadvantage, and institutional failures) in prompting the defendant's "psychotic reactions" and criminal acts. This decontextualized view strengthened the individualist notion of personhood and responsibility advanced by the legal establishment, which, starting from the assumption that each person is responsible for their own "destiny," placed the blame for defendants' difficult life experiences, including histories of child abuse and neglect, on the defendants themselves, thus absolving society from its failures.[23]

Texas prosecutors took this decontextualization one step further, obscuring *any* reference to the defendants' difficult medical and social histories and turning the accused's criminal acts into the totality of their persona. To cloud the defendants' past, they relied heavily on legal instruments such as the "hypothetical question," which, by asking jurors to base their insanity evaluations on theoretical reconstructions of defendants' behavior around the time of the alleged offense, denied the relevance of defendants' medical history and focused jurors' attention on the narrow time frame of the criminal event.[24] To turn the accused's criminal acts into the totality of their being, they exploited psychiatric diagnoses such as psychopathy and antisocial personality disorder to argue that the crimes were a natural expression of the defendant's "true" character and inherent wickedness, rather than the tragic outcome of unfortunate life events.[25] Through these trial tactics, they portrayed defendants as one-dimensional beings devoid of any complexity and contradiction, whose whole personality and future potential could be inferred from, and indeed reduced to, their actions at the time of the offense.[26]

Finally, these tactical and practical obstacles were exacerbated by the value-laden language used by trial actors when conducting mental incapacity evaluations over the twentieth century. On the one hand, psychiatrists and legal actors affirmed their professional legitimacy by establishing apparently scientific and neutral standards to be followed in forensic mental health and criminal culpability assessments. On the other hand, they allowed racial and sexual stereotypes, along with moralizing views about habits and lifestyles, to infiltrate their descriptions of the defendants on trial, along with their conclusions regarding offenders' mental health, criminal culpability, and potential for future violence. As we will see, forensic psychiatrists and trial actors inspired by reactionary ideological frameworks (e.g., the puritan work ethic, Victorian codes of sexual morality, and racialized depictions of dangerousness) regularly pathologized individuals who deviated from shifting standards of appropriateness and "civility," often defined along gendered, racial, and socioeconomic lines. To accomplish this goal, they leveraged stigmatizing diagnostic labels (such as "sexual psychopathy" and "antisocial personality disorder"), which, because of their vague contours and historical malleability, could be reframed to include the personality traits, sexual inclinations, and social behaviors that American society perceived as most threatening to the status quo and therefore in need of being suppressed. State experts and prosecutors involved in Texas capital trials regularly exploited this tendency, weaponizing psychiatric conditions typically associated with immorality and antisocial tendencies against the accused, linking them with personality traits and characteristics that deviated from established standards of "male virtue,"[27] and appealing to public fears of "abnormality" and "difference" to secure death sentences.[28]

Contributions to the Field

In *Judging Insanity, Punishing Difference* I provide theoretical, empirical, and methodological contributions to the field. From a theoretical perspective I advance the critique of scientific positivism and Western Enlightenment principles developed by French postmodern philosophers and by theorists inspired by their approach.[29] Specifically, by revealing the historically contingent nature of representations of mental illness, criminality, masculinity, and blackness in psychiatrists and lay actors' accounts,

I further critical and cultural theorists' challenges to the biological and metaphysical foundations of scientific and legal categorizations[30] and to the positivistic approach that used to inform historical analyses of mental illness and crime in the modern era.[31] Instead of reducing the complexity of human life and behavior to simplistic categories or causes, as experts and lay actors in Texas proceedings tend to do, by deconstructing collective representations and practices through the analysis of individual discourses, I highlight the existence of multiple (and often hidden) points of view and celebrate diversity and complexity as opposed to universal truth.[32] In so doing, I provide a more nuanced and multifaceted understanding of reality, which considers the selective processes through which certain psycho-legal explanations and categories acquire authority and legitimacy as they further the professional interests of mental health experts and legal actors on the one hand, while mirroring society's moral frameworks on the other.

From an empirical point of view, I offer historical support to an existing body of work that has highlighted the difficulty of harmonizing psychiatry and the law's ontological and epistemological assumptions in court settings.[33] Throughout the twentieth century psychiatrists have described offenders as biological machines and/or psychological beings who engage in antisocial behavior as a result of "bad" genes, pathological psychosexual drives, and chemical imbalances, whereas Texas law has invariably depicted them as rational individuals who choose a certain course of action based on internal beliefs, intentions, and motivations. Although the medical approach has led psychiatrists to look for signs of insanity in defendants' bodies and minds, the folk-psychological[34] approach of the criminal law has prompted legal actors to look for it in defendants' behaviors.

This fundamental discrepancy has created a host of difficulties for clinicians who are asked to testify regarding defendants' ability to distinguish right from wrong at the time of the crime in insanity trials. As argued in Chapters 2 and 4, when defendants' behavior before, during, or after the commission of the offense suggested premeditation and/or an attempt at escaping punishment, the insanity defense was unlikely to be successful, no matter how strong the evidence of mental illness presented by the doctors. This finding advances the argument made by several medico-legal scholars who have suggested that the "right and wrong" test fails to consider the complexity of human feelings and behavior highlighted by the medical sciences, creating an almost insuperable barrier for severely mentally ill defendants seeking criminal exculpation.[35] Similarly, the analysis of post-1976 capital punishment cases confirms previous research that has stressed the difficulty of reconciling the theories and methods of psychiatry with the future dangerousness question that experts are asked to solve in Texas courts,[36] with dramatic consequences for the sentencing of mentally ill and intellectually disabled defendants in this jurisdiction.[37] Although other scholars have pointed to the incompatibility between legal and psychiatric understandings of human behavior, in *Judging Insanity, Punishing Difference* I offer a novel perspective on this dissonance by showing how it persists, in different ways, in three different eras of the history of psychiatry (the age of eugenics, the age of psychoanalysis, and the neobiological age of biochemistry).

Besides advancing our understanding of the conflicts between psychiatry and the law in court settings, the cultural analysis conducted in this book illuminates the subtle ways in which stereotypes about race, gender, and sexuality infiltrate experts and lay actors' accounts, both in the theoretical literature and in courtroom practice.[38] As we will see, racist assumptions about African Americans' low intelligence, pathological family dynamics, and propensity for future violence played a central role in psychiatrists and legal actors' accounts, shifting the public's attention from historical patterns of racial and political oppression to endogenous pathological tendencies attributable to genetic differences, negative parenting models, and an overall lack of civility. Similarly, the tendency to medicalize and criminalize behaviors typically associated with socioeconomic disadvantage—including alcohol and drug abuse, irregular employment patterns, and failures to fulfill family obligations—has contributed to reframe defendants' criminal acts as the results of inherent biological and personality defects, rather than of broader social issues. These tendencies have shaped public perceptions of the subjects' mental health, amenability to treatment, and potential for future violence in important ways and are therefore helpful in explaining, alongside the legal considerations outlined earlier, the judicial outcomes of the cases analyzed in this book.

Finally, from a methodological perspective my archival research sheds new light on the daily workings of local county courts and on lower-profile trials that traditionally escape the attention of legal scholars. In the United States, research on mental incapacity and the death penalty tends to focus on state and federal court opinions related to well-known cases that make news headlines for their striking characteristics and appellate histories.[39] In contrast, studies of unpublicized death penalty cases based on a close reading of the trial records are comparatively rare.[40] Scholars' exclusive focus on court opinions and notorious cases is problematic for two reasons. First, the focus on judicial opinions provides a necessarily partial account of the linguistic exchanges and courtroom dynamics that occur in death penalty cases that raise mental incapacity issues, filtered by the institutional perspective of the appellate courts and by the points of contention raised by the appellate lawyers. Second, by focusing exclusively on notorious cases reversed by the higher courts for striking procedural irregularities and constitutional violations,[41] legal researchers have overlooked the daily practices of local county courts, where the destinies of mentally incapacitated defendants are ultimately decided. Indeed, most cases of mentally incapacitated defendants tried in the lower courts will never reach the level of scrutiny dedicated to prominent cases. This is especially true in Texas, where both the TCCA and the Fifth Circuit[42] are reluctant to reverse lower court decisions, even when their practices deviate from the due process standards established by the U.S. Supreme Court.[43] Hence I propose that it is only by looking at the original transcripts of trial court proceedings that we can shed light on the arguments, narratives, and dynamics leading to the regular imposition of death sentences on mentally incapacitated defendants, unfiltered by the institutional perspective of the appellate courts and unmodified by the notoriety of the cases involved.

Texas and Beyond: A Note on Generalizability

At this point, readers may wonder whether the findings and arguments advanced in this book can be generalized to other contexts beyond Texas. This is an important question to address, especially given the local nature of the United States' capital punishment institution. Retentionist states across the country vary significantly in terms of death sentencing and execution patterns, capital punishment statutes and procedures, local penal cultures, political affiliations, religious beliefs, and historical traditions. However, as Paul Kaplan rightly suggests, "regional differences between locations do not entirely determine the ideological content of trial stories," nor do they exclude the possibility that similar prejudices and stereotypes influence the operations of trial actors across multiple settings.[44] Although local legal doctrines and cultural features certainly do play a role in shaping the discourse about mental illness and criminal responsibility in the courtroom, they do not necessarily encourage the emergence of psycholegal frameworks and value systems that could not be found, at least to some extent, in other American retentionist states.

This is particularly true in cases that raise the insanity defense. Twenty-five American states, including Texas, base their insanity evaluations on the English *M'Naghten* rules or some modified version of it.[45] Hence the issues identified in Texas regarding the conflict between the rationalistic approach endorsed by the criminal law and the scientific explanations offered by psychiatric witnesses are likely to be found in several other states. Similarly, court opinions and public opinion polls suggest that the misconceptions and stereotypes that inform lay understandings of mental illness and criminal responsibility in Texas insanity cases mirror, to a large extent, those found among American judges and the general U.S. population.[46]

Turning to sentencing procedures and diminished culpability claims, Texas's capital punishment statute is unusual in that it focuses jurors' sentencing decision on a forecast of the defendant's likelihood to engage in future violent behavior[47] while omitting the mitigation question or significantly narrowing its scope. Because of widespread stereotypes associating "madness" with violence, the Texas statute's emphasis on future dangerousness has encouraged jurors to consider evidence of mental illness and/or intellectual disability as an aggravating, rather than a mitigating, factor at sentencing. As I will show in Chapters 5 and 6, the state's focus on future violence has had a dramatic effect on Texas attorneys and expert witnesses' trial strategies and labeling practices at the sentencing stage of the proceedings, powerfully tipping the scales in favor of death.

Although Texas is peculiar in this respect, some of the misconceptions that emerge in the state's procedural arrangements are likely to be found even in other criminal justice contexts involving future dangerousness predictions. As argued by the U.S. Supreme Court in *Barefoot v. Estelle*,[48] psychiatrists routinely carry out risk assessments at several stages of the criminal justice system, both in Texas and elsewhere. The assumptions guiding future dangerousness predictions in Texas capital cases are probably not radically different from those informing judicial rulings on whether to admit a defendant to bail, parole boards' decisions to grant a prisoner early parole release, or sentencing authorities' behavioral forecasts in noncapital cases. Hence, though Texas's capital punishment statute, pool of prosecutors and expert witnesses, and community values differ from those found in other states, some of the popular misconceptions that inform the state's future dangerousness predictions are likely to be found even beyond Texas's borders.

Indeed, even though Texas's exceptionally high execution rates set the state apart from the rest of the nation, its retributive penal culture and punitive approach to mentally ill and intellectually disabled prisoners are not isolated phenomena. Except for California, Texas holds more representatives than any other state in the U.S. Congress and can therefore exert a powerful influence on national politics. As a result, the federal government and several states have often embraced Texas's retributive philosophy, particularly in the 1980s and 1990s, when the country's prison population and execution rates increased to an extent unknown of before.[49] Moreover, research has shown that other states, such as Florida and Alabama, have deviated from accepted medical standards in evaluating the criminal culpability of defendants with severe mental illnesses,[50] suggesting that some of the misconceptions informing mental health assessments in Texas cases are likely to be found even in other jurisdictions.

Given the generalizability of the Texas case, I propose that this book can be used as a case study to understand how and why many American states perform receptivity to psychiatric expertise while blocking the challenges it poses to outdated ideas of criminal responsibility. As I will show, Texas mental health law, death penalty jurisprudence, and trial practices have adapted to changing medico-legal paradigms to preserve a retributive approach to mentally disabled capital defendants. Although Texas's legal system presents its own peculiar characteristics, the doctrinal developments and trial strategies observed in this context can be analyzed to reveal something about the nature of American criminal law: how it can subdue psychiatric expertise, how its notions of criminal responsibility are impervious to change, and how evidence of mental illness can be weaponized against the accused at sentencing. Within this framework, the choice to focus on Texas capital punishment trials should be seen not as a commitment to advance an argument about Texas's capital punitiveness but as a data-driven decision based on the fact that, when the life of the defendant is at stake, trial actors tend to pay closer attention to issues of mental health and criminal accountability, and the appeals courts tend to preserve a more complete historical record of the cases.

Inside the Texas Archives: A Note on Historical Sources

Having established the relevance of my findings beyond Texas's capital punishment context, a brief note on the book's archival sources is in order. To construct my historical narrative, I relied on a triangulation of sources, including publications in the fields of forensic psychiatry and psychology; Texas mental incapacity doctrines, capital punishment statutes, and case law; trial transcripts, motions, and affidavits; and social and cultural histories of American forensic psychiatry and psychology and Texan penal practices.

The primary documents of this research—the trial transcripts—were collected at the Texas State Library and Archives Commission and at the Texas Court of Criminal Appeals (TCCA) in Austin, Texas. The transcripts are part of the historical records of the TCCA. The TCCA is the highest criminal court in the state and has appellate jurisdiction in all criminal cases. When a Texas county or district court sentences a defendant to death, the case is automatically appealed to the TCCA.[51] The archives of the TCCA therefore include the most thorough, comprehensive, and complete historical collections of trial transcripts of death penalty cases in the state of Texas, providing an invaluable source for the historical analysis conducted in this book.[52]

The case selection was conducted by using the LexisNexis search engine and selecting all Texas death penalty cases appealed between 1909 and 2002 in which the defendant (1) had claimed insanity and/or presented mitigating evidence of mental illness and child abuse, (2) was found guilty of the offense charged and sentenced to death, and (3) had no pending appeals. The selection yielded 86 cases.[53] The cases were divided into three time periods, each one demarcated by important legal, psychiatric, and cultural developments.[54] Defendants' race was identified through a triangulation of data drawn from the ESPY file, a database compiled by M. Watt Espy and John Ortiz Smykla that includes a list of executed inmates in the United States from 1608 to 2002;[55] the Texas Department of Criminal Justice website,[56] which provides a list of executed inmates from 1982 to the present; and research conducted by James Marquart, Sheldon Ekland-Olson, and Jonathan Sorensen,[57] which includes a list of death row prisoners from 1923 to 1988. Although these lists cover information about the race of the defendant, none of them are complete. Whenever possible, the race of the defendants of missing cases was identified through a close reading of the opinions and/or trial transcripts.[58]

Further historical material was gathered from the online archives of forensic psychiatric publications that had a powerful influence on the development of biological and psychological interpretations of mental illness and criminal responsibility in the twentieth century (e.g., *The Journal of Criminal Law and Criminology*, *The American Journal of Insanity*, *The American Journal of Psychiatry*). The papers that discussed the intersection of mental illness and criminal behavior, the insanity defense, criminal responsibility, and the use of medical expert testimonies in criminal proceedings were carefully analyzed to map the development of psychiatric knowledge on the intersection of mental illness and crime over the period under scrutiny. These sources were combined with statutes and court opinions gathered from traditional legal databases to capture as complete a history as possible of the debates about the intersection of mental illness and criminal responsibility in the medical and legal fields.

The decision to rely on forensic psychiatric publications and trial debates was led by two considerations. First, by examining how medical experts frame psychiatric pathological conditions associated with antisocial tendencies, it is possible to identify the characteristics and behaviors that a particular society perceives as most threatening to the social order and therefore in need of medical and legal intervention. These characteristics and behaviors are rarely a neutral assessment of an objective threat; more often than not they are a reflection of a moralistic judgment stemming from deep-seated assumptions and stereotypes that permeate the discourse of the white middle classes, to which most psychiatrists in the United States tend to belong.[59] Given the racial differences and socioeconomic gaps separating forensic psychiatrists from the mentally ill offenders typically trapped in the criminal justice system,[60] psychiatric writings provide the ideal data to explore how scientific discourse can, intentionally or unintentionally, legitimize hegemonic paradigms and historical patterns of political oppression in the name of therapeutic care and public protection.

Second, by examining the rhetorical devices used by defense attorneys and prosecutors to build their theory of the case, and by triangulating these trial tactics with jurors' sentencing decisions, it is possible to discern what sources of authority and belief systems a particular community relates to, and ultimately identifies with, at different points in time. Although jurors' decision-making process is shrouded in mystery and secrecy, their "acceptance of one narrative over another is inevitably a determination, in a strong sense, of [their] own public identity and the identity of [their] community,"[61] and can therefore be used to identify which types of knowledge and ideologies have the most powerful resonance in particular cultural contexts.

Limits of the Sample

Because of a series of practical constraints, my sample excludes several categories of defendants who were worthy of consideration. First, women are rarely sentenced to death in the United States[62] and, as a result, no woman fit the criteria used in the sample selection. Although this problem could have been addressed by including cases of women who successfully claimed insanity or who were sentenced to life imprisonment, this option presented significant problems of its own, as will be discussed later. Another significant exclusion concerns defendants who have yet to exhaust their appeals and are still on death row. The reason for this exclusion is that requesting the trial transcripts of cases currently on appeal can bring inappropriate attention to the case, prompt speedier procedures, and lead to a swifter execution of the inmate.[63]

Finally, and most important, the sample excludes cases of defendants who were charged with a capital crime but were either found not guilty by reason of insanity or sentenced to life imprisonment. In other words, the data set includes only instances of unsuccessful insanity pleas and mitigation claims, an aspect that has a significant impact on the nature and quality of the cases under study. For instance, it is reasonable to speculate that the expert evidence presented in support of a successful insanity plea is typically more powerful and comprehensive than one presented in support of an unsuccessful one. Indeed, a number of defendants included in the data set presented only weak evidence of insanity at trial, either because the symptoms of mental disease were missing or because the attorneys failed to thoroughly investigate the issue.[64] However, as I will show in the next chapters, this limitation was counteracted by the fact that in several instances defendants presented strong evidence of insanity at trial and were, nevertheless, sentenced to death.[65]

The reason for excluding successful insanity and mitigation claims is related to access issues. As mentioned earlier, cases of defendants sentenced to death are automatically appealed to the TCCA. When a case is appealed, the trial court sends the trial transcript to the TCCA, which reviews the petitioner's claims of error in light of the evidence contained in the transcript. After reviewing the case and ruling on the petitioner's claims, the court sends the transcript and all the additional documentation related to the case to its archive, which stores them for future consultations. Once the case has exhausted all its appellate procedures and the ruling is final, the case files are traditionally transferred to the Texas State Archives, which preserves them for the historical record.

In contrast, cases of defendants who are found not guilty by reason of insanity or sentenced to life imprisonment are never or rarely appealed. This is because given Texas's high death sentencing rates, a finding of not guilty by reason of insanity or a sentence of life imprisonment is considered a victory in this jurisdiction. When a case is not appealed to the TCCA, the trial transcripts are difficult to track down, given the decentralized structure of the Texas court system and the lack of regulations regarding the conservation of these legal documents.[66] This means that the transcripts are often either destroyed or simply lost. To address this data limitation, I have abstained from drawing inferences on the possible impact of specific expert and lay testimonies on jurors' decision making and final verdicts. Any such inference would necessarily require a comparison between successful and unsuccessful insanity claims and between cases that led to a death sentence and cases that ended with a life sentence. Rather than emphasizing case outcomes, I have therefore focused on the ways in which courtroom interactions have contributed to the construction of a shared set of meanings at specific points in time, limiting my inferences and generalizations to cases in which defendants were ultimately sentenced to death.

Change and Resistance: A Note on Periodization

Judging Insanity, Punishing Difference is organized into three parts. Each part includes two chapters, one focusing primarily on the psycholegal framework and cultural influences of the time and the second concentrating on their impact on Texas capital punishment proceedings. Part I (Chapters 1 and 2) investigates the era spanning from the rise of biological criminology in the early twentieth century to its decline following the spread of Freudian psychoanalysis in the 1950s. Part II (Chapters 3 and 4) analyzes the period stretching between the emergence of psychoanalytic interpretations of mental illness and criminality in the 1950s and their gradual loss of popularity in the 1970s. Part III (Chapters 5 and 6) covers the time frame spanning from the revival of biological explanations in the 1970s to the U.S. Supreme Court's decision to categorically exclude intellectually disabled defendants from capital punishment in 2002. Despite their difference in focus, all chapters include some illustrative case studies to show how the theoretical developments identified in the forensic psychiatric literature translated in the trial context.

Although there are several overlaps between the psychiatric, legal, and cultural shifts identified in each part of the book, it is important to note that these three spheres advance at different speeds and with different modalities, depending on the context. For example, whereas psychiatrists have pushed for the incorporation of a more holistic view of criminal insanity at least since the mid-nineteenth century,[67] courts and state legislatures across the United States have resisted these critiques, managing to maintain a narrow interpretation of insanity based on a purely cognitive deficit. Similarly, whereas psychiatric and psychological associations have long recognized that clinical predictions of future dangerousness are inaccurate and should therefore be banned from capital punishment proceedings, the U.S. Supreme Court has rejected this argument, stressing that psychiatrists conduct such predictions in many areas of criminal justice and that banning them from the capital punishment context would question their overall legitimacy and open a can of worms with too many ramifications.[68] Finally, although some cultural trends are short-lived and historically specific, others are more long-lasting and impervious to change. For example, whereas the association between homosexuality, criminal psychopathy, and sexual violence was a phenomenon specific to the 1930s and 1950s,[69] the individualist view of human nature that dominated trial debates in the 1980s and 1990s has older ideological roots, stretching back to the eighteenth century, when the Enlightenment notion of the autonomous and rational individual took center stage.[70]

Similarly, the emergence of new psychiatric paradigms in the academic literature often preceded by several decades their adoption by psychiatric experts in trial courts. For example, although psychoanalytic theories were already appearing in U.S. criminological publications in the 1920s and 1930s, it would take until the 1950s before the first defense psychiatrists started using Freudian concepts such as a weakened ego or the Oedipus complex to explain the defendants' emotional difficulties and criminal behaviors. As I will show, the reasons for this time lag are complex and lie in the poor mental health services, delayed forensic psychiatric professionalization, and low levels of legal representation typically provided to indigent capital defendants tried in this jurisdiction. Finally, although the chapters' periodization reflects important paradigmatic shifts, the transition from one paradigm to the next was often gradual and the boundaries separating them blurred. As a result, different psychiatric and cultural paradigms could sometimes coexist within the same trial record, demonstrating the difficulty of clearly identifying sharp shifts or even clear temporal boundaries between the ostensibly dominant frameworks. To capture the temporal disjuncture between psychiatric theory and forensic practice, along with the long transition periods between different psycho-legal frameworks, I use relatively broad time frames of analysis.

Despite the challenges of clearly separating between different paradigms, I identify a series of symbolic dates to demarcate the chapters' periodization and organize the archival data. Part I, for example, starts in 1909, the date of the foundation of the Juvenile Psychopathic Institute in Chicago, the first U.S. research institution dedicated to the psychiatric study of juvenile delinquents. In this institution, which would act as a model for the several child guidance clinics that would emerge over the following years, prominent psychiatrists such as William Healy tested, and ultimately refuted, the dominant criminological theories of the time while advising courts on the most appropriate legal responses and rehabilitative interventions. Part II, on the other hand, begins in 1952, the date when the American Psychiatric Association incorporated psychoanalytic theories into the first edition of its *Diagnostic and Statistical Manual of Mental Disorders* (DSM-I),[71] the first manual aimed at guiding and standardizing American psychiatrists' diagnostic practices both inside and outside courts of law.

Finally, Part III starts in 1976, the year in which the U.S. Supreme Court established that, to pass its constitutional scrutiny, capital trials ought to include a separate sentencing proceeding in which defendants could present any mitigating evidence that might humanize them in the eyes of the jury and call for a life sentence. Whereas in the first two time periods evidence of mental illness could be used only to raise the insanity defense or to claim a lower-level offense based on a lack of mens rea, or criminal intent, in the last era it could also be used to mitigate the sentence and prompt a sympathetic response from the jury after the defendant had been found guilty of a capital crime. As we will see, in Texas courts defendants' right to individualized considerations was significantly compromised as a result of both Texas capital sentencing statute's emphasis on future dangerousness, and its lack of a procedural mechanism that would allow jurors to give effect to the defendant's mitigating evidence in their punishment decision.

Part 1

THE BIOLOGICAL PARADIGM (1909–1952)

ONE

Heredity, Environment, and the Doctrine of Civilization

> There is [a] preliminary of special importance in criminal law in preparation of any effective dealing with punitive justice in this country, and that is the several critics of our system of punitive justice should understand each other; that the point of view of each should be broadened by a comprehension of the point of view of all; that instead of the alienist and the psychologist and the sociologist and the jurist and the economist going their several paths and throwing each his individual light upon our system of punitive justice, the light of all these be concentrated into one ray which shall throw upon our system of punitive justice the combined wisdom of all those who are entitled to bring scientific knowledge to bear upon it.[1]
>
> —ROSCOE POUND

In 1909, during the National Conference on Criminal Law and Criminology held at Northwestern University in Chicago, a group of influential physicians, judges, and lawyers met to design new measures for the observation and treatment of the "deviant classes."[2] In his opening conference speech, American legal scholar Roscoe Pound lamented that, although European forensic psychiatrists such as Emil Kraepelin, Eugen Bleuler, and Charles Goring had studied the physical makeup of prisoners since the mid-nineteenth century, in the United States the law of due process had hindered similar investigations.[3] Consequently, American psychiatrists lacked a comparatively thorough data set that would allow them to generalize about the physical marks of criminal types. According to the conference's committee, this knowledge gap needed to be filled through the creation of a network of laboratories across the United States specifically dedicated to the medical and psychological examination of convicted criminals.[4]

The discussion led to the foundation of the Juvenile Psychopathic Institute in Chicago, the world's first child guidance clinic, directed by Anglo-

American neurologist and criminologist William Healy.[5] At the institute, psychiatrists conducted intensive analyses of the "juvenile delinquents" brought before the juvenile court to identify the underlying causes of their criminal behavior, formulate prevention strategies, and assist judges in determining appropriate forms of correction. Several American states later replicated this model, fulfilling the committee's wish and contributing to the expanding role of American forensic psychiatry in courts of law over the following decades.[6] By virtue of its significant impact on the development of the medical study of criminal behavior in the United States, I use the National Conference on Criminal Law and Criminology as the starting point for this book's historical inquiry.

The conference was the culmination of a series of scientific transformations that had gradually eroded the religious and philosophical foundations that informed legal notions of criminal responsibility in Western thought.[7] Over the nineteenth century the new disciplines of phrenology, neurology, and physiology had questioned the notion of the unitary and rational individual advanced by Christian thinkers and Enlightenment philosophers, proposing an alternative image of man seen as a biological mechanism regulated by natural laws and responding to specific physiological stimuli. These developments fostered a deterministic and mechanistic view of human nature, which described human behavior as the result not of a moral choice or a commitment to religious values but of biological and environmental forces operating beyond the subject's control. Rather than emphasizing man's rationality and personal accountability, the new biomedical sciences stressed his affinity with the animal world and his vulnerability to the pressures of lower instincts and drives. Instead of seeing the human mind and behavior as the unitary expression of individual consciousness, physicians reframed them as the outcome of an internal struggle between conflicting anatomical units, each with their own independent purpose and function.[8] Through this fragmentation the mind had lost control over the body's operations: "The functional units of the human machine each had an independent existence and purpose of their own. . . . Neither function was under the control of the organism, whether animal, or man with a soul."[9] In the late nineteenth and early twentieth centuries this mechanistic view of human nature gave birth to a new notion, "biological man," which exerted a powerful influence on the ways in which lay and expert witnesses framed mental disease and criminal behavior in Texas criminal courts.

Professional Developments

Until the 1880s and 1890s medical and psychiatric explanations of physical and mental disease followed similar paths. However, at the close of the nineteenth century discoveries in the field of pathogenesis and bacteriology prompted a scientific turn in American medicine, making old psychiatric theories seem obsolete. Medicine identified with the new scientific and technological rhetoric and was increasingly framed in biological terms. Psychiatrists, on the other hand, because of their repeated failures in treating mental disease, were gradually relegated to a caregiving function, isolated behind the asylum walls and more worried about managing chronically sick populations than about conducting scientific inquiries into the etiology of mental disease.[10]

In the eyes of the new scientific physician, institutional psychiatry was a remnant of a premodern age, based on enigmatic metaphysical speculations that lacked theoretical rigor and scientific grounding.[11] Psychiatrists were increasingly aware of the gap separating them from the new scientific medicine. Concerned about the risk of being marginalized as representatives of a backward and underdeveloped discipline, they became more receptive to the innovations stemming from the biological sciences. Over the following decades they dedicated significant efforts to scientific research, radically transforming the theories and methods of their discipline to adapt to the new intellectual environment.

Although some psychiatrists highlighted the lack of scientifically grounded etiological explanations,[12] the majority were firmly convinced that a new era of scientific progress and technological advancement was about to radically transform their field. Biological explanations of insanity and criminality were extremely popular, not because of their theoretical or empirical rigor but because they served specific interests and purposes. They enhanced psychiatrists' professional status among the various branches of medicine, justified their claims for authority and expertise over mental disease, and supported their approach to criminal responsibility.[13] In addition, the reframing of insanity as a physical disease distanced psychiatrists from nonexperts, giving them exclusive authority over a specific area of intervention.

Biological Explanations of Mental Illness and Criminality

Encouraged by developments in the fields of neurology and physiology, early twentieth-century psychiatrists turned their attention to human biology as a possible source of criminal behavior. Victor Vaughan,[14] dean of the School of Medicine at the University of Michigan, fully endorsed psychiatrists' physiological approach to human morality when, in front of the American Prison Association, he read the following statement by French scholar Jean-Gabriel De Tarde:

> The moral sense has an organic base (which does not necessarily mean to say a cerebral place) and consequently its disappearance or its deadening can only be explained by means of a gap or a lesion, by an atrophy or an injury to the brain, or by an imperfect nutrition of its cells; by some misfortune in other words.[15]

In the first three decades of the twentieth century, most psychiatrists agreed on the role of organic pathology in the etiology of mental illness and criminality. However, their opinions varied as to the exact physical location of the disease and the mechanism through which it could prompt criminal conduct. For example, Charles Burr, a professor of mental disease at the University of Pennsylvania, joined several other colleagues in focusing on the role of the brain, highlighting that there was a

> widespread, popular belief, that much badness is caused by "pressure" within the skull, the idea being that since the skull is a rigid body surrounding the brain, any injury to the bones, or any disease of the brain, so decreases the volume of the cranial cavity that the brain is squeezed and therefore functions abnormally.[16]

On the other hand, Alfred Gordon, an alienist from Philadelphia, took a holistic and unspecified approach, arguing that mentally imbalanced criminals often presented many "stigmata of physical degeneration, [along with] disturbed functions of the viscera, of tissues, of organs."[17] Similarly, Edgar Doll, a New Jersey clinical psychologist, believed that delinquents' mental instability stemmed from an organic infection affecting "the teeth, tonsils, or gastro-intestinal tract" or a "disturbance of the glands of internal secretion" that upset the equilibrium of the endocrine system.[18] These scholars started from an interrelated view of human biology that argued that "a malfunction in any vital organ could ultimately affect the brain and lead to insanity."[19] In this holistic rationale the human organs were all interconnected; a disease in any single part could ultimately affect the overall functioning of the whole.

Although psychiatrists' opinions varied as to the exact physical origins of disease, most of them agreed that the brain was the primary organ that regulated mental processes, and that lesions to one or more layers of the cortex could degenerate an individual's mental state and prompt antisocial tendencies.[20] For instance, Dr. Michael Osnato, speaking at the annual meeting of the American Medico-Psychological Association, referred to the work of German psychiatrist Aloysius Alzheimer[21] to argue that dementia praecox was "an organic disease of the brain" caused by "lesions in the second and third layers of the cortex," and that such lesions were directly correlated with the mental, affective, and behavioral abnormalities typically found in criminal offenders affected by this medical condition.[22] As discussed in more detail in Chapter 2, until the discovery of technical instruments such as the Wasserman reaction (1906) and the Binet-Simon test (1905), physiological explanations of mental illness and crime relied heavily on the postmortem analysis of organic brain matter, an aspect that would prove problematic for psychiatrists asked to give opinions about living defendants in Texas courts.

The Theory of Reflex Action and the Theory of Instincts

Psychiatrists who argued that criminality stemmed from pathological conditions of the brain drew from two closely intertwined nineteenth-century ideas: the theory of reflex action and the theory of instincts.[23] The theory of reflex action proposed that insanity resulted from lack of inhibition and unchecked expression of impulses, which could easily translate into motiveless and horrendous crimes.[24] According to this theory, the brain controlled and inhibited the natural tendency of the lower reflexes to translate urges and sensations into action.[25] A lesion that undermined the brain's inhibitory faculty over the lower reflexes could therefore prompt automatic movements outside the reach of individual consciousness, as happened in many cases of criminal insanity.

The theory of instincts drew from English biologist Charles Darwin's analogy between the human and the animal world to argue that man's behavior was regulated by animalistic impulses that operated beyond the subject's control. Darwin argued that all species, including humans, descended from a common ancestor and had evolved over millions of years into their present form through a process of natural selection, in which the struggle for survival and adaptation had contributed to eliminate unfavorable genetic traits while maintaining the desirable ones.[26] By stressing that all species descended from "one primordial form," Darwin had broken down the traditional division between men and animals, furthering a secularized view of human nature that framed men as biological machines regulated by the same physical laws that governed the animal kingdom.

Physiological theories based on the Darwinian analogy between men and animals challenged one of the fundamental grounds of legal doctrines of criminal responsibility. By arguing that movements and actions could be the result of unconscious reflexes and impulses rather than of conscious thought processes, they undermined legal notions of the human mind as a rational instrument guiding behavior. However, as I will show in Chapter 2, when transposed into the trial context, explanations of criminality stemming from the reflex action and instincts theories supported the idea that the accused had committed the crime under an irresistible impulse rather than because of a cognitive deficit, falling short of the legal standard required to prove insanity and lack of guilt in Texas criminal courts.

Heredity and Environment

As the somatic approach gathered momentum, in the 1880s and 1890s an increasing number of psychiatrists turned their attention to genetic explanations, arguing that if insanity had an organic basis, it followed that it could be biologically transmitted across generations as much as any other physical pathology.[27] Similarly, a growing number of psychiatrists inspired by Jean-Baptiste Lamarck's theory of "soft inheritance," which proposed that organisms could transmit acquired characteristics and learned abilities to their offspring,[28] argued that children could inherit not only their parents' mental diseases, but also their bad habits and deviant behaviors. In this view, "when a particular mental trait turned into habit, it became embodied in the structure of the nervous system; [and] this acquired structure was passed down to future generations."[29] Criminologists eager to find scientific support for their claims that criminality was an inborn characteristic embraced the Lamarckian theory of soft inheritance with enthusiasm. Inspired by a deterministic view of human biology and conduct, these theorists conceded that there was scope for moral change through education and training during the juvenile years.[30]

However, in the early decades of the twentieth century most psychiatrists embraced a more fixed view of human personality and behavior.[31] Stimulated by August Weissman's refutation of Lamarck's theory[32] and by Gregor Mendel's recently rediscovered heredity laws,[33] they believed that biological characteristics were genetically transmitted without modification from the environment and that the improvement of social conditions was unable to stop the spread of mental disease and moral degeneracy.[34] In the view of Weissman and Mendel's followers, once a particular trait had been acquired, there was no hope for moral recovery. The only solution to the spread of moral degeneracy across generations was eugenic sterilization. A strong supporter of Mendelian heredity theory, Dr. August Drähms emblematically expressed this view when he argued that

> the burden with which the congenital offender comes already laden, and from which he draws his inspirational forces, is purely congenital. It is the product of entailed inheritance from ancestral germ plasms even inoculating that new life with the very germs of theft and murder already stirring in the flood of its progenitors ages back.[35]

Along these lines, Dr. Burr suggested that, rather than resulting from some external precipitating stress factor, criminality was an inborn personality characteristic stemming from an "inherent defect in protoplasm" that could not be cured or corrected.[36]

Genetic and environmental explanations of criminal behavior coexisted in a dialectical relationship throughout the first three decades of the twentieth century.[37] Although some scholars embraced the theories of inborn criminality proposed by eugenicists, several others merged the eugenic and neo-Lamarckian perspectives to develop a more interactive view of criminal causality. According to neo-Lamarckians, delinquent behaviors stemmed from an intricate mix of bad heredity, negative environmental influences, and vicious habits; hence, when asked to assess their patients' moral fiber, psychiatrists needed to observe both the patients' families' genetic pedigrees and their moral upbringing.[38] As I discuss in Chapter 2, experts testifying in Texas courtrooms endorsed this interactive approach, arguing that criminality stemmed from a complex interplay of genetically inherited brain pathologies, immoral habits, and stressful life events.

Cultural Influences and Moral Framework

American Psychiatry and the Doctrine of Civilization

Despite their claims to scientific objectivity, nineteenth- and early twentieth-century psychiatrists interpreted insanity and criminality through the lens of the cultural values and standards of behavior of their time. Inspired by Darwin's evolutionary theories, psychiatrists saw civilization as the most advanced stage of human development, the culmination of a long transition from a primitive condition of savagery and brutality to a civilized status of intellectual refinement, dignity, and self-mastery.[39] In this view, although all human races would eventually reach this stage of evolution, only whites had thus far completed the necessary steps to free themselves from the savagery and violent barbarity of the more archaic stages.[40] Accordingly, nonwhites were yet far from reaching a similar stage of biological and cultural advancement: Civilization was a quintessentially white and, more specifically, male Anglo-Saxon quality.[41]

Forensic psychiatrists influenced by these views described insanity and criminality as fundamental attributes of "uncivilized" men and women. In this view mental illness and criminal behaviors were pathological manifestations of the "eruption of the inner savage," of a loss of control over the unconscious impulses present in every individual, even the most virtuous types.[42] Indulgence in sensual pleasures and failure to conform to the virtuous habits of civilization degenerated individuals' mental and moral condition, transporting them "from a higher plane to a lower plane of living and acting."[43] Following a well-established nineteenth-century tradition, most psychiatrists in the 1910s and 1920s believed that insanity and criminality resulted from "a violation of those physical, mental, and moral laws which, properly understood and obeyed, result not only in the highest development of the race, but [also] in the highest type of civilization."[44] These physical, mental, and moral laws reflected a well-defined view of how individuals should live up to the ideals of appropriateness, dignity, and civility that were thought to distinguish Western culture from the "barbaric" populations of the old European colonies and from the African black slaves now freed from their subjugation.

"Race Science" and Eugenics

Late nineteenth- and early twentieth-century discourse on civilization led many American psychiatrists to believe that mental disease was partly dependent on race. This belief built on an old medical tradition that emphasized the existence of clear anatomical differences between blacks and whites. By the end of the nineteenth century the old American view that racial hierarchies reflected a divine order had been eclipsed by the conviction that the racial power structure "reflected a natural ordering of myriad human groups measurable through the techniques of scientific empiricism."[45] In this framework the races' position in the hierarchical ladder reflected "natural biological divisions" and the innate abilities, temperaments, and destinies of their members. Accordingly, a system that adapted its social, medical, and legal practices to accommodate these differences was neither racist nor discriminatory; it simply acknowledged a scientific fact.

In the 1910s and 1920s most members of the legal and medical profession were firmly convinced that traditional racial hierarchies were rooted in innate biological differences. By then, nineteenth-century biological race theories had evolved into eugenics, an extreme expression of naturalistic racism that reasserted the hierarchical organization of the world's "races along a continuum of intelligence, capacity, and worth" while advocating a strict separation between members of different racial groups to maintain Anglo-Saxon Americans' racial purity and intellectual superiority.[46] In this view racial mixing would inevitably lead to biological and moral degeneration. Hence, white Anglo-Saxon Americans needed to be protected from the genetic contamination of racially inferior and mentally defective individuals, through the enforcement of strict immigration, segregation, and sterilization laws.[47]

The Culture of Character and the Puritan Work Ethic

In the first three decades of the twentieth century, eugenic theories of racial superiority intersected with a culture of character and a puritan work ethic that turned the behavioral characteristics of the white Protestant middle classes into a gold standard of moral rectitude. Over the course of the nineteenth century a puritan ethic of sobriety and simplicity had created the foundations for the emergence of a new class ideology and a vibrant capitalist spirit, which rejected the values and lifestyles of the old feudal aristocracy and celebrated those of the productive and virtuous middle classes.[48] The puritan ethic celebrated industriousness, austerity, and self-discipline as moral virtues leading to spiritual salvation.[49] As Max Weber explains, for the puritans,

> not leisure and enjoyment, but only activity serves to increase the glory of God, according to the definite manifestations of his will. Waste of time is thus the first and in principle the deadliest of sins. . . . Loss of time through sociability, idle talk, luxury, even more sleep than is necessary for health, six to at most eight hours, is worthy of absolute moral condemnation.[50]

Early twentieth-century psychiatrists inspired by the puritan work ethic condemned and criminalized men and women who engaged in "idle" and "self-indulgent" habits and behaviors. Men were most likely to be condemned for their alcohol abuse and sexual promiscuity, which were believed to reduce their industriousness, degrade them to a lower socioeconomic condition, and prompt them to use criminal means to satisfy their needs.[51] In this view, by failing to fulfill their moral duty to create wealth and serve God's will, alcoholic and sexually indulgent men had lost any hope for salvation, in this world as well as in the afterlife.

The social reform movements of the Progressive Era (1890–1920) endorsed the puritan-capitalist framework while rethinking it according to the economic and social developments of their time. Inspired by early twentieth-century Taylorism, progressive reformers aimed to improve the efficiency and productivity of the nation by modernizing and applying scientific criteria to the management of every area of society and government, through the employment of experts selected on purely meritocratic grounds.[52] A number of psychiatrists enthusiastically endorsed the progressive project, recasting hard work, efficiency, and productivity as essential means to achieve not only spiritual salvation but also mental health and social adjustment. In their view mentally ill and intellectually disabled men were "social misfits," individuals incapable of contributing to the economic progress of American society through constant effort and self-control, and therefore most likely to engage in criminal behavior. For example, Dr. Stanley Abbot argued in front of the New York Psychiatrical Society that men affected by dementia praecox displayed "goodness and meekness rather than strength and determination[;] . . . deficient ethical control; unsteadiness of occupation; inefficiency; especially loss of directive energy and initiative, without obvious cause (such as illness)."[53] Following this vein, Dr. Burr associated men's habitual criminality with lack of industriousness, arguing that the inability to pursue a goal with constancy and persistence reflected criminals' lower impulses, their tendency to search for immediate pleasures, and their incapacity to postpone gratification.[54]

Psychiatrists operating in this context described mentally diseased criminals by relying on stereotyped personality and behavioral descriptions associated with social categories that were deemed unfit to function productively within the mechanisms of early twentieth-century capitalism. "Socially problematic" groups, such as immigrant workers from Eastern and Southern Europe and African Americans, were described not only as insane and mentally defective but also as weak, idle, self-indulgent, sexually promiscuous, and highly fertile—all characteristics in sharp contrast with the traits and behaviors cherished by the white Protestant middle classes.[55]

In the South, where the highest proportion of African Americans lived, the association of blackness, madness, and crime had been in vogue since the abolition of slavery in 1865. Shocked by the transformation of race relations brought about by the Civil War, mid-nineteenth-century American psychiatrists started arguing that emancipation increased blacks' likelihood to develop mental diseases and engage in antisocial behaviors. In their view, while slave discipline had thus far restrained blacks' "childish," "emotional," and "instinctive" nature, their newly acquired freedom allowed them to indulge in "unhealthy passions and appetites," which could easily degenerate their mental health condition.[56] Psychiatrists writing in the 1910s and 1920s powerfully embraced these racist arguments, suggesting that, deprived of the supervision of the white slave owner, African Americans had turned into "irresponsible," "lazy," and "unreliable" workers, incapable of coping with the difficulties associated with their new social status and the requirements of "modern civilization."[57] Most important, because of their "deficient . . . perceptive faculty" and "emotional temperament," African Americans lived disconnected from the past, were careless about the future, and were in a constant search for fleeting excitement, all traits that made them particularly inclined to develop antisocial tendencies.[58]

In the late nineteenth and early twentieth centuries the racist stereotypes typically applied to African Americans were extended to Southern and Eastern European immigrants of Catholic faith. At the time, the mass immigration of these ethnic groups to the urban centers of the Northeast were prompting growing concerns among white middle-class Americans, who feared that through their "childish," "beastlike," and "promiscuous" behaviors, Catholic immigrants would create a host of sanitary and political problems that would drain the nation's already scarce resources.[59] American psychiatrists regularly fueled these fears, by arguing that foreign immigrants could be distinguished by their inferior physical characteristics, lower intelligence, and higher propensity to contract mental diseases and engage in criminal conduct.[60] For example, Dr. Milton H. Erickson proposed in 1928 that the immigration of foreign nationals of "defective mentality" had led to a staggering increase in the incidence of crime.[61] "The foreign-born individual of subnormal or deficient intelligence," Erickson argued, "appears to be responsible for an overwhelmingly increased incidence of crime as determined by population ratios. This increased incidence reaches the proportion of 327% of the fair quota for the low-grade morons."[62] To contain this tendency, he proposed that states needed to develop stricter immigration policies, which could limit the entrance of these "low-grade" foreigners and decrease the incidence of crime over the following years.[63]

The Biological Paradigm and Its Diagnostic Limitations

The first three decades of the twentieth century witnessed important developments in the field of diagnostic testing that enhanced psychiatrists and psychologists' image among medical professionals.[64] Instruments such as the Binet-Simon test and the Wasserman reaction gave mental health experts apparently "objective" techniques to assess individuals' mental status, an essential requirement to advance convincing arguments in courts of law. However, when dealing with mental health conditions without a clear organic origin, such as dementia praecox or psychopathy, psychiatrists lacked comparable technical instruments. As a result, they were forced to rely on a purely descriptive approach, based on the observation of behavioral symptoms and physical characteristics, rather than on tests linking the condition to deeper causes.

Diagnostic methods based on physical assessments started from the assumption that evolutionary backwardness was powerfully inscribed in the criminal's body and that, through appropriate measurements and observations, physicians could identify the external marks of moral degeneracy that distinguished the "criminal insane" from the "normal" population. This could be done either by conducting postmortem examinations aimed at identifying brain atrophies and lesions[65] or by measuring the physical parts of living subjects and comparing them to a gold standard of anatomical perfection. For example, after having observed the palates of thousands of mentally diseased or intellectually disabled subjects, Irene Case,[66] a researcher at the Psychopathic Laboratory of the University of Chicago, argued that a disproportionate number of them presented an asymmetric and uncommonly narrow and high palate arch or a smaller than average "space between the bicuspids and the molars of the opposite side."[67] Following a deep-seated nineteenth-century tradition,[68] Dr. Case proposed that such asymmetries were reflective of a concomitant anomaly in the shape of the face and skull, a factor that many psychiatrists saw as a clear sign of the presence of mental abnormalities, intellectual deficiencies, and criminalistic tendencies.[69]

Physicians and alienists who testified in Texas criminal courts were unlikely to rely on similar observations in their mental health assessments. Unless dealing with organic conditions with a measurable symptomatology, such as syphilis or epilepsy, courtroom experts based their evaluations on behavioral observations that were equally available to lay observers without medical expertise. Although clearly informed by the biological paradigm of the time, their evaluations were strikingly untechnical, based as they were on brief conversations with the defendant, superficial physical examinations, and hypothetical reconstructions of the facts of the crime formulated by the attorneys.[70] Given the racist and classist frameworks that shaped much scientific writing of the time, the limited use of medical labels and techniques in early twentieth-century trial proceedings is, of course, cause for celebration. However, experts' reliance on behavioral observations and brief conversations could be equally damaging for the defense, given doctors' failure to translate their diagnoses and descriptions into convincing arguments to spare the defendants' lives based on a finding of criminal insanity.

The reason for the mismatch between psychiatric theory and forensic practice is twofold. First, when testifying on the question of insanity in criminal proceedings, mental health professionals were forced to focus their opinions exclusively on the defendant's cognitive capacities, leaving other areas of potential impairment, whether volitional or emotional, largely unaddressed. Texas courts rely on a particularly narrow version of the "right and wrong" test, which limits the defense to a small number of defendants who, at the time of the charged offense, did not understand that their act was "legally" rather than just "morally" wrong.[71] As shown in Chapters 2–4, Texas's "right and wrong" test powerfully limits the nature, scope, and impact of medical testimonies in insanity trials, filtering out medical explanations that do not fit the cognitive criteria endorsed by the rules, and dismissing theories that would link defendants' mental impairments with a lack of control over the volitional capacities.

The problems associated with the cognitive focus of the "right and wrong" test are exacerbated by the fact that trial actors tend to overestimate the level of mental impairment required to justify an insanity acquittal. For example, most members of the American judiciary and the general public believe that to be found not guilty by reason of insanity, a defendant must show a *complete* lack of "understanding and memory,"[72] an extremely high bar if we consider that even severely mentally disabled defendants usually maintain a part of their cognitive abilities intact.[73] These misconceptions arguably shape the nature of the psychiatric evidence provided in criminal trials, as more subtle explanations of behavior get dismissed for their failure to demonstrate the exceptionally high levels of mental impairment required to justify an insanity acquittal.

Second, the scientific view of human nature advanced by the medical professions contrasts sharply with the folk-psychological view of human behavior that tends to dominate trial contexts. The folk-psychological view that informs mental disability law is a seemingly intuitive theory used by individuals to understand and predict their own and other people's behavior.[74] As legal philosopher Katrina Sifferd explains, "This cognitive capacity allows humans to postulate that behavior is causally related to mental states such as beliefs and desires, and to predict or interpret such behavior based on attribution of mental states."[75] This folk-psychological view is routinely used in the criminal law context to establish defendants' mental state at the time of the crime and their relative level of guilt. Sentencing verdicts thus depend on whether a defendant had the "intent to kill," whether he or she believed that the act was wrong, or on whether the act was committed knowingly or purposefully.

This view of human psychology starts from the assumption that humans are rational beings whose actions and movements are led by mental entities such as beliefs, desires, and intentions. In the early twentieth century this ontological view powerfully shaped the way in which Texas attorneys asked experts to assess defendants' mental state at the time of the crime. Rather than asking the doctors to conduct physical assessments aimed at establishing the presence of anatomical anomalies and cranial asymmetries, they presented them with a hypothetical reconstruction of the defendant's actions before, during, and after the commission of the alleged offense and asked them to use this behavioral evidence to draw conclusions on the defendant's state of mind at the time of the events.[76] Similarly, county court judges openly encouraged jurors and trial actors to follow this approach in assessing whether the defendant had the required mens rea for first-degree murder, when they argued that the defendant's mental state ought to be inferred from an observation of "acts committed, or words spoken."[77] As these examples suggest, the biological causes of defendants' criminal conduct were irrelevant within this framework, because all one needed to know was already inscribed into the defendant's actions and interpretable in behavioral terms.

Structure of Texas Capital Punishment Trials

Before the U.S. Supreme Court established in 1976 that capital punishment trials ought to be split into a guilt phase and a punishment phase, cases carrying the death penalty were tried in the same way as any other criminal case.[78] Traditionally, following an indictment by a grand jury, the county court proceeded with the jury selection, pretrial proceedings, and the trial itself, which aimed at establishing whether the defendant was guilty of the crime charged or of a lower-level offense. If the defendant was found guilty of the crime charged, jurors were given broad discretion to assess the severity of the punishment. Typically, for crimes carrying the death penalty, such as rape and murder in the first degree, the penalty could range between death (by hanging or, after 1923, electrocution) and a minimum of five years of prison detention. In contrast to contemporary practice, the trial proceedings did not include opening and closing statements by the attorneys but only the direct and cross-examination of the witnesses. Importantly, the trial transcripts, which were typically 30–80 pages long, omitted the questions formulated by the lawyers unless they included a hypothetical statement of facts.

Once the parties had presented all their evidence, the trial judge read the charge to the jury and explained the law to be applied to the case at hand. For homicide offenses carrying the death penalty, the charge typically involved an explanation of the mens rea required for first-degree murder. Before reforming its penal code in the mid 1970s, Texas law required the jury to find beyond a reasonable doubt that the homicide was committed with "malice aforethought" to impose the death penalty. "Malice aforethought," the historical equivalent of "intent to kill," was defined as "the *voluntary* and *intentional* doing of an unlawful act by one of *sound memory and discretion*, with the purpose, means and ability to accomplish the reasonable and probable consequences of the act."[79] In some instances, "malice" was described in morally charged terms, as "a condition of the mind which shows a *heart regardless of social duty and fatally bent on mischief*," suggesting that besides establishing voluntariness and intent, jurors ought to assess whether the defendants' actions betrayed a certain level of cruelty.[80] Unless the jury was satisfied beyond a reasonable doubt that the homicide was committed with this state of mind and under circumstances that would neither excuse nor justify the killing, they could not sentence the defendant to more than five years in the penitentiary.

In cases raising the insanity defense, the county judge instructed the jury on the law to be followed in evaluating the defendant's sanity at the time of the alleged offense. From the mid-nineteenth century until 1973 (and again, from 1984 to the present day), the Texas insanity defense was based on the English *M'Naghten* rules, a landmark test developed in 1843 by a panel of common law judges and incorporated by several American states over the nineteenth and twentieth centuries.[81] Also known as the "right and wrong" test, the *M'Naghten* rules provide that individuals affected by a "mental disease or defect" that prevents them from knowing "the nature and quality" of their crime and from understanding its wrongfulness are to be considered not guilty by reason of insanity and excused for their criminal act.[82] Mentally ill defendants who are rationally aware of the wrongfulness of their act are traditionally excluded from legal protection.[83] The only exception to this rule occurs when a defendant maintains a delusional belief that, if true, would justify the offense. An example of this would be if, under the influence of a delusion, a defendant believes that another individual is attempting to take his life and he kills such individual in (supposed) self-defense. All the Texas transcripts analyzed for the 1909–1952 period included a jury instruction modeled on this legal standard.

Empirical Characteristics of the Sample

The sample analyzed in Part I was selected using the LexisNexis search engine and by filtering for cases appealed between 1909 and 1952 that raised the insanity defense. The selection yielded 41 cases, with 39 cases raising insanity claims and 2 cases claiming temporary insanity.[84] According to my estimates, Texas sentenced 437 defendants to death between 1909 and 1952, suggesting that approximately 9% of Texas's capital defendants raised an unsuccessful insanity plea over this time period. These estimates are based on the combination of two lists: one including Texas inmates who were *sentenced to death* from 1923 to 1988[85] and one including Texas inmates who were *executed* from 1608 to 2002.[86] Since the list that stretches back to the beginning of the seventeenth century included only *executed* inmates, my estimate for the 1909–1923 period excludes defendants who were sentenced to death but had their sentences commuted to life. However, until the 1930s, Texas offered minimal procedural protections at the postconviction stage of the proceedings, making commutations of defendants' death sentences highly unlikely over this time period.

Race is a particularly important variable in the analysis of Texas's capital punishment system. The state, like other members of the former Confederacy, has a long history of racial conflict and a discriminatory death penalty system that targets ethnic minority groups. Death penalty research has firmly established that Texas's sentencing patterns are strongly influenced by race-of-defendant and race-of-victim effects, with black defendants who killed or raped white victims being significantly more likely to receive a death sentence than defendants in other victim-offender combinations.[87] According to Marquart and colleagues, in the 1920s and 1930s black defendants were 2.5–3 times more likely to receive a death sentence than their white counterparts in Texas courts.[88] This disproportion started gradually fading in the 1940s and 1950s, possibly reflecting the changed cultural climate that accompanied the emergence of the civil rights movement and the passing of antilynching laws. The 1909–1952 sample included 19 whites, 13 African Americans, 2 Hispanics, and 7 defendants for which the race or ethnicity remains unknown. Interestingly, although 14 (out of 19) white defendants relied on the testimony of a mental health expert to support their insanity claim, only 5 (out of 15) defendants belonging to an ethnic minority group relied on a psychiatric or psychological consultant.[89] This was likely a result of the lower level of legal representation typically afforded to African Americans and Hispanics, because of their relative socioeconomic disadvantage and their status as second-class citizens in early twentieth-century Texan culture.[90]

Given the low number of experts testifying in trials involving ethnic minorities, I was unable to establish whether the racist language linking African Americans to mental defects and criminal backwardness in the psychiatric literature had an equally significant effect on trial discourse.

However, the case analysis reveals that Texas courts used different metrics to evaluate "normal intelligence" among blacks and whites, a fact that indicates that racist stereotypes exerted a significant influence on courts' insanity evaluations.[91] For example, in upholding the death sentence of Woody Maxey, an African American man who claimed to suffer from psychomotor epilepsy, the judges of the Texas Court of Criminal Appeals (TCCA) argued that none of the witnesses had demonstrated that before the homicide the defendant had displayed a behavior consistent with an insane state of mind and that "when not suffering from an attack of epilepsy [the defendant had] shown to have possessed *as much intelligence as the average of his race*."[92] As this passage suggests, in 1912, the year of Maxey's trial, racist prejudices depicting African Americans as intellectually inferior prompted the TCCA to use a lower average of intelligence in evaluating the sanity of black defendants compared with their white counterparts. In so doing, the TCCA legitimized a double standard that could lead to the disproportionate imposition of death sentences on African Americans who, if evaluated according to the level of intellectual functioning expected from white defendants, would have been deemed insane and therefore not culpable for the crime committed.

Hispanic defendants were also expected to display a lower level of intelligence than whites. In the 1943 trial of Juan Gutierrez, a Mexican man charged with the murder of a deputy sheriff in Hidalgo County, the state's expert witness, Dr. W. J. Johnson, argued that the defendant was "of *superior intelligence* considering his education and his environment *for a man of his race*" and used this observation to conclude that Gutierrez was sane at the time of the charged offense.[93] Dr. Johnson started from the assumption, largely shared by psycho-legal authorities and the lay public at the time, that intelligence and morality were closely intertwined and that mental defects inhibited the brain's capacity to control the lower impulses and respond to the pressures of modern life.[94] In the 1910s and 1920s a group of psychologists, later labeled "feeblemindedness theorists," were arguing that most criminals were characterized by a low intellectual endowment and that this mental impairment was particularly widespread among members of the "lower" races.[95] Texas courts' approach to intelligence evaluations in cases involving African Americans and Hispanics suggests that this belief shaped criminal liability in important ways, subtly infiltrating judicial opinions and mental health assessments and perpetuating racial hierarchies based on assumed biological and evolutionary differences between blacks, Hispanics, and whites.

Diagnosing Insanity in Texas Criminal Courts

Indigent capital defendants who are trying to prove insanity and lack of guilt in Texas criminal courts face several challenges. Lack of funding for legal aid,[96] inadequate legal representation,[97] and poor professional ethics among mental health experts[98] undermine the depth, quality, and impact of the evidence presented by the defense, significantly decreasing its chances of success. In the early twentieth century these problems were exacerbated by the lack of specially trained mental health professionals who could convince jurors that the defendant's mental illness undermined his or her ability to behave lawfully. At the time, psychiatrists and psychologists were still establishing themselves as independent professional categories with their own boards, associations, and university degrees.[99] Hence, although the big cities of the Northeast could already rely on a pool of mental health experts, most rural areas in Texas still lacked this kind of professional capacity and had to rely on the opinion of medical doctors without specialized training.[100]

Texas's poor mental health provision was clearly reflected in the low standards of care offered by its mental health institutions. Until the 1960s, when the mental hygiene movement pushed for the deinstitutionalization of psychiatric patients, the state's hospitals were "over-crowded warehouses," holding areas run by poorly trained and underpaid medical staff, in which the limited state budget available was devoted exclusively to custodial expenses.[101] In the 1940s and 1950s psychiatric organizations such as the Texas Society of Mental Hygiene and the Hogg Foundation at the University of Texas at Austin raised awareness about the deplorable conditions of the state's institutionalized population, pushing for legislative reforms and mobilizing resources to restructure the state's mental health system. Although Texas legislators adopted some of their proposed reforms, in 1949 the United States Public Health Service conducted a national survey of state institutions and concluded that "no other state fell as far below the American Psychiatric Association standards of care as Texas."[102]

Partly as a result of the state's substandard mental health services and professional provision, in the first half of the twentieth century Texas attorneys relied mostly, if not exclusively, on lay witnesses for their insanity evaluations. When arguing against an insanity acquittal, lay witnesses tended to limit their testimonies to conclusive statements regarding defendants' ability to distinguish right from wrong at the time of the alleged offense, providing little explanation as to how they reached their conclusions.[103] Their testimonies typically involved statements to the effect that the defendants had always "acted normal" in their presence and that there was nothing in their manner, appearance, and behavior that suggested that their reasoning was impaired or that they were otherwise of "unsound mind." When testifying in support of a finding of criminal insanity, lay witnesses tended to offer more detailed explanations in support of their conclusions; for example, by suggesting that the defendant looked, spoke, and acted bizarrely or struggled to form basic human relationships and to follow social conventions. Frequently cited observations included the defendant looking moody, melancholic, and immersed in deep thought,[104] staring into empty space,[105] having a blank and wild look,[106] staying up all night walking around,[107] being lazy at work,[108] wearing bizarre outfits,[109] refusing to talk to other people,[110] suddenly changing subject in the middle of a conversation,[111] and laughing without apparent reason.[112] By relying heavily on these kinds of testimonies, Texas attorneys reinforced the false idea, shared by many members of the American judiciary, that unless a defendant was so blatantly "crazy" that it could be immediately identified by a bystander without medical training, his mental condition was unlikely to be so severe as to warrant an insanity acquittal.[113]

In the few cases in which physicians were called as expert witnesses, their testimonies generally included a description of their professional experience and diagnostic methods along with their conclusions regarding the defendants' mental health and criminal culpability. The mental health evaluation involved asking defendants a series of questions to identify their level of intelligence, test their sense of reality, and observe their emotional responses to a narration of the circumstances of the case.[114] The questions were particularly designed to ascertain defendants' temperament and uncover whether they or their family members used to indulge in "bad habits," such as excessive drinking or masturbation.[115] Finally, the questions tried to establish whether there was a history of insanity running through the defendant's family.[116] Given the popularity of heredity theories at the time, a finding of a similar pattern across generations was often used to reinforce an otherwise shaky insanity claim.[117]

Although a finding of hereditary insanity could prove useful, a potentially more effective way to convince jurors of the defendant's mental incapacity was to demonstrate that he or she had been, and still was, affected by delusions and hallucinations.[118] Defense psychiatrists trusted this kind of evidence because it could be submitted to traditional standards of examination. It was palpable proof of the presence of mental disease, not a metaphysical speculation. Yet, the outcomes of several cases suggest that even strong evidence of delusions and hallucinations could fail to convince the most skeptical audiences.[119] The cause of this skepticism was that such evidence relied on the defendant's subjective sensations and impressions, an aspect that defense psychiatrists considered important proof but that legal actors and the American public regarded with suspicion. In addition, juries often considered these accounts unreliable because they were based solely on defendants' personal narratives and on psychiatrists' expertise.

The reason for jurors' lack of trust in defendants' accounts and psychiatrists' evaluations is twofold. First, jurors tend to falsely believe that mental illness is "easy to fake" and that defendants are routinely acquitted on the grounds of insanity because of their ability to "put on a show" and convince experts that they suffer from a mental health condition.[120] Second, Texas jurors operate in a context where anti-intellectual sentiments, democratic populist values, and conservative Christian beliefs fuel a lack of trust in scientists and experts, who are perceived as distant elites who would say anything in exchange for an expensive fee and who are too far removed from the problems of "real people" to offer any valuable insight on questions of moral and legal relevance. Although anti-intellectualism is a common feature of American thought,[121] Texas's historical support of populist Republican governors and fundamentalist Christian values has created a political and cultural climate that undermines the authority of scientists and evidence-based knowledge to an extent unknown in other states, both inside and outside courts of law.

Another piece of evidence often adduced in support of insanity claims involves observations of a sudden or gradual change in the defendant's character and behavior. For example, in the trial of Edward Winn, a young man convicted of murder during the commission of a robbery, the defendant's mother cited her son's transformation from a socially adjusted boy with an interest in music to a depressed and withdrawn teenager, a lone wolf who had no interest in social activities or in school, spent most of the time alone in his room, and stood up all night reading the Bible out loud.[122] Psychiatrists testifying in Winn's case attributed this kind of personality change during adolescence with the onset of dementia praecox, a mental condition associated with delusions and hallucinations. In this and comparable cases experts relied on the commonsense belief that if a person behaves irrationally or out of character, there must be something wrong with them.[123]

Besides talking to the defendant, early twentieth-century physicians conducted a medical examination to assess the individual's general physical health. In an attempt to draw a clear line between insanity and criminality and to give their testimony an aura of objectivity, expert witnesses tried to define mental illness according to observable physical criteria. However, courtroom doctors often disagreed on the correct diagnosis in individual cases, and the physical descriptions they needed to corroborate their opinions were often difficult to find. Lacking more sophisticated techniques, physicians based their evaluation on a routine physical examination, which involved simply looking at the defendant's eyes and pupils, measuring blood pressure and heart rate, and testing knee reflexes.[124] In some cases a change in appetite, sleeplessness, and/or headaches were seen as sufficient signs of the presence of mental disease,[125] especially when they followed an accident involving a head injury.[126]

In several cases doctors refrained from conducting a physical examination altogether. In such instances physicians either based their opinions on the observation of defendants' manners and behaviors alone,[127] like any other lay witness, or on the hypothetical questions formulated by the attorneys.[128] Such testimonies generally drew from (1) observations of the defendant's acts and appearance around the time of the crime, during the examination, and in court;[129] (2) testimony adduced at trial; and (3) simple conversations with the defendant whose nature and content remain largely unknown.[130] The reasons for the mystery surrounding doctors' diagnostic methods is that attorneys often failed to ask doctors how the examination was conducted and how they had reached their conclusions. Doctors, on the other hand, were generally vague and reticent when such questions were effectively asked, possibly because the practice of taking notes and keeping a record of the examination was still far from established, even in criminal trials where the life of the defendant was at stake.[131]

To summarize, though informed by the biological and hereditary paradigms of the time, physicians asked to give expert opinions in Texas courts lacked the necessary medical knowledge, diagnostic instruments, and professional rigor to conduct thoughtful and transparent mental health evaluations based on strong scientific methods. Accordingly, with few exceptions, they based their testimonies on superficial medical assessments, formulaic descriptions of diagnostic classifications, and behavioral observations devoid of technical content. As I will discuss in Chapter 2, these diagnostic limitations, coupled with the difficulty of reconciling psychiatric explanations of criminal behavior with the legal questions that experts were required to answer in insanity trials, would have dramatic consequences for the judicial destinies of mentally ill defendants tried in Texas criminal courts.

Conclusion

As we have seen, the first three decades of the twentieth century were characterized by a tension between mental health professionals' scientific aspirations and the value-laden language they used to describe mentally ill offenders' personalities and conduct. On the one hand, psychiatrists and psychologists tried to align with the new scientific medicine by identifying the mechanisms connecting various organic abnormalities and genetic defects with severe mental health conditions and criminal conduct. On the other hand, they provided moralized descriptions of offenders' personalities and behaviors that, drawing from Darwinian evolutionism, "race science," and a puritan work ethic of sobriety and restraint, recast male offenders (particularly if African American or Catholic immigrants) as genetically inferior, morally "primitive," and devoid of "self-control."

In line with the biological and evolutionary framework of the time, psychiatrists writing in the 1910s and 1920s were firmly convinced that mentally ill criminals carried the marks of their mental and moral depravity on their physical bodies. Hence the diagnosis of mental illness and criminality ought to start from a search for external signs of anatomical "abnormality," which might suggest a halt or regression to a more primitive stage of human development. In the research literature, a similar diagnosis involved conducting meticulous physical measurements and observations aimed at identifying tangible features that could help psychiatrists distinguish the mentally ill criminal from the "normal" population. In criminal courts, it entailed carrying out crude behavioral observations and medical evaluations aimed at assessing whether the defendants' mental health condition at the time of the alleged offense was so severe as to deprive them of the necessary cognitive abilities to understand that their conduct was wrong. In the next chapter we will explore the contrasts between forensic psychiatric theories and medical experts' courtroom practices in further detail, paying particular attention to (1) psychiatry's diagnostic limitations when dealing with living individuals and (2) the difficulties of reconciling experts' interpretations of defendants' behavior with the folk-psychological view of human conduct that dominated Texas courtrooms.

TWO

Biology, Insanity, and the Criminal Courts

> A scientific re-examination of the underlying shibboleths, superstitions, and ancient prejudices of our penal law is called for. The great interest in the "crime problem" which is manifest everywhere furnishes the occasion. The marked recent progress of psychiatry, psychology, social case work, and statistical techniques afford the instruments. We must step out of the closed circle of merely legal materials if we would really evaluate the present criminal law and if creative contributions to its improvement are to be made. Not new penal codes spun out of the ingenious a priorisms of criminal lawyers and proceeding upon the same questionable assumptions and prejudices as to "freedom of will" and the value of modern punitive institutions that underly the present regime; not absurdly inadequate tinkerings with the bolts and nuts of an adolescent machine that will probably require basic re-designing and rebuilding; nothing less than a thorough scientific re-examination of the entire situation of society as related to the genesis and control of criminality is needed, if this vital problem is ever to be solved.[1]
>
> —SHELDON GLUECK

Sheldon Glueck, an influential criminologist from Harvard University, echoed the sentiments of many of his colleagues when, in 1928, he called for a radical rethinking of the criminal law in light of recent developments in the medical sciences. A younger colleague and protégé of Roscoe Pound, he shared with his mentor a dissatisfaction with traditional criminal law principles, particularly as applied to juvenile "delinquents" and mentally ill criminals. Starting from a determinist view of human nature and behavior, Glueck and other exponents of the new "scientific" criminology believed that most criminal behavior could be reconducted to an underlying organic pathology,[2] and that mentally ill offenders should be held not responsible for their violent acts and institutionalized in state hospitals for medical treatment. Instead of following traditional principles of retributive justice, they argued, judges and legislators ought to embrace an individualized approach to penal treatment that leveraged current medical knowledge to identify the psychiatric conditions and therapeutic needs of individual offenders and devise appropriate forms of correction.[3]

While progressive medico-legal scholars were pushing for the incorporation of scientific principles into legal doctrines and courtroom practices, conservative legislators and members of the judiciary resisted medical pressures to reform. The legal establishment was generally reluctant to embrace the deterministic assumptions of the new biomedical sciences, preferring to maintain a system of rules based on traditional notions of free will and rational choice. In Texas this conservative pushback manifested itself both in the state's refusal to incorporate the findings of modern medicine into its notions of insanity and criminal responsibility, and in courts' maintenance of practices that were based on commonsense assumptions that had been repeatedly discredited by medical research. For example, despite medical pressures to incorporate an "irresistible impulse" test that would consider potential impairments in the defendant's volitional capacities, Texas decided to maintain the narrow rationalism of the *M'Naghten* rules and focus all the attention on the defendant's ability to distinguish right from wrong. This restrictive legal requirement, coupled with the "epistemological behaviorism"[4] that tends to dominate the trial context, dramatically limited defense attorneys and their experts' ability to build a convincing insanity defense based on current medical knowledge, leading to the imposition of death sentences on several individuals who might have deserved a more compassionate treatment.

In the early twentieth century the challenges presented by the conflicts between psychiatric and legal notions of insanity were exacerbated by the poor levels of legal representation and medical expertise offered to most indigent capital defendants.[5] With few exceptions, defense attorneys lacked the resources to hire qualified expert consultants who could corroborate, with sound medical evidence, the explanations offered by the lay witnesses. Similarly, courtroom physicians missed the technical instruments to back up their diagnoses with "objective" physical proof that could convince the most skeptical jurors. As a result, they typically limited their testimonies to superficial descriptions of the defendant's symptoms and diagnostic label and thus failed to unpack the connection between the defendant's poor mental state and the criminal acts for which he was on trial. In cases involving low-class defendants with weak work ethics and less than "honorable" habits, these problems were amplified by experts' reliance on explanations and word choices that shifted the blame for the defendant's suffering from the mental illness itself to the defendant's "wicked" lifestyle. As we will see, this was particularly apparent in cases involving a diagnosis of syphilis, given its sexually transmitted nature and its puritan association with promiscuity and immorality.

Inside the Texas Courtroom

In the first half of the twentieth century prosecution and defense experts advanced contrasting views on the causes and manifestations of insanity and on their applicability to the case at hand (a pattern that can be observed even in modern courtroom practices). On the one hand, the prosecution experts argued that the defendant was capable of rational reasoning, had a clear motive for attacking the victim, and had demonstrated some level of shrewdness at the time of the offense, all aspects that in their view suggested a lucid and therefore culpable state of mind.[6] On the other hand, the defense alienists claimed that, although the defendant could appear to reason coherently and act purposefully, he might still be harboring some underlying pathology that made him irresponsible for the crime committed. As to the causes of defendants' insanity and criminal behavior, defense psychiatrists generally agreed that most cases could be reconducted to heredity, "a congenital disposition toward lack of moral perceptivity and control."[7] This view had acquired increasing popularity in the 1880s and 1890s, when heredity was used "to explain susceptibility to infectious disease, the occurrence of most chronic illness, and . . . behavioral aberrations of all kinds."[8] Despite growing critiques from psychoanalytic writers, the notion that insanity and criminality could be attributed to hereditary influence continued to shape Texas trial tactics and courtroom testimonies well into the twentieth century, at least until the end of World War II.

Heredity and Environment

Although most early twentieth-century doctors agreed on the hereditary nature of insanity,[9] the extent to which the environment could modify an inherited mental and behavioral "pathology" was a topic of much controversy. Some alienists inspired by Mendel's genetic theories proposed a purely hereditary etiology, arguing that even though most mentally defective criminals came from degenerated and poverty-stricken neighborhoods, these social and cultural conditions were the result of, rather than the cause of, the inhabitants' mental and moral depravity.[10] Others rejected this biologically deterministic and monocausal interpretation, arguing that the environment could play an equally crucial role in precipitating constitutionally defective individuals' already weak mental condition.[11]

Physicians testifying in Texas courts endorsed the latter view of criminal causality. Drawing from a combination of genetic and environmental explanations, they argued that, when facing stressful life events, subjects who had inherited a mental disease from their ancestors were more likely to break down, lose control over their reasoning faculties, and engage in criminal conduct. The exciting causes of insanity were numerous and went from physical problems, such as venereal disease and epilepsy, to more behavioral and psychological issues, such as alcohol abuse, over-worry, and strong feelings of love, hate, and fear. Even though anyone exposed to extreme physical and environmental pressures could potentially develop insanity and lose control over their moral faculties, the argument went, such pressures "acted with far greater malignancy if a taint of insanity were established in the blood."[12] State expert Dr. C. W. Gray clearly synthesized this perspective at the trial of Joe Shield, a man with a history of insanity in his family who was accused of killing his divorced wife and in-laws in 1931. According to the doctor:

> If there is mental unsoundness in the parents or down the line in the family, it predisposes the offspring to mental unbalance. Unbalance of mind is brought about in a great many instances by chronic worry and excessive grief; [for] some forms of insanity where they have weak nervous system or in a weakened condition to start with . . . sudden shocks have a predisposing effect on the mind towards insanity. . . . I have heard of people going suddenly insane

> at the grave of some loved one. . . . [They] do not have any control over their will and do not know anything about right or wrong.[13]

Evidence that a parent, sibling, or relative suffered from some form of mental illness was extremely helpful for the defense, particularly when the defendant's insanity claim was weak. By emphasizing a family history of insanity, defense attorneys could potentially divert the jury's attention from the mental status of the defendant to that of a mentally disordered family member, playing on the determinist idea that if a close relative suffered from a severe mental condition, it followed that their client suffered from some form of mental disease as well.[14] However, defense attorneys often failed to elicit a connection between the mental disorder suffered by the defendant's family member and the one allegedly suffered by the defendant himself, making heredity claims based on family history alone unconvincing.[15] This omission may have been due to a combination of several factors, such as poor investigations driven by a lack of expertise and/or financial constraints, difficulties in retrieving hospital records and conducting interviews with relevant witnesses, and a lack of substantial evidence supporting the legitimacy of the defendant's insanity claim in the first place.

The case of George Duke, a working-class man charged with killing his girlfriend in 1944, offers a typical example of this kind of pitfall. At trial the defense based most of its strategy on the notion that Duke came from a family of "mentally deranged" convicts and that, on the night of the crime, he was under the influence of "intoxicating liquor."[16] Duke's oldest sister, Mandy Miles, testified that their mother, uncle, niece, and brother had all been committed to insane asylums and that two of them had done jail or prison time. She gave the following account of their family history:

> My mother's name was Lurana Duke when she married my father in Bell County, Texas. She was committed to the insane asylum at Austin, but was released several years before she died. She was George's mother. I have an uncle named Jesse Duke. He was in Louisiana but I can't say what town, and he was committed to an insane asylum when I was very small. He is dead now, and died in the insane ward of a jail. My niece, Lucile Landers, was committed to the Wichita Falls insane asylum. They had my sister, Ida Sawyer, in, but I don't think she was ever sentenced to an asylum. I got a report to go to Fairfield, but I didn't go. My brother, Jim David Duke, has

> been committed to an insane asylum, I heard, but I can't be positive as I haven't had a written letter from him. The last I knew he was committed to Huntsville from this court.[17]

The defense's case rested on the idea that Duke had inherited his mother's bad genes, which had weakened his mental faculties, predisposing him to the development of insanity. On the night of the crime the abuse of "intoxicating" liquor further impaired Duke's reasoning powers, prompting him to lose control and unleash his violent attack against the victim. However, the defense presented no expert to corroborate this theory and made no attempt to show that there was a connection between the mental disease suffered by Duke's family members and the one allegedly suffered by Duke himself. Moreover, the state's evidence suggested that Duke had threatened to kill his girlfriend in the past and that he was in the habit of getting heavily drunk, arguing vociferously with the victim, and shooting the pistol in the apartment.[18] Duke's past threats and domestic abuse strongly undermined the notion that the crime stemmed from a temporary lapse in his mental faculties, prompting the jury to conclude that he was fully responsible for the crime committed.

In some cases the defense made some crude attempts to link the defendant's alleged mental health condition to the one suffered by the parents. For example, Joe Shield based his insanity plea primarily on lay witness testimonies suggesting that his father was an alcoholic "sidewalk preacher" who believed he could talk to spirits and make contact with the dead.[19] Although the record contains detailed explanations of the way in which the father's mental health had gradually degenerated,[20] it is strikingly silent as to the defendant's allegedly "unsound" state of mind. Moreover, when the witnesses tried to tie the defendant's insanity claim to his father's mental health problems, they limited themselves to observing that the two resembled each other physically and mentally, providing no explanation as to whether Joe had acquired the eccentricities that made them believe that his father was insane. For example, one of the defendant's cousins limited his description of the resemblances between the two Shields to the following: "Joe very closely resembled his father when he was Joe's age . . . in physical appearance. Physiognomy. Face and head. And quite similar mentally. . . . Joe very closely resembles his father in the contour of his face and head and in his mental traits as far as I can tell."[21] This and similar observations suggest that, at the time of Joe's trial, lay witnesses were subtly influenced by nineteenth-century physiognomic theories,[22] which suggested the existence of a close link between physical structures, particularly the shape of the face and skull, mental illnesses, and criminality. However, they are also indicative of a larger tendency among lay witnesses to rely on observations of defendants' external appearance and behaviors to infer their mental state and draw conclusions regarding their insanity and criminal responsibility.[23]

As these examples suggest, the notion that mentally ill criminals had likely inherited some defective genes from their parents was extremely popular, both among psychiatric authorities and among lay actors and trial attorneys.[24] However, defense strategies based on popular hereditarian and biological theories often failed to secure an insanity acquittal in Texas courts, even when evidence of the defendant's poor mental health was arguably overwhelming. The 1947 trial of Lloyd Ross, a highly respected Harvard-educated surgeon practicing in San Antonio, clearly illustrates this problem. Dr. Ross was charged with the murders of his friend and investment adviser Willard York, York's wife, Gertrude, and two of their children.[25] In the years preceding the killings, Ross had entrusted York with investing a large portion of his savings in a financial portfolio of stocks and bonds.[26] In early 1947 he discovered that York had mismanaged his investments, causing him to lose most of his life savings. Shocked by this discovery and feeling betrayed by his friend, the formerly law-abiding doctor planned a violent retaliation. After having procured a gun, he went to York's home and shot him and his family as they came home in their car, killing all of them except for York's 13-year-old daughter, who managed to escape from the vehicle. At trial the defense tried to show that the violent attacks stemmed from a *combination* of bad heredity and traumatic life events, which had caused the doctor to succumb to the pressures of unrestrained impulses and develop insanity.

In support of the defendant's insanity claim, the defense introduced several lay witnesses, including nurses, doctors, and acquaintances who had known Dr. Ross for several years. They all agreed that he had undergone a radical transformation over the months preceding the killings, particularly following the financial breakdown.[27] From being a respectable, kind, courteous, and professional man, the surgeon started dressing sloppily and became withdrawn, forgetful, and absentminded. He looked nervous, became severely depressed, and lost interest in everything and everyone. His work suffered as a result, to the point that several nurses and doctors who worked with him on a daily basis commented on it.[28] The witnesses all agreed that the murders were completely out of character and concluded that the man must have gone insane to commit a similar action.[29] The fact that Dr. Ross previously was a "perfect gentleman," honorable, and full of virtues made his crime even more difficult to interpret as an act of rational choice.

The defense psychiatrists, Anna Boyd and W. J. Johnson, agreed with the lay witnesses that Dr. Ross was insane at the time of the crime. In their view the defendant had a "schizoid personality" disorder that caused him to experience paranoid delusions, persecutory thoughts, and religious obsessions. Although he had suffered from this condition from an early age, the disease had accumulated over time and manifested itself as he collapsed under the pressures of life.[30] For example, Dr. Boyd testified that shortly after discovering his financial losses, Ross developed

> the idea that everyone was commenting on him, that everyone was watching him as he went down the street, talking about him, saying what a sucker he is. . . . He felt also that the doctors were taking a great delight in his plight; Dr. Ross had had the idea for some time that two San Antonio doctors hated him; that they were spying on him; that they were sending people around to check up on him, and that they were turning patients away from him. Dr. Ross also had the delusion that his wife had turned his daughter against him; he has felt an exaggerated idea of his wife's unfriendliness toward him.[31]

In addition to experiencing these paranoid thoughts, Ross was obsessed with his health and hygiene, refusing to have water in his ear for fear of infections, repeatedly washing his hands, and changing his socks several times a day.[32] Finally, he was firmly convinced that all the events leading up to the murders, including the murders themselves, were part of God's "infinite plan."[33]

On top of this, two physicians testified that Dr. Ross suffered from "rheumatic fever," a disease that could cause him to experience brain hemorrhages, with devastating effects on his mental faculties.[34] The disease, they argued, had degenerated in the months preceding the murder, causing the defendant to suffer an eye hemorrhage, which suggested the possibility of internal brain bleeding. Although Dr. Ross had always had paranoid tendencies, the defense psychiatrists argued, it was the fears associated with the worsening of his physical condition coupled with the pressures associated with his financial losses that precipitated his mental health break.[35]

Finally, the evidence showed that the defendant's mother had died in an insane asylum suffering from a form of paranoia.[36] Several witnesses argued that the defendant closely resembled his mother. They described Mrs. Ross as "gentle and retiring . . . a quiet and reserved woman"[37] who had become mentally "unstable, moody, depressed, and child-like in her manner" as a result of her mental condition.[38] In his youth the defendant shared his mother's reserved character and disposition, as well as her moodiness, depression, and paranoid tendencies. As happened in the *Shield* case, in the absence of more "scientific" methods to assess the hereditary nature of the defendant's mental illness, the lay witnesses relied on physical and characterological similarities to link mother and son's paranoid conditions.

According to the defense, Dr. Ross's congenital paranoia, combined with his medical condition and the emotional strain resulting from his financial loss, gradually undermined his brain's ability to keep the "lower instincts" under control, eventually resulting in an explosion of unrestrained violence with devastating consequences. As one of the physicians who diagnosed the defendant's rheumatic fever explained at trial, "The piling up of emotional stresses and strains one upon the top of the other . . . might cause a so-called blow-up in the mental capacity of the individual, and he might become dangerous and do unheard of things."[39] On appeal the Texas Court of Criminal Appeals (TCCA) upheld Dr. Ross's conviction and death sentence. In response to the defendant's claim that the evidence supporting his insanity plea was so overwhelming as to invalidate the jury's verdict, the TCCA highlighted that

> much of the evidence in the case presents conclusions of witnesses, based on the idea which the witness had that circumstances had developed in the appellant an *irresistible impulse* which drove Dr. Ross to the murder of Willard York, and with him his wife, Gertrude York. . . . [However] the one controlling question in this case is whether or not the accused was so mentally

deranged at the time of the commission of the alleged offense as to make him *incapable of knowing the right from the wrong* in the particular transaction, and that it was a thing he ought not to do.[40]

This, according to the TCCA, the defense had failed to conclusively show.[41] In addition, the circumstances surrounding the murders showed that the defendant had a clear *motive* for wanting to inflict suffering on Willard York and his family, whereas his *actions* following the killings suggested that he understood that his act was wrong. According to the TCCA, "Following the shooting [appellant] returned to San Antonio, went to the police station and surrendered himself to be imprisoned for his crime. It would be singular that a man should do this in the absence of any realization of wrong doing."[42] The court's reasoning in *Ross* clearly illustrates the difficulty of reconciling psychiatry and the law's ontological and epistemological assumptions when trying to establish criminal guilt. Texas courts, like most other judicial bodies, endorse a folk-psychological approach to insanity and criminal responsibility that relies on the observation of external behaviors to infer mental states rather than on scientific explanations highlighting the influence of unconscious impulses on the individual will. As a result, psychiatric evidence that the defendant suffered from a mental illness at the time of the crime may prove useless for the purpose of the insanity defense if the defendant's behavior before and after the commission of the alleged offense suggests the presence of premeditation and/or cover-up. Moreover, psychiatric opinions based on reflex action and heredity theories, such as the ones introduced in Dr. Ross's case, tend to suggest that the defendant acted under an irresistible impulse while maintaining his cognitive abilities intact, falling short of the legal standard of insanity required to prove lack of guilt.

Brain Damage

Besides emphasizing the hereditary nature of mental disease, many early twentieth-century psychiatrists believed that insanity could stem from an organic pathology, especially if the condition affected the individual's brain. Although brain lesions were difficult to locate and identify, psychiatrists were confident that as pathological investigations became more refined, they would eventually reach a full understanding of the physiological causes leading to criminal insanity.[43] Partly as a result of this scientific optimism, the psychiatric literature of the time was filled with speculative explanations of the biological mechanisms connecting various organic defects, mental diseases, and criminal behaviors. Conversely, such explanations rarely, if ever, appeared in the discourse of experts called to testify in Texas capital punishment trials. The reason for this mismatch is that, until a series of technical innovations enhanced psychiatrists' diagnostic abilities—particularly regarding syphilis, feeblemindedness, and epilepsy—somatic explanations of brain pathologies relied primarily on postmortem examinations.

Psychiatrists valued postmortem examinations because they allowed them to identify brain lesions and other organic abnormalities that differentiated insane individuals from the "normal" population.[44] However, because of their inapplicability to living persons, this method was of limited utility for psychiatrists hired to conduct mental health evaluations and to testify in criminal proceedings. As a result, experts typically based their mental health assessments on a simple 20–30-minute conversation aimed at assessing the defendant's cognitive abilities and on the hypothetical questions formulated by the defense and the prosecution. Their opinions drew from information that was equally available to lay observers, such as the defendant's family, medical, and criminal history; his manners, speech, and conduct; his ability to carry on a conversation intelligently and meaningfully; and any marked changes in his personality and conduct following the alleged brain damage.[45] Partly as a result of this epistemological limitation, most insanity trials in the first half of the twentieth century relied almost exclusively on lay witness testimonies, even when defendants' insanity claims were based on organic explanations of mental disease, such as brain damage following traumatic accidents.[46] An analysis of such testimonies suggests that the lay public believed that insanity was closely associated with organic brain defects and that traumatic head injuries could lead to a sudden change in the individual's character and behavior, prompting him to engage in criminal conduct.[47] Traumatic head injuries were, in the mind of many lay witnesses, a useful rationalization for defendants' change of character and criminal actions.

Following a traumatic head injury, lay witnesses argued, defendants would manifest a variety of behavioral symptoms. They would experience severe headaches, insomnia, lapses of memory, and difficulties communicating.[48] They would become melancholic, laugh without reason, talk to themselves, and have persecutory delusions.[49] These were all clear manifestations of insanity, according to the defense. However, evidence that the defendant behaved oddly following a head trauma was typically insufficient to convince the jury that the defendant should be exculpated for his crime, especially if the offense was cruel and/or showed evidence of planning and deception.[50]

The 1923 trial of Ewell Morris, a 21-year-old African American cotton picker, serves as a compelling case study for this point. Morris was charged with the murder of Oliver Marshall, a neighboring white landowner who had recently purchased a ranch where the defendant lived with his mother and two sisters.[51] According to Morris's confession, Marshall inappropriately interfered with the part of land owned by Morris's family, riding over the place on numerous occasions and making excessive use of the communal barn. Upset about Marshall's lack of respect for his property, Morris acquired a shotgun and some shells, hid in a strategic spot of the farm, and shot the victim, killing him instantly.

At trial, Morris raised the insanity defense and presented lay witness testimonies in support of his claim. The witnesses reported that two years before the killing, the defendant had suffered a head injury by falling off the sidewalk and hitting his head on the paved street.[52] Even though Morris recovered shortly after the fall, a few family members testified that they had noticed a marked change in his character and behavior after the accident. Among other things, they reported that Morris started obsessively washing his hands, pulling his fingernails, not speaking and not answering people's questions, speaking and laughing to himself without reason, not sleeping at night, and spitting food and throwing it on the floor.[53] Most important, they argued that in the year before the murder, Morris started to fear sleeping alone at night because he believed that the victim was spying on him at all times with the intent of killing him.[54]

According to the witnesses, it was the traumatic head injury suffered a few years before the murder that had caused Morris's mind to degenerate, undermining his ability to distinguish right from wrong. However, in the absence of medical experts corroborating this hypothesis, the defense's theory lost its explanatory force. The lay witnesses testifying in Morris's case lacked the necessary authority and expertise to explain how the traumatic brain injury may have undermined Morris's ability to reason, make moral judgments, and control his behavior, making an insanity claim based on their opinions alone less powerful. Moreover, the evidence showed that Morris had threatened to kill the victim on numerous occasions before effectively carrying out the murder, and that he had tried to hide at the house of some relatives on the night following the crime.[55] These facts likely led the jury to infer that the murder was premeditated, and that Morris had sufficient mental capacity to distinguish right from wrong at the time of the offense, regardless of the symptoms observed by his family.

Finally, because the case involved a black defendant killing a white victim, and because (white) Texas jurors tend to impose harsher sentences in similar cases,[56] the jury's decision to impose the death penalty was presumably informed not only by lucid considerations regarding Morris's mental health, but also by racist stereotypes that prompted them to explain his criminal act as an expression of his "uncivilized nature" rather than of a mental disorder.[57] In this context, the fact that most defense witnesses were black members of the defendant's family, and most state witnesses were local white landowners and police officers, constituted an additional advantage for the prosecution, which could bet on jurors' likelihood to hold the opinion of the state witnesses in higher regard.[58]

In cases of acute mental disorder and financial hardship, the defendant could be the only (or almost only) witness introduced to support his own insanity claim.[59] In such instances the defendant's testimony was turned into a psychiatric session, a stream of consciousness in which the accused gave a detailed account of his life experiences and of the events leading to, and following, the criminal act itself. In the absence of a medical evaluation, jurors were turned into listening ears with the responsibility of judging, based on their own commonsense views, whether the defendant's manners, appearance, speech, and account of the event suggested that he was mentally deranged at the time of the crime.

The 1935 trial of James Pappas provides an illustrative example in this regard.[60] Pappas was a poor and mentally unstable Greek immigrant with limited knowledge of the English language. Charged with the murder with malice of Bess Burt, a woman he loved but who refused his advances,

Pappas signed a written confession—that he was incapable of reading—in which he admitted to the killing for romantic reasons.[61] Because of his mental condition and linguistic difficulties, Pappas was incapable of cooperating with counsel in his own defense and of providing a list of witnesses who could testify in support of his insanity claim.[62] Hence, Pappas's defense attorneys were forced to rely exclusively on the defendant's own testimony to support their theory that Pappas was mentally ill and legally insane at the time of the killing.[63]

In their motion for a new trial, the defense attorneys argued that "the wild, fantastic, unbelievable story" told by Pappas on the witness stand clearly demonstrated that he was a mentally unbalanced individual.[64] A reading of Pappas's testimony at trial corroborates this conclusion, suggesting that the defendant was extremely confused and had no understanding of his defense strategy. On the one hand, he provided information in support of his insanity claim, testifying that he had been confined in "the crazy hospital" on numerous occasions.[65] On the other hand, in a convoluted, implausible, and incoherent account of the facts, he tried to convince the jury that he was innocent, that he signed the confession although he could not read in English,[66] and that the real perpetrator was an imaginary woman who had killed the victim out of jealousy because she was madly in love with him.[67] An extract of the district attorney's cross-examination clearly illustrates the difficulty of eliciting any meaningful information from the defendant.

Q. Now, when you got in the car the next morning, you had the pistol with you?
A. How do you know I had it?
Q. I am asking you.
A. Do you want me to tell yes or no?
Q. I want you to tell the God's truth?
A. I said a while ago, I said what I had to say.
Q. Did you have the pistol when you got in?
A. Now, I said I told you already, and told the jury and you too. I don't know what I am going to say. You make me like crazy.
Q. I asked you if you had the pistol when you got in the car. The answer is "yes" or "no."

A. I don't remember. . . .
Q. When you got out of the automobile on Jenkins Street, when it was raining, did you not have the pistol then with you?
A. I don't know what you are going to tell me; I don't know what I have. I told you what I was going to say. . . . You make me so dizzy; anything you ask I am going to say "yes." . . . When I got out of the car down there on Jenkins Street, I did not have the pistol with me then.[68]

Given this testimony, the defense attorneys asked the TCCA to grant a new hearing based on newly discovered evidence in support of the defendant's insanity claim. Pappas corroborated his attorneys' statements, arguing that he had only started sharing details about his mental condition following his conviction in 1935.[69] In line with the "brain damage" theory of the time, Pappas believed that his mental condition had degenerated following a head injury suffered during his youth. The injury had allegedly caused him to suffer from severe headaches and lapses of memory, during which he lost his reasoning abilities, "imagined things humanly impossible," and "acted in a wild and crazy manner."[70] To corroborate the defendant's story, the attorneys presented a series of affidavits written by his friends and acquaintances. In these affidavits, Pappas's friends argued that the defendant's mother was insane and was known in their village in Greece as the "Crazy Batziamarkos,"[71] that they had always considered the defendant "a crazy galoot, in other words 'nuts,'" that the defendant "would fly off the handle and was just like a wild man when he got mad,"[72] that he "did not seem to have any control of himself where women were concerned," that he "was unable to carry on a sensible conversation," and that he "seemed to have the mind of a child."[73]

The TCCA ruled that, given Pappas's lack of cooperation in the investigations, the defense attorneys had used "reasonable diligence to obtain testimony touching appellant's mental condition" and that the newly discovered evidence was "certainly material, and calculated, we think, to change the result on another trial."[74] Recognizing that Pappas was probably not a responsible person, the judges reversed the judgment of the trial court and remanded the case for a new hearing. As this example suggests, in extreme cases of mental derangement, the availability of a direct line of communication between the defendant and the court can help unveil mental disorders that would otherwise be filtered, sanitized, and tainted by the language of mental health experts with a partisan interest in securing a conviction. This emerges clearly in the testimony provided by the state experts in this case, who insisted that Pappas was of sane mind despite his bewildering testimony.

Syphilis

Defendants claiming that they suffered from brain pathologies and intellectual defects, such as syphilis and feeblemindedness, were more likely to rely on expert opinions to support their insanity claims. A possible explanation is that such disorders presented clear and specific physical and behavioral symptoms that psychiatrists and psychologists could more confidently identify, even in living individuals. This was particularly true following the development of a series of diagnostic instruments that, by allowing experts to objectively assess the presence of these conditions premortem, legitimized expert testimonies in trial proceedings.

Syphilis, a venereal disease associated with "mucous patches, skin eruptions, and glandular enlargement,"[75] constitutes a case in point. Between 1905 and 1913 psychiatrists concluded that syphilis was caused by a bacterium, *Treponema pallidum*, which could lead to a gradual mental degeneration, general paralysis, and the patient's eventual death.[76] In 1906 they developed the Wasserman reaction, a diagnostic test based on the analysis of a sample of blood or spinal fluid, with an estimated 95% accuracy.[77] In 1909 they discovered a drug, Salvarsan, that proved effective in the treatment of some syphilitic patients. Finally, in 1913 Hideyo Noguchi and J. W. Moore published a study that, based on postmortem examinations, conclusively demonstrated that syphilis caused brain lesions, which in turn led to general paralysis and insanity.[78]

The impact of these discoveries cannot be overstated. In the 1910s, 1920s, and 1930s, psychiatric authorities estimated that general paralysis caused between 10% and 25% of insanity cases found in mental health hospitals across the United States, making it a central public health concern.[79] By showing a link between a recognized organic pathology, such as syphilis, and general paralysis, psychiatrists could claim a scientific status for their discipline and a legitimate place among the medical professions. Moreover, the discovery of a diagnostic test that could identify the presence of the disease while the patient was still alive allowed psychiatrists to overcome the methodological barriers that had limited their premortem evaluations to the external observation of behavioral symptoms. By relying on the analysis of biological matter, the Wasserman reaction dramatically legitimized psychiatrists' diagnoses, giving them an aura of scientific objectivity that traditional psychiatric interviews could hardly achieve.[80]

Discoveries in the field of syphilology opened new horizons to psychiatrists who were called to testify in insanity trials. For the first time in history psychiatrists had the instruments to gather scientific proof of the presence or absence of a brain pathology associated with complete mental incapacitation. The physical nature of this kind of evidence legitimized psychiatrists' claims and, in their view, shielded them from insinuations that they had been deceived by defendants who faked mental illness in order to escape punishment. However, Texas courts were generally suspicious of the defendants' reported symptoms (whether organic or inorganic), even when the psychiatric evaluation was based on physical examinations, scientific measurements, and laboratory tests.[81] In the case of syphilis this overall skepticism was exacerbated by negative stereotypes that, by linking the condition to immoral sexual habits, reframed the criminal act as the result, not of an organic disease operating beyond the subject's control, but of "vicious" lifestyles and behaviors that could have been controlled and therefore corrected. As I will show in the next subsection, by linking defendants' mental health problems and criminal acts to "immoral" behaviors rather than to physical problems, trial actors shifted the criminal blame to the defendants themselves, undermining their insanity claims and powerfully tipping the scales in favor of a guilty verdict.

Syphilis, Immorality, and Crime

Because of its sexually transmitted nature, syphilis was historically associated with sinfulness and moral depravation, a stigmatizing disease that led to social exclusion and public shaming. Although early twentieth-century discoveries in the field of syphilology prompted a growing number of psychiatrists to object to the old view of syphilis as a "carnal scourge,"[82] the traditional association between syphilis and sinfulness survived these critiques. Indeed, several authors writing in the 1910s and 1920s continued to discuss syphilis in morally charged terms, associating the condition with demographic categories whose alleged sexual habits made them particularly prone to contract the disease. For example, in 1914 Dr. Mary O'Malley conducted research into the differential impact of syphilis on white and African American women and concluded that syphilis disproportionately affected the latter group.[83] The reason for such a differential impact, she argued, could be found in African Americans' "animal appetites" and "promiscuous" behavior. Freed from the control of the white "masters," they acted instinctively and disorderly, indulging in various forms of "vices" and excesses, with devastating consequences for their physical and mental health.[84] According to O'Malley, African American women were particularly responsible for the proliferation of syphilis among members of their race. They engaged in premarital sex, had "illegitimate children," and contributed with their "sensual conduct" to the spreading of venereal diseases. Their behavior deviated from puritan white middle-class standards of femininity and was therefore forcefully condemned. In the words of O'Malley:

> The colored women withdraw from all the social laws of white women; many of them do not consider it necessary to enter wedlock, and the number of illegitimate children born to unmarried colored women is very great. Some of them have seven or eight children, although not married. . . . It must necessarily follow from the above facts that venereal disease would be common among them.[85]

Thirty years later, psychiatrists would frame the problem in less crude and judgmental terms. However, the idea that the inherent viciousness of certain social groups made them more prone to contract the disease still lurked beneath the surface. For example, a 1943 article by Dr. W. G. Smillie analyzed the serologic blood tests obtained from 2 million individuals selected for army service between 1940 and 1942 and concluded that syphilis disproportionately affected African Americans across the United States.[86] Although he refrained from the racist comments made by O'Malley, Smillie argued that, at the time, syphilis affected only African Americans and the "lowest" classes of white society, "the ignorant, the careless, the criminal, and the social outcast."[87] Syphilis, he proposed, was the disease of the corrupt and the deviant, a social malady that affected the undesirable categories of the American population.[88]

Discourse on syphilis in Texas capital punishment trials echoed the underlying tension between scientific approaches and moral judgments found in the psychiatric literature. For instance, in the 1936 trial of Donald Covin, a man who was found guilty of murdering a woman he was romantically interested in, the defense attorney repeatedly asked both the defense and the state experts if syphilis could be "innocently acquired," showing a concern that the jury could be negatively influenced by the belief that the defendant had contracted the disease as a result of "immoral conduct" and sexual promiscuity.[89] In response to these questions, the doctors stated that syphilis could be contracted "through innocent means,"[90] either inheritance or some other form of transmission not including sexual intercourse, such as kissing or through "some break in the flesh."[91] However, only 15% of syphilis infections were "innocently acquired" according to one of the experts, with the remaining 85% resulting from promiscuous sexual relations.[92]

The 1944 trial of Harold Miner[93] provides another example of the cultural association between syphilis and immorality that dominated the first half of the twentieth century. Miner, a 47-year-old white man, was on trial for the murder of his divorced wife, Marjorie Miner. According to his testimony, the man had an unhappy childhood resulting from "domestic disturbances" in the home.[94] His father left the family when Miner was 7 years old without providing financial support, forcing his mother to send him and his sister to live with foster parents.[95] Miner contracted syphilis in France during his service in World War I and married the victim, a woman seventeen years younger than him, a few years later in Iowa.[96] His life was defined by his struggle with the disease, which made him restless, sleepless, and depressed; by his continuous moves and changes of occupation; and by his excessive alcohol consumption, both alone and in the company of his wife. This alcohol abuse led to regular conflicts between the two, particularly because of his wife's infidelity and his obsessive jealousy, eventually leading to their separation and divorce.[97] In the defendant's words, "When Marjorie wasn't drinking she was a fine little person, a very lovable person. Unfortunately, under the influence of drink she was very like myself, we both had very nasty ungovernable tempers."[98]

After several failed attempts to persuade his wife to reconcile their differences, Miner threatened to kill her if she did not move back in with him.[99] He sought her out, begged her to return with him and, after a brief altercation in which she tried to run away from him, he shot her and fell, striking his head.[100] According to Miner's version of the facts, after the fall his mind went blank for a few hours, during which he forgot about the whole event. His memory reappeared the following morning, when he read about the shooting in the newspaper, realized what he had done, and decided to give himself up to the police.[101] The jury did not find the defendant's insanity claim and account of the facts convincing, convicted him for "murder with malice aforethought," and sentenced him to death. On appeal the TCCA confirmed the defendant's death sentence.

The opinion of S. D. Swope, a physician and surgeon who testified for the defense, evidences a censorious attitude toward the defendant and his lifestyle and a lack of compassion for his diseased condition, seen more as a consequence of his "over-indulgent behavior" than of some misfortune.[102] Dr. Swope argued that Miner was a psychopathic personality whose upbringing, lack of education, and low intellectual endowment made him unfit to live according to "modern civilized requirements."[103] On top of this, the defendant suffered from syphilis and indulged in excessive alcohol consumption, which, combined, led to a gradual mental and moral degeneration.

> In this state one loses all moral sense of propriety and social relation. He carries on his work for the sole purpose of providing for his *personal indulgence*, and develops into a psychopathic personality which has little regard for law and order and the right of his fellow man. A man thus *depraved* commits the various interdicted crimes and social irregularities without a clear appreciation of any social fault. A mind of this character easily breaks under the stress or strain of emotional association and loses all of his reasoning power and inhibitive sense, where other men with better mental endowment, education and social environment would retain a normal mental state of the appreciation of the rights of others and the necessity for living an upright life. I think the defendant is a psychopathic personality, a man poorly fitted with reasoning power *whose mind has been injured by syphilis and alcohol* to such an extent that his personal acts are not those of a well-balanced sane person.[104]

In view of his examination and of the hypothetical questions provided by the defense attorney, the doctor concluded that at the time of the killing Miner "was not in a normal state of mind" and that he did not know right from wrong.[105]

The language in which Dr. Swope framed his testimony suggests that far from endorsing the detached approach advocated by psychiatric authorities, his opinion was a mix of scientific discourse and moral judgment. On the one hand, his testimony contains a scientific explanation of the association of dementia paralytica with criminal behavior, which proposed that, even though individuals with this condition could normally distinguish right from wrong, if put under extreme pressure—either because of emotional upheavals or the excessive use of alcohol—they were likely to temporarily lose control over their actions, explode in an open manifestation of violence, and potentially forget about the whole event.[106]

On the other hand, Dr. Swope's testimony contains a moral condemnation of the defendant's habits and lifestyle, which deviated from the white Protestant standards of morality and masculinity of the Progressive Era. By associating syphilis and drunkenness with insanity and criminality, Dr. Swope echoed the concerns of rural Protestants, social progressives, and other members of the American temperance movement who, worried about the "moral corruption" brought about by excessive alcohol consumption, in the 1910s and 1920s had advocated and obtained the passage of prohibition laws banning the production and sale of alcoholic beverages across the United States.[107]

Inspired by this dry crusade, several psychiatrists of the time argued that alcohol was a "brain poison" that led to a gradual mental and moral degeneration, which was then transmitted across generations.[108] In this view, alcoholic intoxication removed men's moral inhibitions, undermining their capacity for self-restraint and tempting them to all sorts of indulgences, usually of a sexual nature.[109] In Texas these concerns were fueled by local anxieties about the moral dissipation that was believed to accompany excessive social drinking, particularly among the young men who frequented the saloons. As a temperance woman from Austin explained in a letter to a local editor:

> The social glass ruins more young men than any other form of dissipation—in fact it is the key to all dissipation. They drink to be social, and by the time they have taken two or three glasses, *their sensibilities are blunted and their reason is perverted*, and they do many things of which they are at first ashamed, but after a few repetitions they manifest a *"don't care" spirit*, and in a few years die, that worst of all things, a drunkard.[110]

Mirroring the arguments advanced by early twentieth-century psychiatric writers, the self-declared "Republican lady" believed that young men's alcohol abuse was causing their sensibilities and reason to degenerate, turning them into careless social beings who committed all sorts of immoral actions without feelings of shame or restraint. By recasting Miner's criminal act as the result of his alcoholic and sexual habits rather than of the physical and emotional distress associated with his physical disease, Dr. Swope endorsed this condemning perspective, inadvertently lending credence to the idea that the defendant was morally responsible for the crime committed, as well as for his medical condition.

Feeblemindedness

While psychiatrists explored the links between syphilis and dementia paralytica, a group of influential psychologists, later known as feeblemindedness theorists,[111] developed an explanation of criminal behavior that would influence the defense strategies of several defendants who were claiming insanity in Texas courts. Inspired by the pioneering work of British psychologist and criminologist Charles Goring,[112] feeblemindedness theorists believed that criminals were born with a genetic defect that made them less intelligent than the average citizen, and that this genetic defect could be transmitted to future generations as much as any other hereditary condition.[113] In the 1910s and 1920s these heredity theories merged with eugenic arguments, a marriage that would have dramatic consequences for America's public health policy over the following decades. Indeed, as government officials embraced the notion that feeblemindedness could be inherited and that it was their duty to improve the genetic quality of the U.S. population, a number of states started passing involuntary sterilization laws aimed at curbing the reproduction of "mentally defective" individuals detained in state institutions and deemed a threat to the health and security of the national stock.[114]

The creation of objective instruments for the measurement of intelligence legitimized psychologists' professional authority in this area, raising the status of their discipline among the mental health professions. The most significant advancement in the field of intelligence testing came in 1905 with the development of the Binet-Simon test, a standardized paper-and-pencil test that would become the chief method to assess intelligence levels among juveniles detained in U.S. penal institutions.[115] The Binet-Simon test measured children's level of intellectual development by comparing it with the average level of intelligence for children in a similar age category. If a child's abilities corresponded to those of a younger age group, he or she was classified as mentally defective, the severity of the defectiveness depending on the age of intellectual development reached. This approach to intelligence testing was based on the theory of recapitulation, which proposed that, as children transitioned into adulthood, they would gradually refine their ability to control their lower instincts and drives in the same way as the more "primitive" organisms and races could gradually acquire the biological sophistication and self-control of the more advanced ones.[116]

Whereas most early twentieth-century insanity trials relied on lay witness testimonies, the discovery of a method for the objective assessment of individuals' intelligence prompted a growing number of psychologists to testify in cases in which the defendant claimed to suffer from some form of intellectual impairment.[117] Intelligence tests distanced experts from old subjective methods based on "general impressions" and family pedigree studies,[118] giving them a seemingly scientific instrument that was more likely to hold up against the pressures of cross-examination. However, the use of more refined diagnostic instruments did not necessarily translate into more sophisticated explanations of the mechanisms connecting the intellectual disability with the crime committed. In fact, most psychologists continued to limit themselves to a description of the diagnostic instrument used and of the label applied to the defendant, failing to explain the mechanism through which the defendant's alleged intellectual disability affected the cognitive and emotional capacities required to behave lawfully.[119]

The psychological evidence offered by the defense in the trial of F. M.

Snow clearly illustrates this kind of pitfall. Snow was a 40-year-old white man charged with the killings of his wife, mother-in-law, and stepson in Erath County in 1923.[120] According to the defendant's confession, which was later corroborated by the forensic evidence and various eyewitnesses, Snow had killed the three victims and disposed of their bodies in a brutal yet systematic way. After having killed his stepson by shooting him in the back, Snow took his shoes and trousers, decapitated him with an ax, wrapped his head in a coat, and left it in an old cellar.[121] He then took the victim's beheaded body to a place about eight or nine miles away, where it was later found by the authorities. The following evening, Snow burned the dead bodies of his wife and mother-in-law by placing them in his home's fireplace, a process that took him about seven hours. The police later found human bones and teeth, presumably belonging to the victims, in the defendant's home, confirming the defendant's account of the events and the circumstantial evidence provided by the witnesses.[122]

Snow raised the insanity defense and introduced both lay and expert witnesses in support of his claim. The defense's chief expert witness, a psychologist and social worker named Jean Shepard, administered the standard revision of the Binet-Simon test and concluded that the defendant had the "mentality" of a 9-year-old and could be classified as a moron.[123] The expert explained to the court and the jury how he identified the defendant's age level.

> I gave him what is known as the standard revision of the Binet-Simon test. I began at the six years level. The first question was to give the number of fingers on the right hand and on his left hand. The next one was I exhibited a certain picture and asked him what they were, and he got that on the seven-year level. . . . The next is give a difference between a fly and a butterfly. . . . The next question is what is the thing for you to do, when you have broken something that belongs to someone else, when you are on your way to school and notice that you are in danger of being late.[124]

Despite its scientific appeal, the psychologist's testimony failed to convince the jury that the defendant's intellectual disability undermined his capacity to distinguish right from wrong at the time of the crime. This was partly due to the facts of the crime, which suggested that Snow had dedicated significant efforts to cover up his misdeeds to escape detection,[125] but also to the superficial nature of the expert's testimony. First, the psychologist's questions were clearly tailored for children, making their reliability in assessing the level of intelligence of an adult subject somewhat dubious. Second, though illustrative, the information provided by the psychologist said nothing about why the jury should consider the defendant's mental defectiveness relevant for the establishment of criminal guilt in the context of the alleged offense, an aspect that severely limited the effectiveness of the defendant's insanity claim.

A possible reason for this omission is that, because both psycho-legal authorities and the lay public assumed a strong association between intelligence and morality, neither the attorneys nor the mental health experts believed that such explanations were necessary. For example, lay witnesses at insanity trials tended to falsely assume that intelligence and insanity were closely correlated, and therefore used evidence of intelligence, or the lack thereof, to argue that the defendant was sane or insane at the time of the alleged offense.[126] Similarly, legal and psychological tests aimed at assessing criminal responsibility used intelligence as a proxy for morality and mental health.[127] As discussed in Chapter 1, the legal test of insanity based on the *M'Naghten* rules is grounded in a rationalistic notion of criminal responsibility. It is the product of the Enlightenment, an age that valued intelligence over any other quality, and tended to dismiss the power of feelings, emotions, and impulses over the individual will.

By associating criminality with low intelligence and by using intelligence tests to measure morality, early twentieth-century psychologists aligned with this view. In so doing, they undermined alternative arguments that highlighted how, in the presence of certain mental pathologies, unconscious "irresistible impulses" could overcome the rational will of traditionally intelligent and principled individuals. A conceivable explanation is that, although psychologists had the instruments to measure intelligence, they still lacked an appropriate method to grasp morality and the subject's ability to "resist temptation" and were therefore limited to the use of a strictly cognitive approach.[128] Moreover, intelligence testing fitted nicely with the legal doctrine of criminal insanity embraced by most American courts, providing, for the first time, a linguistic and technical framework that could *potentially* prove effective in courts of law.

Conclusion

In the first half of the twentieth century most forensic psychiatrists and courtroom experts believed in the existence of a close association between organic pathologies and criminal behavior. Although trial doctors dedicated less attention than psychiatric theorists to the biological causes of mental disease, both types of professionals started from the assumption that insanity could be inherited, that brain lesions could lead to mental and moral degeneration, and that syphilis and feeblemindedness were closely associated with criminal conduct. As the trials analyzed in this chapter have shown, Texas doctors' poor psychiatric training, coupled with the discipline's diagnostic limitations when dealing with living individuals, meant that most expert witnesses limited themselves to descriptive accounts of their diagnostic methods and classification systems, failing to provide any meaningful explanation of the ways in which the defendant's mental condition may have rendered him not responsible for the crime committed. This failure was likely exacerbated by the folk-psychological view of human behavior that tended to dominate trial discourse, and to focus expert and lay actors' attention on the defendants' actions at the time of the commission of the offense rather than on the biological causes of their criminal conduct.

Despite its initial popularity, the somatic model of mental disease experienced a rapid decline during World War II, when mental health professionals turned their attention to the psychoanalytic theories of Sigmund Freud.[129] As somatic psychiatrists failed to provide any conclusive proof of the organic nature and genetic origins of mental disorders, Freud's emphasis on environmental influences and developmental psychology became increasingly compelling. Moreover, the war experience gradually revealed that U.S. soldiers without preexisting neuropsychiatric conditions could suffer mental breakdowns because of prolonged combat stress, lending credence to theories that emphasized the importance of environmental traumas over hereditary defects and organic pathologies.[130] Finally, as the world discovered the horrors of Nazi eugenics and information about the Holocaust filled American newspapers, biological theories of racial superiority lost the scientific legitimacy and public approval they had enjoyed in previous decades, paving the way for the rapid diffusion of Freudian psychoanalysis in the 1950s and 1960s.[131]

Part 2

THE PSYCHOANALYTIC PARADIGM (1952–1976)

THREE

Psychoanalysis, the Insanity Defense, and the Family-Centered Ideology

In May 1924 Richard Loeb and Nathan Leopold, two wealthy, accomplished, and highly intelligent teenagers from Chicago, murdered 13-year-old Bobby Franks, a neighbor and family friend, committing what in their view was "the perfect crime."[1] The murder came after seven months of meticulous planning, during which Leopold and Loeb decided that they would abduct and kill Franks after school, hide his body near a lake south of Chicago, and disguise the nature and motive of their crime by making a ransom demand.[2] The plan for ransom collection, which involved a complex system of instructions delivered over the phone, was abandoned when the police found Bobby's dead body in a culvert by the lake. Next to the body was a pair of custom-made glasses that had been purchased by only three individuals in the whole city of Chicago, one of whom was Nathan Leopold.[3] When Leopold and Loeb were brought in for questioning, they immediately confessed to the crime, accusing each other of striking the fatal blows that killed young Franks.[4] The motive for the murder, the boys claimed, was their aspiration to transcend, through their superior intellects, the rules that bound ordinary people.

The Leopold and Loeb trial started in July 1924 in Chicago's Cook County Criminal Court. Because of the social status of the families involved, the offenders' senseless motive, and the careful preparation that went into the crime, the trial attracted exceptional media attention. Leopold and Loeb, who were 18 and 19 at the time of the crime, were not the kind of defendants who typically populated the criminal courts. They came from two of the most affluent and illustrious Jewish families in the city, lived in lavish homes in the wealthy Kenwood area on Chicago's South Side, and were considered child prodigies.[5] Leopold could speak 11 languages, had completed an undergraduate degree at the University of Chicago at age 18, and was about to start at Harvard Law School. Equally precocious, Loeb had graduated from the University of Michigan at age 17, becoming one of the youngest graduates at the school.[6] Nothing in their family pedigree, socioeconomic status, and education was reminiscent of the juvenile delinquents traditionally caught up in the criminal justice system.

The defendants' social privilege meant that they could afford the best possible defense, and at the time that meant hiring renowned criminal defense attorney Clarence Darrow. Instead of filing an insanity plea, as most commentators expected him to do, Darrow decided to have his clients plead guilty and then ask for a mitigation of the sentence based on a claim of mental abnormality.[7] This allowed him to free himself from the restrictive requirements of the insanity test, avoid the often unpopular request for criminal exculpation, and introduce a wide range of expert evidence to build his case for reduced mental capacity. To support his mental abnormality argument, Darrow hired three of the most established Freudian psychiatrists and criminologists in the country: William White, director of the St. Elizabeth Hospital for the Insane in Washington, DC; William Healy, the former director of the Juvenile Psychopathic Institute in Chicago; and Bernard Glueck, the founder of the first prison psychiatric clinic at Sing Sing Prison.[8]

On the witness stand White argued that the key to understanding the boys' behavior lay in their emotional immaturity. The boys, he argued, had experienced a split between their overdeveloped and precocious intellects and their "retarded emotional growth" and were living in a fantasy world in which they played king and slave.[9] Healy gave the boys a mental health evaluation and a battery of psychological tests. He concluded that Leopold was "unbalanced, paranoiac and socially dangerous"[10] and that the two boys were involved in a "strange pathological relationship," a scientific euphemism for their then unspeakable homosexual bond.[11] Further evidence on the sexual aspects of the boys' relationship was offered behind closed doors and alluded to with strategic code words in the news media of the time.[12] Glueck closed the defense's argument by fully endorsing the Freudian theory that, as a result of early childhood experiences, many individuals might find "neurotic satisfaction from the very social reaction that is supposed to deter and frighten them,"[13] making criminal punishment both "useless and absurd."[14]

In addition to the three psychoanalysts, the defense team hired two physicians, Harold S. Hulbert and Karl M. Bowman, to write a report on which the defense could base its theory. After two weeks of intensive evaluations, the doctors produced an 80,000-word document that dissected every detail of the boys' bodily functions, family histories, dreams, and fantasies to find a plausible medical explanation for a morally unexplainable act.[15] What emerged from the boys' accounts was a sober story of privileged but deeply lonely and unusual childhoods. Leopold, according to the report, had been deeply traumatized by the sexual abuse by a governess and by the loss of his mother at age 14. This early loss had played a central role in shifting his view on life in a nihilistic direction and in causing a pathological conflict between his deep sense of inferiority and the "satisfying sense of superiority acquired from his intellectual development."[16] Loeb, on the other hand, had been raised by a well-meaning but overly strict governess who had denied him a normal childhood made of play and hedonistic enjoyment and pushed him "into extreme academic overachievement."[17] Although the blame was here strategically transferred from the parents to the governesses, the message that the boys' thwarted childhoods had played a central role in their emotional immaturity and distorted view on life was made loud and clear. The judge spared the boys the death penalty on the grounds of their age, condemning them to "life imprisonment plus 99 years." Though acknowledging the contribution of the extensive data collected by the defense on the defendants' "physical, mental, and moral" condition, the judge did not consider it in his ruling because "the information was relevant to legislative not judicial action."[18]

The Leopold and Loeb case centers around three themes that will reemerge, to a varied extent, in the trials analyzed in Part II. The first theme concerns the role of parental love and education for the emotional and moral development of the child. "This boy needed more of home, more of love, more directing," Clarence Darrow argued in his closing defense of Richard Loeb. "He needed to have his emotions awakened. He needed guiding hands along the serious road that youth must travel. Had these been given to him, he would not be here today."[19] The second theme relates to the "pathological" link between repressed sex drives, homosexuality, and criminality, although this controversial notion would be fully theorized only in the 1930s and 1950s, when the diagnosis of "sexual psychopathy" took center stage. A final theme is the importance of emotions and, more specifically, emotional maturity alongside intellectual development for the well-being and social adjustment of the individual. No longer was it sufficient to have a high IQ and be born to families free from genetic defects to claim mental well-being and social adjustment; in the new psychoanalytic era the emotional life of the individual was given new independent value, and children were expected to be raised in emotionally, rather than just cognitively and genetically, healthy families. In the 1920s and 1930s psychoanalysis was still an elite instrument of introspection and talk therapy that only a few privileged individuals, such as Leopold and Loeb, could afford to use in a criminal court case. In the 1950s and 1960s it had become the default approach taken by most defense experts, even in cases involving defendants from lower-class backgrounds living far from the urban hubs where psychoanalysts and their well-to-do clientele were initially based.[20] The experience of World War II played a central role in triggering the paradigmatic shift from biological to psychoanalytic explanations of insanity and criminality, not only in the trials of Northern urban elites, but also in those of underprivileged rural Southerners. As mentioned in Chapter 2, during the war thousands of previously healthy soldiers experienced nervous breakdowns after traumatic battle experiences, suggesting that many forms of mental disorder had an environmental, rather than genetic, origin. As the war came to an end, and the world was confronted with the horrific consequences of Nazi Germany's eugenic programs, American psychiatrists turned away from hereditary and somatic approaches, fully embracing a psychoanalytic etiology focusing on early childhood experiences, psychosexual development, and family dynamics.

The turning point for psychoanalysis's influence on American psychiatry, however, came in 1952, when the American Psychiatric Association published the first edition of the *Diagnostic and Statistical Manual of Mental Disorders* (DSM-I). The DSM-I was the first officially recognized diagnostic guideline to be followed in psychiatric evaluations and had a massive impact on the daily practices of mental health professionals across the United States. Because most members of the American Psychiatric Association charged with drafting the manual were trained in the Freudian tradition, psychoanalysis became an integral part of the DSM-I's diagnostic guidelines and thereby of every standardized mental health evaluation conducted until the next radical revision of the manual in 1980 (DSM-III).[21] Through their incorporation into the DSM-I's diagnostic criteria, psychoanalytic principles and concepts had a significant impact on psycho-legal evaluations in Texas criminal proceedings in the 1950s and 1960s, making 1952 the ideal starting point for this chapter's historical inquiry.

The Birth of Psychological Man

The strength and appeal of Freud's ideas lay in their ability to synthesize two distinct intellectual streams. The first one was scientific and started from the Darwinian conceptualization of humans as biological machines regulated by inner instincts and bodily urges.[22] Building on the nineteenth-century theory of reflex action, Freud framed instincts as internal mediators between physiological processes and psychological reactions, while picturing the psyche as a reflexive instrument that mirrored the functioning of the nervous system. However, rather than reducing reflexes to a physical reaction to external stimuli, as nineteenth-century theorists had done, Freud connected the body's physiological processes to the emotional and psychical component of the mind, an aspect that satisfied the medical establishment on the one hand and psychiatrists disappointed with traditional somatic approaches on the other.[23]

The second approach was humanistic and drew from the family tragedies described by William Shakespeare, Johann Wolfgang von Goethe, and Fyodor Dostoyevsky (among others) to stress the moral struggle experienced by human subjects because of their conflicts with parental figures.[24] This literary genre contributed to the diffusion of a commonsense understanding of human psychology, which stressed the importance of inner feelings and healthy family relationships for the individual's psychological well-being and moral upbringing.[25] Freud created a unique synthesis of these two streams of thought, contributing to the discovery of a new object of psychiatric attention: "the idiosyncratic, meaning-saturated, morally inflected psychical life of the human being."[26]

This human subject powerfully resonated with the new notion of personal life that emerged with the crumbling of the Victorian family ideal in the 1890s. In the Victorian era the economy was founded on the traditional family enterprise, which assigned specific roles and identities to its members according to their function within its economic and social organization. In this context individuals' identities were closely related to their role in the family unit; hence, the private and the public sphere were deeply intertwined and the lines separating them blurred.[27] As the mass production and mass consumption associated with the second industrial revolution started transforming Americans' lifestyles (1870–1914) and individuals started working outside the family household, the division between public and private life became clear, and a new notion of personal identity, separate from and outside the family circle, began to emerge.[28]

The founding idea of psychoanalysis, the *unconscious*, embodied this new notion of personal life.[29] Freud's unconscious demarcated an inner symbolic world, an intimate space in which the individual elaborated life experiences and impressions according to subjective needs, feelings, and impulses. It marked a separation between the private and the public, interiority and exteriority, the personal and the social. Psychoanalysis did not assume a correspondence between socioeconomic condition and subjectivity; for the first time, the personal world of the individual was given independent value.

The new notion of the self stimulated by the diffusion of Freudian ideas had a significant impact on the ways in which mental health professionals framed and assessed mental illness and criminality in the 1920s and 1930s. It contributed to the transition from the nineteenth-century notion of "biological man," which saw criminals as organic machines regulated by their physical anatomy and genetic endowment, to a new concept of "psychological man," which framed them as emotional subjects driven by their inner instincts, feelings, and childhood traumas.[30] As we will see, when transposed into the trial context, psychoanalysts' reframing of the human subject in psychological terms helped bridge the traditional gap between folk-psychological and mechanistic explanations of criminal behavior, casting a new light on criminal acts previously perceived as unintelligible to the lay observer.

Psychoanalysis, the Insanity Defense, and Texas Death Penalty Trials

As I argued in Chapter 1, legal notions of mens rea are based on a folk-psychological interpretation of human behavior that theorizes a connection between offenders' mental states—that is, intentions, purposes, and desires—and their criminal conduct.[31] Late nineteenth- and early twentieth-century forensic psychiatrists rejected this teleological interpretation of the mind in favor of a mechanistic and deterministic understanding of human conduct, seen as a manifestation of physiological causes and energy patterns without reference to intent or purpose. Similarly, psychoanalysts writing in the 1950s and 1960s argued that, given their emphasis on the mechanical interaction between physiological mechanisms and psychic structures, their theories were incompatible with the folk-psychological explanation of behavior proposed by the criminal law.[32]

However, despite psychoanalysts' claims to the contrary, their theories introduced a new approach to mental health and criminal behavior that harmonized scientific and teleological interpretations of human conduct.[33] Psychoanalysts relied on technical concepts (e.g., the id, ego, and superego) inspired by the nineteenth-century theory of reflex action, which framed human behavior as a physiological reaction to internal and external stimuli. However, they departed from the nineteenth-century paradigm by linking such concepts to defendants' inner values, emotions, and intentions. For example, when psychoanalysts explained a violent act as the result of a "disruption of [the defendant's] ego,"[34] they meant that the defendant lost control over his aggressive wishes and impulses, not that there was a physical breakdown in an inner machinery that caused an automatic unconscious movement.[35] Whereas the medical model of disease hoped to explain defendants' acts in terms of mathematical relations of cause and effect, mid-twentieth-century psychoanalysts aimed to demonstrate how apparently irrational behaviors could be made intelligible through a technical interpretation based on commonsense understandings of human conduct.[36]

This theoretical innovation proved particularly helpful in elucidating the motivations behind defendants' criminal actions in trial contexts. Whereas expert witnesses inspired by the somatic model of disease had failed to unpack the scientific mechanisms linking defendants' organic conditions with their mental state at the time of the crime, court psychoanalysts started translating their psychiatric theories into a commonsense language understandable to the lay observer. In so doing, they provided compelling theories that connected defendants' difficult family backgrounds, repressed wishes, and emotional difficulties with their conduct at the time of the alleged offense, an aspect that would help expand the psychiatric gaze beyond the simple analysis of symptomatology and diagnostic classification to grasp the deeper meanings of human behavior.

However, although psychoanalysts helped cast a new light on the underlying motivations of defendants' criminal acts, their explanations did not necessarily result in successful insanity claims in Texas courts.[37] The reason can be found in the nature of their scientific reasonings and in their implications for legal doctrines of criminal responsibility. During the twenty years that followed the publication of the DSM-I, criminal defendants tried in Texas county courts continued to be judged, and often convicted, based on the wording of the traditional *M'Naghten* rules. Rather than demonstrating that defendants failed to understand the nature and consequences of their criminal acts as required by the rules, psychoanalytic theories tended to show that they acted under the influence of irresistible impulses, an argument that Texas courts have historically deemed insufficient to prove lack of guilt.[38]

To tackle this issue and tie their theories to a convincing insanity defense, a number of psychoanalysts started arguing that, although defendants' psychological deficiencies did not impair their ability to *intellectually* understand the wrongfulness of their actions, it made it impossible for them to *feel* such wrongfulness at a deeper level.[39] By blurring the lines that traditionally separated cognitive and emotional understandings of wrongdoing, psychoanalysts were able to argue that defendants' emotional deficiencies undermined their ability to distinguish right from wrong and conform their behavior to legal requirements. However, as I argued in Chapter 1, Texas has historically endorsed a cognitive interpretation of legal insanity, which requires defendants to show that they lacked the *intellectual*—rather than the *emotional*—capacity to understand the wrongfulness of their actions in order to prove lack of guilt. This theoretical distinction made insanity claims based on psychoanalytic arguments particularly challenging, especially when defendants' behaviors before, during, and after the commission of the crime suggested the presence of premeditation and/or a cover-up, and the prosecution managed to leverage such behavior to argue that the defendant knew that their conduct was wrong.[40]

Despite these difficulties, forensic mental health professionals testifying in Texas capital punishment trials in the 1950s and 1960s drew heavily from Freudian ideas. The appeal of Freud's theories was twofold. First, although they provided a technical terminology capable of translating medical issues in folk-psychological terms, they never abandoned the scientific paradigm, an aspect that gave them an aura of objectivity and legitimacy. Second, Freud's key theories and concepts reflected powerful concerns with the patient's moral views and ability to incorporate society's moral standards, an aspect that proved particularly helpful in courts of law. Freud's theory of criminality, with its emphasis on the relationship between unconscious drives, rational control mechanisms, and moral standards of behavior, constitutes a particularly illuminating example in this regard.

Psychosexual Development, the Oedipus Complex, and Criminal Behavior

Freud associated psychopathology and criminal behavior with an incorrect functioning of two essential spheres of the human mind: the ego and the superego. In his framework the ego signified the rational section of the mind mediating between unconscious aggressive impulses and external reality, whereas the superego embodied the conscious part of the mind responsible for regulating behavior according to society's moral standards.[41] In assessing the patient's ego, an essential step in every psychoanalytic examination, the therapist was essentially evaluating the individual's awareness of, and capacity to deal with, society's moral standards, including its legal rules and prohibitions.[42] Similarly, when a psychoanalyst evaluated a patient's superego, he or she was effectively judging the person's moral attitudes and the effectiveness of such attitudes in controlling the destructive pressures of the unconscious, or id.[43] Hence psychoanalysts typically discussed psychopathology and criminal behavior as an expression of an excessively "weak," "severe," or "archaic" superego, a framing that directly connected mental illness to a defect in the individual's moral attitudes, and tacitly implied a moral judgment by the psychiatrist using the concept.[44] In this sense, psychoanalytic explanations of criminal behavior included an evaluation of defendants' ethical standards, an aspect that separated them from the neutrality and objectivity stressed by their predecessors and brought them closer to the moralistic approach taken by the criminal law.[45]

Freud associated the ego and superego deficiencies that led to adult criminal conduct with a halt in psychosexual development experienced during the first five years of life. As individuals grew from infancy into adulthood, he argued, they went through five phases of psychosexual development, each one associated with a new erogenous part of the body, which became the main source of libidinal drive and sexual fixation.[46] Sexual frustrations experienced in these early stages prompted pathological copying mechanisms and anxieties that endured into adulthood and turned into neuroses and deviant behaviors.

At the age of 3 the child started feeling sexual attraction for the parent of the opposite sex and secretly desiring to eliminate his or her natural competitor: the parent of the same sex. Freud famously called this infantile desire of incest and murder the Oedipus complex.[47] Once children started experiencing these troubling instincts, anxieties and feelings of guilt started to emerge. Most children would use fantasy, sublimation, and repression to master the conflict internally without acting on their sexual and homicidal impulses. In some cases, however, the impulse was too strong and the mechanisms of repression and sublimation too weak. In such cases the sense of guilt that accompanied the Oedipus conflict survived in the unconscious of the child into adulthood, prompting him or her to commit criminal acts and seek punishment to alleviate their internal suffering. This overwhelming guilt feeling, Freud explained, "derived from the Oedipus complex and was a reaction to the two great criminal intentions of killing the father and having sex with the mother."[48]

Freud's theory of psychosexual development was closely related to his critique of Victorian parental education, with its authoritarian and repressive approach to youth discipline.[49] According to Freud, parents played an essential role in mediating and regulating children's aggressive and sexual impulses. As children grew up, they incorporated the norms and codes inculcated by the parents into their superego, or consciousness. When, because of parents' punitive education, children internalized an excessively harsh superego, they could develop aggressive reactions against their parents or against an authoritative parental tradition, rebel against society's norms, and develop delinquent behavior.[50] To counteract these tendencies, Freud proposed alternative parenting models aimed at encouraging children's healthy sexual exploration and supporting their repression of the Oedipus conflict through early identification with a positive father figure.

Freud's ideas on childhood education would prove deeply inspirational for progressive American psychoanalysts writing from the 1920s onward.[51] Committed to promoting more understanding and tolerant attitudes toward children's emotional needs and sexual impulses, Freud's followers argued that the ego and superego deficiencies leading to neuroses and adult aggression stemmed from insufficient love and warmth received during the childhood years and the consequent inability to identify with the unloving parents.[52] In this view, parental rejection and indifference, along with the use of physical punishment for misbehavior, were counterproductive methods that could hinder or delay the development of a personal conscience, in some cases directly fostering the maturation of delinquent tendencies.

In the Cold War years Freud's progressive views on childhood education encountered numerous critiques from conservative circles. At the time, the geopolitical tension between the Eastern and Western blocs fueled fears and anxieties in the American public, fostering a conformist culture that harshly condemned any form of social deviance.[53] In this political climate, several psychoanalysts and criminal justice officials started warning that excessively permissive or forgiving attitudes might hinder the formation of the internal controls necessary to police children's behavior and help them adapt to society's rules and regulations.[54] These concerns were fueled by the popular media, which, by describing juvenile delinquency as one of the most pressing crime issues of the time (even though no official crime statistics suggested a similar trend), contributed to a revival of parenting models based on strict discipline and control.[55] District attorneys seeking a plausible rationale to undermine the exculpatory potential of evidence of abuse in Texas capital punishment trials strategically endorsed this conservative rationale. In so doing, they framed defendants' parents' use of corporal punishment as a legitimate means to deal with their children's unruly behaviors, lack of discipline, and hostility toward authority.

Nearvel Moon, the Oedipus Complex, and the Debate on Parental Discipline

The case of Nearvel Moon provides an illustrative example of the ways in which the cultural clash between progressive and conservative views on childhood education could manifest itself in a trial context.[56] Moon was an 18-year-old white man charged with the shooting and killing of two men and a boy in a rural area of Harris County in 1959.[57] At the time of the shooting, one of the victims was carrying a whiskey bottle, a detail that would prove extremely significant for the psychoanalytic explanation of the crime provided by the defense. The defendant pleaded not guilty by reason of insanity and presented the testimony of an expert witness, Dr. Robert H. Wagner, to support his claim. A psychiatrist with significant experience in forensic mental health evaluations, Dr. Wagner examined Moon in jail, administered physiological, psychological, and intelligence tests, and interviewed several members of his family.[58] The intelligence test indicated that Moon had an IQ of 70, which classified him as a "borderline mental defective," and the interviews with his family members revealed some disturbing details about his social background and early upbringing.[59]

According to Dr. Wagner, among all the families he had examined throughout his career, "this was one of the most socially degraded families that [he had] ever come in contact with."[60] The interviews revealed that the defendant's father was an alcoholic who repeatedly beat his wife, sons, and daughters and sexually abused one of his daughters.[61] He gave his wife $10 a week to support their eight children and lived in his own place where he spent significantly larger sums on alcohol.[62] He repeatedly came home to his family drunk, and beatings would typically follow. Rather than teaching his sons the difference between right and wrong, he would take them out at night to steal with him and criticize them if they were "crazy" enough to get caught. To give a sense of the moral degradation in which they were brought up, the defendant's siblings reported that their mother once had a miscarriage in the sixth month of pregnancy and his father "showed [the baby's body] to the kids and made a big commotion about it and threw it out to the dogs to eat."[63]

According to the defendant's mother, her husband's beatings were extremely violent.[64] On numerous occasions Moon tried to protect his mother by pointing a shotgun at his father and was beaten into unconsciousness as a result.[65] The defendant resented his father for the violence he submitted his family to and hated alcohol because he associated it with his father's abusive behavior.[66] Shortly before the shootings for which he was on trial, Moon told his mother and brothers that he would kill his father if he ever beat him or his mother again.[67] Drawing from Freud's theory of the Oedipus complex, Dr. Wagner argued that by killing the victim carrying the whiskey bottle, the defendant had symbolically killed his father, satisfying his unconscious impulses and desires.[68] The fact that the defendant took the whiskey bottle and broke it on a rock following the shooting was additional proof of the psychological analogy that might have triggered the homicidal acts. Implicitly supporting a defense of irresistible impulse, the doctor proposed that the view of the older man in the group drinking from the whiskey bottle triggered the defendant's repressed feelings of anger against his father, causing a powerful psychological reaction, which in turn led to the shooting and killing of the three victims.

The prosecution gave a completely different explanation of the defendant's behavior. Rather than portraying the defendant's crime as a pathological reaction to the abuse he suffered at the hands of his father, Assistant District Attorney Frank Briscoe associated it with Moon's antisocial nature and rebellion against authority. To support this contention, Briscoe presented the testimony of two psychiatrists, Dr. Benjamin Sher and Dr. Paul Walter, who minimized Moon's mental disabilities and his difficult family history. For example, Dr. Sher examined the defendant and argued that he was a pleasant individual with a slight intellectual impairment who, because of "some altercations with some authority figures in the past," resented authority figures and felt hostility toward his father.[69] Instead of investigating the defendant's past to identify the deeper origins of this hostility, the doctor simply assumed that it was due to him disliking his father, for no apparent reason.[70] He concluded that the defendant knew the difference between right and wrong at the time of the crime and argued that evidence that Moon was abused and deprived of a moral education as a child would not change his opinion as to his legal sanity.[71]

In contrast to what was proposed by the defense, the prosecution portrayed the beatings as a justified response from a father dealing with uncontrollable children, who would not follow his guidance and would rebel against his patriarchal authority. In this view the children, and particularly the defendant, were physically abused not because their father was an alcoholic, immoral, and violent individual but because they deserved it, the beatings being the result of their own antisocial tendencies. The assistant district attorney's cross-examination of the defendant's brother, General McArthur Moon, clearly illustrates this line of reasoning.

Q. The whippings that you referred to, isn't it true that those things took place after one of you had done something wrong, or had misbehaved in some way?
A. We got one one time for not going over and feeding the dogs for our grandmother.
Q. That is what I had in mind, every time that your father would punish you it would be for some reason or for something that you failed to do?
A. Yes, sir.
Q. He did not punish you without reason, did he?
A. Sometimes he would.
Q. Did your father have any particular favoritism towards any of the children as far as you could tell?
A. Well, he was kind to me because I would do what he told me to do and not jaw back at him. . . .
Q. Are you indicating that Nearvel doesn't do sometimes what he tells him to do and, as you put it, jaws back at him sometimes?

A. He would do it if he wanted to and if he didn't he wouldn't do it.
Q. And that is when the whipping would occur that you have talked about?
A. Yes, sir.[72]

As this passage shows, taking the authoritarian parenting model of the Cold War years to its extreme consequences, the assistant district attorney portrayed the defendant's father's beatings as a legitimate disciplinary measure to manage his son's unruly behavior, rather than as a failure in early parental education that would carry devastating consequences for the child's future mental health and social adjustment.

Alfred Adler, the Theory of Inferiority, and the Masculine Protest

Besides drawing from Freud's theory of the Oedipus complex and from his progressive views on childhood education, defense experts testifying in the 1950s and 1960s were deeply inspired by the work of Alfred Adler. Originally a member of the Viennese Psychoanalytic Society founded by Freud, in 1911 Adler left the group because of his and Freud's conflicting views on the etiology of mental disease.[73] Whereas Freud stressed the role of sexuality, the libido, and the Oedipus complex in fostering the development of mental illnesses and antisocial tendencies, Adler focused on the power of feelings of inferiority, social competition, and compensatory aggression. However, in line with the cultural zeitgeist of their time, the two scholars gave equal importance to the private life and inner psychological world of the individual, and agreed on the negative impact that "pathological" family dynamics could have on patients' sense of self, mental health, and social adjustment.

After his split with Freud, Adler acquired international fame and prestige. In the 1920s, he opened several child education clinics based on his therapeutic principles and pursued an academic career in prestigious European and American institutions. In the 1930s, as fascism and antisemitism spread throughout Europe, Adler, who had Jewish ancestry, decided to emigrate to the United States to take up a professorship at the Long Island College of Medicine in New York. Adler's work at the college encouraged the diffusion of his ideas among American psychoanalysts seeking alternative explanations of mental illness and criminal behavior to the ones proposed by Freud (e.g., the neo-Freudians). His theories on self-esteem, the inferiority complex, and the masculine protest were particularly influential, and would play a crucial role in defense experts' explanations of defendants' criminal behavior in Texas death penalty trials from the 1930s onward.[74]

Adler's theory was that, because of their dependence on adults for their survival, all children were born with a natural feeling of inferiority, an entirely normal sentiment not necessarily associated with a pathological mental health condition.[75] However, for children born with organic weaknesses or raised by pampering or rejecting parents, this feeling of inferiority could become an overwhelming aspect of their life.[76] To compensate for their physical and emotional lacks, these children constantly strove to reach goals that they foresaw would give them a feeling of superiority and a new sense of power and strength.[77] As they struggled for the obtainment of this goal, deeply insecure children became selfish, arrogant, and more vulnerable to break down under the difficulties of life and develop mental health issues.[78] To conceal their sense of inadequacy, they developed "a superiority complex," which manifested itself in a boastful belief in their "superhuman gifts and capacities," in a "vanity in connection with personal appearance," and in a "tyrannical nature," all aspects associated with antisocial tendencies.[79]

Adler's psychology of inferiority was influenced by his feminist views and by his sensitivity to women's social and political battles.[80] Acknowledging that "the *devaluation of woman is the driving force in our civilization*," he argued that children frame the compensatory mechanisms used to overcome their feelings of inferiority as an urge "to become a real man," to move from "below"—a condition associated with weakness, insecurity, and femininity—to "above," a status associated with power, self-confidence, and masculinity.[81] Like children, neurotics tend to classify their memories and experiences according to this false dichotomy, giving them a distorted picture of the world that reinforces their perception of being constantly humiliated and undermined during their social interactions. The desire to be a "real man," which is shared by men and women alike, is the guiding force in the life of the neurotic, who, to overcome his or her original feeling of insecurity, engages in a "masculine protest," a compensatory form of self-assertion that can take the form of violent behaviors.[82]

Robert Freeman, the Inferiority Complex, and the Masculine Protest

The 1958 trial of Robert Freeman provides a compelling example of the ways in which Adler's theory of inferiority shaped psychoanalysts' explanations of defendants' behavior in Texas proceedings. Robert Freeman, a white middle-class 17-year-old, was accused of brutally killing his young girlfriend, Sandra Maywald, after a heated discussion at her family home.[83] On the day of the murder, Freeman had allegedly received a phone call from his girlfriend in which she informed him that she wanted to end their relationship.[84] Distraught, he had gone to Sandra's home to convince her to stay with him, but as it became clear that she was determined to move on, he violently attacked her, cutting her neck with a pocketknife.[85] Immediately after the attack, Freeman called the police. When the officers arrived at the crime scene, they found him at the door entrance, with his shirt, glasses, and face splattered in blood.[86] He immediately confessed to the killing, handed the officers the murder weapon, and directed them to the bedroom, where he had placed Sandra's dead body.

At trial, Freeman pleaded not guilty by reason of insanity and presented several expert witnesses, including two psychiatrists, a clinical psychologist, and a social worker, to support his claim. The defense experts argued that Freeman suffered from paranoid schizophrenia, a condition associated with delusional beliefs and hallucinations, and that his violent attack against the victim was related to deep feelings of inferiority and masculinity issues. For example, Dr. R. M. Finney, a well credentialed psychiatrist with a private practice in Houston, argued that the victim was the only person who made the defendant feel that he was "really a man . . . that he really was masculine," a fact that was supported by the defendant's own confession.[87] "I needed what she had given me," Freeman explained to the officers, "*she made me feel like a man instead of a boy.*"[88] Given this pathological dependence, when Sandra decided to leave him, Freeman felt deprived of his masculinity and thereby of his self-esteem, power, and personal strength.[89] For Robert's weak ego, Sandra's rejection was an unbearable trauma, sufficient to precipitate his mental condition and prompt a loss of control over his aggressive impulses.[90]

The defendant's family dynamics had played a central role in fostering these feelings of inferiority, masculinity issues, and ego deficiencies, the doctors argued. The evidence suggested that the defendant had been adopted by his foster parents when he was 10 months old.[91] In the doctors' opinion, despite their attempts to be "good and loving," adoptive parents could often "become rejecting parents" and cause significant psychological damage in their children.[92] Freeman's father, Dr. Crow explained, "had been an extremely busy man. He is what I call an *absentee father*, that is, his work and his profession carry him outside of his home so much that he really spent more time outside his home than in."[93] In contrast, Freeman's mother had tried to make her son feel accepted but had repeatedly engaged in controlling behaviors that had yielded the opposite result.

> Approximately every year she would give a birthday party and she would, at the birthday, remind Robert that he was adopted, that he was a foster child. Now, intellectually, that sounds good but what does it do to the child. *He feels rejected*. He feels alone, that he does not belong there, and that is exactly what happened to Robert. As the years went by, in this situation, of the *controlling but somewhat rejecting mother and the absentee father*, Robert did not feel that he belonged anywhere, and he grew up with that feeling.[94]

Freeman's family dynamic was extremely common among schizophrenic patients, according to Dr. Crow.[95] In the defendant's case it caused him to withdraw into his own world, an aspect that became more apparent as he was forced into contact with other children at school and his difficulties began to emerge.[96] As a result of his social isolation, he developed the delusion that he came from another planet, that he had flown to the earth on a flying saucer, and that he was a member of a "super race" that did not have to abide by the rules of our society.[97] Freeman's feelings of inadequacy and masculinity issues had prompted compensatory forms of self-assertion that manifested themselves both through a delusional belief in his "superhuman" gifts and capacities and through a violent response to his girlfriend's emotional rejection.[98]

The state's expert, a Harris County psychiatrist named Dr. C. A.

Dwyer, challenged the defense's theory, arguing that the fact that Freeman had called the police after the murder suggested that he knew the difference between right and wrong.[99] The district attorney, Frank Briscoe, reinforced this view in his closing argument when, appealing to the folk-psychological view that actions are logically associated with mental states, he argued:

> Did he know the difference between right and wrong? Well, let's look at what happened. He locked the doors. He sought to exclude others from the house. One of the children got in and saw the blood on this defendant. He was hit, kicked and pushed out of the house. He again locked the doors. He armed himself with a butcher knife—why? Because he was afraid the neighbors would lynch him . . . why was he scared the neighbors would lynch him . . . if he, at that time, did not realize that what he had done was wrong[?] That is the test. Did this defendant know the difference between right and wrong?[100]

Through a well-established prosecutorial strategy, the district attorney diverted the jury's attention away from Freeman's emotional difficulties and psychiatric condition, while focusing it on his behavior at the time of the crime to suggest that his acts betrayed a culpable state of mind.[101] The defense challenged the state expert by arguing that Freeman believed that his violent attack did not cause Sandra any pain or suffering and that, though he was aware of the rules of society, he believed that they did not apply to him because of his alien nature.[102] However, the jury deemed these reasons insufficient to explain the defendant's behavior, finding the explanation provided by the prosecution more logical and in line with their commonsense interpretation of the facts in evidence. As happened in previous decades, when the scientific explanations provided by the trial experts clashed with jurors' commonsense interpretations of defendants' behaviors, the latter would inevitably succeed, regardless of the severity of defendants' mental health conditions and/or personality defects.

The "Pathological" Black Family

Although never fully explicated at trial, Freeman's defense theory was that, while the lack of a strong father figure had hindered his ability to develop an appropriate male sex-role identity, his mother's failure to establish a strong emotional bond had undermined his internal control mechanisms (or ego) and prompted deep feelings of inferiority. The idea that a weak mother-child bond could undermine ego development was typical among mid-twentieth-century psychoanalysts concerned about housewives' ability to fulfill their role as primary caretakers and educators within the (idealized) traditional family structure. Whereas some doctors expressed concerns that too much motherly love might create feelings of dependency and confuse boys' sexual identity,[103] at the time of Freeman's trial most juvenile delinquency experts agreed that a "firm mother-child relationship" was essential to develop the psychological controls that would allow children to mature into self-confident, responsible, and law-abiding citizens.[104]

In the mid-1950s both white and black youth unemployment rates were high, and members of both races turned to criminal activities to compensate for their social and economic marginalization. Hence, until white suburbanization turned "juvenile delinquency" into a "black urban crime," discourse about the criminogenic effects of parental negligence was largely "color-blind."[105] As policymakers expressed their concerns about a "youth crime wave" that was allegedly spreading across the nation, psychoanalysts started blaming female-headed families for undermining boys' sexual identities and pushing them to seek same-sex role models outside the family structure in the world of youth gangs and juvenile delinquents.[106] American boys' criminal activities, the argument went, stemmed from a deep masculinity crisis that could be traced back to the decline of the patriarchal family structure and to mothers' failure to fulfill their role as primary caregivers within or without such structure.[107] As white middle-class families left the racially diverse urban centers for the more homogeneous suburban areas, juvenile delinquency came to be reframed as a black boys' problem, and psychoanalysts turned their attention to the black matriarchal family as a possible breeder of criminality.[108] Although socioeconomic and racial factors played a central role in reinforcing youth marginalization and contributing to criminal involvement, critics typically framed the problem in terms of parental failures.[109]

Black single motherhood, which rose dramatically between 1942 and 1960, became the target of the postwar critique. For example, in 1951 American psychoanalysts Abram Kardiner and Lionel Ovesey argued that in black matriarchal families the quality of maternal care was compromised by male desertion and the related lack of financial support.[110] Abandoned by their husbands and forced to find employment outside the home, black mothers neglected their children and were more likely to lose their temper once home because of work-related fatigue.[111] Their resentment, fear, and distrust of men translated into constant critiques of the father figure, which injured the black boy's paternal ideal, pushing him "to the streets," where he could finally "be a man."[112] Because of these "pathological" gender dynamics and negative family socialization, black male children experienced a masculinity crisis that pushed them to engage in criminal behavior to compensate for their lack of self-love and feelings of inadequacy and inferiority.[113] Even though they recognized the role played by racial discrimination and economic oppression in perpetuating black boys' marginalization, Kardiner and Ovesey's psychoanalytic approach sidelined the role of socioeconomic factors while emphasizing the mother's responsibility for black boys' negative socialization.[114]

The publication of Assistant Secretary of Labor Daniel Patrick Moynihan's *The Negro Family: The Case for National Action* (the Moynihan report) in 1965 brought the critique of the black matriarchal family to the nation's attention. Like Kardiner and Ovesey, Moynihan recognized that racism and historical mistreatment had played a central role in undermining African Americans' socioeconomic prospects; however, he firmly believed that it was the instability of the lower-class black family that was "the fundamental source of weakness" of the black community.[115] The "tangle of pathology," Moynihan argued, stemmed from "the black family's matriarchal structure," which, because of its deviation from American society's patriarchal norm, "retard[ed] the progress of the group as a whole, and impose[d] a crushing burden on the Negro male."[116] "Ours is a society which presumes [and rewards] male leadership in private and public affairs," he explained, "a subculture, such as that of the Negro American, in which this is not the pattern, is placed at a distinct disadvantage."[117] The reversed roles of husband and wife were particularly problematic because it made the black male feel inadequate compared to his white counterpart and the black woman feel "disgusted with her financially dependent husband."[118] The lack of a positive male role model, coupled with black mothers' resentment against men and favoritism toward their daughters, created a significant gender disadvantage for black boys, as reflected in their comparatively low "educational attainment" and high crime rates.[119] Poor academic performances, low mental test scores, and high delinquency rates among African American boys were cast not as signs of genetic inferiority, as happened in the 1910s and 1920s, but as "the effect of broken families" and reversed gender roles, alongside "poverty, failure, and isolation."[120]

As these examples show, in the 1950s and 1960s changes affecting the American family structure and racial relations prompted psychoanalysts to develop new theories of juvenile delinquency based on Adler's individual psychology. Like Adler, they emphasized the link between parental rejection, feelings of inferiority, and criminality; unlike Adler, they used this theory to condemn white and black mothers for their failure to live up to their important roles as primary caretakers. Although parental rejection was recognized as deeply problematic in both white middle-class and black matriarchal families, the psychoanalytic critique of motherly care took different forms depending on the race and social class of the family under scrutiny. White middle-class mothers were often criticized for smothering their sons with love and attention, confusing their sexual identity and delaying their transition into adult manhood.[121] Black single mothers, on the other hand, were accused of resenting and rejecting their sons, favoring their daughters, and "reinforcing a cycle of pathology that was increasingly viewed as the primary problem facing the [African American] community."[122]

In contrast to their white counterparts, in the 1950s and 1960s most ethnic minority defendants tried in Texas criminal courts continued to rely on lay witnesses to support their insanity claims.[123] Hence, it is difficult to evaluate whether and how assessments of minority defendants' mental health and criminal culpability were influenced by psychoanalytic arguments linking the black matriarchal family to criminal behavior. Indeed, my data suggest that out of the six ethnic minority defendants (four African Americans and two Hispanics) who (unsuccessfully) raised the insanity defense between 1952 and 1972, only two relied on an expert consultant to support their claim, a significantly smaller proportion than the one found among their white counterparts (eleven out of fifteen white defendants hired an expert witness).[124] Moreover, even in the small number of cases in which ethnic minority defendants hired a psychiatrist to testify, the experts made no reference to psychoanalytic theories linking their behaviors to emotional difficulties and family history, offering instead poorly substantiated conclusions about their ability to distinguish right from wrong. A possible reason for this phenomenon is that most experts testifying in the 1950s and 1960s drew from the work of mainstream white psychoanalysts who did not write with the black patient and his or her personal and racial struggles in mind. As Martinican psychoanalyst Frantz Fanon argued in 1952:

> Freud and Adler and even the cosmic Jung did not think of the Negro in all their investigations. And they were quite right not to have. It is too often forgotten that neurosis is not a basic element of human reality. Like it or not, *the Oedipus complex is far from coming into being among Negroes.*[125]

"Black psychopathology," Fanon argued, was not rooted in the family dynamics described by Freud but in historical patterns of racial oppression that led to the internalization of a negative racial identity and to pathological feelings of dependency and inadequacy.[126]

The dearth of medical opinions on ethnic minorities' mental health and criminal culpability makes an investigation of the ways in which racist stereotypes affected criminal court cases in the mid-twentieth century complicated. However, the available data, which amount to 21 cases, generally suggest that both lay and expert participants tended to avoid racist arguments connecting minorities' biological characteristics and/or family dynamics with a propensity for mental illness, intellectual deficits, and/or criminality. Instead of indicating a lack of concern for racial matters in forensic mental health assessments, these omissions may reflect changed sensibilities surrounding race and ethnicity following the rise of the civil rights movement, which made openly racist language and discourse socially unacceptable and therefore more strategically disguised.[127] Indeed, research has shown that, although public critiques of white supremacy pushed racial epithets and other remnants of America's shameful past out of the courtroom, in Texas's prison plantations, shielded from public view, prison guards and unit managers continued to use degrading racist language and to beat black prisoners "the old slave way."[128] Given the public nature of the proceedings, trial actors have historically tried to maintain an appearance of impartiality and objectivity by silencing racial issues and giving an appearance of color-blindness. However, as I will show in Chapter 6, this silencing plays the important political function of underplaying the role of social context and historical patterns of racial oppression for minorities' mental health and social adjustment, while reinforcing the individualist notion of criminal responsibility that dominates Texas's criminal law and courtroom ideology.

Conclusion

As mentioned in the Introduction, in the 1950s and 1960s most members of the American Psychiatric Association were trained in the psychoanalytic tradition. As a result, the diagnostic labels included in the first and second editions of the DSM, respectively published in 1952 and 1968,[129] were powerfully influenced by psychoanalytic theories. This influence is particularly striking in the diagnosis of psychopathy or sociopathic personality disorder, a condition associated with specific personality characteristics and antisocial tendencies that has played a crucial role in Texas capital punishment proceedings since the 1950s. In the next chapter I examine the development of this diagnosis as applied to white male offenders, and show how, because of its malleability to shifting cultural values, it is possible to use this diagnostic category to identify the personality characteristics that American society perceived as most threatening to the "hegemonic masculinity"[130] of the time, and therefore deserving of social and, if necessary, penal neutralization.

FOUR

Psychoanalysis and the Construction of the Criminal Psychopath

> The delimitation of psychopathy as a distinct personality type has long been delayed, especially as concerns the finer structure of the personality make-up in these cases. We have been told that they are people who are emotionally rigid, yet no effort has been made to clarify this emotional rigidity, particularly to differentiate it from the emotional rigidity found in other personalities. . . . We have also been told that their behavior is unmodifiable, but how does this trait differ from the behavior of the paranoiac, schizophrenic, manic or epileptic, which too, is well-nigh unmodifiable? We do not know. We have heard it said of psychopathic personalities that they are peculiarly callous and unmoved by the usual human emotions. This rings true, but surely they are not the only ones who display such traits. Wherein, then, do they differ from other individuals displaying such traits of character?[1]
>
> —BENJAMIN KARPMAN

Benjamin Karpman, former director of psychiatry at St. Elizabeth Hospital in Washington, DC, gave voice to widespread concerns when, in 1946, he highlighted the difficulty of identifying the distinguishing features of the "psychopathic personality." Often described as a "waste-basket" or a "catch-all expression" used by psychiatrists to describe "troublesome individuals" with antisocial tendencies, psychopathy has historically puzzled observers for its elusiveness and inexplicability.[2] German psychiatrist J. L. A. Koch first used the label *psychopastische*—literally, "suffering soul"—in 1888, to describe a constitutional or acquired mental dysfunction that could affect both the intellectual and moral realms.[3] Over the following 100 years, psychiatrists invented new labels and definitions, which went from descriptions of psychopaths' "constitutional inferiority" and abnormal body types[4] to identifications of negative personality traits such as egocentrism, lack of empathy, and pathological lying.[5] Despite this diagnostic fluidity, by the mid-twentieth century most authorities agreed that the psychopath's distinctive trait was a tendency to deviate from socially accepted standards of morality and conduct, with or without mental disease or defect.[6]

Because of its uncertain contours and linkage to antisocial behaviors, psychopathy has historically been used as a slate on which society could project its fears and anxieties. The psychiatric establishment has played an important role in this regard, legitimizing stigmatizing descriptions that associate the condition with nonconformist behaviors through the apparently neutral and scientific language of medicine. In the 1950s and 1960s challenges to the traditional gender ideology, family values, and heterosexual norms played a central role in prompting the medicalization and moral condemnation of behaviors that deviated from the standards of the white Anglo-Saxon middle classes, the traditional yardstick for appropriateness and civility in the United States. In Texas capital trials these historical transformations prompted psychiatrists to associate criminal psychopathy with personality traits and sexual inclinations that deviated from dominant standards of manhood, increasing the public stigma attached to particular social groups and encouraging censorious attitudes among Texas jurors.

As we will see, in the decades surrounding World War II, the United States witnessed three cultural transformations that had an important influence on psychiatrists' definitions of criminal psychopathy. The late 1940s and 1950s saw the birth of an "ethic of maturity" and family responsibility that prompted psychiatrists to recast criminal psychopaths as emotionally immature and socially maladjusted subjects, who had failed to fulfill the duties required by a respectable adult life and engaged in criminal activities to satisfy their infantile drives. The late 1930s and 1950s witnessed the spreading of a sex-crime panic that, coupled with advancements in women's sexual liberation and gays' claims for social recognition, prompted psychiatrists to characterize criminal psychopaths as sexual perverts and latent homosexuals, dominated by uncontrollable sexual impulses and ready to attack their victims at every available opportunity. Finally, the 1960s saw the emergence of a bohemian movement and a culture of mass media that, by elevating personal enjoyment and social recognition over family responsibility, led experts to depict criminal psychopaths as narcissistic and egocentric attention cravers who engaged in antisocial behaviors to achieve popularity and other personal gains. In all these instances the male criminal psychopath came to embody the personality characteristics that the American public perceived as most threatening to the social order, at a time when Americans' family values and sense of self were being dramatically overhauled.

The Criminal Psychopath as an "Emotionally Immature" Individual

As argued in Chapter 3, in the mid-twentieth century most members of the American Psychiatric Association were trained in the psychoanalytic tradition. Hence the diagnostic classifications included in the first two editions of the *Diagnostic and Statistical Manual of Mental Disorders* (DSM), published in 1952 and 1968, respectively, were powerfully informed by Freudian ideas. This influence had important implications for psychiatrists' depictions of criminal psychopathy. If biological criminologists writing in the 1910s and 1920s had described psychopaths as "constitutionally" inferior individuals,[7] the new generation of psychoanalysts depicted them as emotionally deficient subjects who, as a result of pathological family dynamics, had failed to compensate for or to sublimate the psychosexual conflicts of early childhood.[8] In this view psychopaths' behavioral problems were the result not of inborn mental and moral defects, as argued by early twentieth-century clinicians, but of negative personality traits and emotional difficulties stemming from early parental failures.

In the aftermath of World War II American society underwent a crucial social transformation that would have deep consequences for psychoanalysts' framing of criminal psychopathy. At the time, the recent experience of fascist totalitarian regimes constantly reminded people of the importance of personal freedom and of its close interconnection with civil and political liberties.[9] To protect themselves from oppressive external interferences by the government and other structures of social organization, Americans retreated into the privacy of family life, an intimate world celebrated for its ability to fulfill men's and women's aspirations in the sentimental as well as vocational sphere.[10] As Americans withdrew into the protective shield of family life, a new ethic of maturity, adulthood, and responsibility began to emerge. Within this ethical framework, for men "'maturity' implied [their] rejection of the homosocial, adolescent world of 'mates' and 'buddies,' their reorientation to the heterosexual dyad, and their acceptance of the responsibilities of marriage, [along with] the acceptance of limits."[11] In the conservative climate of the postwar years, men who escaped the responsibilities associated with family life (e.g., finding a stable occupation and committing to a lifelong monogamous relationship) were seen as psychologically immature and socially maladjusted, two aspects that made them more prone to engage in antisocial activities.[12]

The "ethic of maturity" of the postwar years powerfully shaped psychoanalysts' descriptions of criminal psychopaths.[13] Whereas in the 1910s and 1920s psychiatrists had portrayed them as defective subjects with a poor genetic endowment, psychoanalysts writing in the 1940s and 1950s pictured them as "emotionally immature" and "socially maladjusted" individuals who, because of a halt in their psychosexual development, had failed to acquire the necessary moral standards to live a "responsible" adult life.[14] For example, Harry R. Lipton, a psychiatrist from Georgia with experience in penal institutions, argued in 1949 that as a result of defective development stemming from early family conflicts, the child psychopath tended to cry easily, have sudden and aggressive reactions, rebel against parents and other figures of authority, and run away from home.[15] As the child psychopath transitioned into adulthood, these early symptoms became more marked, crystallizing into permanent personality traits that reflected an "infantile approach" to life. Rather than growing into a mature and well-adjusted citizen, the male psychopath kept behaving like a child, trying "to use on the world those methods which [had] previously been effective with the parents."[16] Because of this emotional immaturity, he denied responsibility for his actions, refused to accept the realities of life, and restlessly searched for the unattainable, failing to understand that "adjustment and success necessitate a long steady pull." Rather than working hard toward a planned goal, he preferred taking chances, expecting to obtain results "by magic rather than by effort."[17]

Karpman shared Lipton's concern with the psychopath's psychological infantilism. Discussing a male psychopath with a long criminal career, he suggested that early family dynamics had turned the subject into an emotionally immature individual, incapable of dealing with the realities of life and of adjusting his behavior to legal requirements.[18] "Weak and delicate" from birth, as a child he craved constant care and attention, an aspect that gradually developed into a fixed personality trait. "Maternal overprotection" had retarded his development, making him emotionally dependent, "sexually conservative," and inapt to approach reality healthily and maturely.[19] As a result of these developmental deficiencies, the man needed long periods of rest and was incapable of engaging in any productive occupation. Bullied at school, the subject started developing early fantasy formations to tackle the difficulties he experienced in real life. Behaviorally, these psychological mechanisms translated into school truancy and fantastic dreams of future achievement, which were regularly frustrated by his indulgence in daydreaming and lack of proper dedication. Because reality kept disappointing him, he increasingly detached from it, living in his own world of fantasies and separating himself from the external world. As his dreamy wishes pressed for fulfillment, they "sought vicarious expression in predatory crimes that would temporarily satisfy his phantasies," immature impulses, and unconscious drives.[20]

The evidence presented in the trial of Riley McCaine suggests that forensic psychiatrists who testified in Texas capital punishment proceedings drew from similar depictions in their evaluations.[21] McCaine, a white working-class man, was charged with the murder of a stranger woman named Elnora Collins in April 1947 and was sentenced to death the following year. In his confession McCaine explained that, on the day of the killing, he saw the young woman on a street in Houston and, "without any provocation or conversation," got out of his car and choked her to death.[22] After the killing, McCaine burned the victim's body, hid it in the woods, and attempted to escape detection by leaving Texas and assuming a different identity, all facts that are typically considered strong commonsense indications of legal sanity in Texas courts.[23] Despite this unfavorable evidence, McCaine contended that, because of a severe mental disease, he did not know the difference between right and wrong at the time of the crime.

To support McCaine's insanity claim, the defense presented the testimony of a few lay and expert witnesses who had met McCaine in the years preceding the murder. Their testimonies depicted a severely depressed man, devastated by two failed marriages, an irregular employment history, and a psychiatric hospitalization.[24] According to the witnesses, at the time of his second divorce proceedings in 1944, the defendant appeared thin, "very nervous," immersed in his own thoughts, and prone to public crying.[25]

The defendant's emotional outbursts were a particular cause for concern. "I don't consider it normal for a man to cry," a psychiatrist who saw the defendant at the end of 1944 explained. "I have seen very few men cry and to me it is quite distressing, and to me it is quite outstanding, something I don't think many people easily forget seeing a man cry."[26] In the witnesses' view, McCaine's inability to control his emotions in public along with his nervous and depressed appearance were strong indications that the man had become mentally ill and was likely to commit a maniacal act.

The defense's chief expert witness, a Texas psychiatrist named John Waterman, examined the defendant following his arrest and concluded that he suffered from "a psychopathic personality with psychotic trends." This personality defect, the doctor explained, was characterized by "periods of mental disturbance which cause[d] [McCaine] to do acts which ordinary people would consider wrong . . . without any recognition of the consequences."[27] Because of a halted development in infancy or childhood, the defendant acted "impulsively," was unable "to look ahead," and seemed to never "learn from experience," even when he expressed regret and repentance for his past actions.[28] When external triggers prompted a psychotic episode, McCaine succumbed under the pressure of primitive urges and obsessions, which could translate into sudden and unexplainable criminal acts, such as the one perpetrated against the victim.[29] McCaine's halted psychological and emotional development, the doctor concluded, undermined his ability to feel love, hate, anger, or guilt for his past actions.[30] Although he had a rational understanding of the moral wrongfulness of the killing, this emotional void impaired his ability to fully appreciate such wrongfulness on an emotional plane.[31]

McCaine's emotional immaturity and impulsivity were reflected in his inability to live a responsible life with regard to family obligations and to hold a job for more than two consecutive years.[32] "He starts out on a job and works two or three months like a house afire and folds up," Dr. Waterman stressed during his testimony. "He can't face responsibility, I mean responsibility we all have to take in regard to family relations and things like that."[33] Although McCaine's first wife explained at trial that both their divorce and McCaine's irregular work pattern were a direct consequence of the Great Depression that followed the 1929 financial crisis,[34] the experts framed them as another symptom of the man's pathological immaturity and inability to make responsible life decisions. In so doing, they condemned McCaine's failure to live up to society's ideal standards of manhood, because of both his family and career instability and his poor emotional control, as reflected by his public crying episodes. By inscribing McCaine's life challenges into his pathological makeup, the experts reinforced the "dispositional" view of mental illness and criminality that tends to dominate the trial context[35] and deemphasized the role of socioeconomic factors in triggering defendants' relational difficulties, professional troubles, and antisocial behaviors.

As this case illustrates, Texas trial experts drew from the association between emotional immaturity and criminal psychopathy advanced by psychoanalytic clinicians. However, if mid-twentieth-century therapists dedicated significant attention to the family dynamics that could cause children to develop psychopathic tendencies, courtroom experts either ignored defendants' family histories altogether[36] or limited their references to cursory mentions of "parental rejection" and "maternal deprivation/overprotection" in defendants' early childhoods.[37] The expert testimony in McCaine's trial clearly illustrates this tendency. Even though Dr. Waterman established that the defendant's psychopathic tendencies, emotional defects, and impulsive behaviors were to be reconducted to a halt in childhood development, he did not explain what parental behaviors might have caused such a developmental problem.[38] This is especially striking given the centrality of family dynamics, particularly mother-child relationships, for the "doctrine of immaturity" endorsed by most expert witnesses, including Dr. Waterman, in the mid-twentieth century.

The reasons for experts' superficial approach to family dynamics in trial proceedings are threefold. First, Texas's insanity standard excludes from the court's consideration any information that, though relevant for a broader understanding of the defendant's personal background and moral blameworthiness, does not help the jury answer the question of whether the defendant could distinguish right from wrong at the time of the crime. Although evidence of parental rejection can be linked to emotional immaturity and aggressive tendencies, arguing that it undermines defendants' awareness of the wrongfulness of their capital crimes is a significant challenge for defense attorneys, deterring them from pursuing its investigation. As I will show in Chapters 5 and 6, the creation in the mid-1970s of constitutional standards requiring courts to consider mitigating evidence of mental illness and child abuse during the sentencing phase created the procedural condition for the introduction of this kind of evidence, freed from the "legal straitjacket" of the "right and wrong" standard.[39]

Second, mid-twentieth-century trial experts worked under significant time and resource constraints and were therefore unable to conduct in-depth evaluations of the defendants' lives and family relationships. The "intensive analytical process" necessary for psychoanalysts to reveal the "unconscious patterning" of a defendant's "psychic life" was difficult to reproduce within the two to three hours allocated for a forensic mental health evaluation, making a complete assessment of a defendant's family conflicts complicated.[40] Finally, in the mid-twentieth century most witnesses were probably reluctant to discuss private family matters in public forums, because of social customs of decorum and fears of social stigma. Even though open communication about intimate aspects of human relationships, including sexual topics, was becoming increasingly commonplace,[41] in many conservative contexts, such as Texas's rural areas, it was still considered taboo and therefore carefully avoided.

The Criminal Psychopath as a "Sexual Pervert"

In the mid-twentieth century American psychiatrists and criminal justice officials developed a new diagnostic category associated with antisocial tendencies: sexual psychopathy.[42] Psychiatrists' interest in this diagnostic classification stemmed from the emergence of a new code of sexual morality, which challenged the traditional notion of "civilized" sexuality by encouraging female sexual exploration outside the boundaries of marriage and procreation. The emergence of this sexual code destabilized traditional family arrangements, prompting concerns among conservatives who feared that, outside the protective patriarchal shield, women would become more vulnerable to assaults by "sexual perverts," "sick" men who had failed to develop proper impulse controls and therefore lived in a constant search for sexual pleasures and erotic satisfaction.

The nineteenth-century notion of "civilized sexuality" restricted sexual intercourse to monogamous marriage and celebrated female abstinence, purity, and self-control as direct paths to moral rectitude and social adjustment.[43] This sexual code fell perfectly in line with somatic psychiatry's association of mental health with control over the lower instincts through the self-restraining power of the brain or rational mind. However, as Freud's ideas gathered momentum, psychoanalysts started questioning this model, highlighting the neurotic effects of sexual repression in female patients and stressing the universal nature of sexual needs across genders. According to Freud and his followers, puritanism was a sterile instrument of repression that led to emotional aridity and pathological controls of instincts and desires, a moralistic and judgmental framework whose only purpose was to curb people's natural drives.

From the 1920s onward, Freud's revolutionary ideas about sexuality and the unconventional sexual behaviors promoted by the new urban bohemian culture helped reframe Americans' understanding of what constituted proper sexual conduct.[44] Influenced by these ideas, the white middle classes started to detach sexuality from procreation, practice family planning, and accept the reality of female sexual desire. Although the puritan framework had theoretically protected women against males' aggressive sexual advances by encouraging a pious and monogamous life, as traditional gender roles became subverted and women claimed more sexual freedom, fears that women and children would become more vulnerable to men's unwarranted attacks began to emerge.[45]

In the late 1930s and early 1950s,[46] these fears were fueled by a series of sex-motivated child murders, which prompted American newspapers to increase their coverage of child rape and molestation.[47] This increased media coverage incited concerns among psychiatrists, legal authorities, and the lay public about a possible sex-crime wave striking the United States, despite a striking lack of evidence to support this contention. By sensationalizing a stereotypical image of sex offenders as uncontrollable beasts possessed by overwhelming sexual instincts and desires,[48] the media prompted several states and the federal government to take special measures to manage and control "sexual psychopaths," individuals incapable of controlling their sexual urges and "likely to attack . . . the objects of [their] uncontrolled and uncontrollable desires."[49]

Beginning in the late 1930s, state governments started instituting special commissions for the investigation of sex crimes, investing in research aimed at the study of sexual psychopaths, and funding specialized institutions aimed at their psychiatric treatment. Most important, twenty-six states and the District of Columbia drafted new "psychopathy laws" that compelled courts to impose indeterminate detentions in psychiatric institutions on defendants diagnosed with sexual deviations.[50] Even though Texas never passed its own psychopathy laws,[51] as progressives in the cities of Austin, Dallas, and Houston pushed for sexually liberating policies, and conservatives held their ground on key issues such as birth control and gay rights, the state became a key battleground for the criminalization of "sexual deviance," particularly in the 1950s and 1960s.[52]

The Sexual Psychopath as an "Insatiable Beast"

Benjamin Karpman, one of the main psychoanalytic contributors to the debate on sexual psychopathy in the 1930s, 1940s, and 1950s, fully embraced the stereotypical image of the sex offender as an "insatiable beast" advanced by the American media.[53] In line with Freud's critique of puritan sexual morality, Karpman argued that parents' tendency to repress and punish children's curiosity in sexual matters, as well as their reticence to provide a frank and open sexual education, hindered the child's natural sexual development, contributing to pathological expressions of sexuality in adulthood. By punishing children's sexual experimentation, parents forced them to repress their natural sexual urges into the unconscious. Once repressed, these natural instincts got distorted and corrupted, only to later reemerge in the form of sexual disorders.

The emotional and psychological immaturity that stemmed from the child's arrested psychosexual development contributed to the formation of a primitive and underdeveloped subject, the sexual psychopath, dominated by his instincts and impulses and incapable of deferring pleasure.[54] The fantasies and dreams of the sexual psychopath were simple and primitive and were focused exclusively on needs and desires. "In a life that is lived on a simple, primitive plane," Karpman explained,

> there is little opportunity for symbolization. . . . Normal judgment and other higher functions are interfered with by the continuous intrusion of primitive instincts that brooks no opposition. The mental organization is not merely savage and primitive but closer to the animal; indeed, individuals of this type are little more than animals in human form.[55]

Whereas later psychoanalysts would argue that the sexual psychopath had an underdeveloped libido, Karpman insisted that they were "insatiable beasts," closer to animals than to humans, always in search of sexual pleasure and erotic satisfaction.[56] Karpman's association of arrested childhood development, primitiveness, and unrestrained expression of lower impulses drew from two central ideas: the instincts theory developed by Freud and inspired by the old notion of reflex action, discussed in Chapter 1, and the notion of childhood development seen as a gradual progression from primitiveness to civilization. The second idea, developed by G. Stanley Hall, a prominent proponent of the progressive education movement, became extremely popular among American psychoanalysts and educators in the first half of the twentieth century. Inspired by nineteenth-century theories of racial evolution,[57] Hall argued that, as children progressed from infancy to adulthood, they followed the same pattern of development followed by the human races, from an early stage of primitiveness and barbarity to a final stage of maturity and civility.[58] It followed from this argument that any interruption in the healthy development of the child could prompt the unleashing of the primitive instincts associated with the early stages of human development and lead to beastlike sexual conduct and criminal behaviors.

In the 1950s and 1960s psychoanalysts' explanations of the nature and origins of "sexual perversions" contributed to a conceptual conflation between criminal psychopathy and various forms of "sexual deviances" in Texas courtrooms.[59] The 1952 trial of Foley Ford Gephart provides an illustrative example in this regard. Gephart, a 37-year-old white man, was charged with the abduction and rape of three children—two girls and a boy between 8 and 10 years of age—in May 1950. The evidence suggested that the defendant, a schoolteacher who had met the victims at a playground some time prior to the offense, had picked up the children at their home and brought them to his apartment, where he had systematically raped them.[60] Called to the stand, the victims reported that this was not an isolated incident, that the two girls had been to the defendant's apartment before, and that each time he had forced them to have sexual intercourse with him.

The defendant pleaded not guilty by reason of insanity. To support his insanity claim, he presented evidence suggesting that in April 1950 he had been committed to Austin State Hospital following a lunacy proceeding.[61] Shortly after his commitment, one of the victims in this case reported that she had been raped by the defendant, and the Travis County court immediately filed an order finding Gephart sane and free to be released. Following his discharge from the hospital, the defendant was arrested for rape of a child under 18 years, at the time a capital offense.

During his stay at Austin State Hospital, the defendant was twice examined by a board of nine physicians, who concluded that he suffered from a severe mental illness. The defense introduced in evidence the minutes from the staff meetings, along with a report of a psychological evaluation conducted at the hospital. In the summary of the second staff meeting, the doctors reported that the defendant complained about "uncontrollable sexual urges to fondle the genitalia of small girls," arguing that "he neither received any pleasure, gratification or sexual stimulation" from this activity but that it had helped him control his passion thus far.[62] Gephart was unable to provide any explanation for these uncontrollable urges, which were episodic and accompanied by confusion that lasted for four to five days at a time. According to the doctors, the evaluation suggested that the patient lacked judgment, insight, and morality and that because of his overwhelming sexual perversions and transient confused states, he had no consideration for other people's well-being. His criminal history, they concluded, coupled with his "childishness at 37 years" and his failure to learn from experience, suggested that Gephart suffered from a "psychosis with psychopathic personality disorder" and therefore should be kept in the hospital for further treatment.

The psychological report echoed these views, adding important considerations regarding the etiology of Gephart's mental condition.[63] As part of his evaluation, the psychological trainee who signed the report administered a series of projective tests, the results of which suggested that the patient was dominated by sexual obsessions and compulsions and therefore tended to "act on the spur of the moment with little thought of the consequences of his actions." Because of "an over attachment to the mother figure" in the early formative years, as a child Gephart had experienced a strong sexual conflict, which had led to an arrest of his psychosexual development at "a pregenital age" and to a marked emotional immaturity.[64] The diagnosis was "over-ideational perschizophrenia with a premorbid obsessive-compulsive adjustment," a particular form of psychosis characterized by obsessions and compulsions.[65]

To counteract this evidence, the state called several expert and lay witnesses to the stand. The state witness list included the doctors who had signed the staff meeting reports at Austin State Hospital,[66] the criminal justice officials who had brought the lunacy charges against the defendant and filed affidavits in support of his hospitalization,[67] and a few experts who had examined Gephart before the death penalty proceedings.[68] The witnesses who had observed and examined Gephart at the time of his civil commitment all testified that in their view he was sane. Although they had previously argued that he was insane and needed to be hospitalized, they explained that those testimonies had the strategic purpose of keeping him locked up for as long as possible for public protection.[69] As the sheriff of Fayette County clarified, when they signed the lunacy proceedings, Gephart had been arrested for sexually assaulting a few young girls but, given Texas's laws on sex offenses, they believed that a traditional proceeding would have led to a maximum prison sentence of two years for aggravated assault, an overly short incarceration time to ensure public safety. As a result, they decided to file a lunacy proceeding against Gephart, hoping that a finding of insanity would lead to a longer period of institutionalization.

As this and other state testimonies suggest,[70] in the absence of "sexual psychopath" laws prescribing the indeterminate detention of sex offenders, Texas officials used civil commitment proceedings to keep such offenders in psychiatric institutions for extended periods without an "objective" medical justification. The practice of using civil commitment proceedings to keep "dangerous sex offenders" in custody was likely a widespread phenomenon, affecting both states that eventually approved a sexual psychopath statute and states that, like Texas, decided against it.[71] Hence, the drafting of sexual psychopathy laws can be read as a strategic move aimed at legitimizing a well-established practice, which utilized the medicalization of sexual deviances to incapacitate and control sex offenders through indeterminate institutionalization, in the interest of public protection.

Despite the contradictory and ethically problematic statements provided by the prosecution's key witnesses, the jury relied on the state's version of the facts, judged Gephart sane at the time of the alleged offense, and sentenced him to death. Once again, one can find a possible explanation for the jury's finding by looking at the medical explanations provided by the defense and at the defendant's behavior following the crime. First, by arguing that the defendant's sexual misconduct was prompted by uncontrollable primitive urges, the psychiatric and psychological reports presented by Gephart's attorney seemed to support a defense of irresistible impulse rather than of legal insanity. Second, the evidence presented by the prosecution suggested that, following the sexual assaults, Gephart had warned the children to never tell anyone about what had happened, threatening to hurt them if they disobeyed and promising gifts if they followed his instructions.[72] As with most cases analyzed in this book, when the defendant's behavior suggests an attempt to escape detection and arrest, the folk-psychological interpretation of human behavior tends to prevail over the medical one, prompting juries to infer a guilty state of mind and impose a death sentence.

The Sexual Psychopath as a "Latent Homosexual"

In the conservative climate of the postwar years, psychoanalysts turned their attention to a particular category of "sexual deviates"—homosexuals—who, through their unconventional sexual preferences, challenged the traditional heterosexual dyad and all the values it represented. In the 1940s and 1950s social institutions for gays and lesbians were raising public awareness about homosexuality, and political movements focusing on gay rights attempted to reframe homosexuality as a positive minority identity.[73] However, until 1973 homosexuality was still categorized as a mental disease, and many American states, including Texas, still criminalized homosexual encounters.[74] The fear that homosexuals could spread their "sexual perversion" among youth and thereby corrupt the entire community might be one of the reasons behind the rapid spread of psychopathy laws.[75] Indeed, between 1949 and 1955 homosexuals were regularly blamed for sex crimes committed against women and children, and "the frequent overlap in use of the terms *sex criminal*, *pervert*, *psychopath*, and *homosexual*, raises the question of whether *psychopath* served in part as a code for *homosexual* at a time of heightened public consciousness of homosexuality."[76]

Psychoanalysts writing in the 1940s and 1950s played a central role in stigmatizing homosexuality as an abnormal sexual orientation stemming from a pathological mental condition.[77] Whereas Freud's early writings on sexuality argued that all human beings had a bisexual disposition free from prescribed gender roles,[78] postwar psychoanalysis refuted this interpretation by associating each gender with a particular sexuality.[79] In this view homosexuals were latent heterosexuals who "feared merging with the pre-oedipal mother" and hoped "to achieve a shot of masculinity in the homosexual act."[80] Rather than being a natural expression of a particular sexual inclination, the homosexual act was the manifestation of an underlying pathology, stemming from the child's original failure to overcome—through a process of sublimation and repression—the Oedipus conflict. As a result of this initial failure, the child developed a pathological sexuality that sought continuous satisfaction through unnatural acts aimed at temporarily restoring his feeling of masculinity.[81]

The association of homosexuality with psychopathy and sexual deviance emerges clearly in one of the affidavits presented by Gephart's attorneys in their motion for a new trial following their client's conviction.[82] In the affidavit Dr. H. J. Hoerster, a physician who had known the defendant for over 18 years, drew from the stigmatization of homosexuals as sexual perverts to argue that Gephart's unnatural sexual compulsions toward children were the result of a *latent homosexuality* that stemmed from an arrested emotional development and had become active following his enlistment in the U.S. Army.[83] The experience of being "taken out of a home environment similar to his and thrust suddenly into rigorous military training among strangers and all males," he proposed, "resulted in a transposition of the latent homosexual and related tendencies into an active condition," and in a pathological acting-out of his hidden sexual perversions on young children as a temporary form of satisfaction.[84]

The trial of Fred Thomas Leath provides another illuminating example of postwar psychoanalysts' labeling of homosexuality as a psychopathic personality disorder associated with sexual perversions.[85] Leath, a 38-year-old white man, was convicted for the shooting and killing of Edward Henry, a 15-year-old boy, in April 1961 and sentenced to death. The defendant's written confession, along with the evidence presented at trial, suggests that the two had been involved in a homosexual relationship and that, shortly before the murder, the officers had informed the defendant "that the deceased had told them every secret he had told the deceased[,] including that he was an ex-convict" and a homosexual.[86]

Leath pleaded not guilty by reason of insanity. To support his claim, he presented the testimony of a Texan psychiatrist, Dr. T. W. Grice, who conducted a 14-minute assessment in the county jail while Leath was awaiting trial and concluded that he suffered from "schizophrenia, paranoid type," a condition associated with paranoid delusions and hallucinations.[87] Dr. Grice's medical conclusion was supported by lay witness testimonies suggesting that Leath was troubled by paranoid fears and persecutory thoughts, manifested by a constant preoccupation with being poisoned[88] or hurt by someone when walking down the street.[89] To challenge the defense's argument, the state presented the testimony of Dr. John T. Holbrook, a renowned hired gun for the prosecution who had examined Leath following his arrest.[90] According to Dr. Holbrook, Leath did not suffer from a severe mental health condition, as argued by Dr. Grice, but from a sociopathic personality disorder,[91] a condition typically affecting "narcotic addicts, alcoholics, and homosexuals" and defined by a marked immaturity and inability to learn from experience.[92]

At the time of Leath's trial, Texas law considered homosexuality a criminal offense and the path toward its destigmatization and social acceptability remained fraught.[93] Dr. Holbrook's testimony reflected this legal and cultural background. First, given the legal prohibitions against homosexuality, the doctor proposed that the defendant's persecutory thoughts should be read as a reflection of legitimate fears that the police and other members of society would go after him for his unlawful sexual inclinations, not as symptoms of a severe mental health condition, as suggested by Dr. Grice.[94] "These people," he argued referring to psychopathic homosexuals, "appear paranoid to the casual observer because they think people are after them. They are correct. People are after them. This includes the police and everybody in society. This is not paranoid thinking. This is based on reality."[95]

Second, drawing from psychoanalytic explanations of sexual psychopathy and from the 1950s stigmatization of homosexuals as "uncontrollable beasts," Dr. Holbrook described the defendant as a lonely individual who, because of a halt in his psychosexual development, had failed to refine his aggressive and sexual instincts and therefore lived at a primitive level, closer to a wild animal than to a civilized human being, alert to any possible danger and always running for his life.[96] Homosexual psychopaths, Dr. Holbrook explained, "have no close relationship with anyone. . . . They live in a jungle *just like a lion or a tiger or any other wild animal*. These animals hear a noise and they run. They know from experience there is trouble ahead."[97]

The postwar stigmatization of homosexuality emerges perhaps even more strikingly in the opinion of the Texas Court of Criminal Appeals (TCCA). In one of his points of contention, Leath complained that the district attorney, in his opening argument, described him as "a blood sucking vampire," an untrue and clearly inflammatory and prejudicial statement.[98] However, the TCCA refused to reverse the conviction on these grounds, stating that

> the argument, when considered in the light of the definition of a vampire as "one who lives by preying on others," particularly the young and healthy, and when weighed in connection with all the facts and circumstances in evidence—the unnatural relationship of the parties and the background and setting in which the killing occurred as shown by the evidence—does not call for a reversal.[99]

As this statement suggests, the judges of the TCCA shared other criminal justice officials and expert witnesses' confusion about the potentially "pathological" undertones and "inhuman" nature of same-sex encounters. By accepting the prosecutors' description of the defendant as a diabolical being who sucked the blood and life of others for his own survival, the TCCA aligned itself with those experts who, by associating homosexuality with sexual perversions such as pedophilia[100] and by linking it with animalistic instincts and sociopathic tendencies,[101] reinforced public stigma around homosexuality, further delaying its decriminalization.

As forensic psychiatric discourse in the Gephart and Leath trials has shown, in the 1950s Texas experts were equally influenced by the scientific developments and moral values of their time. On the one hand, the experts used psychoanalytic theory to argue that negative parental attachments could lead to an arrested psychosexual development and to a pathological unleashing of the individual's primitive sexual impulses in adulthood. On the other hand, they drew from conservative views about what constituted proper sexual conduct to argue that unconventional sexual practices could "corrupt" the mental health of the individual, prompting him to develop pathological conditions associated with antisocial behaviors. In so doing, psychiatrists created an intricate mix of scientific theory and moral judgment that promoted a conceptual conflation between those who deviated from conventional social norms of sexuality and criminal offenders who engaged in violent sexual conduct against vulnerable victims.

The Criminal Psychopath as an "Egocentric Narcissist"

The 1960s witnessed important social and cultural transformations that had long-lasting consequences for psychiatrists' framing of criminal psychopathy. As we have seen, the conservative 1950s celebrated a return to the privacy of family life, with its emphasis on long-term commitment and adult responsibility. In contrast, in the 1960s a new generation of youth started criticizing traditional family values, perceived as limiting and oppressive, and embracing alternative lifestyles that challenged traditional marriage rules and gender roles.[102] At the time, two decades of uninterrupted economic growth and scientific progress had given the new generation an unparalleled sense of power and possibility, prompting the emergence of a "new utopianism" that advocated gender equality and sexual freedom outside the private family unit.[103]

A few commentators associated the new utopianism with the new world of media and advertisement. For example, in 1953 David Riesman argued that the rise of the entertainment industry had prompted Americans to turn away from the private world of the family to embrace the public sphere of mass media.[104] Rather than seeking autonomy from external interference, as the previous generation had done, Americans now sought "mirroring and recognition."[105] Instead of directing their attention inward, they focused on the way others perceived them, constantly working to improve their personal appearance, social skills, and popularity.[106]

The "other-directed personality" described by Riesman recalled Freud's early definition of *narcissism*, a condition associated with an early stage of childhood development characterized by self-love and a constant need for recognition, with potentially pathological undertones.[107] The psychoanalytic establishment (i.e., ego psychologists such as Heinz Hartmann, Ernst Kris, and Rudolph Loewenstein) endorsed the negative connotation of Freud's early definition, attacking the "narcissist" culture of the 1960s for strengthening the primitive unconscious drives of childhood at the expense of the Oedipal authority.[108] Critics used the term *narcissism* to describe the 1960s generation's alleged inability to "make commitments, engage in long term projects, and sacrifice the self for larger purposes," all aspects that were closely associated with their refusal of traditional family values.[109] In this view, by indulging in sensual pleasures, daydreaming, and enjoyment, narcissistic personalities risked turning into irresponsible and maladjusted citizens who engaged in criminal behavior to cope with their real-life frustrations. Moreover, by trying to satisfy their pathological needs and achieve visibility and popularity, these egocentric attention cravers would use their verbal skills to deceive and manipulate others, without concerns for the consequences of their actions.

Notorious forensic psychiatrists shared these concerns and used them to redefine the characteristics of criminal psychopathy according to the new intellectual environment. For example, Hervey Cleckley, an influential psychiatrist who wrote extensively on the psychopathic personality between 1940 and 1975, described the male psychopath as a self-absorbed loner, an egocentric subject who, unable to feel genuine emotions of love and empathy, would carelessly crush other people's feelings to pursue his own needs.[110] Because of a marked impulsivity and hedonistic approach to life, the male psychopath was unable to commit to a coherent life plan and pursue it with steady dedication.[111] Thanks to a normal appearance, a superficial charm, and a pathological tendency to lie, the psychopath was able to hide his underlying disorder, constantly manipulate others, and bend them to his own will.[112] His tendency to lie made him incapable of distinguishing truth from falsehood, taking responsibility for his actions, and feeling guilt and remorse for his misdeeds, all traits that could lead to antisocial tendencies and repeated criminal behaviors.[113]

Although Cleckley and other psychiatrists associated narcissistic and egocentric personalities with social maladjustment and criminality, a few psychoanalytic reformers tried to understand their underlying psychological dynamics in less condemning terms. Heinz Kohut, for example, argued that, because of an early psychological trauma, narcissistic patients needed constant ego reassurance and therefore experienced an "intense hunger for a powerful external supplier of self-esteem and other forms of emotional sustenance in the narcissistic realm."[114] Rather than morally condemning such need, he argued, psychoanalysts "should recognize the legitimacy of patients' need to be mirrored, or to idealize a 'self-object' who made them feel whole and important."[115] By aligning themselves with the changed cultural context and by respecting narcissists' emotional needs, psychoanalytic reformers could express sympathy and understanding for those who rejected family life, pursued activities and professions that served no social purpose, and expressed ideas and beliefs that challenged the established order.[116] In this sense, psychoanalysis could become a symbol of social change and personal freedom rather than one of social conformism and repression.

The trial of Jack Rubenstein (alias Ruby) provides an emblematic example of the way in which the ideological clash between those who framed narcissists as egocentric and hedonistic attention seekers and those who described them as insecure individuals with low self-esteem could translate in the legal arena.[117] Jack Ruby, a Jewish[118] middle-aged white man, was charged with the murder of Lee Harvey Oswald, the man accused of assassinating President John F. Kennedy on November 22, 1963, during a parade in Dallas.[119] Two days after the killing of the president, Ruby shot Oswald, who was surrounded by journalists and television cameras, as he was being transferred from the city jail to the county jail. A few days later, Ruby was indicted for the killing of Oswald and pleaded not guilty by reason of insanity. Thousands of people witnessed Oswald's shooting on television, including ten of Ruby's trial jurors, an aspect that led the TCCA to reverse the judgment of the trial court and order a new proceeding.

The state's theory was that Ruby had premeditated Oswald's killing and was mentally alert at the time of the commission of the offense, two aspects that directly challenged his insanity plea. According to State Attorney Bowie's reconstruction of the events, when Ruby saw Oswald in the basement of the city jail, he

> removed a pistol from his pocket, made a quick and crouched motion toward Lee Harvey Oswald, saying, "you rat son of a bitch, you killed the President," and fired a shot almost simultaneous with the statement. . . . Immediately thereafter he was grappled to the ground, and he there stated . . . "I hope the

> son of a bitch dies" . . . and . . . "I first thought about killing him when I saw him in the show up Friday night."[120]

The admissibility of the state's reconstruction was the object of much controversy, both at trial[121] and on appeal, because Ruby had reported these events, which amounted to a confession of premeditation, during an interrogation at the Dallas police department, before the officers had given him the statutory warnings regarding his right to remain silent and the potentially prejudicial effect of his statements.[122]

The defense experts challenged the interpretation of Ruby's mental state provided by the state attorney. According to their evaluation, Ruby suffered from psychomotor epilepsy—a condition associated with epileptic seizures followed by loss of consciousness and automatic movements—and had killed Oswald during one of these epileptic attacks.[123] In this view, the murder was the result not of a cold and reasoned premeditation, as argued by the state, but of a series of emotional stressors that had accumulated in the days preceding the murder and triggered an aggressive automatic movement at the time of the killing.[124]

Besides emphasizing Ruby's organic condition, the defense experts stressed the role played by his personality characteristics and emotional makeup in prompting his criminal act.[125] They portrayed him as an insecure, impulsive, and emotionally unstable subject who was obsessed with people's social approval and constantly looked for influential connections to improve his self-esteem. For example, Dr. Roy Schafer, a Yale professor and clinical psychologist, gave Ruby a battery of psychological tests[126] that showed that he was extremely preoccupied with his personal appearance, with being liked and appreciated by others, and with acquiring personal prestige by associating with "important" people.[127] On cross-examination District Attorney Henry Wade suggested that these characteristics indicated that Ruby had a narcissistic personality, which prompted him to constantly seek the limelight and other people's attention.[128] The doctor challenged this interpretation, aligning himself with psychoanalytic reformers' view of narcissism as a reflection of the individual's low self-esteem and need for constant ego reassurance. In his view Ruby's

> attraction to people in positions of prestige or class, was typically tied in with the idea of his acquiring some worth, or some feeling of esteem for himself

> since he depends very much on outside sources for feeling self-esteem. But this did not seem to be so much a matter of limelight, as being accepted by people in positions of prestige. The emphasis was on acceptance, rather than being the center of things.[129]

According to the defense expert, Ruby's vanity, along with his desire to appear "tough" and strong,[130] was a compensatory mechanism associated with this feeling of inferiority, a trait shared by many individuals with neurotic and antisocial tendencies. As a result of his poor self-esteem, Dr. Schafer argued, Ruby was emotionally unstable, an aspect that made him more vulnerable to environmental stimulation and inclined to have outbursts of anger, and that played a pivotal role in triggering the loss of consciousness which allegedly accompanied the tragic events.[131]

Echoing this view, Dr. Manfred Guttmacher, an esteemed psychoanalyst employed by the Supreme Court Bench of Maryland,[132] argued that Ruby's impulsivity stemmed from a deep sense of insecurity and from a pressing need to reassert his masculinity.[133] The origin of this feeling of inferiority, he argued, could be traced back to Ruby's early childhood experiences. Raised by a mentally ill mother and an alcoholic father "who tyrannized his family," at the age of 8 Ruby was separated from his siblings and moved between different foster homes until he was considered old enough to take care of himself.[134] This difficult family background had triggered a psychosexual conflict during a crucial stage of Ruby's development, which had contributed to the formation of a "weak ego-structure" that prompted Ruby to constantly reassert "his masculinity by fighting, sexual promiscuity, [and] body building exercises."[135] "His narcissistic concern[s] over his body weight and his baldness," the doctor explained, were further compensatory mechanisms for his feelings of inadequacy, as were his "swaggering boastfulness" and his obsession with "the impression he is going to make on others."[136]

Ruby's "inferiority complex" fueled strong feelings of hostility and aggression, which erupted "in volcanic force" whenever Ruby's control mechanisms would break down, a fact corroborated by his historical involvement in numerous verbal and physical fights.[137] Supporting an irresistible impulse argument, Dr. Guttmacher argued that in the days preceding the killing, the defendant's

> weak ego . . . was constantly assaulted by strong emotional stresses and was suddenly overwhelmed, permitting unconscious, hostile, aggressive impulses to gain ascendency and to rob him of the realization of the wrongfulness of his action, and an inability to control his destructive impulses.[138]

In typical psychoanalytic fashion the expert explained Ruby's emotional involvement with the Kennedys' tragedy in symbolic terms. In his view, "because of his own wretched family life," the defendant saw President Kennedy not only as "the idealized father figure as the head of the state" but also as "the leading member of a perfect family group," which he wished to vicariously join by retaliating against the president's killer.[139] Although Ruby had an intellectual realization of the wrongfulness of his act, his idealized view of the president, coupled with his depiction of the victim as a "rat" to be exterminated, contributed to create a psychological justification for the killing in Ruby's mind and to neutralize any feeling of guilt or remorse for the act committed.[140]

On cross-examination Assistant District Attorney William F. Alexander challenged Dr. Guttmacher's conclusion, suggesting that, rather than being compelled by the defendant's weak ego structure, low self-esteem, and pathological identification with the Kennedys' tragedy, the murder was motivated by his desire to acquire notoriety and gain financial rewards. The following line of questioning clearly illustrates the clash between the prosecution and the defense's interpretations:

> Q. Doctor, if you felt that the real motive for the shooting of Oswald was the desire to gain fame and fortune, and Ruby had misjudged public temperament and public feeling, would that make any difference in your evaluation?
> A. I would certainly think he had sick judgment if he made such—
> Q. If Ruby thought he would be "no billed" by the grand jury, and hailed as a hero for doing what other people didn't have the opportunity or the "guts" to do, would that make any difference?
> A. I think it's sick judgment.
> Q. Sick judgment doesn't mean insane, does it?
> A. That's right.
> Q. Would the fact that Ruby has been able to sell his life story to the newspapers make any difference to you, in your opinion?

A. I don't think it would have anything to do with what happened at the time.[141]

Along these lines, in his cross-examination of defense psychiatrist Dr. Bromberg, District Attorney Wade insinuated that the real reason for the killing could be found not in the defendant's "messianic trend," as argued by the doctor, but in his desire to be seen on television and become a hero in American history. The following extract is illuminating in this regard:

Q. And he had a feeling of wanting to be a hero, is that right?
A. A martyr, rather. He had a definite messianic trend, his motto being to rescue the Jewish people from the charge that they haven't got guts, to put it in his words. . . .
Q. Don't you think, doctor, that shooting a man on television, before quite a number of people, would have the effect on a person having grandiose tendencies, would have the effect, he thought, of making him a hero?
A. I feel at that time he had no such thought because his consciousness was suspended; he was in turmoil and agitation.[142]

As these examples suggest, in Ruby's trial the defense and the prosecution provided two dramatically different interpretations of the defendant's personality and behavior. On the one hand, the defense portrayed him as a brain-damaged, emotionally insecure, and mentally unstable individual who, because of a defect in personality development, had developed a weak ego structure that undermined his ability to control his behavior and act rationally when put under extreme environmental pressure. On the other hand, the prosecution described him as an egotistical and narcissistic personality who had premeditated the killing of Oswald to acquire fame and financial gains and be pictured as a hero by the American media and the wider public.

These conflicting views mirrored the ideological clash that was dividing conservatives and new utopians' standards of behavior in the mid-1960s. By morally condemning Ruby's narcissistic traits as symptoms of his egotistical and attention-craving tendencies, the prosecution endorsed the conservative critique of the world of mass media and advertisement along with its celebration of the 1950s family values of privacy and domesticity. In so doing, the district attorney voiced existing concerns among American conservatives that the new utopianism would create a generation of egocentric narcissists who lived a hedonistic lifestyle, escaped lifelong commitments, and indulged in sensual pleasures. Ruby's habits and personal characteristics coupled with his narcissistic tendencies made him a perfect candidate to embody the negative traits feared by the 1960s establishment, an aspect that played a crucial role in fostering the negative public image promoted by the media and in determining his judicial destiny.

Ruby was a single man, without children, who owned a series of strip clubs in Dallas and who had been repeatedly involved in street fights because of his occupation and heated temperament. The local media leveraged these traits by portraying him as a "Chicago mobster," a "tough guy," and a "strip joint owner,"[143] all characteristics in stark contrast with the ideal model of masculinity as a responsible family man promoted by the conservative worldview. These representations, coupled with the exceptional publicity received by Oswald's shooting on television and with the antisemitic sentiment fueled by the media following the decision to change the defendant's surname from Ruby to Rubenstein during the proceedings, informed strong local prejudice against the defendant, as recognized by the TCCA in its reversal.

In this heated context, the defense's attempt to humanize Ruby by providing some background on his early family upbringing and by explaining his need for attention in terms of low self-esteem fell on deaf ears. Instead, the jury chose to endorse the interpretation provided by the prosecution, which, by insinuating that Ruby had premediated the killings and by describing him as an attention-craving social misfit, aligned more readily with the public image promoted by the media, and with the cultural association of egocentric narcissism and antisocial tendencies promoted by the psychiatric establishment.

Conclusion

As the sources analyzed in the last two chapters have shown, forensic psychiatrists operating in the 1950s and 1960s were still powerfully influenced by the social trends and ideological conflicts of their time. On the one hand, Freud's theory of childhood development, along with his critique of Victorian parental discipline and sexual education, prompted psychoanalytic reformers to stress the potentially pathological and criminogenic effects of harsh parental discipline and sexual and emotional repression experienced in the early formative years. These ideas in turn encouraged the emergence of a series of social movements that challenged traditional family values while promoting alternative lifestyles, sexual liberation, and new modalities of self-presentation. On the other hand, in the conservative climate of the Cold War years, these emancipatory movements prompted a traditionalist backlash, which proposed a return to strict parental discipline and framed the social categories that embraced alternative ways of life as individuals affected by personality disorders associated with antisocial tendencies.

Despite their powerful links with the social and cultural environment, however, forensic psychoanalysts never abandoned the scientific project. On the contrary, their theories and opinions always reflected an ongoing effort to link their moral judgments to psychoanalytic theory. When they identified characteristics such as emotional immaturity, sexual bestiality, and egocentric narcissism in defendants' personality makeups, they always associated them with an interrupted psychosexual development experienced in the early years of life. In so doing, they endorsed Freud's instinct theory, along with his transposition of Darwinian evolutionism into a theory of childhood development, to create a symbolic analogy between the child's emotional progression from infancy to adulthood and the evolution of humanity from a primitive stage of savagery and aggressiveness to a civilized status of self-mastery and intellectual refinement.

Notwithstanding expert witnesses' efforts to link their judgments to psychoanalytic theories, their claims lacked the scientific support of studies showing the empirical validity of such an association. Rather than relying on scientific observations of tangible phenomena, Freud used subjective clinical techniques and drew his inferences from his personal experiences with individual patients, an aspect that might have prompted lay audiences to perceive psychoanalytic explanations as abstract speculations without proper scientific grounding. As I will show in the next two chapters, this issue would become increasingly pressing beginning in the late 1960s, when striking scientific developments prompted a transition to "biopsychosocial" explanations of criminal behavior, which would radically revolutionize expert discourse in Texas trial contexts.

Part 3

THE NEW SCIENTIFIC PARADIGM (1976–2002)

FIVE

The "New" Scientific Psychiatry, Antisocial Personality Disorder, and Future Dangerousness

> There is much that is supremely important in Freud's contribution to psychology, but there is also much that is bad. To eliminate the latter, without losing the former, must be the task of a scientifically-orientated psychology. The answer to the question . . .—What is wrong with psychoanalysis?—is simple: Psychoanalysis is unscientific. It is only by bringing to bear the traditional methods of scientific inference and experimentation that we can hope to reap all the benefit of its founder's genius.[1]
>
> —HANS J. EYSENCK

In the mid-1960s, a number of psychiatrists, psychologists, and philosophers of science started to criticize psychoanalysts' "unscientific" approach to diagnosis and treatment, while promoting a return to the biological paradigm of mental disease.[2] According to detractors of psychoanalytic theory, Freud's subjective approach to clinical evaluations, coupled with his lack of attention to the classification of mental diseases, had led to diagnostic inconsistencies across different evaluators, which in turn undermined the credibility of the psychiatric profession.[3] In its place they proposed a revival of the somatic approach to psychiatric problems first promoted by Emil Kraepelin in the nineteenth century, which emphasized organic causes and the importance of a rigorous diagnostic methodology for the correct administration of treatment. In this changed intellectual context, psychiatrists were encouraged to seek the origin of mental disorder not in the individual's idiosyncratic experience, as proposed by Freud, but "beyond personhood, in biological microstructures that escape uniqueness."[4]

The transition to a biological model of mental disease was fueled by important discoveries in the field of neuroscience. The development of neuroscientific instruments for the observation of the brain, such as magnetic resonance imaging, fostered a wide stream of research into the organic roots of mental health conditions, opening new possibilities in the areas of diagnosis and treatment.[5] These discoveries aligned with important findings in the field of psychopharmacology, which opened new therapeutic horizons and completed the intellectual transition from the psychodynamic to the biological model of disease. Although many antipsychotic drugs presented significant side effects, their ability to eliminate some of the symptoms associated with chronic mental illnesses was seen as a significant improvement over previous therapeutic methods, and was therefore embraced with great enthusiasm.[6]

To mark their departure from Freudian ideas, proponents of the new scientific psychiatry started to reformulate the psychoanalytic categories that had informed the first two editions of the *Diagnostic and Statistical Manual of Mental Disorders* (DSM), while planning the publication of a third edition that would consider the new theoretical climate.[7] The DSM-III, published in 1980, tried to merge the biological and the psychodynamic approaches by associating the former with severe mental illnesses, such as schizophrenia and bipolar disorder (Axis I diagnoses), and the latter with a range of personality disorders, including narcissistic and antisocial personalities (Axis II diagnoses). However, the DSM-III effectively legitimized the biological approach to mental disorder and criminal behavior, while shadowing alternative explanations based on psychological and environmental causes linked to defendants' difficult family upbringings.

These scientific developments were accompanied by a series of cultural and legal changes that, beginning in the mid-1970s, radically transformed the ways in which legal actors and medical experts framed the intersection of mental illness and crime in Texas capital punishment proceedings. The 1980s and 1990s witnessed a punitive turn in American politics that, departing from the rehabilitative approach of the 1960s, promoted an individualist notion of criminal responsibility that framed a defendant's criminal conduct as an act of deliberate choice rather than as the result of social disadvantage and mental health issues. This punitive turn would prove particularly problematic for members of ethnic minorities, given the racial undertones that characterized conservatives' criminal justice agenda and the historical stigma associating African Americans and Hispanics with violence and aggressiveness.

The structure of the Texas capital sentencing statute approved after capital punishment was reinstated in 1976 provided the necessary legal instrument to put this punitive approach into practice in death penalty cases. By placing the issue of future dangerousness at the heart of jurors' punishment decisions, the Texas statute effectively sidelined the mitigation question, promoting instead a powerful theoretical association between previous criminal conduct and future violence. This structure had a strong influence on the ways in which Texas prosecutors and defense attorneys litigated their cases in the 1980s and 1990s, with prosecutors focusing their whole strategy on proving that the defendant would constitute a continuing threat to society, and defense attorneys concentrating their efforts on showing that, despite their antisocial past, defendants were capable of change through treatment and/or rehabilitation.

The political climate and legal paradigm of the 1980s and 1990s[8] would have dramatic consequences for defendants diagnosed with severe mental health conditions and antisocial personality disorders in Texas courts. Despite claims to the contrary, the biological model of mental disease contributed to an increase in the social stigma historically attached to these mental health conditions, supporting jurors' perceptions that the defendant would constitute a continuing threat to society unless permanently incapacitated. For example, by describing defendants' mental disorders as organic defects associated with a "chemical imbalance" in the brain, defense experts reinforced the perception of mentally disordered individuals as dangerous and unpredictable, unless under the constant therapeutic effect of antipsychotic drugs. Similarly, by diagnosing defendants with psychopathy, sociopathy, or antisocial personality disorder (APD)[9] and by describing these diagnostic labels as irredeemable conditions inscribed in defendants' biopsychological makeup, state experts increased jurors' perceptions of defendants' inherent wickedness, powerfully tipping the scales in favor of death.

The crime control rhetoric of the 1980s and 1990s, coupled with the culture of fear advanced by the American media,[10] created an optimal cultural climate for the reception of essentialized explanations of criminal behavior, seen as the simple product of defendants' evil nature rather than of a confluence of complex sociological, psychological, and biological factors. This cultural context, combined with the Texas capital sentencing statute's emphasis on future dangerousness, gave Texas prosecutors a powerful advantage over the defense in death penalty proceedings, allowing them to exploit a diagnosis of APD to undermine defendants' mitigating evidence and turn it into an additional aggravating factor at sentencing.

The Conservative Years and the American Death Penalty

The 1980s and 1990s witnessed a punitive turn in American criminal justice policies. As several scholars have observed, the rise in crime—real or perceived—of the 1960s, coupled with the economic decline and social inequalities triggered by the 1973 oil crisis, prompted a strong conservative reaction among the American public, which found its most powerful resonance in the 1980s, the decade of the Reagan presidency.[11] Opinion polls suggested that, for the first time since the 1930s, most Americans saw crime as the most pressing domestic issue facing the country; they described courts as "too lenient," believed that "criminals were getting off 'too easily,'" and called for criminal justice policies aimed at reestablishing public order.[12] In this political climate, conservative politicians, represented by the New Right, started using rising crime trends as a strategic rhetorical device to attract voters through the promise of tougher crime control policies.[13] These policies, which included the imposition of mandatory sentences, harsher penalties for drug-related offenses, and rarer parole releases, led to an unprecedented growth in the American prison population, which between 1965 and 2000 grew by 600% nationwide and by 1,200% in Texas alone.[14]

The media powerfully amplified public fears about crime and transformed the criminal subject into a scapegoat for society's social ills. As public discourse about crime became sensationalized, criminals were increasingly represented as "mean and/or inferior types of human individuals . . . 'predators' of all kinds, people who are not deserving of our sympathy."[15] Echoing the crime rhetoric of the 1920s and 1930s, when European fascist regimes stressed liberals' failure to properly address the crime problem, in the 1980s and 1990s

> the criminal was represented as a *monstruum*—a being whose features are inherently different from ours and shocking to the well-behaved. . . . The criminal was once again portrayed as an incarnation of the ultimate sin of breaking the fabric of society apart, somebody who had to be contained through incapacitation or death in order to restore the unity and order of society.[16]

Republican politicians leveraged this political climate to their advantage, powerfully exploiting the law and order rhetoric to undermine the work of their Democratic predecessors and establish a new political agenda under their leadership. In so doing, they took issue with the welfare programs and rehabilitative interventions advocated by John F. Kennedy and Lyndon B. Johnson to reduce poverty and tackle social issues, arguing that, by providing easy handouts to criminals while excusing their antisocial behavior, these policies had favored the rise in crime registered in the 1960s.[17] In the view of Richard Nixon and his Republican successors, rather than blaming social circumstances such as poverty or abusive childhoods for offenders' criminal behavior, society should hold offenders fully accountable for their crimes and punish them accordingly.[18]

Starting from an individualist notion of personhood and criminal responsibility,[19] conservatives emphasized individual choice and freedom from societal constraints. They argued that offenders were solely responsible for their antisocial behavior, and that neither the government nor abusive family members, negligent teachers, and/or mental health professionals should be blamed for the crimes committed. In this view, "choosing a career in crime is not the result of poverty or of an unhappy childhood. . . . It is the result of a conscious, willful choice made by some who consider themselves above the law, who seek to exploit the hard work and, sometimes, the very lives of their fellow citizens."[20] The solution to the crime problem, conservatives proposed, was not to blame society for criminals' failures while funding more welfare programs and rehabilitative interventions but to hold offenders fully accountable for their behavior through harsh penal policies and "swift and sure punishment."[21]

The punitive political climate of the late twentieth century had dramatic consequences for the American capital punishment system. Whereas the liberal postwar decades had witnessed gradual declines in death sentences and executions, the conservative 1980s and 1990s registered the most striking increase in the use of the death penalty since the mid-1930s, when the nation's execution rates rose to unparalleled heights.[22] In the 1960s capital punishment's faltering popularity, coupled with social and political factors such as the demands of the civil rights movement and the death toll from the Vietnam War, prompted several states to abolish the death penalty for ordinary murder, in some cases securing total abolition. These national trends captured the attention of the U.S. Supreme Court, which, pressured by growing claims of racial discrimination, turned its attention to the ways in which states were administering the death penalty.

In 1972 the Supreme Court formally recognized the rarity and arbitrariness with which states were administering the death penalty, ordering a moratorium on executions in *Furman v. Georgia*.[23] As they stood, the Court argued, current capital sentencing schemes failed to provide clear guidelines that would ensure that the death penalty was imposed fairly and equally.[24] Abolitionists hoped that the Court's moratorium would strike the final blow against what they saw as an arcane and unjust punishment; however, their wishes would soon be disappointed. In a context of rising crime rates and a punitive upsurge in American politics, the Court's failure to rule the death penalty unconstitutional in all circumstances proved fatal for the abolitionist project. Rather than pushing the country toward total abolition, the Court's moratorium in *Furman* encouraged a punitive backlash, which, through the creation of new capital sentencing schemes, reversed the historical trend of the postwar years, leading to an increase in death sentences and executions in the 1980s and 1990s.

Texas led the way in this punitive turn. Since the U.S. Supreme Court approved Texas's new capital punishment statute in 1976, the state has positioned itself as the leading death sentencer and executioner in the country, sending 958 defendants to death row as of 2013 and 573 prisoners to the death chamber as of 2022.[25] Studies of Texas death rows suggest that a large fraction of the defendants who were sentenced to death between 1976 and 2002 suffered from a severe mental illness and/or intellectual disability, a finding generally confirmed by my own data analysis.[26] Indeed, according to my estimates, in the 1976–2002 time period Texas courts sentenced to death at least eight defendants who raised the insanity defense (three whites, four African Americans, and one Hispanic) and sixteen who made a diminished culpability claim based on mitigating evidence of mental illness and/or child abuse (nine whites, four African Americans, and three Hispanics).[27] Although the legitimacy of these claims was sometimes unsubstantiated,[28] my data show that Texas jurors often dismissed insanity or diminished culpability claims based on mental health issues, even when such claims were based on strong evidence of cognitive and volitional impairment.[29]

The reasons for Texas's punitive approach to mentally disabled capital defendants are multifaceted;[30] however, one aspect that likely played a role is the structure of the Texas capital sentencing statute upheld by the U.S. Supreme Court in *Jurek v. Texas*.[31] The Texas statute required jurors to answer two "special issue" questions at the end of the penalty phase of the capital punishment trial: (1) whether the crime was committed deliberately[32] and (2) whether they believed that the defendant might commit criminal acts of violence in the future.[33] If jurors unanimously answered yes to both special issue questions, they were to impose a death sentence.[34] As we will see, the future dangerousness question would prove exceptionally problematic for defendants presenting evidence of mental illness, given popular beliefs and stereotypes that associated severe mental health conditions with a propensity for future violence.

In the 1970s and 1980s defendants and legal scholars repeatedly challenged the constitutionality of the Texas capital sentencing scheme.[35] They argued that, by failing to include a special issue question asking jurors to consider whether the mitigating evidence presented at trial warranted a life sentence, the Texas statute denied jurors the possibility of making an individualized consideration of the defendants' moral culpability based on his background and circumstances, as required by the U.S. Supreme Court in *Woodson v. North Carolina*.[36] Moreover, by placing future dangerousness predictions at the heart of jurors' sentencing decision, the Texas statute made speculations about the likelihood that the defendant would present "a continuing threat to society," the one and only criterion available to assess a defendant's moral blameworthiness, a particularly controversial issue given the difficulty of making such predictions with a satisfactorily degree of reliability, even with the support of medical experts.[37]

The Supreme Court sanctioned these critiques in the late 1980s in the landmark case of *Penry v. Lynaugh*.[38] According to the *Penry* Court, by forcing jurors to consider evidence of mental disability and/or child abuse within the context of the future dangerousness question, the Texas capital sentencing scheme facilitated the imposition of death sentences on mentally impaired individuals based on a false association between mental illness and future violence.[39] To address this issue, the Texas legislature needed to formulate a statutory mechanism that would allow jurors to give mitigating effect to defendants' diminished culpability evidence at sentencing. Without a similar provision, jurors risked perceiving the special issue questions as requiring them to impose a death sentence, even if the defendant's personal history compelled them to exert mercy.

The *Penry* decision had important implications for Texas's capital punishment procedures. Concerned that future litigation might prompt the Supreme Court to strike down its statute as unconstitutional, in 1991 the Texas legislature amended its capital sentencing scheme to include a mitigation instruction aimed at establishing whether any aspect of the defendant's character or background might warrant a sentence of life rather than death.[40] Despite these legislative changes, until the early 2000s Texas courts continued to deny defendants' right to a mitigation instruction, limiting it to a small number of individuals who could prove[41] (1) that they suffered from a "severe permanent handicap," (2) that there was a direct "nexus" between their mental disability and the crime committed,[42] and (3) that the evidence had a clear aggravating potential when considered within the scope of the future dangerousness question.[43] In the 1990s these legal restrictions resulted in a high number of severely mentally ill defendants being denied a mitigation instruction and receiving a death sentence,[44] raising serious doubts about the legitimacy and constitutionality of the criteria.[45]

Medical Developments, Future Dangerousness, and Reversed Mitigation

By focusing on the future dangerousness question and sidelining the mitigation issue, Texas's capital punishment statute gives the prosecution a significant advantage over the defense in death penalty proceedings. The bifurcation of the capital trial into a guilt and a sentencing phase allows the prosecution to start introducing evidence relevant to the future dangerousness question from the beginning of the proceedings, when everyone's attention is focused on the nature of the crime committed and on the defendant's guilt.[46] On the contrary, unless they are trying to present an exculpatory defense, defense attorneys are not allowed to present any mitigating evidence during the guilt phase, "leaving the jury to focus entirely on the State's case."[47]

To overcome this legal barrier, Texas defense attorneys who work with clients suffering from severe mental disabilities often choose to pursue an insanity defense, even when the evidence supporting a similar claim is arguably insufficient.[48] This allows them to start presenting evidence as to the defendant's mental condition and background during the guilt phase, rather than having to wait until the punishment phase to provide jurors with a counternarrative to the one provided by the state. Moreover, by front-loading their mitigating evidence during the guilt phase of the trial, defense attorneys can overcome the epistemological rupture that separates the strictly "legal" context of the guilt phase from the "human" context of the punishment phase, by presenting a coherent narrative that may help jurors make sense of the defendant's behavior throughout the proceedings.[49]

Although this strategy presents some advantages, the evidence presented in support of an insanity defense during the guilt phase is often inadequate to humanize the defendant in the eyes of the jury. Given its narrow focus on the "right or wrong" question, the insanity defense tends to give jurors the impression that unless the defendant's mental disorder directly prompted him to commit the criminal act, the fact that he suffered from a mental health condition should have no bearing on their sentencing decision.[50] Moreover, by focusing the punishment phase on the future dangerousness question, the Texas statute suggests that the only relevant consideration regarding the defendant's mental condition should be whether it increases or decreases the likelihood that he will commit acts of violence in the future, an aspect that, given the social stigma attached to mental health conditions, shifts the focus in favor of the prosecution. As I show in the next sections, these legal constraints, coupled with developments in the fields of forensic psychiatry and psychology, had a powerful effect on the litigation strategies developed by Texas defense attorneys in the last quarter of the twentieth century.

Prosecutorial Strategies

Texas prosecutors typically rely on three types of evidence to argue that the defendant constitutes a continuing threat to society. The first type of evidence relates to the nature of the crime for which the defendant is on trial and is aimed at demonstrating its peculiar gruesomeness. Texas courts have historically upheld the relevance of this kind of proof for jurors' sentencing determination, arguing that, in some instances, the facts of the crime alone are sufficient to support a finding of future dangerousness.[51] The second type of evidence relates to the defendant's criminal history and relies on lay witness testimonies that describe episodes in which the defendant engaged in antisocial behaviors, especially if these actions were of a violent nature and resulted in criminal convictions. This kind of evidence often includes examples of antisocial behavior that occurred both while at liberty and during incarceration in order to show that even if the defendant is placed in a controlled institutional setting for the rest of his life, he will be unable to control his violent tendencies.

The third kind of evidence, which forms the core of the present discussion, relates to the nature of the defendant himself and aims to demonstrate that, because of an inborn personality defect, the defendant is inherently wicked and unlikely to be rehabilitated. A number of studies suggest that mental health experts who testify for the prosecution on the issue of future dangerousness routinely diagnose defendants with psychopathy, sociopathy, or APD to support their contention that they will constitute a continuing threat to society if their lives were to be spared.[52] These diagnoses are particularly powerful in this context because they encapsulate and medicalize all the characteristics typically associated with future violent behavior, turning them into immutable personality traits that express the defendant's true character. Indeed, a number of simulation studies have shown that defendants' perceived level of psychopathy strongly predicts jurors' support for executions, with interpersonal and affective traits associated with this condition—such as remorselessness, "grandiose self-worth," and a "manipulative interpersonal style"—playing the most significant role in increasing the likelihood of a death sentence.[53]

Jurors' punitive approach to individuals diagnosed with psychopathy, sociopathy, and APD is partly due to the stigmatizing effect of these diagnoses. Traditional notions of psychopathy, such as the ones found in Hervey M. Cleckley's[54] and Robert D. Hare's[55] classic works on the subject, are associated with highly undesirable social traits, such as callousness, lack of empathy, and remorselessness, all characteristics typically associated with "evil" and "badness."[56] The stigma associated with these conditions is further exacerbated by the sensationalized depictions provided by the media, which tend to associate psychopathic traits either with fictional incarnations of evil, such as Hannibal Lecter, or with serial killers who have left a long-lasting impression on the public for their extreme cruelty, such as Ted Bundy or Charles Manson.[57]

The origins of contemporary notions of criminal psychopathy date back to the early twentieth century. Whereas nineteenth-century psychiatrists such as James Pritchard and Isaac Ray depicted apparently unexplainable criminal acts committed by cognitively lucid subjects as pathological manifestations of a mental disease ("moral insanity"), at the turn of the twentieth century psychiatrists started describing them as the natural expression of inherently wicked personalities.[58] Inspired by the biological and evolutionist framework of their time, early twentieth-century psychiatrists viewed criminal psychopathy as a hereditary and organic affliction. In this view, criminal psychopaths' wrongdoings were the manifestation not of a mental health problem but of their true inner self, characterized by "moral insensibility," "coldness of heart," and lack of "scruples of conscience or repentance."[59] Psychiatrists writing in the third quarter of the twentieth century drew heavily from this view, depicting criminal psychopaths as rational yet inherently immoral subjects who strategically and deliberately exploit others through cunning and manipulation.[60] In these formulations, although the main manifestations of the pathology are behavioral, their deeper roots are inherently characterological.[61] For criminal psychopaths antisocial behavior is nothing but a natural expression of their true inner being, an immutable personality trait unlikely to be redeemed.

These descriptions powerfully resonate with Texas prosecutors' dispositional view of defendants' mental states and antisocial behaviors.[62] In this view the defendant's criminal act is an essential element of the defendant's true character, not a behavioral symptom of a mental disorder. When speaking of defendants diagnosed with APD, prosecutors often refer to them as rapists, sexual predators, or "thrill killers," a language that contributes to merge the actor and the action into an indiscernible thing.[63] For example, in the trial of Johnny Paul Penry, District Attorney Joe L. Price started from this ontological perspective to depict the defendant as a "natural born criminal," separate and different from the law-abiding community.

> He's a faker. And he always has been. He's a manipulator. . . . What character have you been shown of him? He's a rapist. He attempts to rape his own brother. He—he rapes women, he kills people. That's his character. . . . You're talking about a sadist, he is one. He is the most sadistical person you will probably ever come into contact with. He is a sexual predator. He is a sadist. He is a cold-blooded killer. He is a sociopath with an antisocial personality. . . . He has no conscience. He's never shown any remorse.[64]

By describing defendants as sexual predators and cold-blooded killers and by labeling their antisocial tendencies as the product of APD, Texas prosecutors have created an ontological association between defendants' capital crime and their inner essence, echoing the characterizations found in conservative media accounts and giving them an aura of scientific legitimacy. In this view, "the potential for dangerousness is inherent in an individual if it is present," and although the environment in which a defendant lives can potentially diminish the expression of that violence, this "doesn't remove the fact that the person poses a threat."[65] Using this line of argument, Texas prosecutors have suggested that defendants diagnosed with APD will always represent a future danger to society, both inside and outside the prison walls, and that the only way to stop them from producing more harm is to physically eliminate them.

An additional factor that makes a diagnosis of APD particularly controversial in Texas capital punishment proceedings is its association with cunning and manipulation. Mid- to late twentieth-century formulations of criminal psychopathy have portrayed individuals affected by this condition as strategic social performers who use their superficial charm[66] and ability to simulate feelings without effectively experiencing them[67] to build relationships of trust with their victims, exploit them, and bend them to their own will. In this view psychopaths are masters at mimicking genuine feelings and at controlling the reactions of their audience, an aspect that requires the maximum attention from experts asked to evaluate their mental competency in capital proceedings. Texas prosecutors regularly exploit this conception, using a diagnosis of psychopathy or APD to argue that the defendant has a pathological tendency to lie and to cast doubt on the reliability of the mitigating evidence presented.[68] For example, in the trial of Samuel Hawkins, state expert Dr. James Grigson, a controversial figure who helped Texas prosecutors secure almost 200 death sentences in the 1980s and 1990s,[69] applied this diagnostic label to suggest that the defendant had used his trial testimony to manipulate the jury, by pretending that his criminal act was due to an underlying mental health condition. The following statement is illustrative of the doctor's argument:

> [The defendant says], "see, I must be sick, something is wrong with me." Now, what he is doing, as most sociopaths will do, they will make minor concessions such as he doesn't mind telling you about his horrible sexual drive and all the terrible things which he has done, but what he hopes to gain from this is a major concession. The con job is, "you have got to see how crazy I am and how sick I am. You can't consider finding me guilty because of what I am."[70]

When Hawkins, who was acting as his own attorney, objected to Dr. Grigson's use of his testimony as evidence of his manipulative tendencies, the district attorney took advantage of his objection to ask the doctor whether, from his observation of the defendant as he stood up in court to object, he noticed any signs of anxiety.[71] Dr. Grigson denied it, arguing that Hawkins was just "trying to get attention and play like an attorney" and that playing this role fed his "ego."[72] By embracing the late twentieth-century characterization of the criminal sociopath as a social performer, always looking for an opportunity to feed his narcissistic needs, Dr. Grigson ridiculed Hawkins's legitimate right to represent himself at trial and used it against him to support his diagnostic conclusion.[73]

A final factor that makes a diagnosis of psychopathy or APD particularly prejudicial for defendants charged with capital murder is the devastating prognosis associated with the condition. Contributing to this bleak view on the possibility of future treatment is the severity of the symptoms linked with the disorder and its lack of association with a known mental disease.[74] The perception of psychopathy's incurability is exacerbated by recent research associating psychopathy with physiological and neurological defects with potentially genetic roots, a framing that "further widens the gap between psychopathy and normality even as it strengthens the case for therapeutic pessimism."[75] In the criminal justice context this unresponsiveness to treatment is further aggravated by the notion that criminal psychopaths cannot feel suffering for their wrongs or for the punishment received as a result of such wrongs. Consequently, they do not learn from their mistakes and are unresponsive to any form of rehabilitative intervention in penal settings.

The trial of James Wilkens Jr. provides a compelling example of the ways in which Texas prosecutors have used the diagnosis of APD to claim that the defendant's criminalistic tendencies are likely to be permanent.[76] Asked by the prosecutor whether the defendant's antisocial traits would likely change over time, state expert Dr. Thomas Allen argued as follows:

> Our basic personality structure is set fairly early in life. There is some flexibility. . . . An individual may become, say, more or less introverted or extroverted, more outgoing or more quiet and reserved over time depending on the circumstances, but if an individual is basically introverted and that's the basic personality structure, then he's going to be introverted pretty much all his life. If an individual's basic personality structure is that of an antisocial personality, it's extremely unlikely that that's ever going to change in his lifetime.[77]

In light of these considerations, Dr. Allen concluded that the prospects for the defendant's rehabilitation were minimal and that his likelihood to continue to represent a future threat to society was high, an opinion shared by all the experts who testified in Wilkens's proceedings.[78]

Given these characterizations, defendants labeled with APD in Texas capital punishment proceedings have a difficult path ahead. Having been cast as emotionally and possibly biologically different from others, inherently inclined to commit antisocial acts, and unresponsive to treatment, defendants' attempts to convince the jury that they are capable of change is likely to fall on deaf ears. Moreover, having been described as manipulative liars whose words and attitudes should always be looked at with suspicion, their efforts to convince jurors to trust the sincerity of their statements rather than seeing them as strategic performances set up to escape punishment can prove to be an almost insurmountable challenge.

Defense Strategies

In the 1980s and 1990s defense attorneys working with capital defendants relied on two main strategies to convince jurors to either find their clients not guilty by reason of insanity or to impose a life sentence. The first strategy consisted in presenting evidence suggesting that the defendant suffered from a severe mental disorder at the time of the crime, and that this condition affected his ability to understand the consequences of his act and/or to control his violent impulses. To support this contention, defense experts typically argued that the defendant suffered from paranoid schizophrenia or some other psychotic condition, and that at the time of the alleged offense he was operating under the influence of paranoid delusions and/or command hallucinations.

The second tactic, which I discuss in Chapter 6, involved presenting background evidence to show that the defendant suffered abuse and neglect as a child, and that this difficult upbringing had a negative impact on his mental health and social adjustment. This kind of evidence relied on a communitarian notion of criminal responsibility, which, challenging the individualist ideology promoted by the conservative establishment, highlighted the role played by failed social institutions in facilitating or preventing the formation of antisocial tendencies in youth. In the following sections, I focus on the first defense strategy and argue that the biological paradigm upon which it was based, coupled with the tactics developed by prosecutors to reverse the mitigating effect of the evidence presented, contributed to increase rather than decrease jurors' perception of the defendant's future dangerousness at sentencing.

The Biological Paradigm and Future Dangerousness

In the last quarter of the twentieth century, medical experts asked to testify regarding defendants' mental health in Texas proceedings tended to describe mental disorders as organic conditions associated with brain defects. As I argued in the Introduction, the publication of the DSM-III in 1980 signaled the beginning of a new era of psychiatric diagnosis and treatment and the triumph of the biological model of mental disease. The main objective of the DSM-III was to address the diagnostic inconsistencies and imprecisions identified in the work of American psychiatrists of psychoanalytic orientation, by providing a unified framework and language that would enhance diagnostic consistency and communication between clinicians.[79] To accomplish this goal, the DSM-III would take an atheoretical approach to etiology, focus on diagnostic categorization, and take a multi-axial approach to classification aimed at integrating the medical and psychosocial components of the clinical evaluation.

Despite its stated objectives, the DSM-III effectively sacrificed the psychosocial component of the evaluation in favor of the biological one. The reasons for this are twofold. First, the drafters of the DSM-III were powerfully influenced by the ideas of the "new psychiatry" movement, a group of scholars who, inspired by Kraepelin's work, emphasized the biological roots of mental disorders while underplaying the sociological and psychological ones.[80] According to representatives of this movement, mental disorders were a chronic condition resulting from a "chemical imbalance" in the brain, which required expert medical treatment through the administration of psychotropic drugs.[81] By endorsing this idea, the drafters of the DSM-III officially sanctioned the biological paradigm of mental disease and the massive use of antipsychotic medications, while delegitimizing alternative explanations based on environmental stressors and therapeutic solutions such as psychotherapy.[82] Second, although the authors of the DSM-III warned that the diagnostic criteria included in the manual should not be taken as a substitute for a thorough clinical evaluation of the patient's background and history, psychiatrists operating inside and outside courts of law typically followed a "check-list" approach, which limited the assessment to a search for symptoms included in the DSM and tended to privilege organic factors over sociopsychological ones.[83]

The biological paradigm has had controversial effects for mentally disordered capital defendants tried in Texas courts. The reasons are threefold. First, by reducing the clinical encounter to "the use of DSM checklists," and by sidelining history taking as a nonessential component of the psychiatric evaluation, the DSM-III discouraged psychiatrists from getting to know the subjects of their evaluations,[84] hindering the humanizing effect of clinical assessments in courts of law. Indeed, regardless of their validity and/or reliability, tentative explanations of how a particular mental disorder came about can help to bring a defendant's history and background to life, contributing to that humanizing effect that courts have repeatedly stressed constitutes one of the core functions of the sentencing phase of capital punishment proceedings.[85] Second, by promoting an image of "disease and disability" rather than of "wholeness and recovery," the biological model of mental disorder negatively affects both patients' trust in their ability to overcome their psychological and behavioral difficulties and the social stigma surrounding their conditions.[86] As Bruce Lachter argues with regard to depressed patients, "There may be a chemical imbalance . . . but the suffering is about loss or fear or hostility or trauma," all psychological aspects that jurors are arguably more likely to relate to.[87]

Finally, by relying on the administration of psychotropic medications, the biological paradigm has promoted an image of mental disorders as chronic and untreatable. In the medical framework, treating is effectively used as a metaphor for tranquilizing: the purpose of the drugs being to sedate the gross symptoms associated with the condition rather than curing the underlying causes of the disease, which are typically assumed rather than proved.[88] This idea tends to suggest that, without the constant therapeutic effect of psychotropic drugs, psychiatric patients are incapable of controlling their emotional and behavioral reactions, making them highly unpredictable and in need of constant supervision. This assumption can have a powerful stigmatizing effect in Texas courts because, as highlighted by a number of expert witnesses in the 1980s and 1990s, one of the main issues encountered in this treatment style is patients' noncompliance, that is, the refusal to take the prescribed medications for fear of their negative side effects.[89]

Empirical research seems to support such claims. For example, a number of studies suggest that the framing of mental disorders as brain diseases tends to increase the public's perception of psychiatric patients as dangerous and unpredictable,[90] whereas associations of mental health conditions with emotional and psychological distress tend to reduce such stigma.[91] Along these lines, some scholars propose that both psychiatrists and laypeople are more likely to see psychological problems as incurable when associated with biological causes, an aspect that increases the stigmatizing effect of diagnostic labeling based on the disease model.[92] Finally, as highlighted by John Read and Niki Harré, "Organizations of 'psychiatric patients' have long railed against the effects of a 'medical model' perspective on their self-esteem, accusing it of increasing stigma while minimizing the complexity of their lives and their capacity for recovery."[93] This evidence suggests that defense psychiatrists' reliance on DSM checklists, coupled with their framing of defendants' mental disorders as biological defects, have the effect of increasing rather than decreasing jurors' perception that the defendant might represent a future threat to society. First, by limiting their diagnosis to an evaluation of the list of symptoms included in the manual, psychiatrists have tended to overlook defendants' social and psychological history and to eschew explanations that go beyond the chemical imbalance theory of the brain. In so doing, they have missed the opportunity to shed light on aspects of the defendant's character, background, and experience that could have helped jurors make sense of the defendant's behavior and decrease the social stigma associated with his mental condition. Second, by endorsing the biological reductionism proposed by the new psychiatry movement, and by arguing that the defendant's antisocial behavior can change only if the underlying medical condition is kept under control through the constant administration of psychotropic drugs, defense experts have supported jurors' perception of mentally disordered defendants as dangerous and unpredictable, depicting them as biologically different and manageable only under particular treatment conditions.[94]

Stanley Burks: Command Hallucination or "Thrill to Kill"?

The trial of Stanley Keith Burks provides a compelling example of the ways in which defense arguments drawing from biological explanations of mental disease can contribute to a finding of future dangerousness in Texas courts.[95] Burks, a 19-year-old African American man, was convicted for the murder and robbery of an elderly man, Mr. Rogers, in April 1979 and sentenced to death. According to his own confession, armed with a hammer and some kitchen knives, Burks entered the victim's house while the man was sleeping, went through his pockets and bedroom drawers, and watched him for about 30 minutes while he was sound asleep.[96] Then, for no apparent reason, he started beating the victim's skull with the hammer for a total of 32 times, slit his throat with a razor, and cut his abdomen open with the knives. Following this brutal killing, he ransacked the house over a three-day period, returning on multiple occasions to collect more items, all in broad daylight.[97]

During the guilt phase of the trial, the defense presented an insanity claim, arguing that Burks suffered from paranoid schizophrenia and that, at the time of the crime, he had experienced a command hallucination ordering him to kill the victim to help him rejoin his deceased wife in heaven.[98] To support its contention, the defense presented extensive lay and expert testimonies suggesting that, since his teenage years, Burks had experienced visual and auditory hallucinations, severe depression, and drug addiction, which had led to several suicide attempts and to numerous, albeit brief, hospitalizations.[99] With regard to his hallucinations, the defense witnesses reported that Burks believed that "devils were chasing him" and that, every time he coughed, an evil spirit named Zodacus would enter his body and temporarily modify his voice, manner, and appearance.[100]

The content of Burks's hallucinations was likely influenced by his strong religious education. The defendant's father, C. L. Burks, was an evangelist preacher for the Church of God and Christ who dealt with spiritualism and seances, the practice of making contact with the dead.[101] He had founded his own evangelistic outreach, the Grain of Mustard Seeds Ministry, whose teachings were disseminated through radio broadcasting and revivals, services conducted for the purpose of eliciting a religious awakening. At the age of 14 the defendant started traveling with his father across the state of Georgia to learn and disseminate his religious teachings.[102] During this time, he attended his father's meetings and seances, was initiated on how to contact "familiar spirits," and was eventually ordained as an evangelist minister.[103] Given Burks's fragile mental health, these experiences likely made a powerful impression on him, affecting his fantasies and thinking patterns.

The state challenged the defense's theory that Burks's crime was prompted by command hallucinations. It argued that the defendant was an incorrigible sociopath and a "thrill killer" who had killed the victim out of sheer hedonistic enjoyment and faked his hallucinations and suicidal tendencies to manipulate his family, friends, and defense experts in order to escape punishment.[104] The assistant district attorney took particular issue with the credibility of the defendant's hallucinations, highlighting that he only mentioned hearing voices after the trial had begun.

> Does it strike you a little bit unusual that he has told no one, no one at all until he talked to Dr. Lett last week that he killed this man because the voices told him to send him up to be with his wife. . . . Only after this man sat in the courtroom with each and every one of you when we explained insanity to you, only then did he go upstairs and tell a psychiatrist, "I was driven to do this by voices." Does that sound believable to you?[105]

The jury endorsed the skeptical view advocated by the state and found the defendant guilty of capital murder. During the punishment phase of the trial, the defense experts' claims that the defendant's actions were directed by command hallucinations once again backfired. In line with the biological paradigm of the time, the defense experts emphasized the organic origin of the defendant's mental health condition but failed to stress the role that his social background might have played in eliciting some of his delusions and hallucinations.[106] As I argued earlier, this biological reductionism tends to reinforce laypeople's association of severe mental disorders with violence, nontreatability, and dangerousness, an aspect that likely contributed to the jury's decision to impose a death sentence. Even the defense's chief expert witness played into this stereotype, when he argued that, because of his mental disorder, there was a risk that Burks would commit unmotivated violent acts against strangers in the future if he heard a voice that ordered him to kill again.[107]

Given its relevance for the second special issue question, the treatability of Burks's mental condition and behavioral difficulties would be a key point of contention between the defense and the prosecution during the punishment phase. According to state expert Dr. Grigson, what made Burks's sociopathic personality disorder particularly threatening was its severity and absolute resistance to treatment. In his view Burks would always represent a danger to society, if kept alive.

> A. This is not a stage he's going through. It's not a passing fancy. As long as he lives, he's going to be a danger to society whether it be inside a prison wall or whether it's outside, wherever it is, as long as he lives.

Q. Eight, nine, ten years from now, twenty years from now?
A. It won't matter.
Q. Can't be rehabilitated?
A. There's absolutely nothing that can be done.[108]

On the other hand, defense expert Dr. Charles Lett argued that the defendant's paranoid schizophrenia could be treated through the use of psychotherapy combined with the administration of antipsychotic drugs.[109] The psychiatrist who treated Burks following his arrest had prescribed him a strong daily dose of Haldol, a potent tranquilizer and antipsychotic drug aimed at controlling Burks's hallucinations and violent impulses.[110] Dr. Lett, who had significant experience in the treatment of psychotic patients, reported that since Burks had started taking this medication his behavior had improved, a finding supported by the testimony of the defendant's mother and stepfather during the punishment phase of the trial.[111] To challenge the idea that Burks's violent tendencies could effectively be controlled, the state presented the testimony of a nurse who argued that Burks had been refusing to take his medications while in jail without manifesting the symptoms typically observed in mentally ill patients who had stopped their treatment.[112]

By highlighting the absence of withdrawal symptoms, the state could pursue a two-pronged strategy. On the one hand, it could use such absence to support its contention that Burks had an antisocial personality disorder and that he did not suffer from a mental illness. This argument relied on a common misconception associated with the use of psychotropic drugs, namely, that it is possible to infer the presence or absence of a mental disorder based on the subject's reactions to treatment. Critics have repeatedly challenged this contention, highlighting that the remission of symptoms following the administration of psychotropic drugs tells us nothing about the effective presence of mental disease and/or about the potential biological underpinnings of an individual's emotional and behavioral difficulties.[113]

On the other hand, the state could argue that, even conceding that the defendant suffered from a severe mental health condition besides his sociopathic personality disorder, the dangers and difficulties involved in the management and control of mentally disordered capital defendants in a prison setting made a life sentence in this case undesirable. By emphasizing the risk that Burks could refuse his medications, the difficulties involved in the monitoring of inmates' compliance with their treatment plan, and the dangerous withdrawal symptoms associated with such noncompliance, the state was able to alert the jury as to the risks involved in relying on medical treatment for the management of violent mentally disordered individuals. Thanks to this strategy, the state was able to (1) undermine the defense's argument that Burks's medical condition and violent tendencies could be managed through the administration of antipsychotic medications and (2) turn it into additional evidence of Burks's unreliability, unpredictability, and future dangerousness.

James Colburn and Deinstitutionalization

The trial of James Blake Colburn provides another illustrative example of the ways in which exculpatory defenses and mitigation strategies based on biological notions of mental disease can backfire in Texas death penalty proceedings.[114] Colburn, a young white man, was convicted for the murder of a lady whom he did not know in 1998 and sentenced to death. The evidence suggested that the woman met the defendant outside his apartment while hitchhiking and asked him for some water.[115] The defendant agreed and led her into his apartment where, after an attempted rape, he strangled her and cut her neck with a kitchen knife. The defendant was arrested shortly thereafter and confessed to the murder. His confession was recorded and played for the jury at trial.

The defense's theory was that Colburn suffered from chronic paranoid schizophrenia, that he experienced visual and auditory hallucinations, and that at the time of the murder a voice had ordered him to kill the victim to fulfill his wish to go to prison.[116] According to the defense, because of his command hallucinations, the defendant did not know the difference between right and wrong at the time of the murder and was therefore insane according to legal standards. The state challenged the defendant's insanity claim, arguing that his criminal act was the result not of a command hallucination, as argued by the defense, but of a rational thought that had prompted him to kill the victim to pursue his plan to get incarcerated.[117] According to the prosecution, Colburn should be seen not as a mentally ill individual succumbing to a sick mind, but as a "mean" criminal who would always represent a "threat" and a "danger" to Texas society.[118]

The defense's explanation of the murder constitutes an emblematic example of the ways in which an apparently exculpatory or mitigating argument can contribute to a finding of future dangerousness in Texas courts. Besides stressing the role of Colburn's command hallucinations in prompting his criminal act, the defense portrayed the murder as the desperate gesture of a man whose mental health condition made life outside a controlled institutional setting unbearable.[119] In this view Colburn's desire to go to prison was the result of an institutional failure on the part of the Texas mental health services, which, by refusing to hospitalize him for a prolonged period of time, had left him with no other choice than to seek "refuge" in the Texas Department of Corrections.[120] As explained by Dr. Walter Quijano, a psychologist famous for his racially charged testimonies in death penalty cases,[121] when Colburn was seeking treatment for his mental health condition antipsychotic medications had become very popular. This popularity was accompanied by a trend toward the rapid discharge of mentally ill patients, no matter how severe their symptoms.

> The United States were closing down state hospitals and the vogue then was to treat the person very rapidly and discharge, to treat them in a hospital in an acute basis. Once the frank symptoms are gone, you discharge them. So, this was the time when long hospitalization was no longer in practice and was criticized if you held somebody too long. . . . The hospital then saw itself as a place to treat acute phase of the illness while the person is actively hallucinating, hearing voices, seeing things, agitation. They would keep them, medicate them to the point they are sedated and if—and they are kept that way for a while and then they are discharged to the community. And the community was supposed to take over through the MHMR [Mental Health and Mental Retardation] system.[122]

However, if the community failed to provide this support network, as happened in most instances,[123] the symptoms were likely to reoccur.

> If the person is discharged from the state hospital, remember only the acute frank symptoms are controlled. The other symptoms of thinking disorder continue, inability to work, inability to socialize, all the other—inability to be independent and to be sufficient are not there. So, when they are sent back,

> somebody has to catch that person and maintain the medication to control the frank symptoms, but also to cultivate the person to do the best they can. If that care is not provided, then the person will become acute again, sent back to the state hospital and thus the revolving door.[124]

In line with this historical trend, Colburn was repeatedly hospitalized for his mental health condition, administered antipsychotic medications, and rapidly released. However, the evidence provided at trial suggests that, given the severity of his mental health condition, life in the community was extremely difficult for Colburn. His ongoing hallucinations, which included seeing devils emerging from his stomach, seeing his face sinking in, and hearing voices ordering him to do things, undermined his ability to hold a job and made him severely depressed, prompting him to commit between 15 and 20 suicide attempts over the years.[125] His mental health problems and adjustment difficulties in turn prompted him to engage in a number of criminal activities, including an attempted burglary and a robbery, which resulted in multiple convictions and seven years of imprisonment.[126] While in prison, Colburn was given food and shelter, regularly administered his medications, and told what to do at all times, all things that gave him a sense of order and helped him cope with his hallucinations and delusions.[127]

Following his release from prison, Colburn fell back into the old pattern of depression, hallucinations, and suicide attempts.[128] Given that the state hospitals had precluded the possibility of prolonged hospitalization, Colburn reasoned that prison was the only option left if he wished to return to an institutional environment where he would be constantly monitored, medicated, and controlled.[129] According to the defense, this reasoning was a clear indication that, at the time of the crime, the defendant had lost touch with society's traditional notions of right and wrong.

> The voice, this command hallucination that Dr. Quijano told you about says kill someone to go to prison. Now, that's crazy. I mean, you and I know you don't kill someone to go to prison. But if he believed this, if he truly believed this, then killing someone was not wrong. . . . He knows if he kills someone, he's going to go back where he's safe. Because Dr. Quijano has told you he needs a structured environment. He needs a place where he doesn't have to make decisions, where he would be told what to do.[130]

The objective of this kind of evidence was threefold. First, it could help support the defendant's insanity claim by arguing that his criminal act was the result of the "crazy" reasoning of a deranged man desperately trying to escape the demons that were populating his mind. Second, it could challenge a finding of future dangerousness during the punishment phase by suggesting that, if placed in a structured environment such as the Texas Department of Corrections, Colburn's symptoms and violent behavior could be kept under control. Finally, it could promote the idea that, by failing to provide the treatment and support he desperately needed, the Texas mental health services were indirectly responsible for Colburn's criminal act, especially given his stated desire to be placed in an institutional setting and his use of the murder to accomplish this goal. In so doing, the defense could further the communitarian notion of criminal responsibility promoted by liberal social reformers, in the hope that it would help distribute the blame across a number of actors who, wittingly or unwittingly, contributed to the tragic events for which Colburn was on trial.

However, the outcome of Colburn's trial suggests that rather than advantaging the defense's case, this evidence backfired. First, by stressing the failure of the Texas mental health services in providing Colburn with constant monitoring and supervision, the defense inadvertently portrayed the defendant as a dangerous and unstable subject, incapable of managing his behavior unless regularly medicated. Second, by stressing that Texas state hospitals tended to rapidly treat patients and release them into the community without further support, the defense indirectly suggested that, if the defendant was judged insane and entrusted to the mental health services, he would shortly be back on the streets, ready to engage in the next violent attack. As a result, this evidence enhanced rather than diminished the perceptions of risk and unpredictability associated with Colburn's mental health condition, undermining both its exculpatory and mitigating potential.

Conclusion

The legal developments that transformed the United States' capital sentencing schemes in the last quarter of the twentieth century created a powerful legal paradox in Texas courts. On the one hand, the U.S. Supreme Court's post-1976 capital punishment jurisprudence encouraged defendants to present a wide range of mitigating evidence during the punishment phase that could prompt jurors to impose a life sentence. On the other hand, by focusing the sentencing decision exclusively on the future dangerousness question, the Texas capital sentencing statute effectively undermined jurors' ability to give effect to such evidence, unless it was directly connected to the crime committed or relevant within the ambit of the future dangerousness issue.

This legal paradox had dramatic consequences for mentally disordered capital defendants tried in the 1980s and 1990s. Emboldened by the advantages presented by the Texas capital sentencing scheme, prosecutors were able to successfully exploit a diagnosis of APD to show that most defendants could represent a continuing threat to society and thereby secure death sentences in a number of cases where the defendant's poor mental health might have warranted a more merciful response. In contrast, defense attorneys' attempts to humanize defendants by demonstrating that they suffered from a chemical imbalance in the brain were often strikingly ineffective. The reasons for this failure are related both to the disadvantages of the Texas capital sentencing scheme, which allowed prosecutors to turn such evidence into an additional indication of the defendant's propensity for violence, and to the social stigma associated with mental health conditions linked to organic causes.

As happened in previous decades, the interpretation of the intersection of mental illness and crime advanced by Texas attorneys and mental health experts in the 1980s and 1990s was powerfully influenced by the historical developments of the time. Taken together, these legal, political, and scientific changes fostered the creation of an essentialized version of the criminal subject, seen either as a mentally ill and biologically different being devoid of personal agency and in constant need of monitoring, or as an inherently evil personality, incapable of feeling basic moral emotions, immune to any rehabilitative intervention, and likely to reoffend at the first available opportunity. By detaching defendants from their social and cultural backgrounds, these essentialized descriptions fostered an ontological association between the defendant and the criminal act while denying jurors the possibility of situating the crime within the broader circumstances surrounding the event.

Defense attorneys and mental health professionals drawing from communitarian notions of criminal responsibility tried to challenge this ontological association. By emphasizing the sociological origins of criminal behavior, advocates of the communitarian framework hoped to make a conceptual separation between the defendant and the criminal act itself and hold Texas institutions accountable for their failure to provide defendants with the necessary care during their formative years. Moreover, by emphasizing the importance of community support for children's healthy development and social adjustment, these actors hoped to demonstrate that, if placed in different social contexts, most capital defendants had the potential and ability to change, regardless of their mental health issues and antisocial past. However, as the cases analyzed in the next chapter will show, the individualist framework that dominated public debate in the 1980s and 1990s, coupled with Texas courts' concern with future dangerousness and incapacitation, meant that in most instances these arguments were insufficient to convince jurors to spare defendants' lives, no matter how compelling the mitigating evidence presented.

SIX

The Abused and Neglected as a "Continuing Threat to Society"

Every marked attitude of a man can be traced back to an origin in childhood.[1]

—ALFRED ADLER

In 1977 Monty Lee Eddings, a 16-year-old white boy, was convicted for the first-degree murder of an Oklahoma police officer and sentenced to death. The evidence presented at his capital trial suggested that on the day of the killing Eddings and a group of younger friends had run away from their homes in Missouri in Eddings's brother's car, carrying a shotgun and two rifles from Eddings's father's firearm collection. As the group reached the Turner Turnpike near Tulsa, Eddings lost control of the vehicle and was pulled over by a police officer of the Oklahoma Highway Patrol. "When the officer approached the car, Eddings stuck [the] loaded shotgun out of the window and fired, killing the officer."[2] Immediately after the shooting, Eddings stated, "I would rather have shot an officer than go back to where I live."[3]

During the penalty phase of the trial, Eddings presented extensive evidence suggesting that he was raised in an abusive and neglectful family environment. As summarized by the U.S. Supreme Court in its ruling on the case:

> His parents were divorced when he was 5 years old, and until he was 14 Eddings lived with his mother without rules or supervision. There is the suggestion that Eddings' mother was an alcoholic and possibly a prostitute. By the time Eddings was 14 he could no longer be controlled, and his mother sent him to live with his father. But neither could the father control the boy. Attempts to reason and talk gave way to physical punishment. The Juvenile Officer testified that Eddings was frightened and bitter, that his father overreacted and used excessive physical punishment: "Mr. Eddings found the only thing that he thought was effectful with the boy was actual punishment, or physical violence—hitting with a strap or something like this."[4]

When Eddings was 7 years old, his mother was briefly married to a police officer who participated in the abuse. The defense argued that this experience was instrumental in prompting Eddings's violent reaction toward the Oklahoma officer. "At the time of the murder," a defense expert explained at trial, "Eddings was in his own mind shooting his stepfather. . . . He acted as a seven-year-old seeking revenge and rebellion."[5] Even though Eddings "did pull the trigger, did kill someone," the difficult circumstances of his upbringing, coupled with his arrested emotional development, undermined his ability to fully appreciate the nature and consequences of his actions.[6] According to the defense, Eddings's abusive childhood was directly linked to his criminal act and should therefore have played a central role in the judge's sentencing decision.

The sentencing judge disagreed with this assessment. After having evaluated all the evidence, he concluded that the defense had presented only one legitimate mitigating circumstance, the defendant's young age, and that this element was insufficient to warrant a life sentence. The defendant's "unhappy upbringing and emotional disturbance," the judge argued, could not be weighed as mitigating evidence because the law prohibited the use of such evidence at sentencing.[7] The Court of Criminal Appeals followed a similar reasoning, arguing that the trial judge was correct in limiting his mitigation considerations to the defendants' young age because evidence of his troubled family history did not "provide a legal excuse from criminal responsibility."[8] The U.S. Supreme Court disagreed, highlighting that legal precedent had clearly established that sentencers should be allowed to consider *any* mitigating evidence—including evidence of a troubled family background—during the penalty phase of a capital trial, regardless of its exculpatory value.[9]

The Supreme Court's receptivity to child abuse evidence in capital cases mirrored broader national trends toward the legal recognition of the devastating effects of abuse on children's emotional well-being. In January 1974 President Richard Nixon signed the Child Abuse Prevention and Treatment Act,[10] the first federal law to acknowledge that many American children were suffering abuse, violence, and neglect at the hands of their parents or guardians. In the 1980s the act encouraged the implementation of child protection laws in several states, including Texas, which imposed the reporting of suspected child abuse cases to the authorities, causing a significant rise in child protection investigations.[11] Until then, it was not unusual to find cases in which the whole community, including neighbors, relatives, friends, and schoolteachers, knew or suspected that a child was being abused but failed to report it.

This legal acknowledgment was accompanied by new discoveries in the field of developmental psychology that suggested that, depending on their severity and duration, child abuse and neglect could undermine victims' capacity for self-control and foster antisocial behaviors in adulthood. Studies conducted in the 1970s, 1980s, and 1990s consistently showed that child abuse and parental mental illness were common among juvenile murderers[12] and that "having been seriously physically abused [as a child], raise[d] the rates of subsequent violence across the board, regardless of the patient's demographic characteristics."[13] Child abuse and neglect, these studies concluded, were essential conditions for the perpetuation of the "cycle of violence" across generations, a pattern commonly found in the lives of capital defendants.[14]

These scientific and legal developments had important implications for defense attorneys representing allegedly mentally ill capital defendants with "troubled" family histories. First, the criminalization of child abuse, coupled with changing sensibilities about the legitimacy of parental discipline and corporal punishment, persuaded more defense witnesses to speak about the defendant's traumatic childhood experiences in their depositions, allowing for the discovery of child abuse instances that previously would have gone undetected. Second, as child protection investigations became more thorough, the likelihood that the defense would find historical records showing that the defendant's case had been reported to the police and social services increased. This presented a significant advantage for the defense, which could use the records to challenge the notion, regularly advanced by prosecutors, that the abuse claim was just a fabrication created post hoc to justify the crime and prompt a compassionate response from the jury.

Despite these improved conditions, in the 1980s, 1990s, and early 2000s most Texas defense attorneys failed to build strong mitigation cases based on their clients' "troubled" childhoods and neglected to examine expert witnesses who could help jurors make sense of such evidence in relation to the charged offense.[15] This holds true even for cases in which clear evidence of abuse emerged, either from the defendant's own account or from other sources, such as family members or social services.[16] The sole exceptions to this rule can be found in cases that made national headlines because of their striking characteristics and appellate histories,[17] and/or in cases involving resourceful defendants who could afford to hire a private attorney and pay adequately for his or her services.[18] As argued in previous chapters, part of the reason for this failure lies in the lack of financial resources and in the low levels of professionalism found among capital defense attorneys in this jurisdiction.[19] However, as I argue later, it is also related to the Texas capital sentencing scheme's emphasis on future dangerousness, and to prosecutors' regular use of a diagnosis of antisocial personality disorder (APD) to turn defendants' mitigating evidence of mental illness and child abuse into additional aggravating factors at sentencing.

Child Abuse, Diminished Culpability, and Future Violence

Defense attorneys advancing diminished culpability claims based on abuse evidence drew from two central ideas. The first idea relied on discoveries in the field of developmental psychology that suggested that negative childhood experiences, especially if combined with mental health issues and/or neurological impairments, could undermine an individual's ability to control his impulses and abide by legal standards.[20] The second idea relied on a "communitarian" notion of criminal responsibility to distribute the blame for defendants' criminal behavior across a variety of social institutions that, over the years, had failed to give defendants the necessary care and support to grow into well-adjusted citizens.

Defense attorneys and medical experts embracing the communitarian view believed that families, schools, and hospitals had a duty to protect and support children, especially if they were struggling with mental health issues and learning disabilities.[21] When such protection and support were missing and the children grew up to become adult criminal offenders, the responsibility for the crimes committed should be distributed across a number of social actors who, directly or indirectly, contributed to turn these disadvantaged children into violent individuals. By taking responsibility for its institutional failures, society acknowledged that many criminal acts could have been prevented through appropriate rehabilitative interventions and that, if caught in the criminal justice system, mentally disordered and/or socially disadvantaged offenders deserved a more lenient treatment, given that society had failed them in the first place.[22]

To challenge these ideas, Texas prosecutors advanced two main arguments. The first argument stressed that "not everybody" who experienced abuse and/or neglect as a child turned to a life of crime as an adult.[23] This kind of reasoning supported the notion that the defendant was "bad from the start" and that his criminal act was the result of a willful choice rather than of his difficult social upbringing.[24] The second argument, which will be the center of the present analysis, appealed to the individualist notion of criminal responsibility advocated by conservative politicians to suggest that the defendant was solely responsible for the difficult life experiences that led to his criminal act, and that his attempt to blame others for his behavior was an additional indication of his maladaptive traits.[25] In this view, social institutions' refusal to educate, hospitalize, and/or treat the defendant over the years ought to be seen as an understandable response to the defendant's criminalistic tendencies, rather than as a sign of parental failure and institutional negligence.[26]

The individualist and communitarian notions of criminal responsibility endorsed by Texas prosecutors and defense attorneys coexisted in a constant state of struggle throughout the 1980s and 1990s. However, the punitive climate promoted by the conservative establishment, coupled with the Texas capital sentencing statute's emphasis on future dangerousness, meant that in many instances the individualist framework advocated by Texas prosecutors tended to prevail, no matter how compelling the mitigating evidence presented. As the trial of James Wilkens Jr. will show, in some cases these background conditions were exacerbated by defense attorneys' failure to thoroughly investigate defendants' family history, and to examine expert witnesses that could help jurors make sense of such evidence in relation to the instant offense.

James Wilkens Jr.: Parental Abuse or "Troubled Social Background"?

James Wilkens Jr. was a 26-year-old white man charged with the attempted murder of his ex-girlfriend, Sandra Williams, and with the murders of her lover, Richard Wood, and of her 4-year-old son, Larry McMillen Jr. The defendant confessed to the killings but pleaded not guilty by reason of insanity. His defense was mainly based on the claim that he had blacked out at the time of the tragic events, could neither remember the exact dynamic of the crime nor some of the events preceding and following the murders, and had experienced a series of auditory and visual hallucinations that had compelled his acts of violence.[27]

According to the defense, Wilkens had a history of child abuse and suffered from severe depression and drug and alcohol addiction. The defendant testified on his own behalf, revealing disturbing details about his traumatic childhood and the effect that these early experiences had on his mental state and behavior. According to Wilkens's testimony, his father physically abused him and his sisters during their upbringing. When he was 5, the State of California took custody of his 6-year-old sister because of the abuse she was suffering at home. As Wilkens explained,

> the reason the State of California took my sister was because my father had started making us bend over a card table while he stood at the end of the hallway and shot us with a pellet gun. And I don't know who called the state, but they came and looked at my sister and took her away. . . . The reason I remember this so well is because that was the only time I ever saw her smile is when she was being taken away.[28]

That same year, Wilkens's father allegedly killed his infant sister as "he was trying to get her to shut up" and, when the police arrived, he told them that the baby had fallen out of the crib.[29]

One day the defendant went home after being hit by some boys at school. His father, who was half drunk, started hitting him as a punishment for being "beat up."[30] The defendant hit him back, ran away, and started living in a garage. Following this episode, his father left the family home and his parents divorced. When the defendant returned home, his mother accused him of driving her husband away and started treating him in a hateful manner.[31] One night, she even went to his room and tried to molest him. Believing that his mother hated him, the defendant ran away and started harboring suicidal and homicidal thoughts.

> I started thinking about killing myself all the time. I didn't have anything to live for . . . and when I was twelve my mother and I got in a fight and I told her I was going to kill myself and she told me that I would be doing her a favor if I did. So, I ran and got a knife and cut my arm. She screamed at me and told me to get out of her house, so I left.[32]

From then on, Wilkens's life would be a continuous succession of tragic events, severe depressions, failed suicide attempts, and drug abuse. His suicide attempts eventually led to his commitment to Rusk State Hospital, where he was treated with antidepressants for five months.[33] Following his release, he started working as a janitor in a restaurant, where he met Sandra Williams, one of the victims in this case.[34] The two had a brief love affair, which ended abruptly because of the woman's romantic involvement with another man, Richard Wood.[35] According to the defendant's account, the discovery of the woman's new relationship precipitated his mental condition, prompting the first auditory hallucinations and the tragic murder of the woman's lover and her 4-year-old son.[36]

Strikingly, the defense failed to introduce official records and/or expert testimonies that could support the defendant's contention that he was physically and emotionally abused as a child and that such abuse had a devastating effect on his mental condition and behavior. Instead, it relied on the testimony of several psychiatrists who had examined Wilkens before his commitment to Rusk State Hospital but had never investigated his family background and early upbringing. The experts agreed that the defendant had an antisocial personality disorder associated with paranoid tendencies and depression, a condition that made him manipulative, paranoid, and provocative but left his ability to distinguish right from wrong intact.[37]

The defense experts provided a detailed description of the symptoms, characteristics, and behaviors associated with their diagnosis; however, they never mentioned Wilkens's history of abuse in their evaluations. In describing the defendant's background, they recounted his history of antisocial behavior, drug abuse, and suicidal attempts but not the painful experiences he went through during his childhood.[38] Rather than highlighting the emotional conflicts and psychological traumas that had characterized Wilkens's social upbringing, their testimonies contributed to portraying Wilkens as a one-dimensional being, whose past history could be reduced to a succession of escalating antisocial behaviors, and whose mental health condition could be simplified through the application of a psychiatric label. Instead of humanizing the defendant, this decontextualized narrative contributed to portray him as a criminal and a drug addict: a dangerous individual who needed to be restrained for his and others' protection.

The prosecution played into this image to undermine the credibility of Wilkens's account and turn his difficult family upbringing into additional evidence of his antisocial tendencies. To accomplish these goals, it relied on a two-pronged strategy. First, it used Wilkens's diagnosis of APD to frame his alleged history of abuse, depression, attempted suicides, and drug addiction as a strategic device used by a narcissistic and manipulative subject to escape from his responsibilities.[39] In this view, Wilkens's constant preoccupation "with what had gone wrong in his life, how his parents had abused him, how people didn't appreciate him," was an indication of "self-pity and projected anger and blame, blaming everybody and taking no responsibility himself," rather than a natural reaction to miserable life circumstances.[40] Through this line of argument, the state delegitimized Wilkens's suffering along with his defense strategy, depicting it as a vile attempt to blame others for his personal choices and avoid the consequences of his criminal act. Second, the state leveraged the negative image painted by the defense and state experts to frame Wilkens's "troubled background"—including his "problems at home," "running away problems," and history of drug abuse—as further evidence of his "maladaptive personality traits" and propensity for future violence.[41] In this view the fact that Wilkens was hit by his father, ran away from home to avoid the beatings, and started abusing drugs as a coping mechanism ought to be seen not as an aspect calling for a more merciful response, but as additional indications of Wilkens's antisocial traits and death-worthiness.

Johnny Penry and the Communitarian Notion of Criminal Responsibility

As Wilkens's case suggests, in the 1980s and 1990s mental health professionals who examined capital defendants before the commission of the offense often failed to thoroughly investigate their family backgrounds and to link their antisocial tendencies to childhood traumas.[42] A similar pattern can be identified in the case of Johnny Paul Penry,[43] whose horrific history of abuse and neglect emerged only after three trials, two reversals from the U.S. Supreme Court,[44] and decades of investigations.

Johnny Penry was charged with the rape and murder of Pamela Carpenter, a woman he barely knew, in 1979. The evidence presented by the defense in his 2002 proceedings suggests that Johnny suffered from severe mental impairments and organic brain damage, had been placed in special institutions for the mentally retarded from an early age, and had a disturbing history of child abuse and torture. According to his family members and acquaintances, Johnny's mother, Shirley Penry, was a mentally disturbed woman who submitted her four children to severe emotional, verbal, and physical abuse and neglect. Although Shirley was abusive with all her children, she was particularly cruel to Johnny. Instead of lovingly helping him deal with his learning difficulties, she "repeatedly beat him, threatened him with a butcher knife, and made him eat his own feces because he had a 'broken brain.'"[45] Sometimes, she forced his siblings to watch her while she was torturing him and to laugh as he cringed with pain.[46]

Throughout Johnny's childhood, his mother would lock him in a pantry, leaving him there for extended periods of time and giving his siblings instructions to never let him out, not even to use the bathroom, "no matter what noises, what banging, what screaming, what crying."[47] While Johnny was locked in the pantry, Shirley would go out drinking with her sister, leaving him and his siblings alone for several hours, and would return late at night visibly intoxicated.[48] On top of physically abusing, humiliating, and torturing Johnny, Shirley kept him out of school and deprived him of the education and support he desperately needed during his developmental years. As a result of his intellectual disability and lack of education, Johnny's development was extremely delayed. At the age of 7, he could communicate only with single words, such as "eat," "no," and "please," and would be fed like an infant.[49] As his cousin explained, "He'd have food that was cut up on a plate and eat with his hands, or he had baby food fed to him like a baby would, out of baby food jars."[50]

Several adult witnesses, including Penry's father, were aware of, or at least suspected, that Johnny was being abused by his mother.[51] However, only one neighbor, Billie Johnson, tried to stop her by contacting Child Protective Services.[52] Unfortunately, the call led to only a brief visit to the Penry residence by the local constable, who did not take further action with regard to the abuse allegations.[53] Most strikingly, when Johnny enrolled at Mexia State School, an institution for mentally retarded children, the employees discovered several scars on his head but failed to report the incident to the authorities, despite the fact that he explained to them that they were the result of his mother's beatings.[54]

To explain to the jury the impact of Shirley's abuse and neglect on Johnny's future behavior, the defense presented several expert witnesses. In line with the communitarian notion of criminal responsibility advocated by social reformers, the defense experts stressed the negative impact that institutional neglect can have on children's emotional development and social adjustment, especially when other sources of support are lacking. For example, Jan Vogelsang, a clinical social worker hired to conduct a biopsychosocial evaluation and a risk assessment, stressed that besides being physically abused and tortured throughout his life, Johnny was deprived of the community support that could have shielded him from the negative consequences of his violent family environment. In abusive and neglecting families, Vogelsang explained, the community can play a crucial role by providing children with a safety net.

> For children who are living in a home that is unsettled, or a home that is violent or a home that has a lot of conflict and problems, the community is often the last resort for that child. What happens when they walk out the door can make a difference in their lives. If the community has schools and churches, has good neighbors, has friends, has social services, services for children with special needs programs, community activities, those are the kind of things

> that can make a real difference in a child's life, if there are severe and chronic problems in the family that are ongoing.[55]

The community in which the Penrys lived, Baicliff, had none of these characteristics. On the contrary, in the 1950s, when "the petrochemical plants came in . . . it became a community that basically had a constable, a justice of the peace, a gas station, a school and a church."[56] The place tended to attract "families who were down on their luck, sometimes people who were running from the law," and offered neither the law enforcement nor the kinds of services that could help a child like Johnny find an external source of help and support.[57] As a result, he was left alone to deal with his mentally ill mother's bizarre abuses amid the indifference of the adults surrounding him. The accumulation of risk factors coupled with the absence of protective factors in Johnny's life, Vogelsang concluded, undermined his already impaired ability to form judgments, make rational decisions, and control his impulses.[58] Hence, "without institutionalization, structure and supervision, he was at high risk to cause harm."[59]

Jonathan Pincus, a professor of neurology at Georgetown University School of Medicine, confirmed Vogelsang's findings. He argued that Johnny suffered from a neurological impairment and that it was the interaction of this neurological condition with his intellectual disability and abusive family environment that had prompted his violent behavior. "The abuse generates the desire or the impulse toward violence," the doctor explained, whereas "the disease of the brain that is represented by neurologic damage and mental illness, lessens the capacity of the person to check and impede that impulse and desire."[60] According to his studies, "Two thirds of murderers have all three factors, and the others have two of the three."[61] Challenging the "not everybody argument" endorsed by the prosecution, the doctor explained that "the three factors that I considered to be important in producing violence can each exist independently without producing it. It's when they combine that we have an electric situation."[62]

The state challenged Penry's mitigating evidence on multiple grounds. First, it minimized the extent of the abuse he suffered as a child and explained it as the result not of the lack of love, understanding, and support of his parents but of his own antisocial tendencies and uncontrollable behavior.[63] Second, it argued that Penry was neither intellectually disabled nor brain damaged, and that the low IQ scores found in his old medical records were either the result of his careless and lazy attitude toward the test or a deliberate attempt to manipulate the system by faking mental retardation.[64] To support these claims, the state experts argued that, from an early age, Penry suffered from a conduct disorder—a natural precursor of APD in adulthood—that inclined him to engage in predelinquent behavior, lie, and manipulate others.[65] This diagnosis enabled the prosecution to argue that some of Shirley's abusive actions, such as locking Johnny up in the pantry, were a criticizable, albeit understandable, reaction to his uncontrollable behavior, rather than an indication of her parental failures. The testimony of state expert Dr. Edward Gripon provides an illustrative example of this kind of reasoning.

Q. We talked about serious violations of the rules, often staying out at night despite parental prohibitions and things of that nature, returning away from home several times, being truant from school and so on. Have you seen instances of that in John Paul Penry's records?

A. Yes. The records reflect actually that he was locked in at night in order to keep him from leaving. Not exactly a parental response I would applaud, but apparently that was what was felt to be necessary at the time.

Q. Parents were afraid he would wander around in the neighborhood . . . and get in trouble?

A. Apparently, they felt . . . that they couldn't control him unless they locked him up.[66]

Besides undermining the mitigating effect of Penry's history of abuse, the diagnosis of conduct disorder allowed the state to challenge the reliability of the results of the numerous IQ tests Penry had taken over the years. According to defense expert Dr. Roger Saunders, Penry's personality disorder artificially lowered his IQ scores, regardless of his effective level of intelligence.

Q. That conduct disorder could interfere with a true evaluation of his IQ?

A. Yes . . . generally speaking, there's oftentimes a lack of motivation, they just don't care, they're easily distracted and are not—are not reinforced by external rewards. . . . They may be more apt to follow impulses or kind of internal drives and impulses and act on them as opposed to conducting themselves appropriately and following the rules.
Q. Such as, just decide I don't want to do it?
A. Right.
Q. I can do it, but I don't want to?
A. I can, right.[67]

Even if one were to concede that Penry was effectively mentally retarded, the state argued, his low IQ scores were due to his lack of education and social deprivation, not to an organic condition as suggested by the defense.[68] By proving this association, the state could claim that, given his disruptive behavior at home and in school, Penry was responsible for his poor achievements, and that neither organic dysfunctions nor parental and institutional neglect could be blamed for his antisocial conduct in adulthood. Assistant District Attorney William Hon forcefully advocated this view in his closing argument on punishment.

> Was he educationally and socially deprived? I think he probably was during the time period . . . but . . . he was not neglected. He was placed in school. His behavior got him kicked out. . . . He was not neglected by the state. I don't think the state of Texas has anything to feel guilty about in any respect in terms of the type of service this man was provided over the years.[69]

Leveraging the stigma associated with a diagnosis of conduct disorder and APD, the state could claim that Penry's criminal acts were the result of his "bad character," rather than of a failure on the part of his family and community to give him the necessary care and support. In so doing, the state managed to turn each piece of mitigating evidence presented by the defense into further proof of Penry's wicked nature and propensity for future violence, and to persuade the jury to impose a death sentence.

Race, Psychopathy, and Future Dangerousness

The historical stigma associating ethnic minorities with a higher propensity for future violence makes a diagnosis of APD particularly prejudicial for African Americans and Hispanics accused of capital murder. Research has consistently shown that the American public tends to see Hispanics and African Americans as more violent and dangerous than whites, a long-standing prejudice rooted in the country's history of racial conflict and in recent developments in criminal justice policy.[70] These racist prejudices powerfully influence the ways in which criminal justice officials interpret African Americans' criminal behaviors in legal settings. Criminological investigations have shown that, although U.S. legal institutions tend to interpret white women's violent acts as a symptom of mental disorder, when African Americans engage in similar behaviors, criminal justice officials tend to frame them as the natural expression of offenders' "dangerous personalities," rather than as a possible manifestation of an underlying mental health condition.[71] Lay individuals seem to share this perception, as demonstrated by their disproportionate use of diagnoses such as conduct disorder and APD—two conditions directly linked with antisocial traits—to describe African Americans in mock forensic psychiatric evaluations.[72] This deep-rooted prejudice emerges particularly prominently in capital punishment proceedings, where both the race of the defendant and the race of the victim have been found to powerfully influence jurors' perceptions of the defendant's potential for future violence.[73]

The law and order rhetoric promoted by the conservative establishment played a central role in strengthening the cultural association of blackness, violence, and criminality in the last quarter of the twentieth century.[74] As the abolition of Jim Crow segregation laws fueled antiblack sentiments, Republicans started to frame drugs as the leading security issue of the time and to link it to failed welfare programs and urban blacks in the public imagination.[75] These arguments were accompanied by the development of discriminatory penal policies, such as the Anti-Drug Abuse Act of 1986, which, by imposing harsher sentences on predominantly African American crack cocaine users, led to the disproportionate growth of the black prison population and to the reinforcement of racial stereotypes linking blackness with violence in the American collective consciousness.[76]

The structure of the Texas capital sentencing statute allowed these racial stereotypes to have a direct bearing on jurors' sentencing decisions in death penalty cases tried in this jurisdiction. As U.S. penal policies led to the disproportionate targeting of African Americans in the 1970s, 1980s, and 1990s, race became a chief determinant of the number of contacts with the criminal justice system likely experienced by individuals during their life span.[77] Modern risk assessors consider a long criminal record as the most powerful predictor of future criminal behavior, and Texas courts have routinely legitimized future dangerousness predictions based on similar assumptions. Given African Americans' higher likelihood to be caught in the criminal justice system, it follows that, by focusing on defendants' criminal records, risk assessors have effectively placed race at the heart of their future dangerousness predictions. This aspect has proven particularly prejudicial for ethnic minorities tried in Texas courts, given the centrality of the future dangerousness question for jurors' sentencing determination in this jurisdiction.

Post-*Furman* investigations into Texas's sentencing patterns have consistently confirmed that racist stereotypes associating blackness with violence have a powerful influence on jurors' decision to impose a death sentence. For example, Sheldon Ekland-Olson compared the racial composition of the Texas death row population with that of the state's arrests in the period between 1974 and 1983 and found that offenders killing white victims were more likely to be sentenced to death regardless of the circumstances of the offense.[78] In particular, black males accused of raping and killing white females were almost five times more likely than average to receive a death sentence, making this offender group the most represented category on Texas death row in the nine-year period under analysis. Given the centrality of the future dangerousness question in the Texas capital sentencing statute, the disproportionate imposition of death sentences on black defendants killing white victims speaks directly to the existence of a powerful racial prejudice associating blackness with violence among Texas jurors.

When an African American or Hispanic defendant is diagnosed with APD, the stigma linking ethnic minorities to a propensity for future violence is exponentially amplified. The prejudicial effect of such stigma in Texas courts is further intensified by experts' tendency to provide decontextualized accounts of defendants' personal history, which denotes a general sociological insensitivity to broader patterns of racial discrimination and a tendency to medicalize social issues. In the following sections I examine two cases that clearly illustrate this trend and argue that, given the prejudicial nature of defendants' accounts and the cultural context in which the trials occurred, the defendants' race likely played a role in jurors' perception of the defendant's future dangerousness and in prompting them to impose a death sentence.

Samuel Hawkins: The "Black Rapist"

The case of Samuel Hawkins provides an illustrative example of the ways in which experts' tendency to medicalize social issues can increase the stigma associated with a defendant's minority status.[79] Hawkins, an African American man, was convicted of the kidnapping, attempted rape, and murder of a 12-year-old white girl, Rhonda Keys, in Amarillo in January 1981 and sentenced to death. Hawkins pleaded not guilty by reason of insanity and asked to represent himself in his trial proceeding, a particularly striking request given the defense he was trying to pursue. The court warned the defendant of the risks involved in self-representation but granted his request following a competency hearing, which found him mentally competent to stand trial.[80] For the first time in Texas history, a capital defendant was going to represent himself in his trial proceedings.

To support his insanity defense, Hawkins testified on his own behalf in narrative form. In his statement, he gave a detailed and disturbing account of his life, claiming that his criminal act was due to an uncontrollable sex drive that, from the age of 12, had prompted him to engage in various illicit sexual activities in a desperate attempt to tame his impulses.[81] According to his own account, Hawkins grew up in a strict and religious family in a rural area near Wadley, a small town in Georgia. His father was a preacher in a Pentecostal Holiness Church and was submissive to white people. There were only two rules in their family:

Go to church, and obey white people's orders. If either of these rules were disobeyed, beatings would follow for both his wife and children.[82] During his life in Georgia, Hawkins explained, his family and generally African American people "suffered a lot of domination by whites," and the schools and services provided for blacks were significantly inferior to the ones offered to whites.[83]

From childhood Hawkins's uncontrollable sexual urges prompted him to masturbate obsessively, seek relief through sexual relations with animals, and sexually molest his younger sisters.[84] To control his sexual obsession, he got fanatically involved in his father's religion, becoming a preacher himself and following strict rules regarding drinking, smoking, and cursing.[85] As he grew up, his sexual urges became increasingly overwhelming, causing him significant difficulties in terms of employment and social adjustment.[86] He was fired from multiple jobs because of his sexual misconduct, which went from obscene acts, such as public masturbation, to actual sexual assaults. His uncontrollable sex drive, coupled with his religious fanaticism, prompted strong feelings of guilt, inferiority, and depression, which led him to seek psychiatric help.[87] He went through several months of therapy but, like his religious commitment, the medical treatment did not improve his ability to control his sexual urges.

In an attempt to escape from his daunting sexual impulses, Hawkins moved from town to town, in the hope that a change of scenery would calm his inner feelings.[88] However, his urges remained unchanged, prompting him to commit a series of rapes in each town he visited. When he was arrested for the attempted rape and murder of Rhonda Keys, he admitted to raping thirteen women, and to killing two of them, just in Amarillo.[89] The seriality of his sexual assaults, coupled with his modus operandi—he always raped white women in their home while pushing a pillow on their face to avoid detection—gained him several media nicknames, including the "Traveling Rapist," the "Black Rapist," and the "Pillow Rapist."[90]

As his multiple attempts to control his impulses failed, Hawkins started to think that he had become an instrument of God and that his rapes were a means to fulfill a divine mission.

> God was the cause and reason for my sex drive and was using me and that in his own time would set me free. I thought I had no choice but submit to his will. I compared my case to several other cases where God did so with other

> men. My victims were white so I thought that God had a mission for me to fulfill with whites and that it would later open eyes to end prejudice.[91]

Hawkins did not feel responsible or guilty for the crimes committed, because he believed that he was helping God to bring social justice through an act of revenge against the white oppressor. This belief made particular sense in light of a statement made by his father to him as a little boy: "The best way to get to the white man [is] through his women."[92] This statement was repeated several times at trial, by Hawkins himself as well as by the expert witnesses, an aspect that likely prompted strong feelings of anger in the white audience and jurors alike, especially if one considers Texas's long history of racial tensions and the punitive approach taken by jurors against black defendants for raping and killing white victims in this jurisdiction.

Besides providing his own testimony, the defendant called Dr. Richard Lee Wall, a clinical psychologist who had examined him in jail, to testify as to his mental condition. Following his evaluation, the expert concluded that Hawkins suffered from paranoia, a condition associated with delusions of persecution and feelings of grandeur, and was therefore legally insane.[93] In the psychological report presented in evidence, the expert explained Hawkins's delusional system in the following terms:

> In this delusional system, whites have oppressed the blacks for a long period of time just as the Egyptians oppressed the Jews. As in biblical times when God appointed prophets and others to gain the release of the Jews, so God has appointed some black people today to gain the blacks' release from white oppression. His attack of the young lady in question was in his mind simply carrying out his assigned task as one of God's appointed. He remembers his father saying that the best way to get to the white man is through his women.[94]

As this passage shows, rather than framing Hawkins's desire for revenge as a member of the black community as a conceivable, albeit violent, reaction to unjust social conditions, the doctor interpreted it as a symptom of a complex psychiatric pathology. In so doing, he transformed Hawkins's reference to African Americans' history of oppression into a delusional belief without foundation in history and fact, thereby delegitimizing his feelings of frustration and outrage against the white community.

The state provided a similarly decontextualized account of Hawkins's rationalizations. Using a well-established prosecutorial strategy, it challenged the credibility of Hawkins's delusions and hallucinations by labeling him as an incorrigible sociopath with a pathological tendency to lie.[95] By framing Hawkins's thoughts, feelings, and behaviors as a simple manifestation of his antisocial tendencies, the state undermined the complexity of Hawkins's social background and the role played by his minority status, peculiar parental education, and pathological sexual urges in prompting his criminal acts. In this essentialized description, while Hawkins's rapes were nothing but the expression of his hedonistic search for pleasure, his explanations were calculated strategic devices used to manipulate the audience and escape responsibility for the crimes committed.[96]

As decades of social scientific research have shown, the lives of African American capital defendants are replete with harsh and brutalizing experiences associated with their minority status, with irreparable consequences for their psychological well-being and future conduct.[97] These brutalizing experiences are often exacerbated by the socioeconomic disadvantage under which most African Americans are brought up, an aspect that deepens the stigma associated with blackness while heightening "the sense of injustice, the righteous outrage that develops in what one commentator has termed a 'subculture of exasperation.'"[98] Given the social context in which Hawkins grew up, and the nature and content of his "delusions," it is reasonable to speculate that his life might have been characterized by similarly brutalizing experiences, and that his desire for revenge against the white oppressor could be the result of the continuous humiliation suffered by him and his community during his formative years.

This contextual analysis in no way excuses Hawkins's criminal behavior, but it does help explain it. Hence, its complete lack of discussion at trial strikes one as a deliberate attempt to silence the role played by racial injustice and oppression in fostering violent reactions among the African American community. In particular, psychiatrists' attempt to medicalize Hawkins's mission to "end racial prejudice" through sexual assaults against white women strikes one as a sociologically insensitive medical strategy, which systematically ignores the social context while framing the defendant's thoughts, as well as his criminal acts, as the manifestation of mental and/or characterological defects rather than as an extreme form of social protest. These medical techniques, coupled with the stigma associated with Hawkins's minority status and alleged personality disorder, likely increased jurors' perception of Hawkins's future dangerousness, powerfully tipping the scales in favor of death.

Steven Alvarado: The Hispanic Gang Member

The trial of Steven Bryan Alvarado provides another powerful example of the ways in which a diagnosis of APD, coupled with experts' failure to highlight the role played by the defendant's social background in prompting his antisocial tendencies, can increase jurors' perception of the defendant's future dangerousness.[99] Alvarado, a 17-year-old Hispanic man, was convicted for the murder of two drug dealers, Manuel Sustaita and his mother, Carmen Sustaita, in El Paso in 1995 and sentenced to death.[100] According to the state's version of the facts, Alvarado and two accomplices had gone to the Sustaitas' residence armed with kitchen knives with the intent of killing the Sustaitas because they had allegedly "cheated" in a drug deal.[101] The defendant had then "intentionally and unjustifiably killed Manuel Sustaita" while his two accomplices killed the other victim.

The defense did not raise an insanity claim. However, it presented extensive mitigating evidence suggesting that Alvarado was a paranoid schizophrenic with a severe drug addiction and a learning disability,[102] who grew up without a stable father figure,[103] and was physically and verbally abused by his mother throughout his childhood.[104] The state counteracted this mitigating evidence by emphasizing Alvarado's history of antisocial behavior.[105] According to the state witnesses, from early adolescence Alvarado had been implicated in a series of violent conflicts with his mother, which on numerous occasions led to police involvement and, in one instance, to the defendant's hospitalization.[106] Connie Edgemon, a psychological associate from Big Spring State Hospital, examined Alvarado as part of a protective custody order following one of these violent episodes.[107] She argued that the defendant, who at the time was only 15, was a violent and dangerous individual with a "full blown anti-social personality disorder."[108] During the interview, Alvarado revealed disturbing details about his past antisocial activities. He told her that he abused and sold intravenous drugs, sold illegal weapons, and had assaulted people with a knife.[109] Most strikingly, he bragged that he was a member of a satanic coven and that during one of its rituals he had personally "engaged in cutting the fat and genitals off live infants and pouring hot wax into their eyes."[110] Besides boasting about his criminal past, Alvarado denied having suffered abusive behaviors from his family members or having experienced academic difficulties at school, all aspects that were challenged by both lay and expert witnesses and that could have worked to his advantage at sentencing.[111]

At first glance, the image projected by Alvarado seems to be entirely consistent with a diagnosis of APD. However, a closer analysis of his social background suggests that Alvarado might have sensationalized some of his accounts to project a macho image of power and invulnerability. The evidence presented at trial suggests that the defendant was a member of a Mexican American criminal street gang in El Paso, Los Midnight Locos, which was known to the authorities for its involvement in drug trafficking and other criminal activities.[112] A number of studies have shown that members of Hispanic street gangs, especially if involved in the consumption and selling of intravenous drugs, tend to project a macho image consistent with the one projected by Alvarado in order to establish their power and prominence on the streets.[113] In this group of men, machismo is seen as a collection of hypermasculine traits based on dominance and aggression, which includes "fighting, drinking, performing daring deeds, seducing women, asserting independence from women, and . . . bragging about escapades."[114]

For individuals who spend most of their time on the streets buying, selling, and consuming drugs, an attitude of dominance, pride, and aggression becomes critical to the establishment of the reputation and defenses necessary to avoid constant victimization and exploitation. In this context, controlling the production and distribution of drugs and showing a willingness to confront threats and fight challengers contribute to projecting an image of toughness that helps drug addicts navigate "a lifeworld in which others constantly seek to exploit vulnerability for personal advantage."[115] Alvarado's criminal history, boastful behavior during his mental health evaluations, defiance of police authorities, and continuous bragging about his drug dealings and violent activities are all consistent with this kind of image.

What made Alvarado's "machismo of the street" particularly problematic in the context of his psychiatric evaluations was that it contributed to a medicalization of his behavior through his labeling as an antisocial personality and paranoid schizophrenic. As mentioned, Alvarado was a young drug addict affiliated with a local Mexican gang, an aspect that should have alerted the mental health professionals who examined him to the possibility that his arrogant and aggressive attitudes during the interview might have been part of an entrenched habit aimed at exerting power and dominance over others as a strategy of identity affirmation and street survival. These aspects were further exacerbated by Alvarado's history of abuse, which likely made him more inclined to use violence and dominance as a means to protect himself after years of repeated domestic victimization.

Research into gang membership has shown that difficult socioeconomic backgrounds and toxic family environments play a central role in fostering a culture of violence and aggressiveness among urban youth.[116] Hence "a given gang member's display of aggressive traits or involvement in violent exchanges is not necessarily pathological; rather it is appropriate behavior in an environment whose socioeconomic conditions are pathological."[117] In cities such as El Paso, where Alvarado grew up, social and political factors such as "institutionalized racism, economic exploitation, and the violence of poverty and deprivation" play a crucial role in pushing young Hispanic men toward drug use and gang involvement, and in making "certain aspects of machismo a necessary means of engaging in certain social-life worlds."[118]

If read against this complex background, Alvarado's history of antisocial conduct, along with his attitude during the mental health evaluations, acquire a different light. However, none of the mental health professionals who examined Alvarado over the years ever considered his behavior in view of his social and cultural context. For example, defense expert Dr. William Follett, an experienced psychiatrist from El Paso, recognized that Alvarado might have exaggerated some of his accounts, particularly the ones associated with his membership in the satanic coven, to project an image of power and domination.[119] However, rather than explaining them as a possible manifestation of the street machismo typically found among drug-addicted gang members, he framed them as the product of fantasies and delusions associated with an underlying psychosis.

> During the course of the examination, [Alvarado] had some rather bizarre fantasies which he gradually and painstakingly revealed to me. This was not at all the type of examination where he came out with all of these things like saying, "I am crazy, doc, and I need to get off for what I have done" in terms of responsibility. He very freely admitted doing things that are against the law and also several things that we felt, both Dr. Gifford and I, the other psychiatrist that examined him, felt that he may even be making up things as maybe part of his illness where, of course, we are not clear on that whether he did some of these things or not, but that was the extent of it. It was just too much, it seemed like.[120]

Dr. Follett's diagnosis helped cast some doubt on the reliability of Alvarado's alleged involvement in satanic ritual abuses, a particularly important function given the national hysteria surrounding these practices at the time of the proceedings.[121] However, by pathologizing Alvarado's attitudes and behaviors, the doctor unwittingly supported the stereotyped image of sickness and unreliability typically associated with mentally ill individuals in the 1990s, while minimizing alternative sociological accounts that could have challenged this association.

Whereas Dr. Follett questioned the reliability of Alvarado's accounts, the state experts took his statements at face value. In their view Alvarado's bragging attitude was nothing but a typical manifestation of his antisocial personality, manipulative tendencies, and narcissistic traits, and an additional indication of his criminalistic tendencies.[122] For example, state expert Dr. Richard Coons, an Austin-based psychiatrist with extensive experience in capital cases, emphasized that narcissists are "full of themselves, they brag, they—they want to be a big shot and act like it," all attitudes consistent with Alvarado's behavior during his evaluation.[123] The defendant's gang membership and macho attitudes, coupled with their labeling as typical expressions of an untreatable personality disorder, projected an image of criminality, dangerousness, and incorrigibility that likely played a pivotal role in jurors' decision to impose a death sentence.

By medicalizing Alvarado's personality and behaviors, the expert witnesses denied the jury the possibility of considering the defendant's antisocial past in light of the difficult life circumstances associated with his ethnic background, socioeconomic conditions, and family history. Although these background considerations might have been insufficient to secure Alvarado a life sentence, they would have given the jury the necessary context to (1) evaluate the credibility of the evidence adduced by the defendant regarding his antisocial past and (2) use these considerations to make an informed assessment as to the defendant's future dangerousness at sentencing.

Conclusion

In cases ending in a death sentence the individualist notion of criminal responsibility advanced by Texas prosecutors tended to prevail over the communitarian view. The reasons for individualism's success are multifaceted and lie in the complex interplay of cultural, legal, and medical frameworks at work in late twentieth-century Texas. As argued in Chapter 5, the punitive turn of the 1980s and 1990s advanced an individualist view of the vicious criminal, detached from his social context and led by opportunistic considerations and self-interest. At the same time, psychiatric labels traditionally associated with criminalistic tendencies, such as psychopathy and APD, contributed to inscribe defendants' violent acts into their personality structure, framing them as dangerous individuals beyond the scope of rehabilitation. Texas's capital sentencing scheme allowed these ontological assumptions to influence jurors' sentencing determinations to an extent unheard of in other states. By sidelining the mitigation question and by focusing jurors' attention on the defendant's probability of reoffending, the state's sentencing framework allowed Texas prosecutors to leverage a diagnosis of APD to reverse the mitigating effect of the evidence of child abuse and neglect, leveraging it as additional proof of the defendant's potential for future violence. Although this strategy was used with defendants of all races, it was particularly effective in cases involving ethnic minorities, given the strength of racial stereotypes associating African Americans and Hispanics with aggressiveness and criminality, and the late twentieth-century tendency to criminalize members of these ethnic groups.

Beyond these local and historically specific patterns, it is possible to identify broader ideological reasons for prosecutors' success. One explanation is related to the strength of the individualist notion of personhood and criminal responsibility embraced by Texas prosecutors, along with its cultural hegemony in Texas capital trials.[124] Research has shown that Anglo-American criminal law and orthodox psychiatric accounts are deeply individualistic, and that the "murder narratives" developed by *both* the defense and the prosecution in capital trial proceedings reflect this underlying ideology.[125] The individualist logic that underpins legal and psychiatric accounts is problematic insofar as it detaches the defendants' mental health conditions and criminal behaviors from the social and political circumstances that contributed to their formation. The law assumes a theoretical social world formed by "equally responsible citizens" who operate in a vacuum, independently from the power dynamics and marginalizing forces that tend to underlie the crime problem.[126] In this theoretical world the logic of individual right and self-interest operates to obscure underlying dynamics of class and conflict. If all citizens are assumed to be equally free to choose whether to behave lawfully, the fact that someone was brought up in poverty, had an abusive childhood, or was exploited and mistreated because of his or her minority status is beyond the point: Fault resides in the individual, not the system.

The insanity test, with its "narrow rationalism," clearly illustrates the law's tendency to base evaluations of criminal responsibility on endogenous causes, in this case the defendant's cognitive capacities.[127] As the historical conflict between psychiatric and legal notions of insanity powerfully attests, psychiatry has consistently pushed for the expansion of the narrow notion of nonresponibility embraced by the criminal law, by proposing more holistic criteria that consider the totality of the individual defendant, including his or her volitional capacities and emotional understanding of wrongdoing. When conducted according to professional guidelines, psychiatric witnesses' mental health assessments can cover a wide range of functions, including the defendant's thinking patterns, emotional reactions, behavioral tendencies, personality traits, ability to form relationships, and capacity to function in his or her environment. Psychiatric testimonies therefore have the potential to offer a more comprehensive and complex picture of the individual on trial than the one that would emerge if the evaluation was limited to an assessment of the defendant's reasoning abilities, as required by the criminal law. Yet none of the functions covered in the mental health evaluation expand the psychiatric and/or legal gaze beyond the patient's individual characteristics to capture the broader social circumstances in which he or she was raised. As legal scholar Alan Norrie convincingly argues:

> [Psychiatry] maintains the law's own project because it does not expose the link between social context and "criminal" behavior, portraying conduct as the result of individual, rather than social, pathology. Psychiatry, like law, decontextualizes social agency, in its case by locating the problem of insanity in the constitution of the individual. Medical discourse hides the social significance of madness by portraying it in terms of individual mental illness.[128]

Psychiatric witnesses' tendency to "decontextualize social agency" manifests itself both in their preference for biological over sociopsychological explanations of mental illness and criminal behaviors[129] and in their use of psychiatric labels to ascribe defendants' behavioral difficulties to mental and characterological defects rather than to pathological influences stemming from their environment. The cases analyzed in the last two chapters offer numerous examples of this kind of tendency, not only among the prosecution witnesses but also among the defense experts. Whereas the state doctors attributed the defendants' criminal acts to permanent negative personality traits associated with a diagnosis of APD, the defense psychiatrists typically linked them to delusions and hallucinations stemming from a chemical imbalance in the brain. The defendant's family histories and wider social backgrounds did not figure in these accounts, and although defense psychiatrists used their medical diagnoses to support an insanity or diminished culpability argument, they reinforced the individualist notion of personhood advanced by the prosecution by depicting defendants' mental health conditions and criminal acts as the result of "internal" physiological and psychological "defects" rather than "external" social pressures. For example, in *Hawkins*, *Burks*, and *Alvarado*, all cases involving ethnic minorities, the defense presented some evidence of the defendants' abusive childhoods and/or "unorthodox" religious educations through the defendant's own accounts or through lay witness testimonies. However, neither the defense attorneys nor their expert consultants linked such evidence to the defendants' mental health problems and criminal offenses, nor did they advance a broader social injustice argument based on defendants' socioeconomic disadvantage and/or ethnic minority status.

Defense teams' lack of attention to defendants' disadvantaged backgrounds may be due to tactical considerations. According to Kaplan, "social injustice arguments" are strategically risky because they challenge the individualist ideology that forms the core of the "American Creed."[130] By arguing that the larger community, in this case U.S. or Texan society, is collectively responsible for the defendant's difficult life conditions and, by proxy, for the madness and violence that ensued, the social injustice argument challenges "the notion that human beings are monadic willful agents."[131] This ontological critique is unlikely to be accepted in a country, like the United States, that places individual rights and freedoms at the center of its legal, cultural, and political identity; hence it is often carefully avoided.[132]

Colburn and Penry's defense teams learned this lesson the hard way. In these two cases the defense attorneys and medical experts presented powerful exculpatory and mitigating evidence suggesting that the defendants suffered from severe mental health conditions and that their suffering was exacerbated by local institutional failures. The state of Texas, the defense teams argued, had failed to provide the necessary mental health support, child protection services, and community networks to support individuals who, like Colburn and Penry, needed constant medical supervision and/or a safety net outside the family unit. The implication of this kind of argument was that because the state and the larger community (represented by the jury members) were partly responsible for Colburn's and Penry's painful life histories and criminal acts, it would be morally wrong for them to sentence these defendants to death. The communitarian view of criminal responsibility underlying this institutional critique subverted the individualist view of the free voluntary agent that dominated Texas courts. As the outcomes of these two cases suggest, this subversive argument failed to elicit a sympathetic response from Texas jurors.

EPILOGUE

Forensic Psychiatry and Trial Practices in the Twenty-First Century

The study of the human mind and its "abnormalities" has changed dramatically since the U.S. Supreme Court abolished the death penalty for the intellectually disabled in 2002.[1] Neuroscience has shed new light on the relationship between brain functions and human emotions, consciousness, and behavior;[2] behavioral genetics has identified a link between inherited enzyme abnormalities, childhood maltreatment, and the risk of future violence;[3] and the new science of psychosis has identified genetic risk factors that make people more vulnerable to the development of schizophrenia.[4] Because of their determinist appeal, some scholars have expressed concerns that these medical discoveries might undermine the notion of personhood and responsibility on which our legal system depends, prompting a radical rethinking of the legal doctrines and penal rationales that guide court judgments in criminal cases.[5] However, recent trends in mental health law and capital punishment jurisprudence suggest that these concerns are largely unfounded. Indeed, rather than causing a complete overhauling of American courts' approach to insanity, mitigation, and future dangerousness, the methods and findings of the new behavioral sciences have been incorporated into everyday trial practices without affecting the overall legal frameworks within which criminal defendants are judged.

Texas offers an emblematic case study in this regard. In striking continuity with the past, in the first two decades of the twenty-first century the state's courts have resisted scientific pressures to reform their mental incapacity doctrines, choosing to maintain narrow and vague criteria that have been repeatedly criticized by the medico-legal community. For example, despite ongoing challenges to the narrowness of the "right and wrong" test,[6] Texas courts continue to implement this standard in their insanity evaluations and to limit its scope to a small pool of mentally disabled defendants who did not know that their act was *legally* wrong at the time of the alleged offense. Similarly, although the mitigation instruction introduced in 1991 has proven to be too vague to provide meaningful guidance at sentencing,[7] Texas courts continue to rely on the wording of the 1991 statute[8] and to condone prosecutors' use of mitigating evidence of mental illness to support a finding of future dangerousness.[9] Finally, notwithstanding ongoing constitutional[10] and scientific[11] challenges, Texas courts continue to base death eligibility on a forecast of the defendant's likelihood of future violence and to allow expert predictions based on subjective (and often unethical) clinical methods to influence jurors' sentencing verdicts.[12]

Whereas Texas's laws on insanity, mitigation, and future dangerousness have remained unaltered, the state's capital sentencing proceedings have undergone a dramatic change over the past 20 years. The reasons for this transformation are multifaceted and include the banning of court restrictions on defendants' right to a mitigation instruction,[13] improved legal assistance for indigent capital defendants,[14] the enforcement of stricter professional standards in capital litigation,[15] and defense lawyers' reliance on a wider range of evidence and experts to build their mitigation cases.[16] Indeed, although Texas and other state and federal courts have been reluctant to expand the law on insanity and diminished culpability based on challenges from the medical professions,[17] they have become increasingly receptive to new scientific evidence that would have been deemed irrelevant or prejudicial at the beginning of the twenty-first century.

Behavioral genetics and cognitive neuroscience constitute a case in point. In the mid-1990s defense attorneys across the United States started using genetic and neurological evidence to build their mitigation cases during the sentencing phase of death penalty proceedings.[18] Whereas until the early 2000s courts were generally reluctant to accept such evidence,[19] over the past 20 years they have become increasingly willing not only to accept genetic tests and brain scans, but also to reverse death sentences in cases where the defendant displayed cognitive and neurological abnormalities and the defense lawyers failed to order the relevant tests.[20] The legitimation and routine use of this kind of evidence has caused some uneasiness in the legal community. For example, some commentators have expressed concerns that, because of their aura of scientific objectivity, genomic tests and neuroimaging techniques might unduly influence jurors' sentencing decisions, trumping other sources of psychological and behavioral evidence that could help to establish defendants' criminal culpability and death-worthiness.[21] However, recent research suggests that genetic and neurological evidence (alone or in combination with environmental factors) has a limited impact on sentencing decisions, with jurors preferring to base their verdicts on the heinousness of the crime and on the defendant's criminal record.[22]

The reasons for jurors' limited receptivity to new scientific evidence lie in three long-standing issues that neither the relaxation of the rules on mitigation nor the availability of more accurate and sophisticated techniques has been able to solve. The first issue concerns the ongoing conflict between the scientific and the folk-psychological view of human behavior that dominates the criminal law. As argued in Chapter 1, criminal law doctrines and trial practices are informed by a commonsense view of human psychology and behavior that assumes that humans are rational decision makers guided by "internal" desires and motivations.[23] When transposed into the trial context, this view of human psychology advances a behavioral approach to responsibility and competence according to which it is possible to infer a defendant's intention based on the analysis of his or her actions. This view contrasts sharply with the one advanced by the behavioral and psychological sciences, which argue that a defendant's conduct can be understood through the analysis of unconscious conflicts,[24] behavioral conditionings,[25] and neural structures[26] operating independently from the rational mind.

Recent discoveries in the field of neuroscience have advanced a mechanistic view of human psychology and behavior that calls into question the notions of "voluntary act" and "criminal intent" that inform criminal law doctrines and trial practices.[27] However, like the numerous scientific critiques that preceded it, the neuroscientific challenge has had little impact on the legal reasoning underlying judges and jurors' assignments of criminal culpability in homicide cases. As the cases analyzed in this book have shown, when asked to determine an individual's guilt and/or moral blameworthiness, jurors tend to look at the defendant's actions before, during, and after the charged offense and to use these behavioral observations to infer the defendant's thoughts and motivations. This approach aligns with the commonsense approach of the criminal law and is minimally affected by the introduction of new scientific evidence on the biological and/or psychological determinants of human conduct. Hence, unless psychiatrists and defense attorneys start translating the new science into the folk-psychological language, the availability of new diagnostic techniques and visual aids supporting a claim of organicity is unlikely to make a difference in jurors' perceptions of defendants' death-worthiness. As legal scholar Stephen Morse explained in 2011, to be legally relevant,

> the biological evidence must be translated into the criminal law's folk psychological criteria. That is, the expert must be able to explain precisely how the neuroevidence bears on whether the agent acted, formed the required *mens rea*, or met the criteria for an excusing condition. If the evidence is not directly relevant, the expert should be able to explain the chain of inference from the indirect evidence to the law's criteria.[28]

According to Morse, this act of translation entails going beyond causal explanations of behavior based on genetic and/or neurological abnormalities—which do not diminish defendants' responsibility for their crimes per se—to explain how these biological defects might excuse defendants for their acts or mitigate their criminal culpability. As we have seen, over the twentieth century courtroom experts regularly failed to translate the deterministic explanations of their time into the law's commonsense approach, offering formulaic descriptions of symptoms, diagnoses, and assessment techniques while leaving the association between the defendant's biological "abnormalities" and the relevant mental state largely unexplored.[29] The hope is that, as social and cognitive neuroscience advances, court experts will be increasingly willing and able to use neuroimaging techniques to "detect specific, legally relevant mental content" and to speak directly to the questions of responsibility and competence that jurors are required to answer.[30]

A second reason for jurors' rejection of scientific evidence of mental health problems relates to defense attorneys' failure to show the *nexus* between the exculpatory or mitigating evidence presented and the charged offense. As argued in Chapters 1 and 2, at the beginning of the twentieth century Texas defense teams often failed to unpack the mechanisms connecting a defendant's mental health problems to the criminal act itself, leaving jurors to wonder how the defendant's medical condition might have affected his or her actions before, during, and immediately after the commission of the offense. An analysis of recent trial transcripts suggests that the same problem emerges in the mitigation strategies advanced by defense teams at the beginning of the twenty-first century.[31] Despite improvements in the quality of the scientific evidence presented, defense attorneys continue to leave the link between the alleged mental disturbance and the criminal act itself unaddressed, explicitly asking experts to avoid questions about past and present criminal offenses and to focus their mental health assessments on the defendant's background and upbringing. Although defense attorneys are under no legal obligation to show that the defendant's mental health problems are directly linked to the criminal act itself,[32] research suggests that their failure to demonstrate the existence of such a link can significantly undermine their mitigation case, even when their argument is strong and supported by sound scientific evidence.[33]

Defense attorneys' decision to avoid questions about the time of the crime is often led by the desire to protect the defendant's Fifth Amendment right against self-incrimination. This is a reasonable strategy, especially in cases where the defendant has claimed innocence and there is a risk that, if questioned, he might reveal details that will raise suspicions about his criminal involvement. As we have seen, in insanity cases the defense team admits that the defendant committed the acts for which he is on trial and focuses the guilt phase on showing that, at the time of the events, the defendant did not know that his criminal act was wrong because of a mental disease or defect. In these cases, if the defendant is found guilty, the defense generally uses the penalty phase to show that, though the defendant's mental illness did not reach the level of legal insanity, it is sufficiently severe to make him less morally blameworthy for the act committed. On the other hand, in innocence cases the defense team argues that the defendant did not commit the charged offense and uses the guilt phase of the proceeding to challenge the prosecution's reconstruction of the criminal event. In these cases, if the defendant is found guilty, the defense can choose between two different courses of action: either changing strategy, admitting guilt, and offering evidence of mental illness that helps to explain the defendant's acts at the time of the offense; or insisting on its innocence claim and presenting mitigating evidence that will appear disconnected from the criminal act itself, because the defense's claim is that the defendant did not commit the act in the first place.

These are difficult dilemmas that can be evaluated only on a case-by-case basis. However, I suspect that unless the evidence of guilt is weak and the case raises serious doubts about the defendant's responsibility for the crime, the defense team should make peace with the jurors' verdict and focus their efforts on constructing the best mitigation case for their client. This entails not only humanizing the defendant through a reconstruction of his difficult life trajectory, but also reconstructing the complex mechanisms that connect his mental disabilities, history of abuse and neglect, and/or patterns of social marginalization with his acts at the time of the offense. When defense experts avoid this topic, prosecutors will invariably point to the gap in their background reconstructions and fill that void with their own interpretation of the murder story. Rather than silencing this aspect in the hope that it will distract jurors from the violence of the act itself, defense attorneys should use their experts to offer an alternative explanation to the one provided by the prosecution, for example, by showing that the defendant's acts were led by delusional thoughts and confused moral standards stemming from severe medical pathologies.

A final reason that jurors often reject sound scientific explanations at mitigation is that evidence of organicity reinforces the dispositional view of mental illness and crime that tends to dominate the trial context. As argued by Arlie Loughnan, through its daily practices the legal system has framed mental illness associated with criminal conduct as dispositional.[34] By this term she means that mental illness is viewed as a relatively *permanent* status or condition, which is inscribed into the *character* of the individual and results in antisocial and deviant behaviors. The dispositional view of mental illness and crime reflects two attribution biases that play an important role in jurors' sentencing decisions. The first is the fundamental attribution error, a cognitive bias that leads humans to overestimate the influence of *personal dispositions* and to underestimate the impact of external circumstances on people's behavior.[35] The second is the trait ascription bias, a psychological tendency that prompts humans to attribute the causes of other people's conduct to *fixed* dispositions of their personality rather than to mutable situational factors.[36] The tendency to attribute people's behavior to fixed personal dispositions has important consequences for jurors' receptiveness to mitigating evidence and predictions of future violence. Research has shown that when jurors see a defendant's conduct as stemming from *permanent* causes, and when they believe that the defendant could have *controlled* the effects of such causes, they are more likely to dismiss the mitigating evidence presented and impose death sentences.[37] In these cases the fact that these *permanent* causes were genetic, neurological, or the result of a genetic and environmental interaction is beside the point: What matters is that the defendant could have controlled the behavioral *effects* of these causes and that these causes are *unlikely to be redeemed*.

To challenge the attribution biases that lead to death sentences, defense experts can resort to two main strategies. The first strategy seeks to problematize the fundamental attribution error by showing that the crime was caused by situational circumstances rather than by dispositional factors. This can be done by contextualizing the defendant's actions by pointing to a series of life events that might have precipitated the defendant's already weak mental health problems, prompting him or her to engage in criminal behavior. As we have seen, examples of similar circumstances abound and include failures on the part of the family to offer a healthy and caring environment in which to grow up; oversights on the part of social institutions such as schools, hospitals, and social services to intervene in cases of mental illness, drug addiction, and child abuse; and negligence on the part of the community to offer alternative sources of support to children growing up in difficult family circumstances. The key to make this evidence effective is to link it to the defendant's conduct at the time of the offense and to use it to show that the crime did not stem from an inherent personality defect but from a "perfect storm" of unfortunate life events.

The second strategy involves challenging the trait ascription bias by showing that the crime stemmed from mutable conditions rather than from fixed character traits. This can be done by leveraging the concept of *neuroplasticity*, a scientific theory that, by demonstrating that the human brain is continuously evolving, challenges the static view on human character that inclines jurors to impose death sentences. Research on neuroplasticity has shown that the brain's neural networks are constantly forging new connections and creating new paths through the cortex.[38] Whereas early studies suggested that by the time a person reached adulthood these paths and connections were already forged and crystallized, late twentieth-century research has revealed that the brain continues to generate new neurons through adulthood, albeit at a slower pace.[39] According to these studies, new learning experiences, environmental influences, and increases or decreases in levels of psychological stress can all alter the structure and function of the brain, leading to important characterological and behavioral changes over an individual's lifespan.[40]

The notion that a person's brain is constantly changing as that person interacts with the environment has exceptional implications for capital defendants tried in Texas courts. First, it challenges the fundamental premise of future dangerousness predictions, namely, that a person's character traits and propensity for future violence can be fixed at a specific point in time: the time of the capital trial.[41] Second, it undermines the argument, regularly advanced by Texas prosecutors and their experts, that individuals diagnosed with psychopathy or antisocial personality disorder (APD) are inherently dangerous and antisocial and that nothing will be able to rehabilitate them.[42] As I showed in Chapters 5 and 6, these labels can be especially prejudicial in Texas death penalty proceedings, given the availability of a pool of unethical doctors who are willing to exploit the diagnosis to make behavioral forecasts based on dubious scientific standards. Although some of the controversial doctors who contributed to the upsurge in death sentences in the 1980s and 1990s have been banned from Texas courtrooms, research suggests that junk science continues to influence trial verdicts and that psychiatric expertise is still weaponized against capital defendants to secure death sentences.[43]

A scientific challenge to the fundamental premise of Texas's future dangerousness question would prove particularly helpful for capital defendants belonging to ethnic minority groups. The reason for this is threefold.

First, research has shown that experts and laypeople tend to misdiagnose African Americans and Hispanics with APD;[44] hence a neuroscientific challenge to the notion that individuals affected by this personality disorder are unlikely to be rehabilitated would prove particularly helpful for members of these ethnic groups. Second, an analysis of recent capital punishment case law reveals that in the 1990s Texas courtroom experts regularly based their behavioral forecasts on racist prejudices linking African Americans with violence and criminality, making the use of future dangerousness predictions especially controversial in cases involving ethnic minorities.[45] Finally, although the U.S. Supreme Court condemned the use of racial categorizations in future dangerousness predictions in 2017 in *Buck v. Davis*, there is reason to believe that this ruling is unlikely to address the subtle prejudices and stereotypes that continue to influence jurors' sentencing decisions.[46]

A closer look at the *Buck* ruling will help elucidate the reasons for this limited efficacy.[47] Buck, an African American man, was convicted of capital murder and sentenced to death by a Texas county court in 1995. During the penalty phase of his capital trial, Buck's attorney called to the stand a future dangerousness expert, Dr. Walter Quijano, who argued that, though Buck was unlikely to constitute a future threat, the fact that he was black increased his risk of future violence.[48] In his appeal to the Supreme Court, Buck argued that by eliciting this kind of testimony from Dr. Quijano, his trial attorney had violated his Sixth Amendment right to effective assistance of counsel. The Court majority, led by Chief Justice Roberts, agreed with Buck and reversed his death sentence, arguing that permitting *explicit* references to race in the context of Texas's future dangerousness question would effectively "allow punishment on the basis of an immutable characteristic," a despicable action that violated one of the fundamental principles of the American justice system and risked undermining the legitimacy of the institution in the eyes of the public.[49]

The *Buck* decision illustrates how even apparently progressive rulings can be used to perpetuate narrow conceptions of racial discrimination that will do little to protect minorities from the biases of the future dangerousness question.[50] On the one hand, by denouncing the overt use of racial classifications in risk assessments, Chief Justice Roberts's majority ruling appears to advance the ongoing battle for racial equality in Texas and other states' capital sentencing processes. On the other hand, by limiting legal censure to *overt* uses of racial categorizations, it allows more insidious racial biases to go unchallenged. As argued by the Harvard Law Review Association, the *Buck* ruling confirms Chief Justice Roberts's commitment to a "colorblind jurisprudence," an approach to racial discrimination that seeks to eliminate racial disparities by banning any *open* discussion of race from America's social institutions, whether for inclusionary or exclusionary purposes.[51] This approach advances the view that race and racism exist "only when specifically mentioned,"[52] a simplistic and culturally insensitive approach that denies the complex ways in which historically entrenched racist prejudices can influence expert and lay opinions, even when not openly disclosed.[53]

As I argue in this book, cultural stereotypes about race and gender operate through subtle references and proxies. It is rare to find witnesses making explicit use of racial categories to draw conclusions that have a direct bearing on a defendant's likelihood to receive a death sentence. Although in the early twentieth century some state experts still used racist associations between ethnic minorities and lack of intelligence to undermine African Americans and Hispanics' insanity claims,[54] since the mid-twentieth century they have tended to avoid openly racist commentaries, even in states such as Texas, where racial tensions were still far from being resolved.[55] Limiting legal censure to those cases in which doctors make explicit references to the defendant's race means leaving unaddressed the numerous other instances in which race matters but is not overtly discussed.[56] Thus, as argued by Justice Sotomayor in 2014, rather than avoiding any discussion of race, as proposed by Chief Justice Roberts, courts should acknowledge the unfortunate role that America's history of racism plays in the judicial process and abandon the naïve view that if individuals stop talking about race, they will also stop thinking about race.[57]

Recognizing the problematic implications of the color-blind approach should prompt a rethinking of the everyday practices of trial actors who, in their many capacities and functions, influence ethnic minorities' judicial destinies. As I argued in Chapter 6, defense attorneys and their experts systematically avoid talking about racial matters in their evaluations and arguments, even when the circumstances of the crime and of the defendants behind these crimes scream for a racial analysis. Although this practice satisfies the Court's constitutional color blindness, it leaves unaddressed important aspects of the defendants' life that had a direct bearing on both their acts at the time of the offense and their evaluation and treatment by medical authorities. Instead of embracing the color-blind approach of the Roberts Court, defense lawyers should unearth the potential effects that America's history of racial oppression and systemic discrimination might have had on the defendants' mental health and criminal involvement, while remaining sensitive to the risks of racial bias in trial actors' arguments and opinions. For their part, defense experts should embrace a social and cultural psychiatry that departs from the discipline's narrow focus on brain pathology to (1) examine the ways in which broader social issues affect defendants' mental health[58] and (2) contextualize the medical encounter to identify potential issues in cultural translation that may lead to misdiagnoses.[59] Although this aspect is particularly relevant for ethnic minorities, it applies equally to the socioeconomically disadvantaged and to individuals in which various categories of social marginalization (e.g., mental illness, homosexuality, minority status) intersect to create unique vulnerabilities to stigma, discrimination, and exclusion.[60]

In this book I have tried to complement the historical record left by generations of attorneys and medical experts who operated in a context where, because of a lack of resources, restrictive legal frameworks, and cultural inclination, the narrative of race, gender, and social disadvantage was largely absent. In the process I have sought to reconstruct this missing narrative, by linking the scattered information emerging in the trial records with an analysis of the broader social issues that affected mentally ill defendants' experience with the medical authorities, both in the time leading up to the arrest and during the trial itself. The aim of the historical reconstruction has been to show the relevance of structural disadvantage for defendants' judicial destinies, but also to problematize the medical categories and legal frameworks used to judge marginalized defendants' mental health conditions and criminal culpability in the courtroom. As we have seen, rather than being based on neutral and objective criteria, these categories and frameworks are deeply influenced by shifting standards of morality and conduct, by public fears of "abnormality" and difference, and by the crime control rhetoric advanced by the popular media. My hope is that, going forward, defense attorneys, expert witnesses, and medico-legal scholars will engage with this contextual information to illustrate the crucial role played by social and cultural factors in defendants' life trajectories, and to question the use and abuse of stigmatizing diagnostic labels that turn defendants' criminal acts into the totality of their being.

Appendix

TABLE 1: Cases Used in Research, 1909–1952

Year	Case	Name of Defendant	Race of Defendant	Mental Incapacity Claim
1910	*Jones v. State*, 131 S.W. 572 (Tex.Crim.App. 1910)	K. C. Jones	Unknown	Insanity
1912	*Maxey v. State*, 145 S.W. 952 (Tex.Crim.App. 1912)	Wood Maxey	African American	Insanity
1913	*Asbeck v. State*, 156 S.W. 925 (Tex.Crim.App. 1913)	William Asbeck	White	Insanity
1913	*Stanton v. State*, 158 S.W. 994 (Tex.Crim.App. 1913)	Floyd Stanton	African American	Insanity
1915	*Harris v. State*, 172 S.W. 975 (Tex.Crim.App. 1915)	Belton Harris	Unknown	Insanity
1915	*Myers v. State*, 177 S.W. 1167 (Tex.Crim.App. 1915)	C. A. Myers	Unknown	Insanity
1916	*Burgess v. State*, 181 S.W. 465 (Tex.Crim.App. 1916)	Robert H. Burgess	White	Insanity
1922	*Apolinar v. State*, 244 S.W. 813 (Tex.Crim.App. 1922)	Clemente Apolinar	Hispanic	Insanity
1923	*Morris v. State*, 255 S.W. 744 (Tex.Crim.App. 1923)	Ewell Morris	African American	Insanity
1924	*Lindsey v. State*, 260 S.W. 862 (Tex.Crim.App. 1924)	Charlie Lindsey	African American	Insanity
1926	*Langhorn v. State*, 289 S.W. 57 (Tex.Crim.App. 1926)	William H. Langhorn Jr.	Unknown	Insanity
1926	*McKenny v. State*, 288 S.W. 465 (Tex.Crim.App. 1926)	Pete McKenny	African American	Insanity

Table 1 *continued*

Year	Case	Name of Defendant	Race of Defendant	Mental Incapacity Claim
1927	*Snow v. State*, 291 S.W. 558 (Tex.Crim.App. 1927)	F. M. Snow	White	Insanity
1928	*Alexander v. State*, 8 S.W.2d 176 (Tex.Crim.App. 1928)	O. T. Alexander	African American	Insanity
1928	*Blake v. State*, 7 S.W.2d 579 (Tex.Crim.App. 1928)	Robert F. Blake	White	Insanity
1928	*Dodd v. State*, 201 S.W. 1014 (Tex.Crim.App. 1928)	Leonard Dodd	White	Temporary insanity
1928	*Francks v. State*, 5 S.W.2d 157 (Tex.Crim.App. 1928)	Clifford Francks	Unknown	Insanity
1931	*Shield v. State*, 38 S.W.2d 76 (Tex.Crim.App. 1931)	Joe Shield	White	Insanity
1932	*Rollins v. State*, 53 S.W.2d 786 (Tex.Crim.App. 1932)	Carter Rollins	African American	Insanity
1933	*Blackshear v. State*, 58 S.W.2d 105 (Tex.Crim.App. 1933)	Barney Blackshear	African American	Insanity
1934	*Dobbins v. State*, 76 S.W.2d 1057 (Tex.Crim.App. 1934)	C. B. Dobbins	White	Insanity
1934	*Thompson v. State*, 77 S.W.2d 538 (Tex.Crim.App. 1934)	Lister Thompson	African American	Insanity
1935	*Arnold v. State*, 79 S.W.2d 130 (Tex.Crim.App. 1935)	Doyle Arnold	White	Insanity
1935	*Pappas v. State*, 78 S.W.2d 619 (Tex.Crim.App. 1935)	James Pappas	White	Insanity
1936	*Covin v. State*, 93 S.W.2d 428 (Tex.Crim.App. 1936)	Donald E. Covin	Unknown	Insanity
1936	*Jordan v. State*, 94 S.W.2d 741 (Tex.Crim.App. 1936)	Henry Jordan	African American	Insanity
1937	*Banks v. State*, 112 S.W.2d 745 (Tex.Crim.App. 1937)	Johnnie Banks	African American	Insanity
1937	*Boss v. State*, 101 S.W.2d 253 (Tex.Crim.App. 1937)	Vince Boss	White	Temporary insanity
1938	*Edwards v. State*, 114 S.W.2d 572 (Tex.Crim.App. 1938)	Charlie Edwards	African American	Insanity

Table 1 *continued*

Year	Case	Name of Defendant	Race of Defendant	Mental Incapacity Claim
1938	*Morgan v. State*, 117 S.W.2d 76 (Tex.Crim.App. 1938)	Collin H. Morgan	White	Insanity
1939	*Winn v. State*, 126 S.W.2d 481 (Tex.Crim.App. 1939)	Edward S. Winn	White	Insanity
1943	*Gutierrez v. State*, 175 S.W.2d 968 (Tex.Crim.App. 1943)	Juan Gutierrez	Hispanic	Insanity
1944	*Duke v. State*, 182 S.W.2d 808 (Tex.Crim.App. 1944)	George Duke	Unknown	Insanity
1944	*Miner v. State*, 178 S.W.2d 268 (Tex.Crim.App. 1944)	Harold A. Miner	White	Insanity
1944	*Murray v. State*, 182 S.W.2d 475 (Tex.Crim.App. 1944)	Allen Murray	African American	Insanity
1948	*McCaine v. State*, 211 S.W.2d 190 (Tex.Crim.App. 1948)	Riley McCaine	White	Insanity
1948	*Ross v. State*, 220 S.W.2d 137 (Tex.Crim.App. 1948)	Lloyd I. Ross	White	Insanity
1949	*Morrow v. State*, 224 S.W.2d 481 (Tex.Crim.App. 1949)	J. W. Morrow Jr.	White	Insanity
1950	*McGee v. State*, 238 S.W.2d 707 (Tex.Crim.App. 1950)	Richard W. McGee	White	Insanity
1951	*Jones v. State*, 243 S.W.2d 848 (Tex.Crim.App. 1951)	William K. Jones	White	Insanity
1951	*McCune v. State*, 240 S.W.2d 305 (Tex.Crim.App. 1951)	Billie George McCune	White	Insanity

Source: Marquart et al. (1998), 201–12; Espy and Smykla (2016).

TABLE 2: Cases Used in Research, 1952–1972

Year	Case	Name of Defendant	Race of Defendant	Mental Incapacity Claim
1952	*Gephart v. State*, 249 S.W.2d 612 (Tex.Crim.App. 1952)	Foley Ford Gephart	White	Insanity
1954	*Brinkley v. State*, 277 S.W.2d 704 (Tex.Crim.App. 1954)	Lonnie Brinkley	White	Insanity

Table 2 *continued*

Year	Case	Name of Defendant	Race of Defendant	Mental Incapacity Claim
1954	*Whitaker v. State*, 268 S.W.2d 172 (Tex.Crim.App. 1954)	Walter E. Whitaker Jr.	White	Insanity
1956	*Bingham v. State*, 290 S.W.2d 915 (Tex.Crim.App. 1956)	Leonard Lionel Bingham	White	Insanity
1956	*Houston v. State*, 287 S.W.2d 643 (Tex.Crim.App. 1956)	Billy Joe Houston	White	Insanity
1957	*Hall v. State*, 301 S.W.2d 161 (Tex.Crim.App. 1957)	Wilburn Monroe Hall	White	Insanity
1958	*Freeman v. State*, 317 S.W.2d 726 (Tex.Crim.App. 1958)	Robert E. Freeman	White	Insanity
1958	*Kizzee v. State*, 312 S.W.2d 661 (Tex.Crim.App. 1958)	Norman Kizzee	African American	Insanity
1959	*Moon v. State*, 331 S.W.2d 312 (Tex.Crim.App. 1959)	Nearvel Moon	White	Insanity
1960	*Martinez v. State*, 333 S.W.2d 370 (Tex.Crim.App. 1960)	Eusebio Regalado Martinez	Hispanic	Insanity
1961	*Leath v. State*, 346 S.W.2d 346 (Tex.Crim.App. 1961)	Fred Thomas Leath	White	Insanity
1961	*Singleton v. State*, 346 S.W.2d 328 (Tex.Crim.App. 1961)	Joe Cephas Singleton	African American	Insanity
1961	*Wilson v. State*, 352 S.W.2d 114 (Tex.Crim.App. 1961)	Donald Ray Wilson	White	Temporary insanity
1962	*Bradley v. State*, 353 S.W.2d 864 (Tex.Crim.App. 1962)	Herbert Lemuel Bradley	African American	Insanity
1962	*Hagans v. State*, 372 S.W.2d 946 (Tex.Crim.App. 1962)	Edward Otho Hagans	Unknown	Insanity
1963	*Welch v. State*, 373 S.W.2d 497 (Tex.Crim.App. 1963)	Eugene Welch	African American	Insanity
1964	*Crain v. State*, 394 S.W.2d 165 (Tex.Crim.App. 1964)	Paul R. Crain	White	Insanity
1965	*Johnston v. State*, 396 S.W.2d 404 (Tex.Crim.App. 1965)	Leon Willis Johnston	White	Insanity

Table 2 *continued*

Year	Case	Name of Defendant	Race of Defendant	Mental Incapacity Claim
1966	*Bryan v. State*, 406 S.W.2d 210 (Tex.Crim.App. 1966)	William Clark Bryan	White	Insanity
1966	*Rubenstein v. State*, 407 S.W.2d 793 (Tex.Crim.App. 1966)	Jack Rubenstein	White	Insanity
1970	*Morales v. State*, 458 S.W.2d 56 (Tex.Crim.App. 1970)	Leopoldo Morales Jr.	Hispanic	Insanity

Source: Marquart et al. (1998), 212–19; Espy and Smykla (2016).

TABLE 3: Cases Used in Research, 1976–2002

Year	Case	Name of Defendant	Race of Defendant	Mental Incapacity Claim
1979	*Adams v. State*, 577 S.W.2d 717 (Tex.Crim.App. 1979)	Randall Dale Adams	White	Mitigation/ aggravation
1979	*Burks v. State*, 583 S.W.2d 389 (Tex.Crim.App. 1979)	Stanley Keith Burks	African American	Insanity
1981	*Hawkins v. State*, 613 S.W.2d 720 (Tex.Crim.App. 1981)	Samuel Hawkins	African American	Insanity
1984	*Smith v. State*, 683 S.W.2d 393 (Tex.Crim.App. 1984)	Larry Smith	African American	Mitigation/ aggravation
1985	*Nethery v. State*, 692 S.W.2d 686 (Tex.Crim.App. 1985)	Stephen Ray Nethery	White	Mitigation/ aggravation
1986	*Granviel v. State*, 723 S.W.2d 141 (Tex.Crim.App. 1986)	Kenneth Granviel	African American	Insanity
1987	*Cordova v. State*, 733 S.W.2d 175 (Tex.Crim.App. 1987)	Joe Angel Cordova	Hispanic	Mitigation/ aggravation
1988	*Holland v. State*, 761 S.W.2d 307 (Tex.Crim.App. 1988)	David Lee Holland	White	Mitigation/ aggravation
1989	*James v. State*, 772 S.W.2d 84 (Tex.Crim.App. 1989)	Johnny James	White	Mitigation/ aggravation
1989	*Lackey v. State*, 819 S.W.2d 111 (Tex.Crim.App. 1989)	Clarence Allen Lackey	White	Mitigation/ aggravation

Table 3 *continued*

Year	Case	Name of Defendant	Race of Defendant	Mental Incapacity Claim
1989	*Sattiewhite v. State*, 786 S.W.2d 271 (Tex.Crim.App. 1989)	Vernon Lamar Sattiewhite	African American	Mitigation/aggravation
1990	*Madden v. State*, 799 S.W.2d 683 (Tex.Crim.App. 1990)	Robert Madden	White	Mitigation/aggravation
1991	*Long v. State*, 823 S.W.2d 259 (Tex.Crim.App. 1991)	David Martin Long	White	Insanity
1992	*Mines v. State*, 852 S.W.2d 941 (Tex.Crim.App. 1994)	Charles E. Mines Jr.	African American	Insanity
1992	*Wilkens v. State*, 847 S.W.2d 547 (Tex.Crim.App. 1992)	James Joseph Wilkens Jr	White	Insanity
1993	*Arnold v. State*, 873 S.W.2d 27 (Tex.Crim.App. 1993)	Jermarr Carlos Arnold	Hispanic	Insanity
1993	*Satterwhite v. State*, 858 S.W.2d 412 (Tex.Crim.App. 1993)	John T. Satterwhite	African American	Mitigation/aggravation
1995	*Alvarado v. State*, 912 S.W.2d 199 (Tex.Crim.App. 1995)	Steven Brian Alvarado	Hispanic	Mitigation/aggravation
1995	*Heiselbetz v. State*, 906 S.W.2d 500 (Tex.Crim.App. 1995)	Earl Carl Heiselbetz	White	Mitigation/aggravation
1996	*Soria v. State*, 933 S.W.2d 46 (Tex.Crim.App. 1996)	Juan Soria	Hispanic	Mitigation/aggravation
1998	*Colburn v. State*, 966 S.W.2d 511 (Tex.Crim.App. 1998)	James Blake Colburn	White	Insanity
1998	*Griffith v. State*, 983 S.W.2d 282 (Tex.Crim.App. 1998)	Michael Durwood Griffith	White	Mitigation/aggravation
1999	*Jackson v. State*, 992 S.W.2d 469 (Tex.Crim.App. 1999)	Donell O'Keith Jackson	African American	Mitigation/aggravation
2005	*Penry v. State*, 178 S.W.3d 782 (Tex.Crim.App. 2005)	John Paul Penry	White	Mitigation/aggravation

Source: Texas Department of Criminal Justice (2022).

TABLE 4: Cases Used in Research and Cases Missing from Archive with Racial Break

Time Frame	African American	Hispanic	White	Unknown	Total
Used in Research	25	8	45	8	86
Period 1 (1909–1952)	13	2	19	7	41
Period 2 (1952–1972)	4	2	14	1	21
Period 3 (1976–2002)	8	4	12	0	24
Missing from Archive	3	0	9	6	18
Period 1 (1909–1952)	1	0	1	6	8
Period 2 (1952–1972)	1	0	0	0	1
Period 3 (1976–2002)	1	0	8	0	9
Total	28	8	54	14	104

Source: Marquart et al. (1998), 201–19; Espy and Smykla (2016); Texas Department of Criminal Justice (2022).

TABLE 5: Expert Witness Used by the Defense by Race and Time Period

Defense Used Expert Witness	Period 1 (1909–1952)	Period 2 (1952–1972)	Period 3 (1976–2002)
White defendant	19	14	12
Yes	14	10	11
No	5	4	1
African American defendant	13	4	8
Yes	5	2	8
No	8	2	0
Hispanic defendant	2	2	4
Yes	0	0	4
No	2	2	0
Unknown race/ethnicity of defendant	7	1	0
Yes	3	1	0
No	4	0	0
Total	41	21	24

Notes

Introduction

1. Speranza (1901), 125–26.

2. Green (1995), 1922.

3. Texas Coalition Against the Death Penalty (2016). These numbers align, and in some respects exceed, broader national trends. Some estimates suggest that retentionist states have collectively executed more than 60 people with severe mental disabilities since the U.S. Supreme Court reinstated the death penalty in 1976, and that between 10% and 70% of current death row prisoners suffer from a severe mental disability. See Perlin (2013), 1.

4. *Atkins v. Virginia*, 536 U.S. 304 (2002).

5. Death Penalty Information Center (2022a).

6. *M'Naghten's Case*, House of Lords, 8 Eng. Rep. 718 (1843); Tex. Penal Code Ann., §8.01 (West 1984).

7. Ray (1962), 42–43; Cardozo (1931), 70, 106, 108; Zilboorg (1943), 273; Gowers (1953), 102; De Grazia (1954), 341; Douglas (1955); Glueck (1962), 46; Brennan (1963); Hermann and Sor (1983), 512.

8. See Shannon (2006), 73.

9. As detailed in Chapter 6, Texas's capital sentencing statute of 1976 required jurors to answer two "special issue" questions at the end of the punishment stage of the proceedings: (1) "whether the conduct of the defendant that caused the death of the deceased was committed deliberately and with the reasonable expectation that the death of the deceased or another would result" and (2) "whether there [was] a probability that the defendant would commit criminal acts of violence that would constitute a continuing threat to society." Tex. Code Crim. Proc. Ann., art. 37.071(b) (West 1974). If jurors unanimously answered yes to both special issue questions, they were to impose a death sentence (Tex. Code Crim. Proc. Ann., art. 37.071(e) (West 1974)). The U.S. Supreme Court upheld Texas's capital sentencing statute in *Jurek v. Texas*, 428 U.S. 262 (1976).

10. *Penry v. Lynaugh*, 492 U.S. 302, 304 (1989).

11. *Penry v. Lynaugh*, at 322–24. See Dix (1976), 1353–55, 1365; Vartkessian (2011); and Vartkessian et al. (2017), 18–19.

12. Tex. Code Crim. Proc. Ann., art. 37.01(b)1–2 (West 1991).

13. See Chapter 5, Section "The Conservative Years and the American Death Penalty."

14. Douglas (1955), 485–95; Hermann and Sor (1983), 499–508; Glueck (1928). For Texas, see Shannon (2006).

15. Vartkessian (2020).

16. Winick (2009); Entzeroth (2011); Slobogin (2003); Ghoshray (2006); Blume and Johnson (2003); Izutsu (2004); Snodgrass and Justice (2007), 81; Bryant (2008); Giardino (2009).

17. See, e.g., Derrida (1973; 1993), Baudrillard and Levin (1981), Foucault (1978; 1980; 1988), and Lyotard (1984).

18. See Valverde (2009), 1–27.

19. See Chapter 1, Section "Diagnosing Insanity in Texas Criminal Courts."

20. See Chapter 3, Section "Psychoanalysis, the Insanity Defense, and Texas Death Penalty Trials."

21. See Chapter 6, Section "Child Abuse, Diminished Culpability, and Future Violence."

22. See Chapter 4, Sections "The Criminal Psychopath as an 'Emotionally Immature' Individual" and "The Criminal Psychopath as a 'Sexual Pervert' "; and Chapter 6, Section "Child Abuse, Diminished Culpability, and Future Violence."

23. See Chapter 6, Section "Child Abuse, Diminished Culpability, and Future Violence." For an interesting case study illustrating how individualism can influence the operations of helping agencies and defense attorneys in ways that facilitate the subject's execution, see Dunn and Kaplan (2009).

24. See Chapter 1, Sections "The Biological Paradigm and Its Diagnostic Limitations" and "Diagnosing Insanity in Texas Criminal Courts."

25. See Chapter 5, Section "Medical Developments, Future Dangerousness, and Reversed Mitigation," Subsection "Prosecutorial Strategies."

26. More broadly, these depictions suggested that the defendants' mental illnesses and criminal behaviors were "dispositional," that is, an expression of their natural disposition and personality and therefore untreatable. See Loughnan (2012), 49–57. As we will see, this ontological view would prove exceptionally prejudicial in Texas capital cases, given the importance placed by the state on defendants' probability of future dangerousness (and, by proxy, their likelihood of rehabilitation and change) for the establishment of death-worthiness.

27. To advance this idea, I draw from R. W. Connell's concept of hegemonic masculinity, an influential framework that has inspired a wave of criminological interest in the ways in which culturally defined standards of manhood can shape men's experience with crime and criminality. In Connell's theory hegemonic masculinity stems from a complex interplay of socioeconomic, political, and cultural

forces that shape the organization of private life and establish the standards that should regulate men's behavior inside and outside the family unit. See Connell (1987), 184; and McFarlane (2013), 323–24. In this framework men who fail to live up to these behavioral standards are cast as "subordinated masculinities," that is, marginalized men who display nonconformist behaviors and characteristics that "undermine or threaten the supremacy of hegemonic masculinity" and therefore need to be suppressed (McFarlane 2013, 324; see also Connell 1987, 183–84). As I will show, psychiatrists and lay actors routinely pathologize and criminalize male offenders who display personalities and lifestyles that deviate from dominant standards of manhood, casting them as emblematic examples of subordinated masculinity in Connell's terms.

28. For a detailed discussion of the theories and literature that inspired this argument, see Deambrogio (2020), 27–68.

29. See, e.g., Derrida (1973; 1993), Baudrillard and Levin (1981), Foucault (1978; 1980; 1988), and Lyotard (1984).

30. See, e.g., Haraway (1988; 2013), Jasanoff (2009), and Ussher (2005).

31. See, e.g., Scull (1981), Rose (1985; 1998; 2010), Foucault (1988), Smith (1981), Wiener (1994), and Porter (2004).

32. Valverde (2009), 1–27.

33. See, e.g., Morse (1978; 1982), Bonnie and Slobogin (1980), Lelling (1993), and Sifferd (2006).

34. See Chapter 1, Section "The Biological Paradigm and Its Diagnostic Limitations."

35. See, e.g., Ray (1838); Glueck (1928); Menninger (1937); Zilboorg (1943), 133; Gowers (1953); and Guttmacher and Weihofen (1952).

36. See, e.g., Monahan (1981); Wiebusch et al. (1995); American Psychiatric Association Task Force (1974); *Barefoot v. Estelle*, 463 U.S. 880, American Psychiatric Association Amicus Curiae in Support of Petitioner (1983); and American Psychological Association (1978).

37. See Dix (1976) and Vartkessian et al. (2017).

38. This analysis builds on previous historical research conducted by Roger Smith on Victorian trials, by Ruth Harris on the Parisian court of the fin de siècle, and by Nicole Rafter on U.S. positivistic criminology in the Progressive Era. See Smith (1981), Harris (1989), and Rafter (1997a; 2008).

39. See, e.g., Slobogin (2003), Denno (2003), Blume et al. (2008), Winick (2009), Entzeroth (2011), and Acker (2017).

40. For exceptions in the United States, see Vartkessian (2011) and Weisman (2008). For exceptions in Europe, see Smith (1981), Harris (1989), and Loughnan (2012).

41. See, e.g., *Penry v. Lynaugh*, 492 U.S. 302 (1989); and *Buck v. Davis*, 137 S.Ct. 759 (2017).

42. The U.S. Court of Appeals for the Fifth Circuit has jurisdiction over three states, including Texas.

43. See, e.g., *Hawkins v. State*, 613 S.W.2d 720 (Tex.Crim.App. 1981); and *Lackey v. State*, 819 S.W.2d 111 (Tex.Crim.App. 1989).

44. Kaplan (2012), 23.

45. The following states base their insanity defense on the *M'Naghten* rules or a modified version of it: Alabama, Alaska, Arizona, California, Colorado, Florida, Georgia, Iowa, Louisiana, Minnesota, Mississippi, Missouri, Nebraska, Nevada, New Jersey, New Mexico, North Carolina, Ohio, Oklahoma, Pennsylvania, South Carolina, South Dakota, Texas, Virginia, and Washington.

46. See Perlin (1989; 1999).

47. Most retentionist states use a weighing process, which involves asking capital jurors to balance the mitigating evidence and the aggravating evidence presented during the sentencing phase. Only one state, besides Texas, relies on the "future dangerousness" question model (Oregon). See Haney et al. (1994), 156.

48. *Barefoot v. Estelle*, 463 U.S. 880, 896–97 (1983).

49. Perkinson (2010), 4–5; Campbell (2011), 659; Campbell (2012), 290–91.

50. Hood and Hoyle (2015), 242. See, in general, Amnesty International (2006).

51. Koeninger (1969), 140.

52. Most of the transcripts selected for analysis were found in two archival collections: the Court of Criminal Appeals Centralized Court Case Files (1909–1990) and the Court of Criminal Appeals Execution Case Files (1968–2012), both held at the Texas State Library and Archives Commission. The Court Case Files document the appeals of all defendants sentenced to death in Texas between January 1909 and December 1990, whereas the Execution Files document approximately 43% of the executions that occurred between November 1993 and December 1998, and all but one of the executions that occurred between January 1999 and April 2012. Missing cases for the period 1993–1999 were found at the TCCA. The catalogue of the Court Case Files is divided into three time periods: 1909–1950, 1950–1975, and 1975–1990, whereas the Execution Files are all listed in the same catalogue; both catalogues are searchable online. See Texas State Library and Archives Commission (n.d., a–d). It is worth noting that the inventory for the 1975–1990 Centralized Court Case Files was full of errors, meaning that several cases were either missing or displaced. This forced me to exclude 18 of the initially selected cases from the final sample, regardless of their empirical relevance for the study. See Appendix, Table 4.

53. See Appendix, Tables 1–3.

54. See the section "Change and Resistance: A Note on Periodization" in this introduction.

55. Espy and Smykla (2016).

56. Texas Department of Criminal Justice (2022).

57. Marquart et al. (1998), 201–33.

58. See Appendix, Tables 1–4.

59. Recent estimates suggest that in 2018 approximately 64% of American psychiatrists were white, 18% were Asian, 9% were Hispanic or Latinx, and 5% were black or African American. Because the average annual pay of a white psychiatrist is

$168,000 a year, and almost all of them have university degrees, their socioeconomic status falls within the upper-middle-class group. See Zippia (2022) and Snider and Kerr (2022).

60. A report by the Prison Policy Initiative based on the 2010 U.S. Census, shows that of the 1.6 million people detained in American prisons, 39% were white, 40% black, and 19% Hispanic. Because the general U.S. population is 64% white, 13% black, and 16% Hispanic, these data suggest that blacks are five times more likely to be incarcerated than whites, and Hispanics twice as likely to be incarcerated. See Sakala (2014) and Guerino et al. (2011).

61. R. P. Burns, (2013), 825.

62. Streib (1989; 2002; 2005).

63. To remedy this issue, a list of desired transcripts was sent to Kate Black, a senior staff attorney at the Texas Defender Service, for approval and vetting.

64. See, e.g., *Jones v. State*, 131 S.W. 572 (Tex.Crim.App. 1910); *Stanton v. State*, 158 S.W. 994 (Tex.Crim.App. 1913); *Asbeck v. State*, 156 S.W. 925 (Tex.Crim.App. 1913); *Gutierrez v. State*, 175 S.W.2d 968 (Tex.Crim.App. 1943); and *Duke v. State*, 182 S.W.2d 808 (Tex.Crim.App. 1944).

65. See, e.g., *Apolinar v. State*, 244 S.W. 813 (Tex.Crim.App. 1922); *McGee v. State*, 238 S.W.2d 707 (Tex.Crim.App. 1950); *Rubenstein v. State*, 407 S.W.2d 793 (Tex. Crim.App. 1966); and *Penry v. State*, 178 S.W.3d 782 (Tex.Crim.App. 2005).

66. Information gathered from conversations with Kate Black (Texas Defender Service) and Elizabeth Vartkessian (Advancing Real Change).

67. See Ray (1838).

68. *Barefoot*, 463 U.S., at 896–98.

69. See Freedman (1987).

70. See Norrie (2014).

71. American Psychiatric Association (1952).

Chapter 1

1. Roscoe Pound, speaking at the National Conference on Criminal Law and Criminology held at Northwestern University in 1909. See American Institute of Criminal Law (1910), 3.

2. Harcourt (2003), 107–8.

3. American Institute of Criminal Law (1910), 93.

4. American Institute of Criminal Law (1910), 26.

5. Beuttler and Bell (2010).

6. Grob (1983), 136–37.

7. As argued by John Burnham, in the eighteenth and early nineteenth centuries most Americans saw the "soul" as the inner "essence" of the individual, something unitary and indivisible that guided people's thoughts and behaviors. Religious and moral belief in the soul provided a strong justification for criminal punishment based on traditional notions of individual responsibility. If the unitary soul was the ultimate source of humans' feelings, thoughts, and actions, it followed that no matter

how physiologically complex a person was, one could assign blame to the individual agent for failing to live up to society's (or God's) moral standards. Burnham (1988), 13.

8. Burnham (1988), 19–21. See also M. Curti (1980), 3–13; and see, in general, Danziger (1979) and Smith (1981).

9. Burnham (1988), 21.

10. Rafter (1997a), 169.

11. Grob (1983), 31.

12. See, e.g., Wechsler (1930). See also Grob (1983), 179.

13. Smith (1981), 34.

14. Vaughan (1914), 690.

15. De Tarde (1912), 177.

16. Burr (1925), 536.

17. A. Gordon (1921), 609.

18. Doll (1921), 366. See also Bandler (1920), 2.

19. Grob (1983), 33.

20. Southard (1910), 119; Orton (1913), 669; Southard and Canavan (1917); Langdon (1917); Gurd (1920), 201–2; Rawlings (1920), 265.

21. Alzheimer (1910).

22. Osnato (1919), 419–20.

23. Burnham (1988), 53–55.

24. Smith (1981), 57. See also, e.g., A. Gordon (1921).

25. Smith (1981), 46–49.

26. Darwin (1985), 455; Darwin (1981).

27. Smith (1981), 54.

28. Lamarck (1914), 113.

29. Smith (1981), 54.

30. See, e.g., P. L. Dodge (1922) and Conklin (1917).

31. Rafter (2008), 128. See also Burnham (1988), 32.

32. Weissman (1889).

33. Mendel (1996).

34. Rafter (2008), 128.

35. Cited in Hunter (1914), 519.

36. Burr (1925), 534–35.

37. See, e.g., Davenport (1911), 252; and Spaulding and Healy (1913), 838–39. See, in general, Ackerknecht (1974); and Grob (1983), 109.

38. Davenport (1911), 265. See also Chapin (1909), 76–77; and P. E. Bowers (1917), 84.

39. Darwin (1981), 34, 386, 404–5; Darwin (1985), 435. See also Spencer (1881), 234–37.

40. Darwin (1985), 459.

41. Darwin (1981), 178, 199, 404–5; Bederman (2008), 98; Cuddy and Roche (2003), 17–22, 32–40.

42. Wiener (1994), 27.

43. Chapin (1909), 77.

44. Grob (1983), 37.

45. López (2006a), 996. See also, e.g., Darwin (1981), 34, 199, 404–5.

46. López (2006a), 997.

47. López (2006a), 997. See also, e.g., Battaglini and Millar (1914), 12–15; Shartel (1925); Carrington (1909); and Laughlin (1914). See, in general, Rosen (1982) and Connelly (2018).

48. Weber (2012), 170–72.

49. Weber (2012), 158.

50. Weber (2012), 157.

51. Kinberg (1914), 573–74. See also Armstrong-Jones (1918), 139.

52. Rafter (2008), 135.

53. E. Abbot (1911), 16.

54. Burr (1925), 534. See also G. G. Fernald (1912), 525.

55. Rafter (2008), 135. See also, e.g., O'Malley (1914), 313–17; Bevis (1921), 70; and Erickson (1928), 618–21. For a discussion of middle-class perceptions of "urban slum dwellers" in Victorian England, see Zedner (1991), 265–66; and Stedman Jones (1971).

56. Roberts (1883), 254; Buchanan (1886); O'Malley (1914), 317–18; Bevis (1921), 69–70.

57. Bevis (1921), 69–70.

58. O'Malley (1914), 314–15, 317; Bevis (1921), 71.

59. Rafter (1997a), 118–19, 127–28.

60. Grob (1983), 40. See also, e.g., Channing (1883), 76–83; Henderson (1893), 13–14; and Drähms (1900), 31.

61. Erickson (1928), 620. See also Vaughan (1914), 690.

62. Erickson (1928), 624.

63. Erickson (1928), 621.

64. See Chapter 2, Section "Inside the Texas Courtroom," Subsections "Syphilis" and "Feeblemindedness."

65. See, e.g., M. R. Fernald et al. (1920), 116.

66. Case (1919), 501–3.

67. Ireland, cited in Case (1919), 501.

68. See, e.g., Peterson (1895); and Talbot (1898), 1210.

69. See, e.g., Healy (1910), 54; and Church and Peterson (1914), 691.

70. The hypothetical question rule affords both parties the right to ask for an expert opinion based on a hypothetical statement of the facts that is reasonably consistent with the evidence presented. The rule provides that if one party gives a poor representation of the facts, the other party has the right to ask the witness a counter-hypothetical question to address any possible lacunae or misrepresentation. In addition, the parties can inquire into the reasons behind the expert's answers, and the court has the duty to oversee that the process is conducted fairly and reasonably. See *Leache v. State*, 3 S.W. 539, 58 Am. Rep. 638 (App. 1886). The U.S. Supreme Court

sanctioned the use of hypothetical questions in the context of future dangerousness predictions in *Barefoot v. Estelle*, 463 U.S., at 903–4.

71. Shannon (2006), 68.

72. *Rex v. Arnold*, 16 St. Tr. 695 (1724), in Howell et al. (1816), 1: 764–65. See also Meynen (2016), 13.

73. For Texas cases showing this tendency among attorneys and lay witnesses, see, e.g., *Penry v. State*, 178 S.W.3d, Asst. Dist. Att'y Hon Quest. McComb, Trial Tr., vol. 42, 224:4–231:12. For psycho-legal scholarship illustrating this pattern, see, e.g., Perlin (1989), 640, 700; Arens et al. (1965), 9; Goldstein (1967), 42; and Hans and Slater (1984), 111.

74. Sellars (1956); Fodor (1987); Carruthers and Smith (1996).

75. Sifferd (2006), 571.

76. *McGee v. State*, 238 S.W.2d, Def. Att'y Simpson Quest. Dr. White, Trial Tr., vol. 1, 155–161¶1. Psychiatrists and courts across the United States have criticized this kind of practice for confusing rather than assisting the jury in evaluating the facts in evidence. See, e.g., Chapin (1909), 92; Reedy (1912); Briggs (1923); Menninger (1928); Bychowski and Curran (1946); and *Clautice v. Murphy*, 180 Md. 558, 409–10 (Md. 1942).

77. *Alexander v. State*, 8 S.W.2d 176 (Tex.Crim.App. 1928), Judge Whit Boyd, Court's Charge, 5§5.

78. This procedural bifurcation was designed to allow capital defendants to present any background evidence that, though insufficient to exculpate them from their crimes, might reduce their moral culpability and call for a sentence of life rather than death. *Gregg v. Georgia*, 428 U.S. 153 (1976); *Woodson v. North Carolina*, 428 U.S. 280 (1976).

79. *Alexander*, Judge Whit Boyd, 5§5; emphasis added.

80. *Alexander*, Judge Whit Boyd, 5§5; emphasis added.

81. Hermann and Sor (1983), 508.

82. *M'Naghten's Case*, 8 Eng. Rep., at 719. See also Fingarette (1972), 12.

83. Slobogin (2000), 1210–11.

84. Appendix, Table 1. This number does not include the eight cases that fit the selection criteria but were excluded from the sample because they were missing from the archive (see Appendix, Table 4).

85. Marquart et al. (1998), 201–33.

86. Espy and Smykla (2016).

87. G. B. Johnson (1941); Garfinkle (1949); Koeninger (1969); Ralph et al. (1992); Brock et al. (1999).

88. Marquart et al. (1998), 68.

89. See Appendix, Table 5.

90. The trial of Allen Murray, an insane African American man sentenced to death for the rape of a 17-year-old white girl in 1944, provides an illuminative example in this regard. In this case the court-appointed defense attorney, T. B. Davis, failed to present *any* evidence in support of the defendant's insanity claim, limiting his strategy to a superficial cross-examination of the state witnesses that did noth-

ing to undermine their credibility. See *Murray v. State*, 182 S.W.2d 475, 475–476 (Tex.Crim.App. 1944), Dr. Hutcheson Test., Trial Tr. 34:25–28, 35:12–14; *Murray*, Jureka Test., Trial Tr. 35:27–38:11; *Murray*, Embry Test., Trial Tr. 39:12–28; *Murray*, Gonzales Test., Trial Tr. 40:9–16; and *Murray*, Allen Test., Trial Tr. 41:8–18. This negligence is particularly striking if one considers that Murray had been recently adjudged insane and committed to an asylum by an Oklahoma court, a factor that facilitated the investigation into his medical history and expanded the list of potential witnesses available to the defense. See *Murray*, at 476–77. Counsel's ineffective legal assistance had severe repercussions on the final verdict, especially if one considers that when a black defendant is accused of raping a white victim in Texas, his chances of receiving a death sentence increase exponentially. See G. B. Johnson (1941), Garfinkle (1949), Koeninger (1969), Ralph et al. (1992), and Brock et al. (1999).

91. See, e.g., *Maxey v. State*, 145 S.W. 952 (Tex.Crim.App. 1912).

92. *Maxey*, at 958–59; emphasis added. See also *Thompson v. State*, 77 S.W.2d 538 (Tex.Crim.App. 1936), Smith Test., Trial Tr. 54.

93. *Gutierrez v. State*, 175 S.W.2d, Dr. Johnson Test., Trial Tr. 51; emphasis added. Since the U.S. Supreme Court decision in *Atkins*, it has become increasingly common for prosecution experts to use " 'ethnic adjustments' to artificially raise minority defendants' IQ scores" and deny them constitutional protection (Sanger 2015, 88). According to Robert Sanger, this practice, which is based on the assumption that ethnic minorities underperform on IQ tests as a result of "testing biases" (stemming from differences in educational and occupational opportunities) and "behavioral factors" (such as "lack of motivation" or "cultural deprivation"), is "not logically and clinically appropriate when computing a person's IQ scores for *Atkins* purposes" (Sanger 2015, 126). Michael Perlin has joined Sanger in criticizing this practice, highlighting the controversial role of prosecutors in "sanctioning the use of 'corrupt science' " to impose death sentences (Perlin 2016, 1437). For examples of Texas cases in which the prosecution advocated the use of "ethnic adjustments" to raise Hispanic defendants' IQ scores, see *Ex parte Rodriguez*, 164 S.W.3d 400, 404 (Tex.Crim.App. 2005); and *Hernandez v. Stephens*, 537 F. App'x 531, 536 (5th Cir. 2013).

94. See, e.g., G. G. Fernald (1912), 525; P. E. Bowers (1917), 83; and A. Gordon (1921), 610.

95. See, e.g., Richmond (1931), 544–45; contra Bronner (1914), 561–62.

96. American Bar Association (2013), xxix–xxxi.

97. American Bar Association (2013), xxx. Since the U.S. Supreme Court decision in *Powell v. Alabama*, 287 U.S. 45 (1932), every defendant facing the death penalty in the United States has been entitled to a court-appointed attorney, a right extended to all criminal defendants in *Gideon v. Wainwright*, 372 U.S. 335 (1963). However, as argued by Stephen Bright (1994), "achieving competent representation in capital and other criminal cases requires much more than the recognition, in *Powell* and in *Gideon* . . . of the vital importance of counsel and of 'thoroughgoing investigation and preparation' " (1836, 1845–46). It requires financial resources, an independent

public defender service, and a group of dedicated and skilled lawyers trained in the complexities of capital litigation. For most of the twentieth century Texas offered none of these assets, a particularly problematic failure if one considers that the state's prosecution offices generally employed experienced criminal lawyers who could rely on a strong network of investigators, forensic experts, and mental health professionals to build their case. See also Bright (2009) and Spangenberg Group (1993).

98. See Ewing (1982).

99. Grob (1983), 234–65.

100. See, e.g., *Burgess v. State*, 181 S.W. 465 (Tex.Crim.App. 1916), Dr. Johnson Test., Trial Tr. 71¶1–2; *Alexander v. State*, 8 S.W.2d, Carothers Test., Trial Tr. 17¶1–21¶1; *Shield v. State*, 38 S.W.2d 76 (Tex.Crim.App. 1931), Dr. Osterhost Test., Trial Tr. 180¶6–181¶1; *Jordan v. State*, 94 S.W.2d 741 (Tex.Crim.App. 1936), Dr. Prentice Hyder Test., Trial Tr. 27; and *Winn v. State*, 126 S.W.2d 481 (Tex.Crim.App. 1939), Dr. Bush Test., Trial Tr. 128:25–129:23.

101. Andrews (2010), 301.

102. Creson (2019).

103. See also *Stanton v. State*, 158 S.W. 994 (Tex.Crim.App. 1913), Mack Test., Trial Tr. 12¶1; *Burgess*, 181 S.W., Carlton Test., Trial Tr. 62¶1; *Duke v. State*, 182 S.W.2d 808 (Tex.Crim.App. 1944), Dr. Bourque Test., Trial Tr. 62¶3–63¶1; *Jones v. State*, 243 S.W.2d 848 (Tex.Crim.App. 1951), Courtney Test., Trial Tr. 108¶3, 110¶2; and *Kizzee v. State*, 312 S.W.2d 661 (Tex.Crim.App. 1958), Corn Test., Trial Tr. 303–4.

104. *Harris v. State*, 172 S.W. 975 (Tex.Crim.App. 1915), Chas Harris Test., Trial Tr. 112:14–15.

105. *Lackey v. State*, 819 S.W.2d, Annabel Lackey Test., Trial Tr. 5253:19–20; *Jones*, 243 S.W.2d, Fudge Test., Trial Tr. 87.

106. *Burgess*, Carlton Test., 57.

107. *Shield*, 38 S.W.2d, Hill Test., Trial Tr. 116¶6.

108. *Arnold v. State*, 873 S.W.2d 27 (Tex.Crim.App. 1935), Lancaster Test., Trial Tr. 64¶2.

109. *Shield*, 38 S.W.2d, Leon Shield Test., Trial Tr. 119¶2.

110. *McKenny v. State*, 288 S.W. 465 (Tex.Crim.App. 1926), Fay Test., Trial Tr. 21¶3.

111. *Harris*, 172 S.W., Reese Test., Trial Tr. 115:9–28.

112. *Bradley v. State*, 353 S.W.2d 864 (Tex.Crim.App. 1962), Dunson Test., Trial Tr. 115:24–116:10.

113. See Perlin (1989), 724.

114. See, e.g., *Morrow v. State*, 224 S.W.2d 481 (Tex.Crim.App. 1949), Dr. Grice Test., Trial Tr. 66¶2–3; *Morrow*, Dr. Crain Test., Trial Tr. 99¶3–100¶3; *Jones*, 243 S.W.2d, Dr. Plasek Test., Trial Tr. 111¶2–112¶1; and *Jones*, Dr. Hawkins Test., Trial Tr. 125¶3–126¶2.

115. See, e.g., *Miner v. State*, 178 S.W.2d 268, 269 (Tex.Crim.App. 1944), Dr. Swope Test., Trial Tr. 91¶1; *Morris v. State*, 255 S.W. 744 (Tex.Crim.App. 1923), Def. Att'y Dunlap Quest. Dr. Shield, Trial Tr. 174¶3–176¶1.

116. *Shield*, 38 S.W.2d, Dr. Gray Test., Trial Tr. 222¶2–5.

117. See Chapter 2, Section "Inside the Texas Courtroom," Subsection "Heredity and Environment."

118. See, e.g., *Lindsey v. State*, 260 S.W. 862, 862, 864 (Tex.Crim.App. 1924); and *Alexander*, 8 S.W.2d, Carothers Test., Trial Tr. 17¶1. For later cases, see *Hawkins v. State*, 613 S.W.2d, Dr. Wall Test., Trial Tr. vol. 9, 14–25; *Satterwhite v. State*, 858 S.W.2d 412, 426 (Tex.Crim.App. 1993); and *Robison v. State*, 720 S.W.2d 808, 488 (Tex.Crim.App. 1994).

119. See, e.g., *Morris*, 255 S.W. 744, Rosa Lee Morris Test., Trial Tr. 51¶2–52¶1; *Ross v. State*, 220 S.W.2d 137 (Tex.Crim.App. 1948), Dr. Boyd Test., Trial Tr. 243¶1–245¶1; *Ross*, Dr. Johnson Test., Trial Tr. 275¶5–277¶4; and *McGee*, 238 S.W.2d, Dr. White Test., Trial Tr. vol. 2, 132¶3. For later cases, see *Burks v. State*, 583 S.W.2d 389 (Tex. Crim.App. 1979), Debra Ann Burks Test., Trial Tr. vol. 1, 412:8–413:8; and *Colburn v. State*, 966 S.W.2d 511 (Tex.Crim.App. 1998), Dr. Quijano Test., Trial Tr. vol. 25, 248:7–249:2.

120. Perlin (1987), 98. See also Perlin (1989), 713–20.

121. See Hofstadter (1963).

122. *Winn*, 126 S.W.2d, Weaver Test., Trial Tr. 77:25–79:4, 80:2–82:18. See also *Colburn*, 966 S.W.2d, Fitszimmons Test., Trial Tr. vol. 25, 171:13–184:20.

123. See also *Ross*, 220 S.W.2d, Dr. Stout Test., Trial Tr. 131¶2–132¶1.

124. See, e.g., *Arnold*, 79 S.W.2d, Dr. Nies Test., Trial Tr. 175; *Covin v. State*, 93 S.W.2d 428 (Tex.Crim.App. 1936), Dr. Rowe Test., Trial Tr. 132:7–11; and *Morgan v. State*, 117 S.W.2d 76 (Tex.Crim.App. 1938), Dr. Swope Test., Trial Tr. 104¶2.

125. *Jones*, 243 S.W.2d, Dr. Plasek Test., Trial Tr. 112¶1.

126. *McGee*, 238 S.W.2d, Dr. David Test., Trial Tr. vol. 1, 206¶5–208¶1.

127. *Jones*, Dr. Plasek Test., 111¶3.

128. *Shield*, 38 S.W.2d, Dr. Allen Test., Trial Tr. 147¶5–172¶1; *Shield*, Dr. Osterhost Test., Trial Tr. 173¶6–179¶1; *Shield*, Dr. Gray Test., 203¶5–225¶1; *Shield*, Dr. Snyder Test., Trial Tr. 228¶3–234¶1.

129. Texas prosecutors regularly play into jurors' dislike of defendants' apparent coldness during the proceedings to argue for a death sentence. See, e.g., *Covin*, 93 S.W.2d, Cavanaugh Test., Trial Tr. 20:7–15; and *Burks*, 583 S.W.2d, Dr. Grigson Test., Trial Tr. vol. 2, 771:19–20.

130. See, e.g., *Burks*, Dr. Grigson Test., vol. 2, 770:10–771:12; and *Lindsey*, 260 S.W. 862, at 862, 863.

131. *Edwards v. State*, 114 S.W.2d 572 (Tex.Crim.App. 1938), Dr. Holt Test., Trial Tr. 17¶1–18¶2.

Chapter 2

1. See, e.g., Glueck (1928), 181.

2. See, e.g., Southard (1910), 126; Mott (1922), 445; Rutherford (1922), 581; and Shelton (1934).

3. Glueck (1964), 328–34.

4. I use the term *epistemological behaviorism* to indicate the tendency to infer mental states from the external observation of behaviors, typical of the folk-psychological view of the criminal law. See Chapter 1, Section "The Biological Paradigm and Its Diagnostic Limitations."

5. See Brennan (1963).

6. See, e.g., *Winn v. State*, 126 S.W.2d, Def. Att'y (n.n.) Quest. Dr. Duncan, Trial Tr. 157:20–158:1.

7. Rosenberg (1968), xiv.

8. Rosenberg (1968), 100.

9. See Battaglini and Millar (1914), 12.

10. See, e.g., Burr (1925), 534–35. See, in general, M. Curti (1980), 275.

11. Davenport (1911), 265, 252; Chapin (1909), 76–77; P. E. Bowers (1917), 84.

12. See Rosenberg (1968), 125.

13. *Shield v. State*, 38 S.W.2d, Dr. Gray Test., Trial Tr. 222¶2–224¶1.

14. Historically, this was believed to be an effective strategy. As a journalist for *The Nation* argued in a commentary on the trial of Charles Guiteau, a mentally deranged man who killed President James Garfield in 1881, if the defense could demonstrate that several members of the accused's family had suffered from mental disease, "it would do more to establish a doubt in the minds of an ordinary jury than all the testimony of all the experts in the country with regard to hereditary insanity" (cited in Rosenberg 1968, 100).

15. See, e.g., *McKenny v. State*, 288 S.W., Mose McKenny Test., Trial Tr. 19; and *McKenny*, Julia McKenny Test., Trial Tr. 19–20. The defendant in this case based his insanity claim exclusively on family members' testimony to the effect that a number of relatives, including the defendant's cousin and one of his sisters, were insane. See also *Gutierrez v. State*, 175 S.W.2d, Nicola Test., Trial Tr. 42–43; *Gutierrez*, Rev. Flores Test., Trial Tr. 44–45; *Shield v. State*, 38 S.W.2d; and *Duke v. State*, 182 S.W.2d.

16. *Duke*, at 808.

17. *Duke*, Miles Test., Trial Tr. 52¶2–53¶1.

18. *Duke*, Miles Test., 809§2, 810§5.

19. Gene Deason [journalist for the *Bromwood Bulletin*] to M. Watt Espy, May 14, 1976, Correspondence 1962–2007, Box 61, Folder 1M, Watt Espy Papers. 1730–2008, National Death Penalty Archive, M. E. Grenander Special Collections and Archives, State University of New York, Albany, p. 2, https://archives.albany.edu/description/catalog/apap301aspace_ebb546723281017b82b494fb508975c2.

20. See, e.g., *Shield*, 38 S.W.2d, W. H. Thompson Test., Trial Tr. 62¶1–2; *Shield*, E. P. Thompson Test., Trial Tr. 63¶3–64¶3.

21. *Shield*, Leon Shield Test., Trial Tr. 121¶2. See also *Shield*, Ethel Shield Test., Trial Tr. 126¶2.

22. See Chapter 1, Section "The Biological Paradigm and Its Diagnostic Limitations."

23. See, e.g., *Shield*, Leon Shield Test., 122¶6–123¶1; *McGee v. State*, 238 S.W.2d, Eva McGee Test., Trial Tr. vol. 3, 469–470; *Houston v. State*, 287 S.W.2d 643 (Tex.

Crim.App. 1956), Def. Att'y Stinson Quest. W. H. Houston, Trial Tr. 166:10–12; and *Lackey v. State*, 819 S.W.2d, Annabel Lackey Test., Trial Tr. 5253:19–20. Along these lines, Nicola Lacey (2010) argues that in eighteenth-century England "the trial was focused not on internal questions about the defendant's state of mind but rather on external facts of conduct," a tendency that survives even in twentieth-century penal practices (117). See also Loughnan (2012), 59.

24. For Texas court experts advocating this approach, see *Shield*, Dr. Allen Test., Trial Tr. 150¶3–152¶2; *Pappas v. State*, 78 S.W.2d 619 (Tex.Crim.App. 1935), Dr. Greenwood Test., Trial Tr. 62; and *Ross v. State*, 220 S.W.2d, Dr. Johnson Test., Trial Tr. 263¶2. For psychiatric publications advancing this kind of argument, see Chapin (1909), 76–77; P. E. Bowers (1917), 84; and Conklin (1917); see, in general, Burnham (1988), 57.

25. *Ross*, 220 S.W.2d.

26. *Ross*, at 138. See also "Trial of San Antonio Doctor Will Begin Monday," *Paris News*, July 27, 1947, p. 9, https://www.newspapers.com/clip/825116/lloyd-ross-md/ (accessed April 21, 2022).

27. *Ross*, Lewis Test., Trial Tr. 93¶2–94¶1; *Ross*, Dr. Maxwell Test., Trial Tr. 153¶4–155¶1.

28. *Ross*, Sister Bernice Test., Trial Tr. 137¶3.

29. *Ross*, Dr. Scott Test., Trial Tr. 123¶1; *Ross*, Dr. Cooper Test., Trial Tr. 144¶1; *Ross*, Dr. Maxwell Test., 156¶2.

30. *Ross*, Dr. Johnson Test., Trial Tr. 263¶2.

31. *Ross*, Dr. Boyd Test., Trial Tr. 243¶1; *Ross*, Dr. Johnson Test., 264¶1.

32. *Ross*, Dr. Johnson Test., 277¶5–278¶1.

33. *Ross*, Dr. Boyd Test., 243¶2–244¶2; *Ross*, Dr. Johnson Test., 275¶5–276¶3.

34. *Ross*, Dr. Helfer Test., Trial Tr. 222¶2–223¶1; *Ross*, Dr. Scott Test., 116¶3, 118¶2.

35. *Ross*, Dr. Johnson Test., 267¶4–5, 278¶5–6.

36. *Ross*, Dr. Bennett Test., Trial Tr. 125¶3–126¶1.

37. *Ross*, Tuzuh Stahl Test., Trial Tr. 200¶4.

38. *Ross*, Renna Ross Test., Trial Tr. 218¶2.

39. *Ross*, Dr. Scott Test., 122¶1. See also *McCune v. State*, 240 S.W.2d 305 (Tex. Crim.App. 1951), Dr. Thomas Test., Trial Tr. 115¶1–2.

40. *Ross*, 220 S.W.2d, at 139; emphasis added.

41. *Ross*, at 141.

42. *Ross*, at 141.

43. See Rosenberg (1968), 174.

44. See, e.g., Southard (1910) and Gurd (1920).

45. See, e.g., *Morris v. State*, 255 S.W., Dr. Shields Test., Trial Tr. 172–73; *Pappas*, 78 S.W.2d, Dr. York Test., Trial Tr. 58–59; *Pappas*, Dr. Appleby Test., Trial Tr. 60–61; *Morrow v. State*, 224 S.W.2d, Dr. Grice Test., Trial Tr. 66¶2–3; *Morrow*, Dr. Crain Test., Trial Tr. 99¶3–100¶3; *Jones v. State*, 243 S.W.2d, Dr. Plasek Test., Trial Tr. 111¶2–112¶1; and *Jones*, Dr. Hawkins Test., Trial Tr. 125¶3–126¶2.

46. See, e.g., *Stanton v. State*, 158 S.W., Mack Test., Trial Tr. 12; *Morris*, 255 S.W.,

Rosa Lee Morris Test., Trial Tr. 51; *Apolinar v. State*, 244 S.W., Susana Apolinar Test., Trial Tr. 23; *Apolinar*, Ricardo Apolinar Test., Trial Tr. 27; *Apolinar*, Heard Test., Trial Tr. 28; *Apolinar*, Vasquez Test., Trial Tr. 28; *Morrow*, 224 S.W.2d, Ragan Test., Trial Tr. 56¶5–57¶6; and *Jones*, 243 S.W.2d, Gray Test., Trial Tr. 103¶2. For a later case relying on similar evidence to support an insanity claim, see *Bradley v. State*, 353 S.W.2d, Dunson Test., Trial Tr. 110:22–23; and *Bradley*, Nelson Test., Trial Tr. 137:22–138:7.

47. Recent studies have shown that a traumatic brain injury affecting the frontal lobes can undermine an individual's ability to control impulses and form judgment, increasing a person's risk of criminal involvement. See Lynch et al. (2021), 216. This is reflected in the high proportion of brain-damaged individuals currently populating American prisons (60.25% of the overall offender population according to recent estimates) and in the regularity with which criminal defendants present neurological evidence pointing to a similar trauma, particularly in death penalty cases. See Shiroma et al. (2010); and Moriarty et al. (2013), 702. See, in general, Giardino (2009), 2955; and Seiden (2003), 395.

48. *Stanton*, 158 S.W., Mack Test., Trial Tr. 12; *Stanton*, Grabtree Test., Trial Tr. 13; *Morrow*, 224 S.W.2d, Griffith Test., Trial Tr. 42¶3.

49. *Morris*, 255 S.W., Mildred Morris Test., Trial Tr. 67–68; *Morrow*, 224 S.W.2d, Sutton Test., Trial Tr. 79¶3–80¶6; *Morrow*, Mr. Murrell Test., Trial Tr. 86¶6–87; *Morrow*, Mrs. Murrell Test., Trial Tr. 93; *Bradley*, 353 S.W.2d, Dunson Test., Trial Tr. 111:25–112:4; *Bradley*, Nelson Test., Trial Tr. 135:4–11.

50. See, e.g., *Jones*, 243 S.W.2d, at 849. Recent studies have corroborated this finding. For example, Paul Litton has argued that, unless accompanied by other factors, evidence of traumatic brain injury is generally insufficient to secure an insanity acquittal. This is because, although "cognitive impairments from [traumatic brain injury] can [in rare cases] rise to the level of insanity, the effects are more often relevant to a judgment of diminished responsibility, which is relevant in mitigation at sentencing" (Litton 2018, 44).

51. *Morris*, 255 S.W.2d, at 746.

52. *Morris*, Rosa Morris Test., Trial Tr. 51.

53. *Morris*, Rosa Morris Test., 48–53. See also *Morris*, Mildred Morris Test., Trial Tr. 67–68; *Morris*, Maxwell Morris Test., Trial Tr. 79–80; and *Morris*, Buelah Johnson Test., Trial Tr. 89–91.

54. *Morris*, Rosa Morris Test., 51–52, 57; *Morris*, Mildred Morris Test., 69.

55. *Morris*, Hicks Test., Trial Tr. 112–114¶1; *Morris*, Osby Test., Trial Tr. 114¶3–116¶1.

56. G. B. Johnson (1941); Garfinkle (1949); Koeninger (1969); Ralph et al. (1992); Brock et al. (1999).

57. As argued in Chapter 1, in the early twentieth century psychiatrists and laypeople saw African Americans as genetically inferior, "uncivilized," and lacking in intelligence and self-control. See Gilman (1985), 142. However, these racist characterizations did not entail, for the law or for jurors, the conclusion that black defendants

lacked the ability to distinguish right from wrong and conform their behavior to legal requirements. A possible reason for this dissonance is that jurors tended to interpret blacks' criminal behavior as a natural manifestation of their psychological tendencies rather than as the result of some underlying pathology calling for criminal exculpation. See, e.g., Sniderman and Piazza (1993), Quillian and Pager (2001), and Chiricos and Eschholz (2002). Alternatively, it may be that rather than being based on legal logic, jurors' decision to impose death sentences on African Americans was driven by their interest in maintaining whites' historical supremacy over blacks and by a biopolitical (and eugenic) desire to eliminate "undesirable" populations in the name of public protection. On the concept of biopolitics and its relationship to racism, see Foucault (1990), 139–40; and Foucault (2004), 254–58. See also Agamben (1998).

58. Note that Morris's trial was held in 1923, only five years after the Red Summer of 1919, a period of intensified race riots and mob violence during which "hundreds of people, most of them black, were killed, and thousands were injured and forced to flee their homes" (Waxman 2019). Although several states tangled with racial conflicts during this period, Texas witnessed some of the most violent attacks against the black population on its own soil. See, e.g., Durham (1980).

59. *Pappas*, 78 S.W.2d, Pappas Test., Trial Tr. 26–49; *Edwards v. State*, 114 S.W.2d, Edwards Test., Trial Tr. 11–19; *McCune*, 240 S.W.2d, Billie McCune Test., Trial Tr. 49–86; *Miner v. State*, 178 S.W.2d, Miner Test., Trial Tr. 37–63, 67–78; *Jordan v. State*, 94 S.W.2d, Jordan Test., Trial Tr. 16–27. See also *Stanton*, 158 S.W., Stanton Test., Trial Tr. 22¶1. For a later case in which the defendant's testimony, and performance as his own defense attorney, played a crucial role in jurors' decision making, see *Hawkins v. State*, 613 S.W.2d, Hawkins Test., Trial Tr. vol. 9, 1678–1730.

60. *Pappas*, 78 S.W.2d.

61. *Pappas*, Pappas Conf., Trial Tr. 64–67.

62. *Pappas*, Def. Att'ys Francis and Van Dobson Hr'g on Mot. for New Trial, Trial Tr. 3–4§2.

63. *Pappas*, Pappas Test., 26–49.

64. *Pappas*, Def. Att'ys Francis and Van Dobson Hr'g on Mot. for New Trial, 5§3.

65. *Pappas*, Pappas Test., 48–49.

66. *Pappas*, Pappas Test., 29.

67. *Pappas*, Pappas Test., 33–39.

68. *Pappas*, Pappas Test., 40–41.

69. *Pappas*, Pappas on Mot. for Cont., Trial Tr. 19.

70. *Pappas*, Pappas on Mot. for Cont., 19–20.

71. *Pappas*, Zgouridos Aff. Hr'g on Mot. for New Trial, Trial Tr. 26.

72. *Pappas*, Henckel Aff. Hr'g on Mot. for New Trial, Trial Tr. 13.

73. *Pappas*, Agurastos and Agurastos Aff. Hr'g on Mot. for New Trial, Trial Tr. 23–24.

74. *Pappas*, 78 S.W.2d, at 620–21.

75. *Covin v. State*, 93 S.W.2d, Dr. Leake Test., Trial Tr. 37:11–12.

76. See, e.g., *Jordan*, 94 S.W.2d, Dr. Prentice Hyder Test., Trial Tr. 28¶2–5.
77. Grob (1983), 132; Lunbeck (1996), 50. See also "Syphilis and Insanity," *The Lancet*, November 22, 1919, p. 935.
78. Noguchi and Moore (1913).
79. Lunbeck (1996), 48; Grob (1983), 188. See also *Covin*, 93 S.W.2d, Dr. Rowe Test., Trial Tr. 128¶4.
80. Lunbeck (1996), 50.
81. See *Covin*, 93 S.W.2d, Dr. Witt Aff. Ex. C, First Am. Mot. for New Trial, 38¶3–39¶1; *Covin*, Dist. Att'y Williams State's Answer to Am. Mot. for New Trial, 49§4; and *Covin*, Dr. Witt Aff. Resp. to State's Answer to Am. Mot. for New Trial, 51¶4.
82. Lunbeck (1996), 50.
83. O'Malley (1914), 317–18.
84. O'Malley (1914), 317.
85. O'Malley (1914), 318.
86. Smillie (1943).
87. Smillie (1943), 366.
88. But see Fullilove (1943); and Sampson (1943), 764.
89. *Covin*, 93 S.W.2d, Dr. Leake Test., Trial Tr. 43:3–17.
90. *Covin*, Dr. Leake Test., 43:3.
91. *Covin*, Dr. Pierson Test., Trial Tr. 78:18. See also *Covin*, Dr. Veazey Test., Trial Tr. 87:13–15.
92. *Covin*, Dr. Leake Test., 43:8–10.
93. *Miner*, 178 S.W.2d.
94. *Miner*, at 268.
95. *Miner*, Harold Miner Test., Trial Tr. 38¶1.
96. *Miner*, Harold Miner Test., 39¶3, 44¶3.
97. *Miner*, Harold Miner Test., 46¶2, 47¶4–48¶6, 53¶2–3.
98. *Miner*, Harold Miner Test., 48¶6.
99. *Miner*, Harold Miner Test., 73¶2.
100. *Miner*, Harold Miner Test., 74¶1.
101. *Miner*, Harold Miner Test., 74¶2–75¶1.
102. *Miner*, Dr. Swope Test., Trial Tr. 91¶1.
103. *Miner*, Dr. Swope Test., 90¶5.
104. *Miner*, Dr. Swope Test., 91¶1–2; emphasis added. See also *Miner*, 178 S.W.2d, at 269.
105. *Miner*, Dr. Swope Test., 93¶3–94¶2.
106. *Miner*, Dr. Swope Test., 91¶2. See also *Jordan*, 94 S.W.2d, Dr. Prentice Hyder Test., Trial Tr. 30¶6–31¶1; and *Jordan*, Dr. D. C. Hyder Test., Trial Tr. 35¶3.
107. See Burnham (1988), 170–83; and Rafter (2008), 138–39. For Texas, see Wuthnow (2014), 58–62.
108. Armstrong-Jones (1918), 136.
109. Armstrong-Jones (1918), 136.

110. Cited in Wuthnow (2014), 60; emphasis added.

111. Rafter (2008), 128–33.

112. Goring et al. (1972).

113. Rafter (2008), 126, 128–33. See, e.g., Goddard (1912); Spaulding and Healy (1913), 837; and Richmond (1931), 537, 544–45; contra Bronner (1914), 561–62; Stevens (1915), 191–95; and M. W. Curti (1926). The work of Charles Davenport at the Eugenics Record Office and the research conducted at the Human Betterment Foundation in Pasadena, California, are particularly relevant in this regard; see Cuddy and Roche (2003), 12–14; and Larson (1996).

114. Cuddy and Roche (2003), 13. The U.S. Supreme Court upheld the constitutionality of these laws in *Buck v. Bell*, 274 U.S. 200 (1927). For a list of enacted or proposed sterilization statutes, see Laughlin (1922). For a critique of sterilization laws resulting from the lack of scientific evidence supporting such measures, see Hunter (1914), 521.

115. Rafter (2008), 140.

116. Burnham (1988), 55.

117. See, e.g., *Snow v. State*, 291 S.W. 558 (Tex.Crim.App. 1927), Shepard Test., Trial Tr. 186–196; *McCune*, 240 S.W.2d, Dr. Thomas Test., Trial Tr. 113–115; *Moon v. State*, 331 S.W.2d 312 (Tex.Crim.App. 1959), Dr. Wagner Test., Trial Tr. 186:25–187:7, 210:1–22; and *Welch v. State*, 373 S.W.2d 497 (Tex.Crim.App. 1963), Dr. Wells Test., Trial Tr. 395:5–398:3.

118. See, e.g., Goddard (1912).

119. See, e.g., *Snow*, 291 S.W., Shepard Test., Trial Tr. 188¶4–192¶2; and *Welch*, 373 S.W.2d, Dr. Wells Test., Trial Tr. 397:12–398:15, 411:9–430:14. For exceptions, see, e.g., *McCune*, 240 S.W.2d, Dr. Thomas Test., Trial Tr. 115¶1–2; and *Penry v. State*, 178 S.W.3d, Dr. Pincus Test., Trial Tr. vol. 51, 232:4–233:24. In contrast, the psychological literature of the time was replete with explanations of the process through which intellectual disabilities could weaken men's moral sense and capacity for self-control. See, e.g., A. Gordon (1921), 610; G. G. Fernald (1912), 525; and P. E. Bowers (1917), 83.

120. *Snow*, 291 S.W.2d, at 560.

121. *Snow*, at 561.

122. *Snow*, at 562.

123. *Snow*, 291 S.W.2d, Shepard Test., 188¶4. See also *Snow*, Dr. Bozeman Test., Trial Tr. 197¶2.

124. *Snow*, Shepard Test., 189¶2.

125. *Snow*, Shepard Test., 193¶4. See also *Snow*, 291 S.W.2d, at 560–62.

126. See, e.g., *Arnold*, 873 S.W.2d, Beaird Test., Trial Tr. 81¶1; and *Arnold*, Sarrels Test., Trial Tr. 117¶2.

127. See G. G. Fernald (1912), 545.

128. G. G. Fernald (1912), 545.

129. Hale (1995), 4–5, 190; Grob (1991), 190–91.

130. Grob (1991), 190–91; Grob (1983), 41–69; Hale (1995), 190, 207.

131. Hale (1995), 209.

Chapter 3

1. Lane (1995), 106–7.

2. Statement of Nathan F. Leopold Jr., May 31, 1924, Northwestern University, pp. 2–9, https://homicide.northwestern.edu/docs_fk/homicide/5866/LeopoldStatement.pdf (accessed April 28, 2022).

3. "The Perfect Crime: In Love with Murder," transcript, *PBS*, April 10, 2018, https://www.pbs.org/wgbh/americanexperience/films/perfectcrime/#transcript (accessed April 28, 2022).

4. *Chicago Daily News*, July 29, August 4, and September 10, 1924, p. 3; Statement of Nathan F. Leopold Jr., 9.

5. Fass (1993), 922.

6. McKernan (1924), 54.

7. Fass (1993), 931.

8. Fass (1993), 932–33.

9. Covert, cited in Hale (1995), 92.

10. Hale (1995), 92–93.

11. *Chicago Daily News*, August 1, 1924.

12. Fass (1993), 940–41; Hale (1995), 93.

13. Glueck (1932), 33.

14. Hale (1995), 93.

15. Fass (1993), 933–34.

16. Dr. H. S. Hulbert, cited in Sellers (1926), 30.

17. Fass (1993), 934.

18. Hale (1995), 93. See McKernan (1924), 378–79.

19. Sellers (1926), 174.

20. See, e.g., *Gephart v. State*, 249 S.W.2d 612 (Tex.Crim.App. 1952); *Moon v. State*, 331 S.W.2d; and *Leath v. State*, 346 S.W.2d 346 (Tex.Crim.App. 1961).

21. American Psychiatric Association (1980).

22. Zaretsky (2005), 332.

23. Burnham (1988), 53, 33. See Freud (1953); and Watson (1919), 195; and in general, see Bernard (1925) and Liddell (1960).

24. Zaretsky (2005), 332–33.

25. For expert witness testimonies using defendants' difficult relationships with their parents to explain their mental illnesses, personality disorders, and criminal behaviors, see, e.g., *Morgan v. State*, 117 S.W.2d, Dr. Swope Test., Trial Tr. 105; *Freeman v. State*, 317 S.W.2d 726 (Tex.Crim.App. 1958), Dr. Crow Test., Trial Tr. vol. 2, 359:10–361:3, 362:15–363:8; and *Bryan v. State*, 406 S.W.2d 210 (Tex.Crim.App. 1966), Dr. Crow Aff. Def's Hr'g on Am. Mot. for New Trial, 622¶4.

26. Zaretsky (2005), 333.

27. Schorske (1980).

28. Zaretsky (2005), 5, 23.

29. Zaretsky (2005), 5–6.

30. See Rieff (1979), 329–57.

31. Fingarette (1972), 86.

32. See, e.g., Hoedemaker (1948), 7; Committee on Psychiatry and Law (1954), 6; and Roche (1958), 229–30.

33. Fingarette (1972), 86–91; Waelder (1960).

34. *Rubenstein v. State*, 407 S.W.2d, Dr. Guttmacher Test., Trial Tr. vol. 5, 1086:17–1087:5.

35. See Chapter 1, Section "Biological Explanations of Mental Illness and Criminality," Subsection "The Theory of Reflex Action and the Theory of Instincts."

36. Fingarette (1972), 87–88.

37. See, e.g., *McCaine v. State*, 211 S.W.2d 190 (Tex.Crim.App. 1948); *Gephart*, 249 S.W.2d; *Moon*, 331 S.W.2d; and *Rubenstein*, 407 S.W.2d.

38. See, e.g., *Morgan*, 117 S.W.2d, Dr. Swope Test., Trial Tr. 109–110; *McCaine*, 211 S.W.2d, Dr. Waterman Test., Trial Tr. 82: 21–83:15; *Gephart*, 249 S.W.2d, Def's Ex. 4, Report of Staff Meeting of Austin State Hospital of April 25, 1950 vol. 2, 115; *Gephart*, Def's Ex. 5, Psychological Report Dated March 28, 1950, vol. 2, 115; *Freeman*, 317 S.W.2d, Dr. Crow Test., Trial Tr. vol. 2, 362:1–14, 374:10–25; and *Rubenstein*, 407 S.W.2d, Dr. Guttmacher Test., Trial Tr. vol. 5, 1122:15–20.

39. See, e.g., *Morgan*, Dr. Swope Test., 113¶2–3; *McCaine*, Dr. Waterman Test., 85:4–22; *Freeman*, 317 S.W.2d, Dr. Finney Test., Trial Tr. vol. 1, 127:18–128:2; *Freeman*, Dr. Crow Test., vol. 2, 355:24–356:13; *Rubenstein*, Dr. Guttmacher Test., vol. 5, 1115:1–17, 1116:16–22; and *Bryan*, 406 S.W.2d, Dr. Crow Aff. Def's Hr'g on Am. Mot. for New Trial, 623¶2.

40. See, e.g., *McCaine*, 211 S.W.2d, Dist. Att'y Winborn Quest. Dr. Waterman Test., Trial Tr. 91:22–92:13; *Freeman*, 317 S.W.2d, Asst. Dist. Att'y Briscoe Quest. Dr. Dwyer Test., Trial Tr. vol. 1, 285:7–289:25, contra *Freeman*, Dr. Crow Test., vol. 2, 355:1–23; *Moon*, 331 S.W.2d, Asst. Dist. Att'y Briscoe Quest. Dr. Walter Test., Trial Tr. vol. 2, 257:13–21; and *Rubenstein*, 407 S.W.2d, State Att'y Bowie Hyp. Quest. Dr. Stubblefield Test., Trial Tr. vol. 6, 1264:21–1265:17.

41. Freud (1961a), 28, 34–39, 55–56. See Denno (2005), 617–18.

42. Fingarette (1972), 110–11.

43. Fingarette (1972), 112–13. See also Nunberg (1948), 192–93.

44. Fingarette (1972), 113–14.

45. See also Wolberg (1954), 516; Waelder (1960), 187; and Kubie (1960), 155–56.

46. Freud (1957b), 332–33; Freud (1961a), 52; Freud (1961b), 186–87. See, in general, Fenichel (1945); Rapaport (1960); and Fitzpatrick (1976), 69.

47. Freud (1957b), 332–33.

48. Freud (1957b), 333. Freud never developed his ideas into a fully fledged criminological theory. However, his brief analysis on the relationship between childhood development and criminality inspired the work of several neo-Freudian theorists—including August Aichhorn, Melanie Klein, Franz Alexander, Hugo Staub, Otto Fenichel, Fritz Redl, and David Wineman—who would deeply influence the American debate on mental illness and crime in the 1950s and 1960s.

49. See Hale (1995), 47, 53, 89–90; and Freud (1961c; 2014).

50. See Freud (1957b), 333; and Freud (1961a).

51. See Hale (1995), 89–91.

52. See, e.g., Healy and Bronner (1943); Friedlander (1949), 206, 214; F. Alexander and Staub (1956); Aichhorn (1963); Spock (1956; 1963); and Kawin (1963).

53. Hartman (2008), 56.

54. For psychoanalytic critiques of the tolerant approach to childhood education, see, e.g., A. M. Johnson (1949), 225, 228, 235; and Bergler and Meerloo (1963). See, in general, Hale (1995), 231, 233–34; and Zaretsky (2005), 278–79. For critiques by criminal justice officials, see Hoover (1943; 1963).

55. According to Andrew Hartman (2008), "The Cold War panic over juvenile delinquency was metaphorical: what was often mistaken for delinquent behavior was, in fact, nothing more than a superficial teenage subculture that failed to conform to stricter-than-usual adult norms and expectations, a stringency born of the anxieties associated with the Cold War" (56). But see Hoover (1963), 663.

56. *Moon*, 331 S.W.2d. See also *Alvarado v. State*, 912 S.W.2d 199 (Tex.Crim.App. 1995); and *Penry v. State*, 178 S.W.3d.

57. *Moon*, at 312.

58. *Moon*, Dr. Wagner Test., Trial Tr. vol. 2, 184:15–185:10.

59. *Moon*, Dr. Wagner Test., vol. 2, 186:25–187:1.

60. *Moon*, Dr. Wagner Test., vol. 2, 187:23–25.

61. *Moon*, Dr. Wagner Test., vol. 2, 188:1–189:17.

62. *Moon*, Dr. Wagner Test., vol. 2, 190:11–18.

63. *Moon*, Dr. Wagner Test., vol. 2, 191:14–23.

64. *Moon*, W. V. Moon Test., Trial Tr. vol. 2, 338:7–339:24.

65. *Moon*, Dr. Wagner Test., vol. 2, 193:2–10.

66. *Moon*, Dr. Wagner Test., vol. 2, 194:19–22.

67. *Moon*, Dr. Wagner Test., vol. 2, 193:15–19.

68. *Moon*, Dr. Wagner Test., vol. 2, 204:6–205:5.

69. *Moon*, Dr. Sher Test., Trial Tr. vol. 2, 231:20–232:19.

70. *Moon*, Dr. Sher Test., vol. 2, 234:21–235:1, 237:8–21, 247:24–248:18.

71. *Moon*, Dr. Sher Test., vol. 2, 250:7–14. See also *Moon*, Dr. Walter Test., Trial Tr. vol. 2, 257:8–259:19, 264:8–265:12.

72. *Moon*, Asst. Dist. Att'y Briscoe Quest. Gen. McArthur Moon Test., Trial Tr. vol. 2, 316:14–317:14.

73. Zaretsky (2005), 92.

74. See, e.g., *Morgan*, 117 S.W.2d, Dr. Swope Test., Trial Tr. 114¶2; *Freeman*, 317 S.W.2d, Dr. Finney Test., Trial Tr. vol. 1, 101:21–102:3, 120:1–121:12; *Freeman*, Dr. Crow Test., Trial Tr. vol. 2, 355:18–357:15; *Rubenstein*, 407 S.W.2d, Dr. Guttmacher Test., Trial Tr. vol. 5, 1096:4–17, 1097:13–15; *Morales v. State*, 458 S.W.2d 56 (Tex. Crim.App. 1970), Dr. Zyporyn Dep. Def's Mot. for New Trial, 14:12–16, 18:8–21; *Lackey v. State*, 819 S.W.2d, Ann Lackey Test., Trial Tr. vol. 32, 5249:12–5251:5; and *Lackey*, McBride Test., Trial Tr. vol. 32, 5301:13–5302:19.

75. A. Adler (1924), 13.

76. Ansbacher and Ansbacher (1956), 118.

77. A. Adler (1924), 14.

78. Ansbacher and Ansbacher (1956), 261.

79. Ansbacher and Ansbacher (1956), 261.

80. Zaretsky (2005), 94.

81. Ansbacher and Ansbacher (1956), 118; emphasis added.

82. Ansbacher and Ansbacher (1956), 250.

83. *Freeman*, 317 S.W.2d, at 727; *Freeman*, Freeman Conf., Trial Tr. vol. 1, 74:1–7.

84. *Freeman*, Freeman Conf., vol. 1, 75:6–8.

85. *Freeman*, Freeman Conf., vol. 1, 75:8–76:24.

86. *Freeman*, 317 S.W.2d, at 727–28.

87. *Freeman*, Dr. Finney Test., Trial Tr. vol. 1, 101:22–24.

88. *Freeman*, Freeman Conf., vol. 1, 75:14–18; emphasis added.

89. *Freeman*, Dr. Finney Test., vol. 1, 120:21–121:12.

90. According to Dr. Howard G. Crow, a Texan psychiatrist who had served in the army in various psychiatric evaluation units, Robert's feeling of "not being a man" was typical among individuals affected by paranoid schizophrenia: "The male, the man with the mental illness, fundamentally complains about his masculinity. Am I a man? Am I adequate? Do I fit in? He has feelings of terrible inferiority, of inadequacy of *not being a man*" (*Freeman*, Dr. Crow Test., Trial Tr. vol. 2, 357:11–15; emphasis added).

91. *Freeman*, Dr. Finney Test., vol. 1, 119:4–10.

92. *Freeman*, Dr. Crow Test., vol. 2, 359:19–25.

93. *Freeman*, Dr. Crow Test., vol. 2, 360:2–6; emphasis added.

94. *Freeman*, Dr. Crow Test., vol. 2, 360:18–23; emphasis added.

95. *Freeman*, Dr. Crow Test., vol. 2, 360:23–361:2.

96. *Freeman*, Dr. Crow Test., vol. 2, 361:2–7.

97. *Freeman*, Dr. Crow Test., vol. 2, 361:7–21; *Freeman*, Dr. Finney Test., vol. 1, 145:19–22.

98. *Freeman*, Dr. Crow Test., vol. 2, 356:16–357:6, 361:25–362:14.

99. *Freeman*, Dr. Dwyer Test., Trial Tr. vol. 2, 288:18–289:12.

100. *Freeman*, Dist. Att'y Briscoe Cl. Arg., Trial Tr. vol. 3, 8:12–24.

101. *Freeman*, Dist. Att'y Briscoe Quest. Dr. Finney Test., Trial Tr. vol. 1, 111:21–112:17.

102. *Freeman*, Dr. Crow Test., vol. 2, 355:24–356:18, 361:19–21.

103. See, e.g., Levy (1943), Strecker (1946), and Gorer (1948).

104. See, e.g., Levy (1937); Friedlander (1949); and Bowlby (1951), 2: 11. See, in general, Polat (2021).

105. Lindquist (2012), 159.

106. Lindquist (2012), 161, 163–64.

107. See Levy (1937); Friedlander (1949); and Bowlby (1951), 2: 11. Whereas psychoanalysts traced the cause of the American "masculinity crisis" (and its associated criminal involvement) back to failures in early parenting, public intellectuals such as

William Whyte and Arthur Schlesinger Jr. linked it to the loss of individual male autonomy stemming from the advent of mass conformism and white-collar work. See Whyte (2013) and Schlesinger (1958). In this view, as the American male escaped the "unendurable burden of freedom" and retreated into the protective "womb" of social conformism and corporate culture, he lost his sense of self and, with it, his gender identity and masculine prowess (Schlesinger 1958).

108. Lindquist (2012), 161.

109. See, e.g., Hoover (1956–1957).

110. Lindquist (2012), 164–65.

111. Kardiner and Ovesey (1967), 65.

112. Kardiner and Ovesey (1967), 302; Lindquist (2012), 164.

113. Kardiner and Ovesey (1967), 345; Lindquist (2012), 166.

114. Lindquist (2012), 164.

115. Moynihan (1965), 5; Lindquist (2012), 180.

116. Moynihan (1965), 29.

117. Moynihan (1965), 29.

118. Pettigrew (1964), 15–16; Lindquist (2012), 175.

119. Moynihan (1965), 31, 38–40; Lindquist (2012), 181.

120. Moynihan (1965), 36, 38.

121. This view was popularized by nonspecialized writers. For example, in his bestselling collection of essays *Generation of Vipers*, fiction and satire author Philip Wylie coined the concept of Momism, a derogatory term used to describe American men's excessive attachment to their mothers and the negative consequences of this attachment for their sense of manhood (Wylie 1942, 48–51, 184–204). For an insightful discussion of the ideological dimension of this debate, see Cuordileone (2012), 124–66.

122. Lindquist (2012), 174.

123. Ethnic minority defendants' ongoing reliance on lay witnesses is likely related to the lack, until *Ake v. Oklahoma*, 470 U.S. 68 (1985), of a constitutional mandate requiring states to offer a free psychiatric consultation to indigent defendants raising an insanity claim.

124. See Appendix, Table 5.

125. Fanon (2008), 117; emphasis added.

126. Fanon (2008), 118–19.

127. See López (2006a), 998.

128. Perkinson (2010), 236.

129. American Psychiatric Association (1968).

130. Connell (1987), 184.

Chapter 4

1. Karpman (1946), 281.

2. See Maughs (1941); Graham (1962), 446; Pichot (1978); Werlinder (1978); Rafter (1997b; 2004); and Horley (2014), 92.

3. Koch (1892). See Kiehl and Hoffman (2011). The term *psychopath* had already

appeared in an Austrian psychiatric textbook by Ernst von Feuchtersleben in 1845 (Werlinder 1978, 86n2; Rafter 1997b, 241). However, rather than indicating a specific personality disorder that manifested itself in delinquent tendencies, it was used as an umbrella category that included various mental disabilities affecting the "empirical" (i.e., the "psycho-physical") rather than the "ethical" spheres of the human mind (C. L. Burns 1954, 193).

4. Healy (1915); Glueck (1918a; 1918b; 1923).

5. Cleckley (1941).

6. Graham (1962), 446.

7. Hulbert (1939). See Rafter (1997a), 168, 173–74.

8. Cleckley (1941), 273–76; Bromberg (1948), 166–67.

9. Zaretsky (2005), 284.

10. Zaretsky (2005), 284–85.

11. Zaretsky (2005), 285.

12. For an influential writing illustrating Americans' concern with psychological immaturity, emasculation, and its potential dangers for the United States' geopolitical influence during the Cold War, see Schlesinger (1949). For a general discussion of the links between the "ethics of maturity" and postwar anticommunist propaganda, see Hartman (2008), 58.

13. See Lindner (1956), 183; Rieff (1990), 8; Passerini (1997), 2: 322; and Zaretsky (2005), 285.

14. See, e.g., Levine (1940); Glueck and Glueck (1943); Banay (1943); Lindner (1944); Karpman (1935; 1946; 1948); Bromberg (1947); Bromberg (1953–1954), 172; and Mayer (1948), 578.

15. Lipton (1949), 584–86.

16. Lipton (1949), 586.

17. Lipton (1949), 587.

18. Karpman (1935), 274–75.

19. Karpman (1935), 274.

20. Karpman (1935), 275. See also Bromberg (1948), 112; Hoedemaker (1948); Bender (1947); Bromberg (1953–1954); and Graham (1962).

21. *McCaine v. State*, 211 S.W.2d, Dr. Waterman Test., Trial Tr. 81:28–82:12, 84:20–24. See also *Gephart v. State*, 249 S.W.2d, Def's Ex. 4, Report of Staff Meeting of Austin State Hospital of April 25, 1950, vol. 2, 115; *Gephart*, Def's Ex. 5, Psychological Report Dated March 28, 1950, vol. 2, 115; *Bingham v. State*, 290 S.W.2d 915 (Tex. Crim.App. 1956), Dr. Koeninger Test., Trial Tr. 307; *Bingham*, Dr. Schinkler Test., Trial Tr. 333; and *Bingham*, Dr. Grice Test., Trial Tr. 351.

22. *McCaine*, 211 S.W.2d, at 192.

23. *McCaine*, at 192–93.

24. *McCaine*, Dr. Choate Test., Trial Tr. 75:1–4; *McCaine*, Melba McCaine Test., Trial Tr. 53:14–21, 58:25–28.

25. *McCaine*, Dr. Choate Test., 74:17–75:4, 75:15–22; *McCaine*, Melba McCaine Test., 54:8–28; *McCaine*, Curtis Test., Trial Tr. 51:22–52:17.

26. *McCaine*, Dr. Choate Test., 76:3–6.
27. *McCaine*, Dr. Waterman Test., 81:28–82:4.
28. *McCaine*, Dr. Waterman Test., 82:5–9.
29. *McCaine*, Dr. Waterman Test., 82:21–83:15.
30. *McCaine*, Dr. Waterman Test., 82:13–21.
31. *McCaine*, Dr. Waterman Test., 85:4–22.
32. *McCaine*, Dr. Waterman Test., 84:20–24. See also *McCaine*, Melba McCaine Test., 63:16–20. Along these lines, the expert witnesses testifying in the trial of Leonard Lionel Bingham, a white man convicted of murder in 1956, diagnosed the defendant with a psychopathic personality disorder, describing him as an emotionally immature, impulsive, and irresponsible individual who, because of an early halt in psychosexual development, was unable to postpone immediate gratification in view of future rewards. See *Bingham*, 290 S.W.2d, Dr. Koeninger Test., Trial Tr. 297, 299, 302; *Bingham*, Dr. Schinkler Test., 334; and *Bingham*, Dr. Grice Test., 352–353.
33. *McCaine*, Dr. Waterman Test., 84:21–24.
34. The defendant's first wife, Melba McCaine, explained their divorce in the following terms: "I found it necessary to divorce the defendant primarily because of financial difficulties. It was Depression times. He didn't have a job and he changed frequently. He never kept a job very long" (*McCaine*, Melba McCaine Test., 53:14–17).
35. Arlie Loughnan first used the term *dispositional* to describe the ontological view of mental illness at its intersection with crime advanced by the criminal law. By this term, she means that mental illness is viewed as a relatively fixed personal characteristic, which is embedded in the psychological makeup of the individual and can manifest itself in various antisocial behaviors. This notion seems to suggest a deep-seated tendency in criminal law to frame mental illness as a mix of internal disposition and action, something inscribed into the character of the individual and interpretable in behavioral terms. See Loughnan (2012), 49–57.
36. See, e.g., *Bingham*, 290 S.W.2d, Dr. Koeninger Test., Trial Tr. 294–309; and *Leath v. State*, 346 S.W.2d, Dr. Grice Test., Trial Tr. 134–146.
37. For a parental rejection argument, see, e.g., *Johnston v. State*, 396 S.W.2d 404 (Tex.Crim.App. 1965), Dr. Rubin Test., Trial Tr. 176:3–178:21; and *Freeman v. State*, 317 S.W.2d, Dr. Crow Test., Trial Tr. vol. 2, 360:18–23. For theories linking maternal overprotection with pathological sexual conduct, see, e.g., *Gephart*, 249 S.W.2d, Def's Ex. 5, Psychological Report Dated March 28, 1950, vol. 2, 115.
38. *McCaine*, Dr. Waterman Test., 82:5–9.
39. *Woodson v. North Carolina*, 428 U.S. 280 (1976); *Lockett v. Ohio*, 438 U.S. 536 (1978); and *Eddings v. Oklahoma*, 455 U.S. 104 (1982).
40. Polat (2021), 274.
41. See Fass (1993), 942–44.
42. For a discussion of the historical processes that prompted the transition from an understanding of sexual deviance as "motivated by racial or biological dispositions" to an interpretation of it as a psychological pathology and personality disorder requiring close psychiatric attention, see Hamm (2001), 38–41.

43. Hale (1995), 4.

44. Freedman (1987), 86; Hale (1971); Burnham (1973); Robinson (1976).

45. Freedman (1987), 86–87, 89.

46. According to U.S. historian Estelle Freedman, "The legitimization of male aggression during World War II and the shift of national attention toward external enemies combined to reduce the focus on violent sexual crimes" in the 1940s (Freedman 1987, 96).

47. Freedman (1987), 83–84. See also Glueck (1937).

48. Freedman (1987), 94. See, e.g., Hoover, cited in Frosch and Bromberg (1939); and Hoover (1947).

49. Freedman (1987), 84. See also Swanson (1960); and Brakel and Rock (1971), 362–65.

50. Lave (2008), 549.

51. Bowie and Williamson (1959), 915.

52. See De Orio (2017).

53. Karpman (1947), 206–7.

54. Karpman (1947), 207–8.

55. Karpman (1947), 221.

56. Freedman (1987), 91; Karpman (1940), 204; Karpman (1954), 501. See also Rouke (1950), 451; and Geil (1945; 1948).

57. See Chapter 1, Section "Cultural Influences and Moral Framework," Subsection "American Psychiatry and the Doctrine of Civilization."

58. Hartman (2008), 18; Hall (1904).

59. For examples of expert witnesses conflating homosexuality, sex offenses, and criminal psychopathy, see *Gephart*, 249 S.W.2d, Dr. Hoerster Aff. Def's First Am. Mot. for New Trial, 72¶2–73¶1; and *Leath*, 346 S.W.2d, Dr. Holbrook Test., Trial Tr. 241:11–24. For later cases drawing from psychoanalytic theory to explain "pathological" sexual assaults, see, e.g., *Gribble v. State*, 808 S.W.2d 65, 75–76 (Tex.Crim. App. 1990).

60. *Gephart*, 249 S.W.2d, at 614.

61. *Gephart*, at 615.

62. *Gephart*, Def's Ex. 4, vol. 2, 115.

63. *Gephart*, Def's Ex. 5, vol. 2, 115.

64. The chief defense expert in the trial of Leon Willis Johnston, a white man convicted of the rape of an 8-year-old girl, similarly associated the defendant's pathological relationship with his parents with his sexually deviant behaviors, which included masturbating obsessively, engaging in homosexual relations, and repeatedly raping his 2-year-old child. See *Johnston v. State*, 396 S.W.2d, Dr. Rubin Test., Trial Tr. 176:3–178:21.

65. See also *Gephart*, Dr. Boelsch Test., Trial Tr. vol. 1, 117¶2,4–119¶1, 121¶3–4.

66. *Gephart*, Dr. Martin Test., Trial Tr. vol. 1, 156¶2–163¶1.

67. *Gephart*, Flournoy Test., Trial Tr. vol. 1, 74¶4–78¶2; *Gephart*, Hart Test., Trial Tr. vol. 1, 164¶2–171¶1.

68. *Gephart*, Dr. Waide Test., Trial Tr. vol. 1, 78¶3–90¶3; *Gephart*, Dr. Hanretta Test., Trial Tr. vol. 1, 104¶3–114¶1; *Gephart*, Dr. Kuehne Test., Trial Tr. vol. 1, 90¶4–104¶1.

69. *Gephart*, Flournoy Test., vol. 1, 77¶2–78¶1.

70. *Gephart*, Dr. Martin Test., vol. 1, 158¶1; *Gephart*, Hart Test., vol. 1, 165¶4–166¶1, 167¶3–168¶1. The state experts who evaluated Gephart's mental state before the capital punishment proceedings concurred with the other state witnesses that the defendant was a sane individual and a "sex pervert." See *Gephart*, Dr. Waide Test., vol. 1, 79¶2; *Gephart*, Dr. Kuehne Test., vol. 1, 91¶3–92¶2; and *Gephart*, Dr. Hanretta Test., vol. 1, 105¶2–106¶2.

71. For a history of civil commitment laws for violent sex offenders in the United States, see Walsh (2017), 880–87. In the 1990s and early 2000s, Texas and 20 other states passed sexually violent predator laws, which allow for the civil commitment of violent sex offenders if they are deemed to be at risk of reoffending following their release from prison. See, e.g., Turner et al. (2015). Despite their potential for abuse, the U.S. Supreme Court has repeatedly upheld the constitutionality of such statutes. See *Kansas v. Hendricks*, 521 U.S. 346 (1997); and *Kansas v. Crane*, 534 U.S. 407 (2002).

72. *Gephart*, 249 S.W.2d, at 614.

73. Freedman (1987), 103. For Texas, see De Orio (2017), 56–57.

74. Texas decriminalized same-sex sodomy in the early 2000s, when the U.S. Supreme Court held sodomy laws unconstitutional in *Lawrence v. Texas*, 539 U.S. 558 (2003).

75. Freedman (1987), 103–4. See East (1946); Haines et al. (1948), 425; De River (1949); Gerassi (1966); and Bowman and Engle (1953), 117–19. See, in general, Schmeiser (2008).

76. Freedman (1987), 103.

77. Zaretsky (2005), 299–300.

78. Zaretsky (2005), 111. See Freud (1955), 100, 110–12; and Freud (1964), 188.

79. See, e.g., Ràdo (1940); Socarides (1979), 246; and Bayer (1981), 28–30.

80. Socarides, cited in Bayer (1981), 36.

81. Zaretsky (2005), 300; Lewes (1988), 74–93.

82. *Gephart*, 249 S.W.2d, Dr. Hoerster Aff. Def's First Am. Mot. for New Trial, 72–74.

83. *Gephart*, Dr. Hoerster Aff., 72¶2–73¶1; cf. Lorand (1939), 178.

84. *Gephart*, Dr. Hoerster Aff., 72¶3, 73¶2.

85. *Leath*, 346 S.W.2d.

86. *Leath*, at 347.

87. *Leath*, Dr. Grice Test., Trial Tr. 138:11–139:2, 141:1–6.

88. *Leath*, Dr. Grice Test., 109:20–25.

89. *Leath*, Dr. Grice Test., 110:1–111:5, *Leath*, Guynes Test., Trial Tr. 178:3–13, 178:20–179:16; contra *Leath*, Debets Test., Trial Tr. 304:1–11; and *Leath*, Campbell Test., Trial Tr. 341:1–4.

90. *Leath*, Dr. Holbrook Test., Trial Tr. 231:13–17.

91. *Leath*, Dr. Holbrook Test., 245:21–246:1.

92. *Leath*, Dr. Holbrook Test., 241:11–24.

93. See De Orio (2017).

94. *Leath*, Dr. Holbrook Test., 241:24–242:16.

95. *Leath*, Dr. Holbrook Test., 241:24–242:16.

96. *Leath*, Dr. Holbrook Test., 265:21–266:21.

97. *Leath*, Dr. Holbrook Test., 265:21–266:21; emphasis added.

98. *Leath*, 346 S.W.2d, at 348.

99. *Leath*, 346 S.W.2d, at 348.

100. *Gephart*, 249 S.W.2d, Dr. Hoerster Aff., 72¶2–73¶1; *Johnston*, 396 S.W.2d, Dr. Rubin Test., Trial Tr. 178:1–20.

101. *Leath*, Dr. Holbrook Test., 241:11–24, 265:21–266:5.

102. Zaretsky (2005), 309–10.

103. Zaretsky (2005), 307.

104. Riesman et al. (1961).

105. Zaretsky (2005), 310.

106. See also Susman (2012), xix–xxviii.

107. Zaretsky (2005), 110. See Freud (1957a), 88, 91, 95–97; and Freud (1958), 318.

108. Zaretsky (2005), 312–13; Lowenfeld and Lowenfeld (1970).

109. Zaretsky (2005), 314. See, e.g., Kernberg (1975).

110. Cleckley (1941), 241–42. See also H. M. Adler (1920); and Hulbert (1939), 5, 8.

111. Cleckley (1941), 255.

112. Cleckley (1941), 238, 240.

113. Cleckley (1941), 239–40, 246.

114. Kohut (1978), 479.

115. Zaretsky (2005), 314.

116. Zaretsky (2005), 315. See Kohut (1978), 803; and Kohut (1971), 64, 46.

117. *Rubenstein*, 407 S.W.2d. For later cases in which the expert witnesses framed psychopaths as charismatic and manipulative subjects, see, e.g., *Adams v. State*, 577 S.W.2d 717 (Tex.Crim.App. 1979), Dr. Grigson Test., Trial Tr. 1408:6–15; *Burks v. State*, 583 S.W.2d, Dr. Buch Test., Trial Tr. vol. 1, 527:11–529:22; *Burks*, Dr. Grigson Test., Trial Tr. vol. 1, 7624:22–7626:1; *Hawkins v. State*, 613 S.W.2d, Dr. Grigson Test., Trial Tr. vol. 9, 1815:19–1819:19; and *Alvarado v. State*, 912 S.W.2d, Edgemon Test., Trial Tr. vol. 38, 62:12–24, 66:21–67:7.

118. The relevance of Ruby's Jewish ancestry for an understanding of the climate surrounding his capital punishment proceeding will become evident later.

119. *Rubenstein*, 407 S.W.2d, at 794.

120. *Rubenstein*, State Att'y Bowie Hyp. Quest. Dr. Stubblefield Test., Trial Tr. vol. 6, 1264:21–1265:17.

121. *Rubenstein*, Dist. Att'y Wade Quest. Dr. Bromberg Test., Trial Tr. vol. 7, 1414:4–1420:23.

122. *Rubenstein*, 407 S.W.2d, at 794–95.

123. *Rubenstein*, Dr. Schafer Test., Trial Tr. vol. 4, 863:11–22; *Rubenstein*, Dr. Gut-

tmacher Test., Trial Tr. vol. 5, 1056:13–25, 1086:1–8; *Rubenstein*, Dr. Bromberg Test., Trial Tr. vol. 7, 1395:11–1396:8.

124. *Rubenstein*, Dr. Schafer Test., vol. 4, 928:12–929:4, 937:2–8; *Rubenstein*, Dr. Guttmacher Test., vol. 5, 1086:17–1087:20; *Rubenstein*, Dr. Bromberg Test., vol. 7, 1396:5–23.

125. *Rubenstein*, Dr. Schafer Test., vol. 4, 872:16–873:2, 924:21–926:4, 928:12–929:4; *Rubenstein*, Dr. Guttmacher Test., vol. 5, 1086:10–25, 1092:23–1093:14.

126. *Rubenstein*, Dr. Schafer Test., vol. 4, 867:9–16.

127. *Rubenstein*, Dr. Schafer Test., 848:14–649:1, 916:6–22, 917:13–918:2. See also *Rubenstein*, Dr. Guttmacher Test., vol. 5, 1093:21–1094:20.

128. *Rubenstein*, Dist. Att'y Wade Quest. Dr. Schafer Test., Trial Tr. vol. 4, 953:12–17.

129. *Rubenstein*, Dr. Schafer Test., vol. 4, 953:21–954:3.

130. See also *Rubenstein*, Howard Test., Trial Tr. vol. 3, 658:5–23.

131. *Rubenstein*, Dr. Schafer Test., vol. 4, 928:12–929:4. See also *Rubenstein*, Dr. Guttmacher Test., vol. 5, 1093:21–1094:20.

132. *Rubenstein*, Dr. Guttmacher Test., vol. 5, 1059:2–4.

133. *Rubenstein*, Dr. Guttmacher Test., vol. 5, 1094:22–25.

134. *Rubenstein*, Dr. Guttmacher Test., vol. 5, 1079:16–1080:4. See also *Rubenstein*, Dr. Bromberg Test., vol. 7, 1426:3–1427:11.

135. *Rubenstein*, Dr. Guttmacher Test., vol. 5, 1086:17–25, 1094:22–25.

136. *Rubenstein*, Dr. Guttmacher Test., 1096:4–17, 1097:13–15. The defense experts' emphasis on Ruby's sense of inferiority and masculinity issues, along with their association with his difficult family relationships, recalls Adler's theories of the inferiority complex and the masculine protest discussed in Chapter 3, Section "Alfred Adler, the Theory of Inferiority, and the Masculine Protest." See Ansbacher and Ansbacher (1956), 108–12, 114–19, 249–50, 257–61.

137. *Rubenstein*, Dr. Guttmacher Test., 1097:17–21. See also *Rubenstein*, Templin Test., Trial Tr. vol. 3 615:10–616:9, 618:20–25, 620:19–621:3; *Rubenstein*, Howard Test., Trial Tr. vol. 3, 648:5–11, 649:10–14; and *Rubenstein*, Dr. Towler Test., Trial Tr. 982:7–984:6.

138. *Rubenstein*, Dr. Guttmacher Test., vol. 5, 1122:15–20.

139. *Rubenstein*, Dr. Guttmacher Test., vol. 5, 1100:4–10.

140. *Rubenstein*, Dr. Guttmacher Test., vol. 5, 1109:7–9, 1115:1–17, 1116:16–22.

141. *Rubenstein*, Asst. Dist. Att'y Alexander Quest. Dr. Guttmacher Test., Trial Tr. vol. 5, 1152:17–1153:19. *Rubenstein*, Att'y Wade Quest. Howard Test., Trial Tr. vol. 3, 656:1–22, 658:5–23.

142. *Rubenstein*, Dist. Att'y Wade Quest. Dr. Bromberg Test., Trial Tr. vol. 7, 1435:20–1436:18.

143. *Rubenstein*, 407 S.W.2d, at 796.

Chapter 5

1. Eysenck (2014), 206.

2. Zaretsky (2005), 334. See, e.g., Gitelson (1964), 462–63; Grünbaum (1984); Kurzweil (1989), 252; and Luhrmann (2000), 173, 176.

3. Andreasen (2006), 108. See, e.g., Kendell et al. (1971; 1975) and Rosenhan (1973).

4. Grünbaum, cited in Zaretsky (2005), 335.

5. Zaretsky (2005), 335.

6. See, in general, Murray (2006) and Kaut (2011).

7. Zaretsky (2005), 334.

8. See Melossi (2008), 197–252.

9. In this chapter I use the diagnoses of psychopathy, sociopathy, and antisocial personality disorder interchangeably, in line with contemporary practice. Weisman (2008), 197.

10. See Garland (2001) and Simon (2007).

11. Melossi (2008), 199–200. See also Perkinson (2010), 294–97, 334–37.

12. Perkinson (2010), 295–96. See Cronin et al. (1981), 60, 69, 75; and Carter (1996), 30.

13. Perkinson (2010), 296–97.

14. Perkinson (2010), 6.

15. Melossi (2008), 205, 210.

16. Melossi (2008), 219. See, e.g., Bennett et al. (1996).

17. Perkinson (2010), 296–97.

18. During his eight-year presidency (1993–2001), Bill Clinton criticized the right's radical individualism for disintegrating America's social and moral fabric and advocated for a return to community values of social inclusion and mutual obligation. However, rather than translating these ideals into a rehabilitative criminal justice program aimed at reintegrating criminal offenders into "healthy" communities of living, he engaged in a bidding war against his political opponents "to increase penalties for crime" and gather electoral support from the American people. This political competition became strikingly clear in 1994, when Clinton signed a federal crime bill (the Violent Crime Control and Law Enforcement Act, Pub.L. 103–322) that created harsher sentencing laws and offered states federal funding to incentivize the construction of prisons, prompting the steepest rise in incarceration rates ever registered under an American president (Ofer 2019). On Bill Clinton's relationship to communitarianism, see Marshall (2012) and Etzioni (1993).

19. See Glass and Rud (2012), 95–99.

20. Reagan, cited in Beckett (1999), 49–50. See Perkinson (2010), 334.

21. Perkinson (2010), 334, 296, 340. See Nixon (1967); Beckett (1999), 38; Parenti (2000), 8; Ivins and Dubose (2000), 154; and Robison (1995), A29.

22. Steiker and Steiker (2012), 224–25. In the 1930s the United States executed an average of 167 prisoners each year. In 1998, when the modern peak in executions occurred, a total of 98 prisoners were taken to the death chamber. See Death Penalty Information Center (2022b).

23. *Furman v. Georgia*, 408 U.S. 238 (1972).

24. Steiker and Steiker (2012), 225–26.

25. Death Penalty Information Center (2022a).

26. See, e.g., Texas Coalition Against the Death Penalty (2007; 2016).

27. See Appendix, Tables 3 and 4. Data on the racial breakdown of my sample was obtained from the Texas Department of Criminal Justice website. See Texas Department of Criminal Justice (2022).

28. See *Sattiewhite v. State*, 786 S.W.2d 271 (Tex.Crim.App. 1989).

29. See, e.g., *Burks v. State*, 583 S.W.2d; *Colburn v. State*, 966 S.W.2d; and *Penry v. State*, 178 S.W.3d.

30. For example, scholars have pointed to the inadequate legal representation provided to indigent capital defendants in the state's county courts, the numerous instances of official misconduct found in Texas capital punishment cases, and Texas courts' reliance on unethical and improper expert opinions to establish the defendants' mental state and/or predict their future behavior. See Bright (1994); Williams (2004), 635–43; and Acker (2017).

31. *Jurek v. Texas*, 428 U.S. 262 (1976). See Vartkessian (2011), 11–14.

32. Tex. Code Crim. Proc. Ann., art. 37.071(b) (1) (West 1974).

33. Tex. Code Crim. Proc. Ann., art. 37.071(b) (2). If the evidence raised the issue of provocation, jurors were required to answer a third "special issue" question, namely, "whether the conduct of the defendant in killing the deceased was unreasonable in response to the provocation, if any, by the deceased" (Tex. Code Crim. Proc. Ann., art. 37.071(b) (3)).

34. Tex. Code Crim. Proc. Ann., art. 37.071(f) (West 1974).

35. See, e.g., *Penry v. Lynaugh*, 492 U.S. 302 (1989); *Lackey v. State*, 819 S.W.2d; *Mines v. State*, 852 S.W.2d 941 (Tex.Crim.App. 1994); *Satterwhite v. State*, 858 S.W.2d; Dix (1976), 1343–1414; and Vartkessian et al. (2017).

36. *Woodson v. North Carolina*, 428 U.S. 280 (1976).

37. See Monahan (1981) and Wiebusch et al. (1995).

38. *Penry v. Lynaugh*, 492 U.S. 302 (1989).

39. For empirical research showing that mental illness, offered as a mitigating factor at sentencing, is often interpreted as aggravating, see, e.g., Berkman (1989).

40. Tex. Code Crim. Proc. Ann., art. 37.01(b)1–2 (West 1991); Vartkessian et al. (2017), 4.

41. These criteria were first established by the U.S. Court of Appeals for the Fifth Circuit. See *Turner v. Johnson*, 106 F.3d 1178, 1189 (5th Cir. 1997); *Wilkerson v. Collins*, 950 F.2d 1054, 1060 (5th Cir. 1992); and *Hughes v. Johnson*, 991 F.Supp 621, 632 (Dist. Ct.Tex.-Galveston 1998).

42. *Harris v. Johnson*, 81 F.3d 535, 539 (5th Cir. 1996); *Jones v. Johnson*, 171 F.3d 270, 276 (5th Cir. 1999); *Lackey*, 819 S.W.2d, at 134–36; *Goss v. State*, 826 S.W.2d 162, 165 (Tex.Crim.App. 1992); *Nobles v. State*, 843 S.W.2d 503, 506 (Tex.Crim.App. 1992); *Richardson v. State*, 879 S.W.2d 874, 6–7 (Tex.Crim.App. 1993); *Satterwhite*, 858 S.W.2d, at 427; *Robison v. State*, 720 S.W.2d 808, 487 (Tex.Crim.App. 1994); contra *Mines*, 852 S.W.2d, at 952–56, 959–60.

43. *Ex parte Smith*, 309 S.W.3d 53, 60 (Tex.Crim.App. 2010); following the Fifth Circuit's reasoning in *Roy Gene Smith v. Quarterman*, 515 F.3d 392 (5th Cir. 2008). See also *Lackey*, 819 S.W.2d, at 131–32; and *Satterwhite*, 858 S.W.2d, at 426.

44. Amnesty International (2006); Texas Coalition Against the Death Penalty (2007).

45. See, e.g., *Lackey*, 819 S.W.2d; *Satterwhite*, 858 S.W.2d; *Robison*, 720 S.W.2d; and *Mines*, 852 S.W.2d. In 2004 the U.S. Supreme Court ruled that Texas's restrictions on defendants' right to a mitigation instruction were unconstitutional. See *Tennard v. Dretke*, 542 U.S. 274 (2004). Strikingly, interviews conducted with Texas capital jurors in the post-*Penry* era suggest that even when defendants were granted a mitigation instruction, such instruction had a limited effect on jurors' sentencing determination. See Vartkessian et al. (2017).

46. Vartkessian (2011), 135–36.

47. Vartkessian (2011), 136.

48. See, e.g., *Burks*, 583 S.W.2d; *Mines*, 852 S.W.2d; *Satterwhite*, 858 S.W.2d; and *Colburn*, 966 S.W.2d. For exceptions, see, e.g., *Alvarado v. State*, 912 S.W.2d.

49. Cheng (2010), 41.

50. Between 1974 and 1984 Texas substituted the traditional "right and wrong" test with a modified version of the American Law Institute's insanity standard. Tex. Penal Code Ann., § 8.01[a] (West 1974). Although Texas's new test extended the scope of the protection to include defendants who were "*incapable* of conforming [their] conduct to the requirements of the law [they] allegedly violated," there is no evidence to suggest that this short-lived change significantly modified the nature of the evidence presented at trial and/or jurors' receptivity to such evidence in capital punishment proceedings. See *Burks*, 583 S.W.2d; and *Hawkins v. State*, 613 S.W.2d; emphasis added. One reason for this is that, although the Texas legislature added a volitional prong to the traditional rules, it limited its impact by requiring defendants to demonstrate that they were "incapable" of conforming their conduct to legal requirements, an exceptionally high threshold that significantly limited the scope of the protection. See Bubany (1974), 312.

51. *Mitchell v. State*, 650 S.W.2d 801, 812 (Tex.Crim.App. 1983); *Smith v. State*, 683 S.W.2d 393, 407 (Tex.Crim.App. 1984); *Keeton v. State*, 724 S.W.2d 58, 61 (Tex.Crim. App. 1987); *Johnson v. State*, 853 S.W.2d 527, 531 (Tex.Crim.App. 1992).

52. Edens and Cox (2012), 239, 248; Edens et al. (2013), 175.

53. Edens et al. (2013), 175.

54. Cleckley (1976).

55. Hare (1993).

56. Cavadino (1998), 5–6.

57. Edens et al. (2013), 175.

58. Weisman (2008), 191–96.

59. Krafft-Ebing (1905), 623; Weisman (2008), 195.

60. Cleckley (1976), 337–64; Hare (1998), 106.

61. Weisman (2008), 198.

62. Loughnan (2012), 49–57.

63. See, e.g., *Penry*, 178 S.W.3d, Dr. Gripon Test., Trial Tr. vol. 46, 97:16–23; *Penry*, Asst. Dist. Att'y Hon Quest. Dr. Pincus Test., Trial Tr. vol. 51, 233:21–234: 2;

Penry, Asst. Dist. Att'y Hon Cl. Arg. on Punishment, vol. 58, 31:24–32:10; *Burks*, 583 S.W.2d, Dr. Grigson Test., Trial Tr. vol. 2, 557:16–566:16; *Burks*, Dr. Holbrook Test., Trial Tr. vol. 2, 796:11–798:22, 807:8–808:19; and *Burks*, Asst. Dist. Att'y Ludwick Cl. Arg. on Punishment, Trial Tr. vol. 2, 823:2–13.

64. *Penry*, Dist. Att'y Price Cl. Arg. on Punishment, vol. 58, 112:10–15.

65. *Penry*, Asst. Dist. Att'y Hon Quest. Dr. Gripon Test., Trial Tr. vol. 46, 113: 10–17.

66. Cleckley (1976), 434.

67. Hare (1993), 46–51.

68. See, e.g., *Burks*, 583 S.W.2d, Asst. Dist. Att'y Garrigan Cl. Arg. on Guilt or Innocence, Trial Tr. vol. 2, 698:9–703:8; *Wilkens v. State*, 847 S.W.2d 547 (Tex.Crim. App. 1992), Asst. Dist. Att'y Henry Quest. Dr. Allen Test., Trial Tr. vol. 31, 79:23–88:2; *Wilkens*, Asst. Dist. Att'y Henry Quest. Dr. McNeel Test., Trial Tr. vol. 31, 15:8–24:3; and *Penry*, 178 S.W.3d, Dr. Saunders Test., Trial Tr. vol. 43, 236:23–240:3.

69. See Tolson (2004); and Acker (2017), 764.

70. *Hawkins*, 613 S.W.2d, Dr. Grigson Test., Trial Tr. vol. 9, 1818:13–23.

71. *Hawkins*, Dist. Att'y Curtis Quest. Dr. Grigson Test., Trial Tr. vol. 9, 1819:14–17.

72. *Hawkins*, Dr. Grigson Test., vol. 9, 1819:18–19.

73. This practice was openly condemned by the TCCA on appeal. See *Hawkins*, 613 S.W.2d, at 727–29.

74. Weisman (2008), 199. See, e.g., Arrigo and Shipley (2001), 328–29.

75. Weisman (2008), 199. See, e.g., A. Abbott (2001), 296–98; and Blair et al. (2005).

76. *Wilkens*, 847 S.W.2d; but see *Alvarado*, 912 S.W.2d, Dr. Follett Test., Trial Tr. vol. 38, 168:18–170:10.

77. *Wilkens*, 847 S.W.2d, Dr. Allen Test., Trial Tr. vol. 33, 85:20–86:12.

78. *Wilkens*, Dr. Allen Test., vol. 33, 87:13–88:17. See also *Wilkens*, Dr. McNeel Test., Trial Tr. vol. 33, 26:19–31:16, 32:15–33:17.

79. Andreasen (2006), 110–11.

80. See, e.g., Kaut (2011), 205, 217. See, in general, Leeman (2007) and B. Lewis (2010).

81. Murray (2009), 285. See Kuppin and Carpiano (2006).

82. Murray (2009), 287–88; Murray (2011), 287.

83. Andreasen (2006), 111.

84. Andreasen (2006), 111.

85. *Woodson v. North Carolina*, 428 U.S., at 303–4; *Lockett v. Ohio*, 438 U.S., at 601–4; *Eddings v. Oklahoma*, 455 U.S., at 117–19 (Justice O'Connor, concurring).

86. Andreasen (2006), 111.

87. Lachter (2001), 313.

88. Murray (2006), 310–11; Murray (2011), 287–88; Jackson (2006); Joseph and Ratner (2013).

89. *Burks*, 583 S.W.2d, Dr. Vogtsberger Test., Trial Tr. vol. 1, 320:9–25, 325:3–7; *Colburn*, 966 S.W.2d, Dr. Quijano Test., Trial Tr. vol. 25, 219:22–220:6, 223:9–224:2.

90. Read and Harré (2001), 223–25; Sarbin and Mancuso (1970); Golding et al. (1975), 109; Schwartz and Schwartz (1977).

91. Mehta and Farina (1997).

92. Herman (2001).

93. Read and Harré (2001), 225. See O'Hagan (1992).

94. The evidence on jurors' reception of exculpatory and mitigating evidence based on organic causes (e.g., neuroscience and neuroimaging techniques) is mixed and somewhat discouraging. On the one hand, scholars have shown that defendants presenting evidence of brain injury are more likely to be found not guilty by reason of insanity than others who did not present such evidence (Gurley and Marcus 2008, 92). On the other hand, recent studies suggest that genetic and neurological evidence, whether alone or in combination with environmental factors, have a limited effect on jurors' decision at sentencing (N. Gordon and Greene 2018; Schweitzer and Saks 2011). I hypothesize that in Texas the structure of the state's capital sentencing scheme is more likely to turn evidence of organicity into a two-edged sword that promotes an image of dangerousness and death-worthiness rather than one of vulnerability and diminished responsibility.

95. *Burks*, 583 S.W.2d.

96. *Burks*, Burks Conf., Trial Tr. vol. 1, 308:7–310:13.

97. *Burks*, 583 S.W.2d, at 390.

98. *Burks*, Dr. Lett Test., Trial Tr. vol. 2, 656:7–16, 659:22–660:23.

99. *Burks*, Def. Att'y Cunningham Op. Arg. on Guilt or Innocence, Trial Tr. vol. 1, 312:1–313:21; *Burks*, Dr. Lewis Test., Trial Tr. vol. 1, 370:12–371:14; *Burks*, Dr. Harrington Test., Trial Tr. vol. 1, 380:11–19; *Burks*, Tillman Test., Trial Tr. vol. 1, 385:14–387:22; *Burks*, Robinson Test., Trial Tr. vol. 1, 393:13–396:7; *Burks*, Kimberly Burks Test., Trial Tr. vol. 1, 340:16–344:10; *Burks*, Debra Ann Burks Test., Trial Tr. vol. 1, 414:23–417:3; *Burks*, C. L. Burks Test., Trial Tr. vol. 1, 478:13–482:16.

100. *Burks*, Beecham III Test., Trial Tr. vol. 1, 111:3; *Burks*, Debra Ann Burks Test., vol. 1, 412:8–413:25.

101. *Burks*, C. L. Burks Test., vol. 1, 466:18–23, 368: 24–470:17.

102. *Burks*, C. L. Burks Test., vol. 1, 475:15–22, 477:20–478:12.

103. *Burks*, C. L. Burks Test., vol. 1, 485:11–486:25.

104. See, e.g., *Burks*, Dr. Bolch Test., Trial Tr. vol. 2, 494:13–497:24; *Burks*, Dr. Buch Test., Trial Tr. vol. 2, 526:5–529:22; *Burks*, Dr. Grigson Test., Trial Tr. vol. 2, 557:16–566:16.

105. *Burks*, Asst. Dist. Att'y Garrigan Cl. Arg. on Guilt or Innocence, Trial Tr. vol. 2, 700:24–701:9.

106. This tendency is particularly evident in psychiatrists' continuous emphasis on psychotropic drug treatment. See, e.g., *Burks*, Dr. Vogtsberger Test., Trial Tr. vol. 1, 316:20–318:14; and *Burks*, Dr. Lett Test., vol. 2, 634:24–635:13. For a similarly decontextualized approach, see *Colburn*, 966 S.W.2d, Dr. Quijano Test., Trial Tr. vol. 25, 216:8–25, 232:17–234:17.

107. *Burks*, 583 S.W.2d, Dr. Lett Test., vol. 2, 669:2–18.

108. *Burks*, Dr. Grigson Test., vol. 2, 779:17–25. See also *Wilkens*, 847 S.W.2d, Dr. Allen Test., Trial Tr. vol. 33, 87:13–88:17; and *Wilkens*, Dr. McNeel Test., Trial Tr. vol. 33, 26:19–31:16, 32:15–33:17.

109. *Burks*, Dr. Lett Test., vol. 2, 634:19–435:10.

110. *Burks*, Dr. Vogtsberger Test., vol. 1, 316:20–318:14.

111. *Burks*, Dr. Lett Test., vol. 2, 634:13–18; *Burks*, Bobbie Rolen Test., Trial Tr. vol. 2, 817: 9–19; *Burks*, Lorene Rolen Test., Trial Tr. vol. 2, 820:7–11.

112. *Burks*, Stacey Test., Trial Tr. vol. 1, 344:24–346:24, 349:4–16.

113. Murray (2011), 288.

114. *Colburn*, 966 S.W.2d.

115. *Colburn*, Asst. Dist. Att'y Hileman Op. Arg. on Guilt or Innocence, Trial Tr. vol. 23, 4:1–6:11.

116. *Colburn*, Def. Att'y Crow Cl. Arg. on Guilt or Innocence, Trial Tr. vol. 26, 367:9–368:22.

117. *Colburn*, Asst. Dist. Att'y Hileman Op. Arg., vol. 23, 7:1–9:14.

118. *Colburn*, Asst. Dist. Att'y Hileman Cl. Arg. on Guilt or Innocence, Trial Tr. vol. 26, 403:8–11, 403:20–404:3.

119. *Colburn*, Dr. Quijano Test., vol. 25, 251:21–252:14.

120. *Colburn*, Def. Att'y Stover Cl. Arg. on Guilt or Innocence, Trial Tr. vol. 26, 383:16–18.

121. See *Buck v. Davis*, 137 S.Ct., at 764; Grissom (2011); and Acker (2017), 769–75.

122. *Colburn*, Dr. Quijano Test., vol. 25, 236:25–238:1.

123. Gronfein (1985).

124. *Colburn*, Dr. Quijano Test., vol. 25, 238:12–24.

125. *Colburn*, Fitzsimmons Test., Trial Tr. vol. 25, 178:4–15, 184:7–13, 184:21–185:15, 186:19–21.

126. *Colburn*, Fitzsimmons Test., vol. 25, 187:8–18.

127. *Colburn*, Fitzsimmons Test., vol. 25, 189:2–19.

128. *Colburn*, Fitzsimmons Test., vol. 25, 188:5–189:1.

129. *Colburn*, Fitzsimmons Test., vol. 25, 190:9–15, 192:4–7.

130. *Colburn*, Def. Att'y Stover Cl. Arg., vol. 26, 385:16–386:7.

Chapter 6

1. A. Adler (1924), 10.

2. *Eddings v. Oklahoma*, 455 U.S., at 872.

3. *Eddings*, at 873n1.

4. *Eddings*, at 872–73 (citation omitted).

5. *Eddings*, at 873n2 (citation omitted).

6. *Eddings*, at 873n2.

7. *Eddings*, at 873.

8. *Eddings*, at 874.

9. *Eddings*, at 876–78. See also *Woodson v. North Carolina*, 428 U.S. 280 (1976); *Lockett v. Ohio*, 438 U.S. 536 (1978); and *Skipper v. South Carolina*, 476 U.S. 1 (1986).

10. Pub. L. 93–247.

11. Despite these developments, child abuse is still underreported and has been so throughout the twentieth century. For instance, a study conducted in 1981 by the National Center for Child Abuse and Neglect estimated that only 33% of known child maltreatment cases were reported across the United States that year. These percentages are significantly lower when one focuses on incest, with one study showing that in 1984 only 2% of known cases of intrafamilial abuse were reported to the authorities (Russell 1983).

12. D. O. Lewis et al. (1979; 1988a; 1988b); Feldman et al. (1986); Widom (1989a; 1998b). See, in general, Haney (1995), 569–74.

13. Monahan (2001), 55. For similar arguments, see Gambarino, cited in Haney (1995), 547–609; Widom (1992), 1; K. A. Dodge et al. (1990), 1682; and Monahan (2001), 48.

14. Arenella (1995), 708; Feldman et al. (1986); D. O. Lewis et al. (1986); McCord (1994).

15. See *Wilkens v. State*, 847 S.W.2d; *Hawkins v. State*, 613 S.W.2d; and *Alvarado v. State*, 912 S.W.2d. This pattern is particularly striking if one considers that, already in 1989, the American Bar Association required capital defense attorneys to investigate defendants' family histories—including instances of emotional, sexual, and physical abuse—for the purpose of sentencing mitigation; see American Bar Association (1989; 2003). The U.S. Supreme Court turned this professional requirement into a constitutional mandate in *Wiggins v. Smith*, 539 U.S. 510 (2003).

16. See, e.g., *Wilkens*, 847 S.W.2d; *Hawkins*, 613 S.W.2d; and *Alvarado*, 912 S.W.2d. For exceptions, see *Gribble v. State*, 808 S.W.2d, at 75–76; and *Penry v. State*, 178 S.W.3d. *Strickland v. Washington*, 466 U.S. 668 (1984), a landmark U.S. Supreme Court ruling that established the minimum standards required to fulfill the Sixth Amendment's right to counsel in criminal cases, did little to address this professional negligence, given its "highly deferential" approach to the performance of defense counsel and the laxity of the two-pronged criteria used to establish whether such performance was ineffective.

17. See, e.g., *Rubenstein v. State*, 407 S.W.2d; and *Penry*, 178 S.W.3d.

18. See, e.g., *Freeman v. State*, 317 S.W.2d.

19. See Bright (1994), 1845–46, 1852–55; and Bright (2009), 2.

20. D. O. Lewis et al. (1979; 1986).

21. See, e.g., *Alvarado*, 912 S.W.2d, Def. Att'y Gates Op. Arg. on Punishment, Trial Tr. vol. 38, 5:21–6:6; *Alvarado*, Def. Att'y Harney Quest. Edgemon, Trial Tr. vol. 38, 82:19–83:3; and *Alvarado*, Dr. Follett Test., Trial Tr. vol. 38, 167:1–25.

22. These ideas were rooted in a wider communitarian ideology that, in the 1980s and 1990s, criticized the radical individualism and antigovernment populism of the Reagan presidency (1981–1989) while stressing the importance of communal rights

and bonds for the restoration of America's social fabric (Burke 2014). According to exponents of the communitarian view (which included then-president Bill Clinton), the neoliberal policies of the 1980s had gradually disintegrated America's social institutions and practices, creating a "mix of social anarchy and moral withdrawal" (Burke 2014). In this view, unless the United States balanced the individual rights and duties championed by the conservative establishment with social responsibilities toward the local communities, American society would become increasingly "normless," "self-centered," and ultimately criminogenic (Burke 2014). For criminologists drawing from the communitarian view, see, e.g., Currie (1994; 2019) and Young (1999).

23. *Alvarado*, 912 S.W.2d, Asst. Dist. Att'y Morgan Cl. Arg. on Punishment, Trial Tr. vol. 39, 392:14–393:3.

24. Haney (1995), 597. For examples of prosecutors advancing these arguments, see, e.g., *Penry*, 178 S.W.3d, Dr. Cunningham Test., Trial Tr. vol. 53, 290:23–294:7, 297:19–298:22; *Penry*, Asst. Dist. Att'y Hon Quest. Vogelsang Test., Trial Tr. vol. 50, 296:19–298:3; and *Penry*, Asst. Dist. Att'y Hon Quest. Dr. Pincus Test., Trial Tr. vol. 51, 146:3–147:2, 180:8–191:22. For scientific studies challenging this approach, see, e.g., D. O. Lewis et al. (1988a) and Masten and Garmezy (1985).

25. *Wilkens*, 847 S.W.2d.

26. See also *Alvarado*, 912 S.W.2d, Asst. Dist. Att'y Morgan Cl. Arg., vol. 39, 385:24–387:23; and *Penry*, 178 S.W.3d, Asst. Dist. Att'y Hon Cl. Arg., Trial Tr. vol. 58, 37:21–39:25.

27. *Wilkens*, 847 S.W.2d, Wilkens Jr. Test., Trial Tr. vol. 30, 71:13–79:20.

28. *Wilkens*, Wilkens Jr. Test., vol. 30, 12:10–22.

29. *Wilkens*, Wilkens Jr. Test., vol. 30, 13:2–7.

30. *Wilkens*, Wilkens Jr. Test., vol. 30, 19:9–23.

31. *Wilkens*, Wilkens Jr. Test., vol. 30, 20:9–15.

32. *Wilkens*, Wilkens Jr. Test., vol. 30, 20:17–21:6.

33. *Wilkens*, Wilkens Jr. Test., vol. 30, 40:15–42:8.

34. *Wilkens*, Wilkens Jr. Test., vol. 30, 52: 19–53:20.

35. *Wilkens*, Wilkens Jr. Test., vol. 30, 61:9–23, 66:10–67:8.

36. *Wilkens*, Wilkens Jr. Test., vol. 30, 71:13–77:6.

37. *Wilkens*, Dr. Crow Test., Trial Tr. vol. 29, 68:9–70:4, 71:21–72:8, 75:8–14; *Wilkens*, Dr. Hatton Test., Trial Tr. vol. 29, 128:16–23, 129:8–15; *Wilkens*, Dr. Rodriguez Test., Trial Tr. vol. 29, 156:5–158:10.

38. *Wilkens*, Dr. Crow Test., vol. 29, 68:9–70:4; *Wilkens*, Dr. Rodriguez Test., vol. 29, 157:18–158:5, 160:14–24.

39. See, e.g. *Wilkens*, Asst. Dist. Att'y Henry Quest. Dr. Allen Test., Trial Tr. vol. 31, 79:23–88:2; and *Wilkens*, Asst. Dist. Att'y Henry Quest. Dr. McNeel Test., Trial Tr. vol. 31, 15:8–24:3. See also *Burks v. State*, 583 S.W.2d, Dr. Bolch Test., Trial Tr. vol. 2, 494:13–497:24; *Burks*, Dr. Buch Test., Trial Tr. vol. 2, 526:5–529:22; and *Burks*, Dr. Grigson Test., Trial Tr. vol. 2, 557:16–566:16.

40. *Wilkens*, Asst. Dist. Att'y Henry Quest. Dr. Allen Test., vol. 31, 75:13–19.

41. *Wilkens*, Dr. Rodriguez Test., vol. 29, 157:18–158:5.

42. See also *Alvarado*, 912 S.W.2d, Edgemon Test., Trial Tr. vol. 38, 65:17–24; and *Alvarado*, Iglecias Test., Trial Tr. vol. 38, 287:14–288:18.

43. *Penry v. State*, 178 S.W.3d.

44. *Penry v. Lynaugh*, 492 U.S. 302 (1989); *Penry v. Johnson*, 532 U.S. 779 (2001).

45. *Penry v. State*, 178 S.W.3d, at 796; *Penry*, Gonzalez Test., Trial Tr. vol. 49, 71:7–75:24; *Penry*, Trudy Ross Test., Trial Tr. vol. 49, 148:24–158:19, 166:24–171:11; *Penry*, Kasicky Jr. Test., Trial Tr. vol. 47, 186:16–197:1; *Penry*, Barnett Test., Trial Tr. vol. 47, 163:7–166:14.

46. *Penry*, Dr. Pincus Test., Trial Tr. vol. 51, 240:5–9.

47. *Penry*, Kasicky Jr. Test., Trial Tr. vol. 47, 202:5–7.

48. *Penry*, Kasicky Jr. Test., vol. 47, 191:2–192:5.

49. *Penry*, Kasicky Jr. Test., vol. 47, 206:2–7.

50. *Penry*, Kasicky Jr. Test., vol. 47, 207:8–10.

51. *Penry*, Trudy Ross Test., vol. 49, 233:10–234:15; *Penry*, Vogelsang Test., Trial Tr. vol. 50, 105:21–107:18.

52. *Penry*, Johnson Test., Trial Tr. vol. 47, 255:17–258:8.

53. *Penry*, Vogelsang Test., vol. 50, 105:21–107:7.

54. *Penry*, Vogelsang Test., vol. 50, 135:8–137:14.

55. *Penry*, Vogelsang Test., vol. 50, 99:2–13.

56. *Penry*, Vogelsang Test., vol. 50, 100:3–6.

57. *Penry*, Vogelsang Test., vol. 50, 100:7–12.

58. *Penry*, Vogelsang Test., vol. 50, 182:14–186:12.

59. *Penry*, Vogelsang Test., vol. 50, 186:10–12.

60. *Penry*, Dr. Pincus Test., vol. 51, 146:23–147:2.

61. *Penry*, Dr. Pincus Test., vol. 51, 148:11–13. See D. O. Lewis et al. (1986; 1988a).

62. *Penry*, Dr. Pincus Test., vol. 51, 191:19–22.

63. *Penry*, Asst. Dist. Att'y Hon Cl. Arg. on Punishment, Trial. Tr. vol. 58, 37:21–39:10.

64. *Penry*, Dr. Gripon Test., Trial Tr. vol. 46, 37:4–22, 46:7–17, 48:22–50:10.

65. *Penry*, Dr. Saunders Test., Trial Tr. vol. 43, 213:2–218:4.

66. *Penry*, Dr. Gripon Test., vol. 46, 52:10–53:1.

67. *Penry*, Dr. Saunders Test., vol. 43, 236:25–237:16.

68. *Penry*, Dist. Att'y Price Quest. Dr. Price Test., Trial Tr. vol. 52, 124:14–125:13.

69. *Penry*, Asst. Dist. Att'y Hon Cl. Arg., vol. 58, 39:11–16, 22–25.

70. Hicks (2004), 23.

71. Sniderman and Piazza (1993); Quillian and Pager (2001); Chiricos and Eschholz (2002).

72. Hicks (2004), 22–23. See Kilgus et al. (1995), Iwamasa et al. (2000), and Delbello et al. (2001).

73. Baldus et al. (1997); Haney (2005).

74. Radelet and Vandiver (1986); Zimring (2004); Wacquant (2009); M. Alexander (2010); Perkinson (2010); Campbell (2011; 2012).

75. Perkinson (2010), 296–99, 303–4, 334–37.

76. Perkinson (2010), 336. See Hallinan (2003), 45; Mauer (2006), 61, 155–56; Abramsky (2007), 54; Wacquant (2009); Bosworth (2009); and M. Alexander (2010).

77. Harcourt (2015), 238–40.

78. Ekland-Olson (1988). See also W. J. Bowers and Pierce (1980).

79. *Hawkins*, 613 S.W.2d.

80. *Hawkins*, at 722–23.

81. *Hawkins*, Hawkins Test., Trial Tr. vol. 9, 1678:20–1679:2.

82. *Hawkins*, Def's Ex. 1, 7-page Handwritten Statement by Mr. Hawkins, 1958–1959.

83. *Hawkins*, Hawkins Test., vol. 9, 1679:2–4.

84. *Hawkins*, Hawkins Test., vol. 9, 1679:5–18, 1680:10–13.

85. *Hawkins*, Hawkins Test., vol. 9, 1679:10–1680:9.

86. *Hawkins*, Hawkins Test., vol. 9, 1682:19–1683:22.

87. *Hawkins*, Hawkins Test., vol. 9, 1682:11–18, 1684:2–1685:16.

88. *Hawkins*, Hawkins Test., vol. 9, 1686:16–24.

89. *Hawkins*, Hawkins Test., vol. 9, 1686:25–1687:3.

90. *Hawkins*, Boyett Jr. Test., Trial Tr. vol. 9, 1731:15–25.

91. *Hawkins*, Def's Ex. 1, 1961–1962.

92. *Hawkins*, Dr. Wall Test., Trial Tr. vol. 9, 1758:24–25.

93. *Hawkins*, Dr. Wall Test., vol. 9, 1754:23–1755:2, 1756:2–6, 1757:22–1758:2.

94. *Hawkins*, Def's Ex. 4, Psychological Summary from Dr. Richard Lee Wall on Samuel Hawkins, Date of Examination January 16 and 17, 1978, 1962§5.

95. *Hawkins*, Dr. Grigson Test., Trial Tr. vol. 9, 1811:13–1816:16.

96. *Hawkins*, Dr. Grigson Test., vol. 9, 1816:17–1818:24.

97. Haney (1995), 579–83.

98. Harvey, cited in Haney (1995), 582.

99. *Alvarado*, 912 S.W.2d.

100. *Alvarado*, at 203–4.

101. *Alvarado*, at 207.

102. *Alvarado*, Def. Att'y Gates Op. Arg. on Punishment, Trial Tr. vol. 38, 5:1–21; *Alvarado*, Dr. Follett Test., Trial Tr. vol. 38, 168:1–17, 164:24–165:21, 171:17–172:8.

103. *Alvarado*, Dr. Follett Test., vol. 38, 170:20–171:16.

104. *Alvarado*, Iglecias Test., Trial Tr. vol. 38, 242:20–249:22.

105. *Alvarado*, Gagnon Test., Trial Tr. vol. 38, 10:7–15:3; *Alvarado*, Meyers Test., Trial Tr. vol. 38, 53:4–54:12; *Alvarado*, Nava III Test., Trial Tr. vol. 38, 148:7–150:4.

106. *Alvarado*, Williams Test., Trial Tr. vol. 38, 24:6–26:3, 33:4–40:5, 43:8–15; *Alvarado*, Plaza Test., Trial Tr. vol. 38, 124:12–126:21.

107. *Alvarado*, Edgemon Test., Trial Tr. vol. 38, 58:19–20.

108. *Alvarado*, Edgemon Test., vol. 38, 62:18–19.

109. *Alvarado*, Edgemon Test., vol. 38, 69:19–70:15.

110. *Alvarado*, Edgemon Test., vol. 38, 70:19–23.

111. *Alvarado*, Edgemon Test., vol. 38, 65:17–24, 80:14–81:1; contra *Alvarado*, Iglecias Test., vol. 38, 239:19–241:2, 242:20–249:22; and *Alvarado*, Dr. Follett Test., vol. 38, 171:17–172:8.

112. *Alvarado*, Williams Test., vol. 38, 40:16–41:1.

113. Quintero and Estrada (1998), 152–53.

114. Casavantes (1976), 149.

115. Quintero and Estrada (1998), 155–56, 158.

116. Haney (1995), 585–88.

117. Jankowski, cited in Haney (1995), 587.

118. Quintero and Estrada (1998), 163.

119. *Alvarado*, Dr. Follett Test., vol. 38, 166:2–12.

120. *Alvarado*, Dr. Follett Test., vol. 38, 161:25–162:14.

121. See, e.g., Lanning (1992); Stidham et al. (2012); and Hughes (2017), 691.

122. *Alvarado*, Edgemon Test., vol. 38, 66:24–67:7, 68:23–69:11; *Alvarado*, Asst. Dist. Att'y Morgan Quest. Dr. Follett Test., Trial Tr. vol. 38, 186:14–187:16; *Alvarado*, Dr. Coons Test., Trial Tr. vol. 39, 336:18–337:12.

123. *Alvarado*, Dr. Coons Test., vol. 39, 337:6–8.

124. Paul Kaplan reached a similar conclusion in *Murder Stories* (2012), a study of capital punishment trials in early 2000s California.

125. Kaplan (2012), 85–132; Norrie (2014).

126. Norrie (2014), 29.

127. Norrie (2014), 262.

128. Norrie (2014), 263.

129. See, e.g., *Rubenstein*, 407 S.W.2d, Def. Att'y Belli Quest. Dr. Towler, Trial Tr. vol. 4, 967:6–971:14; *Lackey v. State*, 819 S.W.2d, Def. Att'y Brown Quest. Dr. McBride, Trial Tr. vol. 32, 5296:14–5305:13; and *Penry*, 178 S.W.3d, Def. Att'y Smith Quest. Dr. Pincus, Trial Tr. vol. 51, 103:19-132:19.

130. Kaplan (2012), 139–40.

131. Kaplan (2012), 140.

132. Another possible explanation is that late twentieth-century defense teams lacked the financial resources to conduct a thorough investigation into the defendants' social backgrounds, or that they were so imbued in the individualist logic that they never considered this aspect to be relevant.

Epilogue

1. *Atkins v. Virginia*, 536 U.S. 304 (2002).

2. Denno (2015; 2016).

3. N. Gordon and Greene (2018); Denno (2011).

4. Brown and Patterson (2011), 1.

5. Denno (2009), 330, 351–52; Denno (1996), 254.

6. *Clark v. Arizona*, 548 U.S. 735 (2006); Shannon (2006).

7. Vartkessian et al. (2017).

8. Tex. Code Crim. Proc. Ann., art. 37.01(b)1–2 (West 1991).

9. See *Sprouse v. State*, No. AP-74933, 2007 WL 283152 (Tex.Crim.App Jan. 31, 2007).

10. See, e.g., the case of Billy Joe Wardlow, a Texas death row inmate who challenged the constitutionality of the state's future dangerousness question for defendants under age 21 based on evidence showing that the parts of the brain linked to self-control continue to develop until the early 20s (Caplan 2020; Death Penalty Information Center 2020). For other examples, see Acker (2017).

11. See, e.g., Monahan (1981); Wiebusch et al. (1995); American Psychiatric Association Task Force (1974); *Barefoot v. Estelle*, 463 U.S. 880, American Psychiatric Association Amicus Curiae in Support of Petitioner (1983); and American Psychological Association (1978).

12. See, e.g., *Saldano v. State*, 70 S.W.3d 873, 885 (Tex.Crim.App. 2002); *Coble v. State*, 330 S.W.3d 253, 277–80 (2011); and *Buck v. Davis*, 137 S. Ct., at 769.

13. See *Tennard v. Dretke*, 542 U.S., at 274–75.

14. The Texas Defender Service, founded in 1995, offers both legal representation to capital defendants and professional training to trial lawyers across the state. According to the organization's website, the work of the service has "achieved countless victories for clients who faced the death penalty because of their mental illness, intellectual disability, and race," directly contributing to the steady decline in executions in the state (https://www.texasdefender.org/, accessed November 16, 2022).

15. See *Wiggins v. Smith*, 539 U.S. 510, at 2530–31; and State Bar of Texas (2006), 966–77.

16. *Sprouse*, 2007 WL 283152; *Milam v. State*, No. AP-76379, 2012 WL 1868458 (Tex.Crim.App. May 23, 2012); *Green v. State*, No. AP-76458, 2012 WL 4673756 (Tex. Crim.App. Oct. 3, 2012).

17. See, e.g., *Clark*, 548 U.S., at 2711–12; and *Kahler v. Kansas*, 140 S.Ct. 1021, 1022–24 (2020).

18. Denno (2009), 321; Denno (2015), 495, 503–4.

19. Denno (2009), 321.

20. Denno (2011), 993–94, 1014–15; Denno (2015), 507–11.

21. Denno (2009), 330, 351–52; Denno (1996), 254; Denno (2016), 75.

22. See Appelbaum et al. (2015), 134; Appelbaum and Scurich (2014); N. Gordon and Greene (2018); and Schweitzer and Saks (2011); but see also Gurley and Marcus (2008), 85–97.

23. See Chapter 1, Section "The Biological Paradigm and Its Diagnostic Limitations."

24. Freud (1957b).

25. Skinner (1972; 1985).

26. See, e.g., Libet (1985).

27. Libet (1985).

28. Morse (2011), 604.

29. See, e.g., *Snow v. State*, 291 S.W., Shepard Test., Trial Tr. 188–194. For exceptions, see *Penry v. State*, 178 S.W.3d, Dr. Pincus Test., Trial Tr. vol. 51, 232: 4–233:24.

30. Morse (2011), 611.

31. See, e.g., *Milam*, 2012 WL 1868458; and *Green*, 2012 WL 4673756.

32. *Tennard*, 542 U.S., at 274–75.

33. See Vartkessian et al. (2017).

34. Loughnan (2012), 49–57.

35. Heider (1958); Bordens and Horowitz (2002), 76.

36. Kammer (1982); Jones and Nisbett (1971).

37. Stevenson et al. (2010). See N. Gordon and Greene (2018), 79.

38. See, e.g., Fuchs and Flügge (2014).

39. Casey et al. (2008); Blakemore (2012); Caballero et al. (2016); S. Johnson (2022).

40. Davidson and McEwen (2012); Park and Huang (2010); Shaffer (2016).

41. This argument was first advanced by Wardlow's attorneys in their 2019 petition to the U.S. Supreme Court to stay Wardlow's execution. See *Wardlow v. Texas*, On Pet. for Writ of Cert. to the Tex. Crim. App. (U.S. 2019).

42. See, e.g., *Burks v. State*, 583 S.W.2d, Dist. Att'y Whaley Quest. Dr. Holbrook, Trial Tr. vol. 2, 796:11–798:15; and *Penry*, 178 S.W.3d, Dist. Att'y Cl. Arg. on Punishment, Trial Tr. vol. 58, 121: 13–16, 125:18–25. For a study suggesting that brain regulation interventions can be effective in the treatment of criminal psychopaths, see Konicar et al. (2015).

43. See Acker (2017), Harvard Law Review Association (2017), Sanger (2015), and Perlin (2016).

44. Research suggests that psychiatrists and lay individuals disproportionately use diagnoses such as conduct disorder and antisocial personality disorder to describe African Americans in mock forensic psychiatric evaluations. See Hicks (2004), 22–23; Kilgus et al. (1995); Iwamasa et al. (2000); and Delbello et al. (2001).

45. *Saldano*, 70 S.W.3d, at 885. See Acker (2017), 769–73.

46. *Buck*, 137 S.Ct., at 776–80.

47. *Buck*, 137 S.Ct., at 776–77.

48. *Buck*, at 769. Dr. Quijano used racist stereotypes to inform his future dangerousness predictions in five other cases in the 1990s, and all ended in a death sentence. In 1996 the Texas attorney general ordered that the defendants in these cases be granted a new sentencing hearing because of Dr. Quijano's prejudicial statements. However, he refused to grant a new hearing to Buck because, although in the other cases the prejudicial testimony was elicited by the state attorney, in Buck's trial it was presented by the defense lawyer. See *Buck*, at 769–70, 778–79 (citations omitted).

49. *Buck*, at 778.

50. In his dissenting opinion Justice Thomas recognized, and lauded, the limited impact that the *Buck* ruling would have on cases with slightly different sets of facts. *Buck*, at 781 (Justice Thomas, dissenting).

51. Harvard Law Review Association (2017), 271. The theory of constitutional color blindness was first developed by Justice Harlan in *Plessy v. Ferguson*, 163 U.S. 537 (1896) (Justice Harlan, dissenting).

52. López (2006b), 161.

53. See Steiker and Steiker (2015).

54. See Chapter 1, Section "Empirical Characteristics of the Sample."

55. See Chapter 3, Section "The 'Pathological' Black Family."

56. See Chapter 6, Section "Race, Psychopathy, and Future Dangerousness."

57. In the words of Justice Sotomayor, "The way to stop discrimination on the basis of race is to speak openly and candidly on the subject of race, and to apply the Constitution with eyes open to the unfortunate effects of centuries of racial discrimination" (*Schuette v. Coalition to Defend Affirmative Action*, 134 S. Ct. 1623, 1676 (2014) (Justice Sotomayor, dissenting)).

58. Ingle (2019); Di Nicola (2019); Kirmayer et al. (2011).

59. See Alarcón (2009).

60. On intersectionality theory, see, e.g., Cho et al. (2013), Carbado (2013), and Carbado et al. (2013).

References

Cases

Adams v. State, 577 S.W.2d 717 (Tex.Crim.App. 1979)
Ake v. Oklahoma, 470 U.S. 68 (1985)
Alexander v. State, 8 S.W.2d 176 (Tex.Crim.App. 1928)
Alvarado v. State, 912 S.W.2d 199 (Tex.Crim.App. 1995)
Apolinar v. State, 244 S.W. 813 (Tex.Crim.App. 1922)
Arnold v. State, 873 S.W.2d 27 (Tex.Crim.App. 1993)
Asbeck v. State, 156 S.W. 925 (Tex.Crim.App. 1913)
Atkins v. Virginia, 536 U.S. 304 (2002)
Barefoot v. Estelle, 463 U.S. 880 (1983)
Bingham v. State, 290 S.W.2d 915 (Tex.Crim.App. 1956)
Bradley v. State, 353 S.W.2d 864 (Tex.Crim.App. 1962)
Bryan v. State, 406 S.W.2d 210 (Tex.Crim.App. 1966)
Buck v. Bell, 274 U.S. 200 (1927)
Buck v. Davis, 137 S.Ct. 759 (2017)
Burgess v. State, 181 S.W. 465 (Tex.Crim.App. 1916)
Burks v. State, 583 S.W.2d 389 (Tex.Crim.App. 1979)
California v. Brown, 479 U.S. 538 (1986)
Clark v. Arizona, 548 U.S. 735 (2006)
Clautice v. Murphy, 180 Md. 558 (Md. 1942)
Coble v. State, 330 S.W.3d 253 (2011)
Colburn v. State, 966 S.W.2d 511 (Tex.Crim.App. 1998)
Covin v. State, 93 S.W.2d 428 (Tex.Crim.App. 1936)
Duke v. State, 182 S.W.2d 808 (Tex.Crim.App. 1944)
Eddings v. Oklahoma, 455 U.S. 104 (1982)
Edwards v. State, 114 S.W.2d 572 (Tex.Crim.App. 1938)
Ex parte Rodriguez, 164 S.W.3d 400 (Tex.Crim.App. 2005)
Ex parte Smith, 309 S.W.3d 53 (Tex.Crim.App. 2010)

Freeman v. State, 317 S.W.2d 726 (Tex.Crim.App. 1958)
Furman v. Georgia, 408 U.S. 238 (1972)
Gephart v. State, 249 S.W.2d 612 (Tex.Crim.App. 1952)
Gideon v. Wainwright, 372 U.S. 335 (1963)
Goss v. State, 826 S.W.2d 162 (Tex.Crim.App. 1992)
Green v. State, No. AP-76458, 2012 WL 4673756 (Tex.Crim.App. Oct. 3, 2012)
Gregg v. Georgia, 428 U.S. 153 (1976)
Gribble v. State, 808 S.W.2d 65 (Tex.Crim.App. 1990)
Gutierrez v. State, 175 S.W.2d 968 (Tex.Crim.App. 1943)
Harris v. Johnson, 81 F.3d 535 (5th Cir. 1996)
Harris v. State, 172 S.W. 975 (Tex.Crim.App. 1915)
Hawkins v. State, 613 S.W.2d 720 (Tex.Crim.App. 1981)
Hernandez v. Stephens, 537 F. App'x 531 (5th Cir. 2013)
Houston v. State, 287 S.W.2d 643 (Tex.Crim.App. 1956)
Hughes v. Johnson, 991 F.Supp 621 (Dist.Ct.Tex.-Galveston 1998)
Johnson v. State, 853 S.W.2d 527 (Tex.Crim.App. 1992)
Johnston v. State, 396 S.W.2d 404 (Tex.Crim.App. 1965)
Jones v. Johnson, 171 F.3d 270 (5th Cir. 1999)
Jones v. State, 131 S.W. 572 (Tex.Crim.App. 1910)
Jones v. State, 243 S.W.2d 848 (Tex.Crim.App. 1951)
Jordan v. State, 94 S.W.2d 741 (Tex.Crim.App. 1936)
Jurek v. Texas, 428 U.S. 262 (1976)
Kahler v. Kansas, 140 S.Ct. 1021 (2020)
Kansas v. Crane, 534 U.S. 407 (2002)
Kansas v. Hendricks, 521 U.S. 346 (1997)
Keeton v. State, 724 S.W.2d 58 (Tex.Crim.App. 1987)
Kizzee v. State, 312 S.W.2d 661 (Tex.Crim.App. 1958)
Lackey v. State, 819 S.W.2d 111 (Tex.Crim.App. 1989)
Lawrence v. Texas, 539 U.S. 558 (2003)
Leache v. State, 3 S.W. 539, 58 Am. Rep. 638 (App. 1886)
Leath v. State, 346 S.W.2d 346 (Tex.Crim.App. 1961)
Lindsey v. State, 260 S.W. 862 (Tex.Crim.App. 1924)
Lockett v. Ohio, 438 U.S. 536 (1978)
Maxey v. State, 145 S.W. 952 (Tex.Crim.App. 1912)
McCaine v. State, 211 S.W.2d 190 (Tex.Crim.App. 1948)
McCune v. State, 240 S.W.2d 305 (Tex.Crim.App. 1951)
McGee v. State, 238 S.W.2d 707 (Tex.Crim.App. 1950)
McKenny v. State, 288 S.W. 465 (Tex.Crim.App. 1926)
Milam v. State, No. AP-76379, 2012 WL 1868458 (Tex.Crim.App. May 23, 2012)
Miner v. State, 178 S.W.2d 268 (Tex.Crim.App. 1944)
Mines v. State, 852 S.W.2d 941 (Tex.Crim.App. 1994)
Mitchell v. State, 650 S.W.2d 801 (Tex.Crim.App. 1983)
M'Naghten's Case, House of Lords, 8 Eng. Rep. 718 (1843)

Moon v. State, 331 S.W.2d 312 (Tex.Crim.App. 1959)
Morales v. State, 458 S.W.2d 56 (Tex.Crim.App. 1970)
Morgan v. State, 117 S.W.2d 76 (Tex.Crim.App. 1938)
Morris v. State, 255 S.W. 744 (Tex.Crim.App. 1923)
Morrow v. State, 224 S.W.2d 481 (Tex.Crim.App. 1949)
Murray v. State, 182 S.W.2d (Tex.Crim.App. 1944)
Nobles v. State, 843 S.W.2d 503 (Tex.Crim.App. 1992)
Pappas v. State, 78 S.W.2d 619 (Tex.Crim.App. 1935)
Penry v. Johnson, 532 U.S. 779 (2001)
Penry v. Lynaugh, 492 U.S. 302 (1989)
Penry v. State, 178 S.W.3d 782 (Tex.Crim.App. 2005)
Plessy v. Ferguson, 163 U.S. 537 (1896)
Powell v. Alabama, 287 U.S. 45 (1932)
Richardson v. State, 879 S.W.2d 874 (Tex.Crim.App. 1993)
Robison v. State, 720 S.W.2d 808 (Tex.Crim.App. 1994)
Ross v. State, 220 S.W.2d 137 (Tex.Crim.App. 1948)
Roy Gene Smith v. Quarterman, 515 F.3d 392 (5th Cir. 2008)
Rubenstein v. State, 407 S.W.2d 793 (Tex.Crim.App. 1966)
Saldano v. State, 70 S.W.3d 873 (Tex.Crim.App. 2002)
Satterwhite v. State, 858 S.W.2d 412 (Tex.Crim.App. 1993)
Sattiewhite v. State, 786 S.W.2d 271 (Tex.Crim.App. 1989)
Schuette v. Coalition to Defend Affirmative Action, 134 S. Ct. 1623 (2014)
Shield v. State, 38 S.W.2d 76 (Tex.Crim.App. 1931)
Skipper v. South Carolina, 476 U.S. 1 (1986)
Smith v. State, 683 S.W.2d 393 (Tex.Crim.App. 1984)
Snow v. State, 291 S.W. 558 (Tex.Crim.App. 1927)
Sprouse v. State, No. AP-74933, 2007 WL 283152 (Tex.Crim.App. Jan. 31, 2007)
Stanton v. State, 158 S.W. 994 (Tex.Crim.App. 1913)
Tennard v. Dretke, 542 U.S. 274 (2004)
Thompson v. State, 77 S.W.2d 538 (Tex.Crim.App. 1936)
Turner v. Johnson, 106 F.3d 1178 (5th Cir. 1997)
Wardlow v. Texas, On Pet. for Writ of Cert. to the Tex. Crim. App. (U.S. 2019)
Welch v. State, 373 S.W.2d 497 (Tex.Crim.App. 1963)
Wiggins v. Smith, 539 U.S. 510 (2003)
Wilkens v. State, 847 S.W.2d 547 (Tex.Crim.App. 1992)
Wilkerson v. Collins, 950 F.2d 1054 (5th Cir. 1992)
Winn v. State, 126 S.W.2d 481 (Tex.Crim.App. 1939)
Woodson v. North Carolina, 428 U.S. 280 (1976)

Statutes

Child Abuse Prevention and Treatment Act (CAPTA), Pub.L. 93–247 (1974)
Tex. Code Crim. Proc. Ann., art. 37.01(b) 1–2 (West 1991)
Tex. Code Crim. Proc. Ann., art. 37.071(b) 1–3 (West 1974)

Tex. Code Crim. Proc. Ann., art. 37.071(f) (West 1974)
Tex. Penal Code Ann. §8.01 (West 1984)
Tex. Penal Code Ann. §8.01(a) (West 1974)
U.S. Constitution, Amendment V
Violent Crime Control and Law Enforcement Act, Pub.L. 103–322 (1994)

Academic References and Other Sources

Abbot, E. (1911). Meyer's Theory of the Psychogenic Origin of Dementia Praecox: A Criticism. *American Journal of Insanity*, 68, 15–22.

Abbott, A. (2001). Into the Mind of a Killer. *Nature*, 410, 296–98.

Abramsky, S. (2007). *American Furies: Crime, Punishment, and Vengeance in the Age of Mass Imprisonment.* Beacon Press.

Acker, J. R. (2017). Snake Oil with a Bite: The Lethal Veneer of Science and Texas's Death Penalty. *Albany Law Review*, 81, 751–806.

Ackerknecht, E. H. (1974). The History of the Discovery of the Vegetative (Autonomic) Nervous System. *Medical History*, 18(1), 1–8.

Adler, A. (1924). *The Practice and Theory of Individual Psychology.* Routledge, Trench, Trubner.

Adler, H. M. (1920). The Criminologist and the Courts. *Journal of the American Institute of Criminal Law and Criminology*, 11, 419–25.

Agamben, G. (1998). *Homo Sacer: Sovereign Power and Bare Life.* Stanford University Press.

Aichhorn, A. (1963). *Wayward Youth.* Viking Press.

Alarcón, R. D. (2009). Culture, Cultural Factors, and Psychiatric Diagnosis: Review and Projections. *World Psychiatry*, 8(3), 131–39.

Alexander, F., and Staub, H. (1956). *The Criminal, the Judge, and the Public: A Psychological Analysis*, rev. ed. Free Press.

Alexander, M. (2010). *The New Jim Crow: Mass Incarceration in the Age of Colorblindness.* New Press.

Alzheimer, A. (1910). *Beiträge zur Kenntnis der Pathologischen Neuroglia und Ihrer Beziehungen zu den Abbauvorgängen im Nervengewebe.* G. Fischer.

American Bar Association. (1989). *Guidelines for the Appointment and Performance of Counsel in Death Penalty Cases.* https://www.americanbar.org/content/dam/aba/administrative/death_penalty_representation/1989guidelines.pdf (accessed April 23, 2022).

American Bar Association. (2003). *Guidelines for the Appointment and Performance of Counsel in Death Penalty Cases.* https://www.americanbar.org/content/dam/aba/administrative/death_penalty_representation/2003guidelines.pdf (accessed April 23, 2022).

American Bar Association. (2013). *Evaluating Fairness and Accuracy in State Death Penalty Systems: The Texas Capital Punishment Assessment Report—Summary of the Report.* American Bar Association.

American Institute of Criminal Law. (1910). *Proceedings of the First National Confer-*

ence on Criminal Law and Criminology: Called in Celebration of the Fiftieth Anniversary of the Founding of Northwestern University School of Law, Chicago, Illinois, June 7 and 8, 1909. Northwestern University.

American Psychiatric Association. (1952). *Diagnostic and Statistical Manual of Mental Disorders.* American Psychiatric Association.

American Psychiatric Association. (1968). *DSM-II: Diagnostic and Statistical Manual of Mental Disorders.* American Psychiatric Association.

American Psychiatric Association. (1980). *DSM-III: Diagnostic and Statistical Manual of Mental Disorders.* American Psychiatric Association.

American Psychiatric Association Task Force. (1974). *Clinical Aspects of the Violent Individual.* American Psychiatric Association.

American Psychological Association. (1978). Report of the Task Force on the Role of Psychology in the Criminal Justice System. *American Psychologist*, 33, 1099–1110.

Amnesty International. (2006). *The Execution of Mentally Ill Offenders.* AMR 51/003/2006. Amnesty International.

Andreasen, N. C. (2006). DSM and the Death of Phenomenology in America: An Example of Unintended Consequences. *Schizophrenia Bulletin*, 33(1), 108–12.

Andrews, N. (2010). To Do No Harm: Medicine and the Death Penalty in England and Texas. In G. M. Bakken (ed.), *Invitation to an Execution: A History of the Death Penalty in the United States*, 285–320. University of New Mexico Press.

Ansbacher, H. L., and Ansbacher, R. R. (1956). *The Individual Psychology of Alfred Adler.* Basic Books.

Appelbaum, P. S., and Scurich, N. (2014). Impact of Behavioral Genetic Evidence on the Adjudication of Criminal Behavior. *Journal of the American Academy of Psychiatry and the Law*, 42, 91–100.

Appelbaum, P. S., Scurich, N., and Raad, R. (2015). Effects of Behavioral Genetic Evidence on Perceptions of Criminal Responsibility and Appropriate Punishment. *Psychology, Public Policy, and Law*, 21(2), 134–44.

Arenella, P. (1995). Demystifying the Abuse Excuse: Is There One? *Harvard Journal of Law and Public Policy*, 19, 703–9.

Arens, R., Granfield, D. D., and Susman, J. (1965). Jurors, Jury Charges, and Insanity. *Catholic University Law Review*, 14(1), 1–29.

Armstrong-Jones, R. (1918). The Relation of Alcohol to Mental States. *American Journal of Psychiatry*, 75(1), 133–54.

Arrigo, B. A., and Shipley, S. (2001). The Confusion over Psychopathy (I): Historical Considerations. *International Journal of Offender Therapy and Comparative Criminology*, 45, 325–44.

Baldus, D. C., Woodworth, G., Zuckerman, D., and Weiner, N. A. (1997). Racial Discrimination and the Death Penalty in the Post-*Furman* Era: An Empirical and Legal Overview with Recent Findings from Philadelphia. *Cornell Law Review*, 83, 1638–1770.

Banay, R. (1943). Immaturity and Crime. *American Journal of Psychiatry*, 100(2), 100–170.

Bandler, S. W. (1920). *The Endocrines*. W. B. Saunders.

Battaglini, G. Q., and Millar, R. W. (1914). Eugenics and the Criminal Law. *Journal of the American Institute of Criminal Law and Criminology*, 5(1), 12–15.

Baudrillard, J., and Levin, C. (1981). *For a Critique of the Political Economy of the Sign*. Telos Press.

Bayer, R. (1981). *Homosexuality and American Psychiatry: The Politics of Diagnosis*. Basic Books.

Beckett, K. (1999). *Making Crime Pay: Law and Order in Contemporary American Politics*. Oxford University Press.

Bederman, G. (2008). *Manliness and Civilization: A Cultural History of Gender and Race in the United States, 1880–1917*. University of Chicago Press.

Bender, L. (1947). Psychopathic Behavior Disorders in Children. In R. M. Lindner and R. V. Seliger (eds.), *Handbook of Correctional Psychology*, 360–77. Philosophical Library.

Bennett, W. J., DiIulio, J. J., and Walters, J. P. (1996). *Body Count: Moral Poverty and How to Win America's War Against Crime and Drugs*. Simon & Schuster.

Bergler, E., and Meerloo, J. A. M. (1963). *Justice and Injustice: The Origin of the Sense of Justice and Its Relation to Everyday Life, the Law, and the Problems of Juvenile Delinquency and Crime*. Grune & Stratton.

Berkman, E. F. (1989). Mental Illness as an Aggravating Circumstance in Capital Sentencing. *Columbia Law Review*, 89(2), 291–309.

Bernard, L. L. (1925). *Instinct: A Study in Social Psychology*. Henry Holt.

Beuttler, F. W., and Bell, C. C. (2010). *For the Welfare of Every Child: A Brief History of the Institute for Juvenile Research, 1909–2010*. University of Illinois.

Bevis, W. M. (1921). Psychological Traits of the Southern Negro with Observations as to Some of His Psychoses. *American Journal of Psychiatry*, 78(1), 69–78.

Blair, J., Mitchell, D., and Blair, K. (2005). *The Psychopath: Emotion and the Brain*. Blackwell.

Blakemore, S. J. (2012). Development of the Social Brain in Adolescence. *Journal of the Royal Society of Medicine*, 105(3), 111–16.

Blume, J. H., and Johnson, S. L. (2003). Killing the Non-Willing: Atkins, the Volitionally Incapacitated, and the Death Penalty. *South Carolina Law Review*, 55(1), 93–143.

Blume, J. H., Johnson, S. L., and Seeds, C. (2008). Of Atkins and Men: Deviations from Clinical Definitions of Mental Retardation in Death Penalty Cases. *Cornell Journal of Law and Public Policy*, 18(3), 689–733.

Bonnie, R. J., and Slobogin, C. (1980). The Role of Mental Health Professionals in the Criminal Process: The Case for Informed Speculation. *Virginia Law Review*, 66(3), 427–522.

Bordens, K. S., and Horowitz, I. A. (2002). *Social Psychology*. Erlbaum Associates.

Bosworth, M. (2009). *Explaining U.S. Imprisonment*. Sage.

Bowers, P. E. (1917). The Criminal Insane and Insane Criminals. *American Journal of Psychiatry*, 74(1), 77–87.

Bowers, W. J., and Pierce, G. (1980). Arbitrariness and Discrimination Under Post-*Furman* Capital Statutes. *Crime and Delinquency*, 26, 563–635.

Bowie, A. D., and Williamson, J. M. (1959). The Sexual Psychopath: An Unsolved Problem in Texas. *Texas Law Review*, 38, 915–20.

Bowlby, J. (1951). *Maternal Care and Mental Health*, vol. 2. World Health Organization.

Bowman, K. M., and Engle, B. (1953). California Sexual Deviation Research. In *Review of Scientific Literature on Sexual Deviation*, 115–16. California State Department of Mental Hygiene.

Brakel, S. J., and Rock, R. S. (1971). *The Mentally Disabled and the Law*. University of Chicago Press.

Brennan, J. (1963). Law and Psychiatry Must Join in Defending Mentally Ill Criminals. *American Bar Association Journal*, 49(3), 239–43.

Briggs, L. V. (1923). Medico-Legal Insanity and the Hypothetical Question. *Journal of the American Institute of Criminal Law and Criminology*, 14(1), 62–74.

Bright, S. B. (1994). Counsel for the Poor: The Death Sentence not for the Worst Crime but for the Worst Lawyer. *Yale Law Journal*, 103(7), 1835–83.

Bright, S. B. (2009). Right to Counsel in Death Penalty and Other Criminal Cases: Neglect of the Most Fundamental Right and What We Should Do About It. *Journal of Law and Society*, 11(1–2), 1–30.

Brock, D. E., Sorensen, J., and Marquart, J. W. (1999). Racial Disparities in Capital Punishment in Texas After *Penry*. *Criminal Justice Studies*, 12(2), 159–72.

Bromberg, W. (1947). Emotional Immaturity and Antisocial Behaviour. *Journal of Clinical Psychopathology*, 8(3), 432–52.

Bromberg, W. (1948). *Crime and the Mind: An Outline of Psychiatric Criminology*. Lippincott.

Bromberg, W. (1953–1954). American Achievements in Criminology (1938 to 1950). *Journal of Criminal Law, Criminology and Police Science*, 44(2), 166–76.

Bronner, A. F. (1914). Research on the Proportion of Mental Defectives Among Delinquents. *Journal of the American Institute of Criminal Law and Criminology*, 5(4), 561–68.

Brown, A. S., and Patterson, P. H. (2011). Introduction. In A. S. Brown and P. H. Patterson (eds.), *The Origins of Schizophrenia*, 1–2. Columbia University Press.

Bryant, B. C. (2008). Expanding *Atkins* and *Roper*: A Diagnostic Approach to Excluding the Death Penalty as Punishment for Schizophrenic Offenders. *Missouri Law Journal*, 78(4), 905–37.

Bubany, C. P. (1974). The Texas Penal Code of 1974. *Southwestern Law Journal*, 28, 292–339.

Buchanan, J. M. (1886). Insanity in the Colored Race. *New York Medical Journal*, 44, 67–70.

Burke, R. H. (2014). The Case for a Radical Moral Communitarianism. *British Journal of Community Justice*, December 17. https://mmuperu.co.uk/bjcj/articles/the-case-for-a-radical-moral-communitarianism/ (accessed March 20, 2023).

Burnham, J. C. (1973). The Progressive Era Revolution in American Attitudes Toward Sex. *Journal of American History*, 59, 885–908.

Burnham, J. C. (1988). *Paths into American Culture: Psychology, Medicine, and Morals*. Temple University Press.

Burns, C. L. (1954). A Forgotten Psychiatrist—Baron Ernst von Feuchtersleben, MD, 1833. *Proceedings of the Royal Society of Medicine, Section of the History of Medicine*, 47(3), 190–94.

Burns, R. P. (2013). The Jury as a Political Institution: An Internal Perspective. *William & Mary Law Review*, 55(3), 805–35.

Burr, C. W. (1925). Crime from a Psychiatrist's Point of View. *Journal of the American Institute of Criminal Law and Criminology*, 16(4), 519–36.

Bychowski, G., and Curran, F. J. (1946). Current Problems in Medico-Legal Testimony. *Journal of Criminal Law and Criminology*, 37(1), 16–36.

Caballero, A., Granberg, R., and Tseng, K. Y. (2016). Mechanisms Contributing to Prefrontal Cortex Maturation During Adolescence. *Neuroscience and Biobehavioral Reviews*, 70, 4–12.

Campbell, M. C. (2011). Politics, Prisons, and Law Enforcement: An Examination of the Emergence of "Law and Order" Politics in Texas. *Law and Society Review*, 45(3), 631–65.

Campbell, M. C. (2012). Ornery Alligators and Soap on a Rope: Texas Prosecutors and Punishment Reform in the Lone Star State. *Theoretical Criminology*, 16(3), 289–311.

Caplan, L. (2020). Should Billy Joe Wardlow Be Executed for a Crime Committed When He Was Eighteen? *The New Yorker*, June 30. https://www.newyorker.com/news/news-desk/should-billy-joe-wardlow-be-executed-for-a-crime-committed-when-he-was-eighteen (accessed December 16, 2022).

Carbado, D. W. (2013). Colorblind Intersectionality. *Signs*, 38(4), 811–45.

Carbado, D. W., Crenshaw, K. W., Mays, V. M., and Tomlinson, B. (2013). Intersectionality: Mapping the Movements of a Theory. *Du Bois Review: Social Science Research on Race*, 10(2), 303–12.

Cardozo, B. (1931). What Medicine Can Do for Law. In B. Cardozo, *Law and Literature and Other Essays and Addresses*, 70–120. Harcourt, Brace.

Carrington, C. (1909). Sterilization of Habitual Criminals. *Virginia Medical Semi-Monthly*, 13, 421–22.

Carruthers, P., and Smith, P. K. (eds.) (1996). *Theories of Theories of Mind*. Cambridge University Press.

Carter, D. T. (1996). *From George Wallace to Newt Gingrich: Race in the Conservative Counterrevolution, 1963–1994*. Louisiana State University Press.

Casavantes, E. J. (1976). *El Tecato: Social and Cultural Factors Affecting Drug Use Among Chicanos*. National Coalition of Spanish Speaking Mental Health Organizations.

Case, I. (1919). The Correlation Between Mental Defect and Anomalies of the Hard Palate. *American Journal of Psychiatry*, 75(4), 501–20.

Casey, B. J., Getz, S., and Galvan, A. (2008). The Adolescent Brain. *Developmental Review*, 28(1), 62–77.

Cavadino, M. (1998). Death to the Psychopath. *Journal of Forensic Psychiatry*, 9(1), 5–8.

Channing, W. (1883). A Consideration of the Causes of Insanity. *Journal of Social Science*, 18, 68–92.

Chapin, J. B. (1909). The Insanity Defense for Crime. *American Journal of Psychiatry*, 66(1), 71–82.

Cheng, J. (2010). Frontloading Mitigation: The "Legal" and the "Human" in Death Penalty Defense. *Law and Social Inquiry*, 35(1), 39–65.

Chiricos, T., and Eschholz, S. (2002). The Racial and Ethnic Typification of Crime and the Criminal Typification of Race and Ethnicity in Local Television News. *Journal of Research in Crime and Delinquency*, 39(4), 400–420.

Cho, S., Crenshaw, K. W., and Mccall, L. (2013). Toward a Field of Intersectionality Studies: Theory, Applications, and Praxis. *Signs*, 38(4), 785–810.

Church, A., and Peterson, F. (1914). *Nervous and Mental Diseases*. Saunders.

Cleckley, H. (1941). *The Mask of Sanity: An Attempt to Reinterpret the So-Called Psychopathic Personality*. Henry Kimpton.

Cleckley, H. (1976). *The Mask of Sanity: An Attempt to Reinterpret the So-Called Psychopathic Personality*. Mosby.

Committee on Psychiatry and Law. (1954). *Criminal Responsibility and Psychiatric Expert Testimony*. Report no. 25. Group for the Advancement of Psychiatry.

Conklin, E. G. (1917). The Development of the Personality. *American Journal of Insanity*, 74(1), 123–28.

Connell, R. W. (1987). *Gender and Power*. Stanford University Press.

Connelly, M. T. (2018). *The Response to Prostitution in the Progressive Era*. University of North Carolina Press.

Creson, D. A. (2019). Mental Health. In *The Texas State Historical Association Handbook of Texas*. https://www.tshaonline.org/handbook/entries/mental-health (accessed January 6, 2022).

Cronin, T. E., Cronin, T. Z., and Milakovich, M. E. (1981). *U.S. v. Crime in the Streets*. Indiana University Press.

Cuddy, L. A., and Roche, C. M. (2003). *Evolution and Eugenics in American Literature and Culture, 1880–1940: Essays on Ideological Conflict and Complicity*. Bucknell University Press.

Cuordileone, K. A. (2012). *Manhood and American Political Culture in the Cold War*. Routledge.

Currie, E. (1994). *Reckoning: Drugs, the Cities, and the American Future*. Macmillan.

Currie, E. (2019). Market, Crime, and Community: Toward a Mid-Range Theory of Post-Industrial Violence. In L. M. Friedman and G. Fisher (eds.), *The Crime Conundrum: Essays on Criminal Justice*, 17–44. Routledge.

Curti, M. (1980). *Human Nature in American Thought: A History*. University of Wisconsin Press.

Curti, M. W. (1926). The New Lombrosianism. *American Institute of Criminal Law and Criminology*, 17(2), 247–51.

Danziger, K. (1979). The Materialist Repudiation of Wundt. *Journal of the History of Behavioural Sciences*, 15, 205–30.

Darwin, C. (1981 [1871]). *The Descent of Man, and Selection in Relation to Sex*. Princeton University Press.

Darwin, C. (1985 [1859]). *On the Origin of Species by Means of Natural Selection or the Preservation of Favoured Races in the Struggle for Life*. Penguin Classics.

Davenport, C. B. (1911). *Heredity in Relation to Eugenics*. Henry Holt.

Davidson, R. J., and McEwen, B. S. (2012). Social Influences on Neuroplasticity: Stress and Interventions to Promote Well-Being. *Nature Neuroscience*, 15(5), 689–95.

Deambrogio, C. (2020). The Mind on Trial: Mental Illness and Capital Punishment in America's Highest Execution State. PhD diss., University of Oxford.

Death Penalty Information Center. (2020). Neuroscience Experts: Brain Science Shows Texas' Use of Future Dangerousness to Sentence Those Under 21 to Death Is Unreliable, Unconstitutional. June 23. https://deathpenaltyinfo.org/news/neuroscience-experts-brain-science-shows-texas-use-of-future-dangerousness-to-sentence-those-under-21-to-death-is-unreliable-unconstitutional (accessed December 16, 2022).

Death Penalty Information Center. (2022a). Death Sentencing Rates. https://deathpenaltyinfo.org/facts-and-research/sentencing-data/death-sentencing-rates (accessed April 22, 2022).

Death Penalty Information Center. (2022b). Facts About the Death Penalty. https://documents.deathpenaltyinfo.org/pdf/FactSheet.pdf (accessed December 12, 2022).

De Grazia, E. (1954). The Distinction of Being Mad. *University of Chicago Law Review*, 22, 339–55.

Delbello, M. P., Lopez-Larson, M. P., Soutullo, C. A., and Strakowski, S. M. (2001). Effects of Race on Psychiatric Diagnosis of Hospitalized Adolescents: A Retrospective Chart Review. *Journal of Child and Adolescent Psychopharmacology*, 11(1), 95–103.

Denno, D. W. (1996). Legal Implications of Genetics and Crime Research. In G. Bock and J. Goode (eds.), *Genetics of Criminal and Antisocial Behaviour*, 248–64. Wiley.

Denno, D. W. (2003). Who Is Andrea Yates? A Short Story About Insanity. *Duke Journal of Gender Law and Policy*, 10, 1–139.

Denno, D. W. (2005). Criminal Law in a Post-Freudian World. *University of Illinois Law Review*, 601–774.

Denno, D. W. (2009). Behavioral Genetics Evidence in Criminal Cases: 1994–2007. In N. A. Farahany (ed.), *The Impact of Behavioral Sciences on Criminal Law*, 317–54. Oxford University Press.

Denno, D. W. (2011). Courts' Increasing Consideration of Behavioral Genetics Evidence in Criminal Cases: Results of a Longitudinal Study. *Michigan State Law Review*, 967–1047.

Denno, D. W. (2015). The Myth of the Double-Edged Sword: An Empirical Study of Neuroscience Evidence in Criminal Cases. *Boston College Law Review*, 56, 493–551.

Denno, D. W. (2016). The Place for Neuroscience in Criminal Law. In D. Patterson and M. S. Pardo (eds.), *Philosophical Foundations of Law and Neuroscience*, 69–83. Oxford University Press.

De Orio, S. (2017). The Invention of Bad Gay Sex: Texas and the Creation of a Criminal Underclass of Gay People. *Journal of the History of Sexuality*, 26(1), 53–87.

De River, J. P. (1949). *The Sexual Criminal: A Psychoanalytic Study*. Blackwell Scientific.

Derrida, J. (1973). *Speech and Phenomena, and Other Essays on Husserl's Theory of Signs*. Northwestern University Press.

Derrida, J. (1993). Structure, Sign, and Play in the Discourse of the Human Sciences. In J. Natoli and L. Hutcheon (eds.), *A Postmodern Reader*, 223–42. SUNY Press.

De Tarde, G. (1912). *Penal Philosophy*. Little, Brown.

Di Nicola, V. (2019). "A Person Is a Person Through Other Persons": A Social Psychiatry Manifesto for the 21st Century. *World Social Psychiatry*, 1, 8–21.

Dix, G. E. (1976). Administration of the Texas Death Penalty Statutes: Constitutional Infirmities Related to the Prediction of Dangerousness. *Texas Law Review*, 55(8), 1343–1414.

Dodge, K. A., Bates, J. E., and Pettit, G. S. (1990). Mechanisms in the Cycle of Violence (How Child Abuse Affects Later Aggressive Behavior). *Science*, 250(4988), 1678–83.

Dodge, P. L. (1922). Environment as It Influences the Development of the Juvenile Delinquent. *American Journal of Psychiatry*, 78(4), 629–36.

Doll, E. A. (1921). Classification of Defective Delinquents. *Journal of the American Institute of Criminal Law and Criminology*, 12(3), 360–68.

Douglas, W. O. (1955). The Durham Rule: A Meeting Ground for Lawyers and Psychiatrists. *Iowa Law Review*, 41, 485–95.

Drähms, A. (1900). *The Criminal, His Personnel and Environment*. Macmillan.

Dunn, K., and Kaplan, P. J. (2009). The Ironies of Helping: Social Interventions and Executable Subjects. *Law and Society Review*, 43(2), 337–68.

Durham, K. R., Jr. (1980). The Longview Race Riot of 1919. *East Texas Historical Journal*, 18(2), 13–24.

East, N. W. (1946). Sexual Offenders. *Journal of Nervous and Mental Diseases*, 103(6), 626–66.

Edens, J. F., and Cox, J. (2012). Examining the Prevalence, Role and Impact of Evidence Regarding Antisocial Personality, Sociopathy and Psychopathy in Capital Cases: A Survey of Defense Team Members. *Behavioral Sciences and the Law*, 30(3), 239–55.

Edens, J. F., Davis, K. M., Fernandez Smith, K., and Guy, L. S. (2013). No Sympathy for the Devil: Attributing Psychopathic Traits to Capital Murderers Also Predicts Support for Executing Them. *Personality Disorders: Theory, Research, and Treatment*, 4(2), 175–81.

Ekland-Olson, S. (1988). Structured Discretion, Racial Bias, and the Death Penalty: The First Decade After *Furman* in Texas. *Social Science Quarterly*, 69, 853–73.

Entzeroth, L. (2011). Challenge and Dilemma of Charting a Course to Constitutionally Protect the Severely Mentally Ill Capital Defendant from the Death Penalty. *Akron Law Review*, 44, 529–82.

Erickson, M. H. (1928). Study of the Relationship Between Intelligence and Crime. *American Institute of Criminal Law and Criminology*, 19(4), 592–635.

Espy, M. W., and Smykla, J. O. (2016). Executions in the United States, 1608–2002: The ESPY File. *Inter-University Consortium for Political and Social Research*. https://doi.org/10.3886/ICPSR08451.v5 (accessed March 5, 2020).

Etzioni, A. (1993). Is Bill Clinton a Communitarian? *National Civic Review*, 82(3), 221–25.

Ewing, C. P. (1982). Dr. Death and the Case for an Ethical Ban on Psychiatric and Psychological Predictions of Dangerousness in Capital Sentencing Proceedings. *American Journal of Law and Medicine*, 8(4), 407–28.

Eysenck, H. J. (2014 [1963]). *Uses and Abuses of Psychology*. Hauraki.

Fanon, F. (2008). *Black Skin, White Masks*. Grove Press.

Fass, P. S. (1993). Making and Remaking an Event: The Leopold and Loeb Case in American Culture. *Journal of American History*, 80(3), 919–51.

Feldman, M., Mallouh, K., and Lewis, D. O. (1986). Filicidal Abuse in the Histories of 15 Condemned Murderers. *Journal of the American Academy of Psychiatry and the Law*, 14(4), 345–52.

Fenichel, O. (1945). *The Psychoanalytic Theory of Neurosis*. W. W. Norton.

Fernald, G. G. (1912). The Defective Delinquent Class Differentiating Tests. *American Journal of Psychiatry*, 68(4), 523–94.

Fernald, M. R., Hayes, M. H. S., Dawley, A., and Ruml, B. (1920). *A Study of Women Delinquents in New York State*. Century.

Fingarette, H. (1972). *The Meaning of Criminal Insanity*. University of California Press.

Fitzpatrick, J. J. (1976). Psychoanalysis and Crime: A Critical Survey of Salient Trends in the Literature. *Annals of the American Academy of Political and Social Science*, 423(1), 67–74.

Fodor, J. A. (1987). *Psychosemantics: The Problem of Meaning in the Philosophy of Mind*, vol. 2. MIT Press.

Foucault, M. (1978). Nietzsche, Genealogy, History. *Semiotexte*, 3(1), 78–94.

Foucault, M. (1980). *Power/Knowledge: Selected Interviews and Other Writings, 1972–1977*. Pantheon.

Foucault, M. (1988). *Madness and Civilization: A History of Insanity in the Age of Reason*. Vintage.

Foucault, M. (1990). *The History of Sexuality*, vol. 1, *An Introduction*. Vintage Books.

Foucault, M. (2004). *Society Must Be Defended: Lectures at the Collège de France, 1975–76.* Penguin.

Freedman, E. B. (1987). "Uncontrolled Desires": The Response to the Sexual Psychopath, 1920–1960. *Journal of American History*, 74(1), 83–106.

Freud, S. (1953 [1905]). Three Essays on the Theory of Sexuality. In J. Strachey, A. Freud, and C. L. Rothgeb (eds.), *The Standard Edition of the Complete Psychological Works of Sigmund Freud*, vol. 7 (1901–1905), *A Case of Hysteria, Three Essays on Sexuality, and Other Works*, 123–246. Hogarth Press and the Institute of Psycho-Analysis.

Freud, S. (1955 [1918]). From the History of an Infantile Neurosis. In J. Strachey, A. Freud, and C. L. Rothgeb (eds.), *The Standard Edition of the Complete Psychological Works of Sigmund Freud*, vol. 17 (1917–1919), *An Infantile Neurosis and Other Works*, 7–123. Hogarth Press and the Institute of Psycho-Analysis.

Freud, S. (1957a [1914]). On Narcissism: An Introduction. In J. Strachey, A. Freud, and C. L. Rothgeb (eds.), *The Standard Edition of the Complete Psychological Works of Sigmund Freud*, vol. 14 (1914–1916), *On the History of the Psycho-Analytic Movement, Papers on Metapsychology, and Other Works*, 67–102. Hogarth Press and the Institute of Psycho-Analysis.

Freud, S. (1957b [1916]). Some Character-Types Met Within Psycho-Analytic Work. In J. Strachey, A. Freud, and C. L. Rothgeb (eds.), *The Standard Edition of the Complete Psychological Works of Sigmund Freud*, vol. 14 (1914–1916), *On the History of the Psycho-Analytic Movement, Papers on Metapsychology, and Other Works*, 309–33. Hogarth Press and the Institute of Psycho-Analysis.

Freud, S. (1958 [1913]). The Disposition to Obsessional Neurosis. In J. Strachey, A. Freud, and C. L. Rothgeb (eds.), *The Standard Edition of the Complete Psychological Works of Sigmund Freud*, vol. 12 (1911–1913), *The Case of Schreber, Papers on Technique, and Other Works*, 311–27. Hogarth Press and the Institute of Psycho-Analysis.

Freud, S. (1961a [1923]). The Ego and the Id. In J. Strachey, A. Freud, and C. L. Rothgeb (eds.), *The Standard Edition of the Complete Psychological Works of Sigmund Freud*, vol. 19 (1923–1925), *The Ego and the Id and Other Works*, 1–66. Hogarth Press and the Institute of Psycho-Analysis.

Freud, S. (1961b [1928]). Dostoevsky and Parricide. In J. Strachey, A. Freud, and C. L. Rothgeb (eds.), *The Standard Edition of the Complete Psychological Works of Sigmund Freud*, vol. 21 (1927–1931), *The Future of an Illusion, Civilization and Its Discontents, and Other Works*, 173–94. Hogarth Press and the Institute of Psycho-Analysis.

Freud, S. (1961c [1930]). Civilization and Its Discontents. In J. Strachey, A. Freud, and C. L. Rothgeb (eds.), *The Standard Edition of the Complete Psychological Works of Sigmund Freud*, vol. 21 (1927–1931), *The Future of an Illusion, Civilization and Its Discontents, and Other Works*, 64–225. Hogarth Press and the Institute of Psycho-Analysis.

Freud, S. (1964 [1940]). An Outline of Psychoanalysis. In J. Strachey, A. Freud, and

C. L. Rothgeb (eds.), *The Standard Edition of the Complete Psychological Works of Sigmund Freud*, vol. 23 (1937–1939), *Moses and Monotheism, an Outline of Psychoanalysis, and Other Works*, 183–94. Hogarth Press and the Institute of Psycho-Analysis.

Freud, S. (2014 [1908]). *Civilized Sexual Morality and Modern Nervous Illness*. Read Books.

Friedlander, K. (1949). Latent Delinquency and Ego Development. In K. Eissler and P. Federn (eds.), *Searchlights on Delinquency: New Psychoanalytic Studies Dedicated to Professor August Aichhorn on the Occasion of His Seventieth Birthday, July 27, 1948*, 205–15. Imago.

Frosch, J., and Bromberg, W. (1939). The Sex Offender: A Psychiatric Study. *American Journal of Orthopsychiatry*, 9, 761–67.

Fuchs, E., and Flügge, G. (2014). Adult Neuroplasticity: More than 40 Years of Research. *Neural Plasticity*, 1–11.

Fullilove, R. E. (1943). Syphilis and the Negro [letter to the editor]. *Journal of the American Medical Association*, 122(6), 764.

Garfinkle, H. (1949). Research Note on Inter- and Intra-Racial Homicides. *Social Forces*, 27(4), 369–81.

Garland, D. (2001). *The Culture of Control: Crime and Social Order in Contemporary Society*. University of Chicago Press.

Geil, G. A. (1945). The Similarity in Rorschach Patterns of Adult Criminal Psychopaths and Pre-Adolescent Boys. *Rorschach Research Exchange*, 9(4), 201–6.

Geil, G. A. (1948). The Goodenough Test as Applied to Adult Delinquents. *Journal of Clinical and Experimental Psychopathology*, 9(1), 62–82.

Gerassi, J. (1966). *The Boys of Boise: Furor, Vice, and Folly in an American City*. Macmillan.

Ghoshray, S. (2006). Tracing the Moral Contours of the Evolving Standards of Decency: The Supreme Court's Capital Jurisprudence Post-*Roper*. *Journal of Catholic Legal Studies*, 45(561), 600–606.

Giardino, A. E. (2009). Combat Veterans, Mental Health Issues, and the Death Penalty: Addressing the Impact of Post-Traumatic Stress Disorder and Traumatic Brain Injury. *Fordham Law Review*, 77(6), 2955–95.

Gilman, S. L. (1985). *Difference and Pathology: Stereotypes of Sexuality, Race, and Madness*. Cornell University Press.

Gitelson, M. (1964). On the Identity Crisis in American Psychoanalysis. *Journal of the American Psychoanalytic Association*, 12(3), 451–76.

Glass, G. V., and Rud, A. G. (2012). The Struggle Between Individualism and Communitarianism: The Pressure of Population, Prejudice, and the Purse. *Review of Research in Education*, 36(1), 95–112.

Glueck, B. C. (1918a). *Concerning Prisoners*. National Committee for Mental Hygiene, Incorporated.

Glueck B. (1918b). A Study of 608 Admissions to Sing Sing Prison. *Mental Hygiene*, 2, 85–151.

Glueck, B. (1923). *Types of Delinquent Careers.* National Committee for Mental Hygiene.

Glueck, S. (1928). Psychiatry and the Criminal Law. *Virginia Law Review*, 14(3), 155–81.

Glueck, S. (1932). Mental Hygiene and Crime. *Psychoanalytic Review*, 19(1), 23–35.

Glueck, S. (1937). Sex Crimes and the Law. *Nation*, September 25, pp. 318–20.

Glueck, S. (1962). *Law and Psychiatry: Cold War or Entente Cordiale?* Johns Hopkins University Press.

Glueck, S. (1964). Roscoe Pound and Criminal Justice: A Memoir in Appreciation of the Dean of American Legal Scholars. *Crime and Delinquency*, 10(4), 299–352.

Glueck, S., and Glueck, E. (1943). *Criminal Careers in Retrospect.* New York Commonwealth Fund.

Goddard, H. H. (1912). *The Kallikak Family: A Study in the Heredity of Feeble-Mindedness.* Macmillan.

Golding, S. L., Becker, E., Sherman, S., and Rappaport, J. (1975). The Behavioural Expectations Scale: Assessment of Expectations for Interaction with the Mentally Ill. *Journal of Consulting and Clinical Psychology*, 43(1), 109.

Goldstein, A. S. (1967). *The Insanity Defense.* Yale University Press.

Gordon, A. (1921). Medico-Legal Aspect of Morbid Impulses. *Journal of the American Institute of Criminal Law and Criminology*, 12(4), 604–16.

Gordon, N., and Greene, E. (2018). Nature, Nurture, and Capital Punishment: How Evidence of a Genetic-Environment Interaction, Future Dangerousness, and Deliberation Affect Sentencing Decisions. *Behavioral Sciences and the Law*, 36(1), 65–83.

Gorer, G. (1948). *The American People: A Study in National Character.* W. W. Norton.

Goring, C., Pearson, K., and Driver, E. D. (1972 [1913]). *The English Convict: A Statistical Study: Including the Schedule of Measurements and General Anthropological Data.* Patterson Smith.

Gowers, S. E. (1953). *Report of the Royal Commission on Capital Punishment (1949–1953).* HMSO.

Graham, J. J. (1962). What to Do with the Psychopath? *Journal of Criminal Law, Criminology, and Police Science*, 53(4), 446–52.

Green, T. A. (1995). Freedom and Criminal Responsibility in the Age of Pound: An Essay on Criminal Justice. *Michigan Law Review*, 93(7), 1915–2053.

Grissom, B. (2011). Lawyers Seek Reprieve for Death Row Inmate in Racially Tinged Case. *Texas Tribune*, August 31.

Grob, G. N. (1983). *Mental Illness and American Society, 1875–1940.* Princeton University Press.

Grob, G. N. (1991). From Hospital to Community: Mental Health Policy in Modern America. *Psychiatric Quarterly*, 62(3), 187–212.

Gronfein, W. (1985). Psychotropic Drugs and the Origins of Deinstitutionalization. *Social Problems*, 32(5), 437–54.

Grünbaum, A. (1984). *The Foundations of Psychoanalysis: A Philosophical Critique*, vol. 2. University of California Press.

Guerino, P., Harrison, P. M., and Sabol, W. J. (2011). *Prisoners in 2010*. U.S. Department of Justice, Bureau of Justice Statistics, December. https://bjs.ojp.gov/content/pub/pdf/p10.pdf (accessed December 16, 2022).

Gurd, A. E. (1920). The Structural Brain Lesions of Dementia Praecox. *American Journal of Psychiatry*, 77(2), 201–11.

Gurley, J. R., and Marcus, D. K. (2008). The Effects of Neuroimaging and Brain Injury on Insanity Defenses. *Behavioral Sciences and the Law*, 26(1), 85–97.

Guttmacher, M. S., and Weihofen, H. (1952). *Psychiatry and the Law*. Norton.

Haines, W. H., Hoffman, H. R., and Esser, R. A. (1948). Commitments Under the Criminal Sexual Psychopath Law in the Criminal Court of Cook County, Illinois. *American Journal of Psychiatry*, 105(6), 420–25.

Hale, N. G., Jr. (1971). *Freud and the Americans: The Beginning of Psychoanalysis in the United States, 1876–1917*. Oxford University Press.

Hale, N. G., Jr. (1995). *The Rise and Crisis of Psychoanalysis in the United States: Freud and the Americans, 1917–1985*. Oxford University Press.

Hall, G. S. (1904). The Natural Activities of Children as Determining the Industries in Early Education. *Journal of the Proceedings and Addresses of the Forty-Third Annual Meeting of the National Education Association*, 443–47.

Hallinan, J. T. (2003). *Going Up the River: Travels in a Prison Nation*. Random House.

Hamm, T. (2001). *Rebel and a Cause: Caryl Chessman and the Politics of the Death Penalty in Postwar California, 1948–1974*. University of California Press.

Haney, C. (1995). Social Context of Capital Murder: Social Histories and the Logic of Mitigation. *Santa Clara Law Review*, 35(2), 547–609.

Haney, C. (2005). *Death by Design: Capital Punishment as a Social Psychological System*. Oxford University Press.

Haney, C., Sontag, L., and Costanzo, S. (1994). Deciding to Take a Life: Capital Juries, Sentencing Instructions, and the Jurisprudence of Death. *Journal of Social Issues*, 50(2), 149–76.

Hans, V. P., and Slater, D. (1984). "Plain Crazy": Lay Definitions of Legal Insanity. *International Journal of Law and Psychiatry*, 7(2), 105–14.

Haraway, D. (1988). Situated Knowledges: The Science Question in Feminism and the Privilege of Partial Perspective. *Feminist Studies*, 14(3), 575–99.

Haraway, D. J. (2013). *Simians, Cyborgs, and Women: The Reinvention of Nature*. Routledge.

Harcourt, B. E. (2003). The Shaping of Chance: Actuarial Models and Criminal Profiling at the Turn of the Twenty-First Century. *University of Chicago Law Review*, 70(1), 105–28.

Harcourt, B. E. (2015). Risk as a Proxy for Race: The Dangers of Risk Assessment. *Federal Sentencing Reporter*, 27(4), 237–43.

Hare, R. D. (1993). *Without Conscience: The Disturbing World of the Psychopaths Among Us*. Pocket Books.

Hare, R. D. (1998). Psychopathy, Affect, and Behavior. In D. J. Cooke, A. E. Forth, and R. D. Hare (eds.), *Psychopathy: Theory, Research, and Implications for Society*, 105–38. Kluwer Academic.

Harris, R. (1989). *Murders and Madness: Medicine, Law, and Society in the Fin de Siècle*. Oxford University Press.

Hartman, A. (2008). *Education and the Cold War: The Battle for the American School.* Palgrave Macmillan.

Harvard Law Review Association (2017). Sixth Amendment, Ineffective Assistance of Counsel, Race, and Sentencing, *Buck v. Davis*. *Harvard Law Review*, 131(1), 263–72.

Healy, W. (1910). Individual Study of the Young Criminal. *Journal of the American Institute of Criminal Law and Criminology*, 1, 50–62.

Healy, W. (1915). *The Individual Delinquent: A Textbook of Diagnosis and Prognosis for All Concerned in Understanding Offenders*. Little, Brown.

Healy, W., and Bronner, A. F. (1943). *New Light on Delinquency and Its Treatment.* Yale University Press.

Heider, F. (1958). *The Psychology of Interpersonal Relations*. Wiley.

Henderson, C. R. (1893). *An Introduction to the Study of the Dependent, Defective, and Delinquent Classes*. D. C. Heath.

Herman, H. (2001). The Need for Mental Health Promotion. *Australian and New Zealand Journal of Psychiatry*, 35(6), 709–15.

Hermann, D. H., and Sor, Y. S. (1983). Convicting or Confining? Alternative Directions in Insanity Law Reform: Guilty but Mentally Ill Versus New Rules for Release of Insanity Acquittees. *Brigham Young University Law Review*, 1983(3), 499–508.

Hicks, J. W. (2004). Ethnicity, Race, and Forensic Psychiatry: Are We Color-Blind? *Journal of the American Academy of Psychiatry and the Law Online*, 32(1), 21–33.

Hoedemaker, E. D. (1948). Irresistible Impulse as a Defense in Criminal Law. *Washington Law Review and State Bar Journal*, 23(1), 1–7.

Hofstadter, R. (1963). *Anti-Intellectualism in American Life*. Vintage.

Hood, R., and Hoyle, C. (2015). *The Death Penalty: A Worldwide Perspective*. Oxford University Press.

Hoover, J. E. (1943). "Blaming the Parents." *Lapham's Quarterly*. https://www.laphamsquarterly.org/youth/blaming-parents (accessed December 12, 2022).

Hoover, J. E. (1947). How Safe Is Your Daughter? *American Magazine*, July 1947, p. 32.

Hoover, J. E. (1956–1957). Punish the Parent? *The Rotarian*, October 1956, pp. 24–26; March 1957, pp. 14–16; and May 1957, p. 2.

Hoover, J. E. (1963). Juvenile Delinquency or Youthful Criminality? *Syracuse Law Review*, 15, 660–68.

Horley, J. (2014). The Emergence and Development of Psychopathy. *History of the Human Sciences*, 27(5), 91–110.

Howell, T. J., Cobbett, W., and Jardine, D. (eds.). (1816). *A Complete Collection of*

State Trials and Proceedings for High Treason and Other Crimes and Misdemeanors: From the Earliest Period to the Year 1783, with Notes and Other Illustrations. T. C. Hansard for Longman, Hurst, Rees, Orme & Brown.

Hughes, S. (2017). American Monsters: Tabloid Media and the Satanic Panic, 1970–2000. *Journal of American Studies*, 51(3), 691–719.

Hulbert, H. S. (1939). Constitutional Psychopathic Inferiority in Relation to Delinquency. *American Institute of Criminal Law and Criminology*, 30(1), 3–21.

Hunter, J. D. (1914). Sterilization of Criminals. *Journal of the American Institute of Criminal Law and Criminology*, 5(4), 514–39.

Ingle, M. (2019). A Social Psychiatry Manifesto That Takes Social Context Seriously. Mad in America, October 17. https://www.madinamerica.com/2019/10/social-psychiatry-manifesto-takes-social-context-seriously/ (accessed December 16, 2022).

Ivins, M., and Dubose, L. (2000). *Shrub: The Short but Happy Political Life of George W. Bush*. Vintage.

Iwamasa, G. Y., Larrabee, A. L., and Merritt, R. D. (2000). Are Personality Disorder Criteria Ethnically Biased? A Card-Sort Analysis. *Cultural Diversity and Ethnic Minority Psychology*, 6(3), 284–96.

Izutsu, L. T. (2004). Applying *Atkins v. Virginia* to Capital Defendants with Severe Mental Illness. *Brooklyn Law Review*, 70, 995–1043.

Jackson, G. E. (2006). A Curious Consensus: "Brain Scans Prove Disease?" *Ethical Human Psychology and Psychiatry*, 8(1), 55–60.

Jasanoff, S. (2009). *Science at the Bar: Law, Science, and Technology in America*. Harvard University Press.

Johnson, A. M. (1949). Sanctions for Superego Lacunae of Adolescents. In K. Eissler and P. Federn (eds.), *Searchlights on Delinquency: New Psychoanalytic Studies Dedicated to Professor August Aichhorn on the Occasion of His Seventieth Birthday, July 27, 1948*, 225–45. Imago.

Johnson, G. B. (1941). The Negro and Crime. *Annals of the American Academy of Political and Social Science*, 217, 93–104.

Johnson, S. (2022). Why Is 18 the Age of Adulthood If the Brain Can Take 30 Years to Mature? Big Think, January 31. https://bigthink.com/neuropsych/adult-brain/ (accessed December 16, 2022).

Jones, E. E., and Nisbett, R. E. (1971). The Actor and the Observer: Divergent Perceptions of the Causes of Behavior. In E. Jones, D. E. Kanouse, H. H. Kelley, R. E. Nisbett, S. Valins, and B. Weiner (eds.), *Attribution: Perceiving the Causes of Behavior*, 79–94. General Learning Press.

Joseph, J., and Ratner, C. (2013). The Fruitless Search for Genes in Psychiatry and Psychology: Time to Re-Examine a Paradigm. In S. Krimsky and J. Gruber (eds.), *Genetic Explanations: Sense and Nonsense*, 94–106. Harvard University Press.

Kammer, D. (1982). Differences in Trait Ascriptions to Self and Friend: Unconfounding Intensity from Variability. *Psychological Reports*, 51(1), 99–102.

Kaplan, P. (2012). *Murder Stories: Ideological Narratives in Capital Punishment.* Lexington Books.

Kardiner, A., and Ovesey, L. (1967 [1951]). *The Mark of Oppression: Exploration in the Personality of the American Negro.* Meridian Books.

Karpman, B. (1935). *The Individual Criminal: Studies in the Psychogenetics of Crime.* Nervous and Mental Disease Publishing.

Karpman, B. (1940). The Principles and Aims of Criminal Psychopathology. *Journal of Criminal Psychopathology,* 1, 187–218.

Karpman, B. (1946). Psychopathy in the Scheme of Human Typology. *Journal of Nervous and Mental Disease,* 103(3), 276–88.

Karpman, B. (1947). Passive Parasitic Psychopathy: Toward the Personality Structure and Psychogenesis of Idiopathic Psychopathy (Anethopathy). *Psychoanalytic Review,* 34(2), 198–222.

Karpman, B. (1948). The Myth of the Psychopathic Personality. *American Journal of Psychiatry,* 104, 523–34.

Karpman, B. (1954). *The Sexual Offender and His Offenses: Etiology, Pathology, Psychodynamics, and Treatment.* Julian Press.

Kaut, K. (2011). Psychopharmacology and Mental Health Practice: An Important Alliance. *Journal of Mental Health Counseling,* 33(3), 196–222.

Kawin, E. (1963). *Parenthood in a Free Nation,* vol. 1. Macmillan.

Kendell, R. E. (1975). Psychiatric Diagnosis in Britain and the United States. *British Journal of Psychiatry,* 9, 453–61.

Kendell, R. E., Cooper, J. E., Gourlay, A. J., Copeland, J. R., Sharpe, L., and Gurland, B. J. (1971). Diagnostic Criteria of American and British Psychiatrists. *Archives of General Psychiatry,* 25, 123–30.

Kernberg, O. (1975). *Borderline Conditions and Pathological Narcissism.* J. Aronson.

Kiehl, K. A., and Hoffman, M. B. (2011). The Criminal Psychopath: History, Neuroscience, Treatment, and Economics. *Jurimetrics,* 51(4), 355–98.

Kilgus, M. D., Pumariega, A. J., and Cuffe, S. P. (1995). Influence of Race on Diagnosis in Adolescent Psychiatric Inpatients. *Journal of American Academy of Child Adolescence Psychiatry,* 34, 67–72.

Kinberg, O. (1914). Alcohol and Criminality. *Journal of the American Institute of Criminal Law and Criminology,* 5(4), 569–89.

Kirmayer, L. J., Narasiah, L., Munoz, M., Rashid, M., Ryder, A. G., Guzder, J., Hassan, G., Rousseau, C., and Pottie, K. (2011). Common Mental Health Problems in Immigrants and Refugees: General Approach in Primary Care. *Canadian Medical Association Journal,* 183(12), E959–E967.

Koch, J. L. A. (1892). *Die Psychopathischen Minderwertigkeiten,* vol. 2. Maier.

Koeninger, R. C. (1969). Capital Punishment in Texas, 1924–1968. *Crime and Delinquency,* 15(1), 132–41.

Kohut, H. (1971). *The Analysis of the Self.* International Universities Press.

Kohut, H. (1978). Thoughts on Narcissism and Narcissistic Rage. In H. Kohut,

The Search for the Self, ed. P. H. Ornstein, 2: 615–58. International Universities Press.
Konicar, L., Veit, R., Eisenbarth, H., Barth, B., Tonin, P., Strehl, U., and Birbaumer, N. (2015). Brain Self-Regulation in Criminal Psychopaths. *Scientific Reports*, 5(1), 1–7.
Krafft-Ebing, R. (1905). *Textbook of Insanity, Based on Clinical Observations*. F. A. Davis.
Kubie, L. (1960). *Practical and Theoretical Aspects of Psychoanalysis*. Praeger.
Kuppin, S., and Carpiano, R. M. (2006). Public Conceptions of Serious Mental Illness and Substance Abuse, Their Causes, and Treatments: Findings from the 1996 General Social Survey. *American Journal of Public Health*, 96(10), 1766–71.
Kurzweil, E. (1989). *The Freudians: A Comparative Perspective*. Yale University Press.
Lacey, N. (2010). Psychologising Jekyll, Demonising Hyde: The Strange Case of Criminal Responsibility. *Criminal Law and Philosophy*, 4(2), 109–33.
Lachter, B. (2001). "Chemical Imbalance": A Clinical Non Sequitur. *Australasian Psychiatry*, 9(4), 311–15.
Lamarck, J. B. (1914 [1809]). *Zoological Philosophy: An Exposition with Regard to the Natural History of Animals*. Hugh Elliot.
Lanning, K. (1992). *Investigator's Guide to Allegations of Ritual Child Abuse*. National Center for the Analysis of Violent Crime, Federal Bureau of Investigation. http://www.darksidecollective.org/RitualChildAbuse.pdf (accessed December 3, 2019).
Lane, B. (1995). *Chronicle of 20th Century Murder*. Berkley Books.
Langdon, F. W. (1917). Biologic Aspects of Dementia Praecox. *American Journal of Psychiatry*, 73(4), 681–92.
Larson, E. J. (1996). *Sex, Race, and Science: Eugenics in the Deep South*. Johns Hopkins University Press.
Laughlin, H. H. (1914). *The Legal, Legislative, and Administrative Aspects of Sterilization*. Eugenics Record Office, Bulletin 10A.
Laughlin, H. H. (1922). *Eugenical Sterilization in the United States*. Psychopathic Laboratory of the Municipal Court of Chicago.
Lave, T. R. (2008). Only Yesterday: The Rise and Fall of Twentieth Century Sexual Psychopath Laws. *Louisiana Law Review*, 69(3), 549–91.
Leeman, E. (2007). The Costs of Compliance. *Journal of the American Academy of Psychoanalysis and Dynamic Psychiatry*, 35(2), 179–87.
Lelling, A. E. (1993). Eliminative Materialism, Neuroscience, and the Criminal Law. *University of Pennsylvania Law Review*, 141(4), 1471–1564.
Levine, M. (1940). Normality and Maturity. *The Family*, 21(1), 18–26.
Levy, D. M. (1937). Primary Affect Hunger. *American Journal of Psychiatry*, 94(3), 643–52.
Levy, D. M. (1943). *Maternal Overprotection*. Columbia University Press.
Lewes, K. (1988). *The Psychoanalytic Theory of Male Homosexuality*. Simon & Schuster.
Lewis, B. (2010). *Moving Beyond Prozac, DSM, and the New Psychiatry: The Birth of Postpsychiatry*. University of Michigan Press.

Lewis, D. O., Lovely, R., Yeager, C., Ferguson, G., Friedman, M., Sloane, G., and Pincus, J. H. (1988a). Intrinsic and Environmental Characteristics of Juvenile Murderers. *Journal of the American Academy of Child and Adolescent Psychiatry*, 27(5), 582–87.

Lewis, D. O., Pincus, J. H., Feldman, M., Jackson, L., and Bard, B. (1986). Psychiatric, Neurological, and Psychoeducational Characteristics of 15 Death Row Inmates in the United States. *American Journal of Psychiatry*, 143(7), 838–45.

Lewis, D. O., Pincus, J. H., Bard, B., Richardson, E., Prichep, L. S., Feldman, M., and Yeager, C. (1988b). Characteristics of 14 Juveniles Condemned to Death in the United States. *American Journal of Psychiatry*, 145(5), 584–89.

Lewis, D. O., Shanok, S. S., Pincus, J. H., and Glaser, G. H. (1979). Violent Juvenile Delinquents: Psychiatric, Neurological, Psychological, and Abuse Factors. *Journal of the American Academy of Child Psychiatry*, 18(2), 307–19.

Libet, B. (1985). Unconscious Cerebral Initiative and the Role of Conscious Will in Voluntary Action. *Behavioral and Brain Sciences*, 8(4), 529–39.

Liddell, E. G. T. (1960). *The Discovery of Reflexes*. Clarendon Press.

Lindner, R. M. (1944). *Rebel Without a Cause: The Hypnoanalysis of a Criminal Psychopath*. Grune & Stratton.

Lindner, R. M. (1956). *Must You Conform?* Rinehart.

Lindquist, M. A. (2012). *Race, Social Science, and the Crisis of Manhood, 1890–1970: We Are the Supermen*. Routledge.

Lipton, H. R. (1949). The Psychopath. *Journal of Criminal Law and Criminology*, 40(5), 584–96.

Litton, P. (2018). Traumatic Brain Injury and a Divergence Between Moral and Criminal Responsibility. *Duquesne Law Review*, 56(35), 1–21.

López, I. F. H. (2006a). A Nation of Minorities: Race, Ethnicity, and Reactionary Colorblindness. *Stanford Law Review*, 59(4), 985–1063.

López, I. [F.] H. (2006b). *White by Law: The Legal Construction of Race*. New York University Press.

Lorand, S. (1939). Perverse Tendencies and Fantasies: Their Influence on Personality. *Psychoanalytic Review*, 26, 178–90.

Loughnan, A. (2012). *Manifest Madness: Mental Incapacity in the Criminal Law*. Oxford University Press.

Lowenfeld, H., and Lowenfeld, Y. (1970). Our Permissive Society and the Superego: Some Current Thoughts About Freud's Cultural Concepts. *Psychoanalytic Quarterly*, 39(4), 590–608.

Luhrmann, M. (2000). *Of Two Minds: An Anthropologist Looks at American Psychiatry*. Vintage.

Lunbeck, E. (1996). *The Psychiatric Persuasion: Knowledge, Gender, and Power in Modern America*. Princeton University Press.

Lynch, A. J., Perlin, M. L., and Cucolo, H. (2021). "My Bewildering Brain Toils in Vain": Traumatic Brain Injury, the Criminal Trial Process, and the Case of Lisa Montgomery. *Rutgers University Law Review*, 74(1), 215–70.

Lyotard, J. F. (1984). *The Postmodern Condition: A Report on Knowledge*, vol. 10. University of Minnesota Press.

Marquart, J. W., Ekland-Olson, S., and Sorensen, J. R. (1998). *The Rope, the Chair, and the Needle: Capital Punishment in Texas, 1923–1990*. University of Texas Press.

Marshall, W. (2012). The Forgotten Communitarian. *Democracy Journal*, summer. https://democracyjournal.org/magazine/25/the-forgotten-communitarian/ (accessed December 12, 2022).

Masten, A. S., and Garmezy, N. (1985). Risk, Vulnerability, and Protective Factors in Developmental Psychopathology. In B. B. Lahey and A. E. Kazdin (eds.), *Advances in Clinical Child Psychology*, 1–52. Springer.

Mauer, M. (2006). *Race to Incarcerate*. New Press.

Maughs, S. (1941). A Concept of Psychopathy and Psychopathic Personality: Its Evolution and Historical Development. *Journal of Criminal Psychopathology*, 2, 329–56, 465–99.

Mayer, E. E. (1948). Prefrontal Lobotomy and the Courts. *Journal of Criminal Law and Criminology*, 38(6), 576–83.

McCord, J. (1994). Aggression in Two Generations. In L. R. Huesmann (ed.), *Aggressive Behavior: Current Perspectives*, 241–51. Plenum.

McFarlane, H. (2013). Masculinity and Criminology: The Social Construction of Criminal Man. *Howard Journal of Criminal Justice*, 52(3), 321–35.

McKernan, M. (1924). *The Amazing Crime and Trial of Leopold and Loeb*. Plymouth Court Press.

Mehta, S., and Farina, A. (1997). Is Being "Sick" Really Better? Effect of the Disease View of Mental Disorder on Stigma. *Journal of Social and Clinical Psychology*, 16, 405–19.

Melossi, D. (2008). *Controlling Crime, Controlling Society: Thinking About Crime in Europe and America*. Polity.

Mendel, G. (1996 [1865]). Experiments in Plant Hybridization. https://www.mendelweb.org/mendel.html (accessed January 7, 2019).

Menninger, K. A. (1928). Medicolegal Proposals of the American Psychiatric Association. *Journal of the American Institute of Criminal Law and Criminology*, 19(3), 367–77.

Menninger, K. A. (1937). *The Human Mind*. Knopf.

Meynen, G. (2016). *Legal Insanity: Explorations in Psychiatry, Law, and Ethics*. Springer International.

Monahan, J. (1981). *The Clinical Prediction of Violent Behavior*. U.S. Government Printing Office.

Monahan, J. (2001). *Rethinking Risk Assessment: The MacArthur Study of Mental Disorder and Violence*. Oxford University Press.

Moriarty, J. C., Langleben, D. D., and Provenzale, J. M. (2013). Brain Trauma, PET Scans, and Forensic Complexity. *Behavioral Sciences and the Law*, 31(6), 702–20.

Morse, S. J. (1978). Crazy Behavior, Morals, and Science: An Analysis of Mental Health Law. *Southern California Law Review*, 51(4), 527–656.

Morse, S. J. (1982). Failed Explanations and Criminal Responsibility: Experts and the Unconscious. *Virginia Law Review*, 68(5), 971–1084.

Morse, S. J. (2011). The Status of Neurolaw: A Plea for Current Modesty and Future Cautious Optimism. *Journal of Psychiatry and Law*, 39(4), 595–626.

Mott, F. (1922). Insanity and the Reproductive Glands. *British Medical Journal*, 1(3194), 445–46.

Moynihan, D. P. (1965). *The Negro Family: The Case for National Action*. U.S. Government Printing Office.

Murray, T., Jr. (2006). The Other Side of Psychopharmacology: A Review of the Literature. *Journal of Mental Health Counseling*, 28(4), 309–37.

Murray, T., Jr. (2009). The Loss of Client Agency into the Psychopharmaceutical-Industrial Complex. *Journal of Mental Health Counseling*, 31(4), 283–308.

Murray, T., Jr. (2011). The Role of Psychopharmacology in Mental Health: A Response to Kaut. *Journal of Mental Health Counseling*, 33(4), 283–94.

Nixon, R. (1967). What Has Happened to America? *Reader's Digest*, October. http://college.cengage.com/history/ayers_primary_sources/nixon_1967.htm (accessed May 23, 2020).

Noguchi, H., and Moore, J. W. (1913). A Demonstration of *Treponema pallidum* in the Brain in Cases of General Paralysis. *Journal of Experimental Medicine*, 17(2), 232–38.

Norrie, A. (2014). *Crime, Reason, and History: A Critical Introduction to Criminal Law*. Cambridge University Press.

Nunberg, H. (1948). *The Practice and Theory of Psychoanalysis*. International Universities Press.

Ofer, U. (2019). How the 1994 Crime Bill Fed the Mass Incarceration Crisis. *ACLU News and Commentary*, June 4. https://www.aclu.org/news/smart-justice/how-1994-crime-bill-fed-mass-incarceration-crisis (accessed December 12, 2022).

O'Hagan, M. (1992). On Being "Not Quite Human": A Psychiatric Survivor's Perspective on Stigma. In D. Patten (ed.), *Public Attitudes to Mental Illness*, xvii–xxii. Health Research Services, New Zealand Department of Health.

O'Malley, M. (1914). Psychoses in the Colored Race. *American Journal of Psychiatry*, 71(2), 309–37.

Orton, S. T. (1913). A Study of the Brain in a Case of Catatonic Hirntod. *American Journal of Insanity*, 69(4), 669–731.

Osnato, M. (1919). A Critical Review of the Pathogenesis of Dementia Praecox, with a Discussion of the Relation of Psychoanalytic Principles. *American Journal of Psychiatry*, 75(3), 411–31.

Parenti, C. (2000). *Lockdown America: Police and Prisons in the Age of Crisis*. Verso.

Park, D. C., and Huang, C. M. (2010). Culture Wires the Brain: A Cognitive Neuroscience Perspective. *Perspectives on Psychological Science*, 5(4), 391–400.

Passerini, L. (1997). Youth as a Metaphor for Social Change: Fascist Italy and America in the 1950s. In G. Levi and J. C. Schmitt (eds.), *A History of Young People in the West: Stormy Evolution to Modern Times*, 2: 281–340. Harvard University Press.

Perkinson, R. (2010). *Texas Tough: The Rise of America's Prison Empire.* Picador/Henry Holt.

Perlin, M. L. (1987). Supreme Court, the Mentally Disabled Criminal Defendant, and Symbolic Values: Random Decisions, Hidden Rationales, or Doctrinal Abyss. *Arizona Law Review*, 29(1), 1–98.

Perlin, M. L. (1989). Unpacking the Myths: The Symbolism Mythology of Insanity Defense Jurisprudence. *Case Western Reserve Law Review*, 40(3), 599–731.

Perlin, M. L. (1999). Half-Wracked Prejudice Leaped Forth: Sanism, Pretextuality, and Why and How Mental Disability Law Developed as It Did. *Journal of Contemporary Legal Issues*, 10, 3–36.

Perlin, M. L. (2013). *The Shame of the States. Mental Disability, and the Death Penalty.* Rowman & Littlefield.

Perlin, M. L. (2016). Your Corrupt Ways Had Finally Made You Blind: Prosecutorial Misconduct and the Use of Ethnic Adjustments in Death Penalty Cases of Defendants with Intellectual Disabilities. *American University Law Review*, 65(6), 1437–60.

Peterson, F. (1895). Craniometry and Cephalometry in Relation to Idiocy and Imbecility. *American Journal of Psychiatry*, 52(1), 73–89.

Pettigrew, T. F. (1964). *A Profile of the Negro American.* Van Nostrand.

Pichot, P. (1978). Psychopathic Behaviour: A Historical Overview. In R. D. Hare and D. Schalling (eds.), *Psychopathic Behaviour: Approaches to Research*, 55–70. Wiley.

Polat, B. (2021). Mental Hygiene, Psychoanalysis, and Interwar Psychology: The Making of the Maternal Deprivation Hypothesis. *Isis*, 112(2), 266–90.

Porter, R. (2004). *Madmen: A Social History of Madhouses, Mad-Doctors, and Lunatics.* Tempus.

Quillian, L., and Pager, D. (2001). Black Neighbors, Higher Crime? The Role of Racial Stereotypes in Evaluations of Neighborhood Crime. *American Journal of Sociology*, 107(3), 717–67.

Quintero, G. A., and Estrada, A. L. (1998). Cultural Models of Masculinity and Drug Use: "Machismo," Heroin, and Street Survival on the U.S.-Mexico Border. *Contemporary Drug Problems*, 25(1), 147–68.

Radelet, M., and Vandiver, M. (1986). Race and Capital Punishment. *Crime and Social Justice*, 25, 94–113.

Ràdo, S. (1940). A Critical Examination of the Concept of Bisexuality. *Psychosomatic Medicine* 2(4), 459–67.

Rafter, N. H. (1997a). *Creating Born Criminals.* University of Illinois Press.

Rafter, N. H. (1997b). Psychopathy and the Evolution of Criminological Knowledge. *Theoretical Criminology*, 1(2), 235–59.

Rafter, N. H. (2004). The Unrepentant Horse-Slasher: Moral Insanity and the Origins of Criminological Thought. *Criminology*, 42(4), 979–1008.

Rafter, N. H. (2008). *The Criminal Brain: Understanding Biological Theories of Crime.* New York University Press.

Ralph, P. H., Sorensen, J. R., and Marquart, J. W. (1992). A Comparison of Death-

Sentenced and Incarcerated Murderers in Pre-*Furman* Texas. *Justice Quarterly*, 9, 185–209.

Rapaport, D. (1960). *The Structure of Psychoanalytic Theory: A Systematizing Attempt.* International University Press.

Rawlings, E. (1920). The Histopathologic Findings in Dementia Praecox. *American Journal of Psychiatry*, 76(3), 265–84.

Ray, I. (1838). *A Treatise on the Medical Jurisprudence of Insanity.* Little, Brown.

Ray, I. (1962 [1838]). *A Treatise on the Medical Jurisprudence of Insanity.* Winfred Overholser.

Read, J., and Harré, N. (2001). The Role of Biological and Genetic Causal Beliefs in the Stigmatisation of "Mental Patients." *Journal of Mental Health*, 10(2), 223–35.

Reedy, R. E. (1912). Insanity and Criminal Responsibility. *Journal of the American Institute of Criminal Law and Criminology*, 2(4), 521–45.

Richmond, F. C. (1931). The Criminal Feebleminded. *American Institute of Criminal Law and Criminology*, 21(4), 537–52.

Rieff, P. (1979). *Freud: The Mind of the Moralist.* University of Chicago Press.

Rieff, P. (1990). *The Feeling Intellect: Selected Writings.* University of Chicago Press.

Riesman, D., Glazer, N., and Denney, R. (1961). *The Lonely Crowd: A Study of the Changing American Character.* Yale University Press.

Roberts, J. D. (1883). Insanity in the Colored Race. *North Carolina Medical Journal*, 12, 249–59.

Robinson, P. (1976). *The Modernization of Sex: Havelock Ellis, Alfred Kinsley, William Masters, and Virginia Johnson.* Elek.

Robison, C. (1995). Bush Signs "Tough Love" Juvenile Crime Bill: Punishment Boosted for Young Offenders. *Houston Chronicle*, June 1.

Roche, P. Q. (1958). Criminal Responsibility and Mental Disease. *Tennessee Law Review*, 26, 222–31.

Rose, N. (1985). *Psychology, Politics, and Society in England, 1869–1939.* Routledge.

Rose, N. (1998). *Inventing Our Selves: Psychology, Power, and Personhood.* Cambridge University Press.

Rose, N. (2010). At Risk of Madness. In T. Baker and J. Simon (eds.). *Embracing Risk: The Changing Culture of Insurance and Responsibility*, 209–37. University of Chicago Press.

Rosen, R. (1982). *The Lost Sisterhood: Prostitution in America, 1900–1918.* Johns Hopkins University Press.

Rosenberg, C. E. (1968). *The Trial of the Assassin Guiteau: Psychiatry and the Law in the Gilded Age.* University of Chicago Press.

Rosenhan, D. L. (1973). On Being Sane in Insane Places. *Science*, 179, 250–58.

Rouke, F. L. (1950). Recent Contributions of Psychology to the Study of Criminogenesis. *Journal of Criminal Law and Criminology*, 41(4), 446–55.

Russell, D. E. (1983). The Incidence and Prevalence of Intrafamilial and Extrafamilial Sexual Abuse of Female Children. *Child Abuse and Neglect*, 7(2), 133–46.

Rutherford, H. R. C. (1922). Insanity and the Endocrine Glands [letter to the editor]. *British Medical Journal*, 1(3197), 581.

Sakala, L. (2014). *Breaking Down Mass Incarceration in the 2020 Census: State-by-State Incarceration Rates by Race/Ethnicity*. Prison Policy Initiative, May 28. https://www.prisonpolicy.org/reports/rates.html (accessed December 16, 2022).

Sampson, W. C. (1943). Syphilis and the Negro [letter to the editor]. *Journal of the American Medical Association*, 122(6), 764.

Sanger, R. M. (2015). IQ Intelligence Tests, Ethnic Adjustments, and *Atkins*. *American University Law Review*, 65(1), 87–150.

Sarbin, T. R., and Mancuso, J. C. (1970). Failure of a Moral Enterprise: Attitudes of the Public Toward Mental Illness. *Journal of Consulting and Clinical Psychology*, 35, 159–73.

Schlesinger, A. M., Jr. (1949). *The Vital Center: The Politics of Freedom*. Houghton-Mifflin.

Schlesinger, A. M., Jr. (1958). The Crisis of American Masculinity. *Esquire*, November 1. https://classic.esquire.com/article/1958/11/1/the-crisis-of-american-masculinity (accessed December 12, 2022).

Schmeiser, S. R. (2008). The Ungovernable Citizen: Psychopathy, Sexuality, and the Rise of Medico-Legal Reasoning. *Yale Journal of Law and the Humanities*, 20(2), 163–240.

Schorske, C. E. (1980). *Fin-de-siècle Vienna: Politics and Culture*. Knopf.

Schwartz, R. D., and Schwartz, I. (1977). Reducing the Stigma of Mental Illness. *Diseases of the Nervous System*, 38, 101–3.

Schweitzer, N. J., and Saks, M. J. (2011). Neuroimage Evidence and the Insanity Defense. *Behavioral Science and the Law*, 29, 592–607.

Scull, A. (1981). *Madhouses, Mad-Doctors, and Madmen: The Social History of Psychiatry in the Victorian Era*. University of Pennsylvania Press.

Seiden, J. A. (2003). The Criminal Brain: Frontal Lobe Dysfunction Evidence in Capital Proceedings. *Capital Defense Journal*, 16, 395–420.

Sellars, W. (1956). Empiricism and the Philosophy of Mind. In H. Feigl, M. Scriven, and W. Sellars (eds.), *The Foundations of Science and the Concepts of Psychoanalysis*, 253–329. University of Minnesota Press.

Sellers, A. V. (1926). *The Loeb-Leopold Case, with Excerpts from the Evidence of the Alienists and Including the Arguments to the Court by Counsel for the People and the Defense*. Classic.

Shaffer, J. (2016). Neuroplasticity and Clinical Practice: Building Brain Power for Health. *Frontiers in Psychology*, 7(1118), 1–12.

Shannon, B. D. (2006). The Time Is Right to Revise the Texas Insanity Defense: An Essay. *Texas Tech Law Review*, 39(1), 67–100.

Shartel, B. (1925). Sterilization of Mental Defectives. *Journal of the American Institute of Criminal Law and Criminology*, 16(4), 537–54.

Shelton, E. K. (1934). The Physical Make-Up as Related to Criminality. *Annals of the American Academy of Political and Social Science*, 175(1), 230–35.

Shiroma, E. J., Ferguson, P. L., and Pickelsimer, E. E. (2010). Prevalence of Traumatic Brain Injury in an Offender Population: A Meta-Analysis. *Journal of Correctional Health Care*, 16(2), 147–59.

Sifferd, K. L. (2006). In Defense of the Use of Commonsense Psychology in the Criminal Law. *Law and Philosophy*, 25(6), 571–612.

Simon, J. (2007). *Governing Through Crime: How the War on Crime Transformed American Democracy and Created a Culture of Fear.* Oxford University Press.

Skinner, B. F. (1972). *Beyond Freedom and Dignity.* Vintage.

Skinner, B. F. (1985). Cognitive Science and Behaviourism. *British Journal of Psychology*, 76(3), 291–301.

Slobogin, C. (2000). An End to Insanity: Recasting the Role of Mental Disability in Criminal Cases. *Virginia Law Review*, 86(6), 1199–1247.

Slobogin, C. (2003). What *Atkins* Could Mean for People with Mental Illness. *New Mexico Law Review*, 33, 293–314.

Smillie, W. G. (1943). Syphilis in the United States: Primarily a Negro Problem. *Journal of the American Medical Association*, 122(6), 365–66.

Smith, R. (1981). *Trial by Medicine: Insanity and Responsibility in Victorian Trials.* Edinburgh University Press.

Snider, S., and Kerr, E. (2022). Where Do I Fall in the American Economic Class System? *U.S. News and World Report*, August 25. https://money.usnews.com/money/personal-finance/family-finance/articles/where-do-i-fall-in-the-american-economic-class-system (accessed December 16, 2022).

Sniderman, P. M., and Piazza, T. (1993). *The Scar of Race.* Harvard University Press.

Snodgrass, L., and Justice, B. (2007). Death Is Different: Limits on the Imposition of the Death Penalty to Traumatic Brain Injuries. *Developments in Mental Health Law*, 26(2), 81–98.

Socarides, C. W. (1979). The Psychoanalytic Theory of Homosexuality with Special Reference to Therapy. In I. Rosen (ed.), *Sexual Deviation*, 243–77. Oxford University Press.

Southard, E. E. (1910). A Study of the Dementia Praecox Group in the Light of Certain Cases Showing Anomalies or Scleroses in Particular Brain-Regions. *American Journal of Psychiatry*, 67(1), 119–76.

Southard, E. E., and Canavan, M. M. (1917). The Stratigraphical Analysis of Finer Cortex Changes in Certain Normal-Looking Brains in Dementia Praecox. *Journal of Nervous and Mental Disease*, 45(2), 97–129.

Spangenberg Group. (1993). Executive Summary. In *A Study of Representation in Capital Cases in Texas*, i–xiii. Report prepared by the Spangenberg Group for the State Bar of Texas. https://capitalpunishmentincontext.org/files/resources/representation/Spangenberg%20Group%202.pdf.

Spaulding, E. R., and Healy, W. (1913). Inheritance as a Factor in Criminality. *Journal of the American Institute of Criminal Law and Criminology*, 4, 837–58.

Spencer, H. (1881 [1857]). *Progress: Its Laws and Causes.* Fitzgerald.

Speranza, G. C. (1901). The Medico-Legal Conflict over Mental Responsibility. *Green Bag*, 13, 123–26.

Spock, B. (1956). *Baby and Child Care*. Bodley Head.
Spock, B. (1963). *Problems of Parents*. Bodley Head.
State Bar of Texas. (2006). Guidelines and Standards for Texas Capital Counsel. *Texas Bar Journal*, November, 966–77.
Stedman Jones, G. (1971). *Outcast London: A Study in the Relationship Between Classes in Victorian Society*. Clarendon.
Steiker, C. S., and Steiker, J. M. (2012). Entrenchment and/or Destabilization: Reflections on (Another) Two Decades of Constitutional Regulation of Capital Punishment. *Law and Inequality: A Journal of Theory and Practice*, 30(2), 211–44.
Steiker, C. S., and Steiker, J. M. (2015). The American Death Penalty and the Invisibility of Race. *University of Chicago Law Review*, 1, 243–94.
Stevens, H. C. (1915). Eugenics and Feeblemindedness. *Journal of the American Institute of Criminal Law and Criminology*, 6(2), 190–97.
Stevenson, M. C., Bottoms, B. L., and Diamond, S. S. (2010). Jurors' Discussions of a Defendant's History of Child Abuse and Alcohol Abuse in Capital Sentencing Deliberations. *Psychology, Public Policy, and Law*, 16, 1–28.
Stidham, D., Fitzgerald, H., and Baldwin, J. (2012). Satanic Panic and Defending the West Memphis Three: How Cultural Differences Can Play a Major Role in Criminal Cases. *University of Memphis Law Review*, 42(4), 1061–1104.
Strecker, E. (1946). *Their Mothers' Sons: The Psychiatrist Examines an American Problem*. Lippincott.
Streib, V. L. (1989). Death Penalty for Female Offenders. *University of Cincinnati Law Review*, 58, 845–80.
Streib, V. L. (2002). Gendering the Death Penalty: Countering Sex Bias in a Masculine Sanctuary. *Ohio State Law Journal*, 63(1), 433–74.
Streib, V. L. (2005). Rare and Inconsistent: The Death Penalty for Women. *Fordham Urban Law Journal*, 33(2), 101–32.
Susman, W. (2012). *Culture as History*. Pantheon.
Swanson, A. (1960). Sexual Psychopath Statutes: Summary and Analysis. *Journal of Criminal Law, Criminology, and Police Science*, 51, 228–35.
Talbot, E. S. (1898). *Degeneracy: Its Causes, Signs, and Results*, vol. 35. Scott.
Texas Coalition Against the Death Penalty. (2007). Mental Illness and the Death Penalty in Texas: Know the Facts. https://tcadp.org/wp-content/uploads/2010/06/MIDP-Fact-Sheet-03-08.pdf (accessed March 18, 2020).
Texas Coalition Against the Death Penalty. (2016). Texas Death Penalty Developments in 2016: The Year in Review. https://tcadp.org/2016/12/15/texas-death-penalty-developments-2016-year-review/ (accessed March 18, 2020).
Texas Department of Criminal Justice. (2022). Death Row Information: Executed Inmates. https://www.tdcj.texas.gov/death_row/dr_executed_offenders.html (accessed December 16, 2022).
Texas State Library and Archives Commission. (n.d., a). *Texas Court of Criminal Appeals: An Inventory of Court of Criminal Appeals Centralized Court Case Files*

(Part I: File Numbers 2 thru 25000) at the Texas State Archives, 1909–1950. https://txarchives.org/tslac/finding_aids/50104.xml (accessed March 30, 2015).

Texas State Library and Archives Commission. (n.d., b). *Texas Court of Criminal Appeals: An Inventory of Court of Criminal Appeals Centralized Court Case Files (Part II: File Numbers 25001 thru 49719) at the Texas State Archives, 1950–1975.* https://txarchives.org/tslac/finding_aids/50105.xml (accessed March 30, 2015).

Texas State Library and Archives Commission. (n.d., c). *Texas Court of Criminal Appeals: An Inventory of Court of Criminal Appeals Centralized Court Case Files (Part III: File Numbers 49720 thru 71207) at the Texas State Archives, 1975–1990.* https://txarchives.org/tslac/finding_aids/30190.xml (accessed March 30, 2015).

Texas State Library and Archives Commission. (n.d., d). *Texas Court of Criminal Appeals: An Inventory of Court of Criminal Appeals Execution Case Files at the Texas State Archives, 1968–2012.* https://txarchives.org/tslac/finding_aids/30112.xml (accessed March 30, 2015).

Tolson, M. (2004). Effect of "Dr. Death" and His Testimony Lingers. *Houston Chronicle*, June 17.

Turner, D. B., Boccaccini, M. T., Murrie, D. C., and Harris, P. B. (2015). Jurors Report That Risk Measure Scores Matter in Sexually Violent Predator Trials, But That Other Factors Matter More. *Behavioral Sciences and the Law*, 33(1), 56–73.

Ussher, J. M. (2005). Unravelling Women's Madness: Beyond Positivism and Constructivism and Towards a Material-Discursive-Intrapsychic Approach. In W. Chan, D. E. Chunn, and R. Menzies (eds.), *Women, Madness, and the Law: A Feminist Reader*, 19–41. Glasshouse.

Valverde, M. (2009). *Law's Dream of a Common Knowledge.* Princeton University Press.

Vartkessian, E. S. (2011). Fatal Distraction: Does the Texas Capital Sentencing Statute Discourage the Consideration of Mitigating Evidence? PhD diss., University of Oxford.

Vartkessian, E. S. (2020). Including Assets-Based Mitigation in Sentencing. *Criminal Justice Policy Review*, 31(6), 857–85.

Vartkessian, E., Sorensen, J., and Kelly, C. (2017). Tinkering with the Machinery of Death: An Analysis of Juror Decision-Making in Texas Death Penalty Trials During Two Statutory Eras. *Justice Quarterly*, 34(1), 1–24.

Vaughan, V. C. (1914). Crime and Disease. *Journal of the American Institute of Criminal Law and Criminology*, 5(5), 688–94.

Wacquant, L. (2009). *Punishing the Poor: The Neoliberal Government of Social Insecurity.* Duke University Press.

Waelder, R. (1960). Basic Theory of Psychoanalysis. *Journal of the American Psychoanalytic Association*, 32, 587–602.

Walsh, K. (2017). Antisocial Personality Disorder and Donald DD: Distinguishing the Sex Offender from the Typical Recidivist in the Civil Commitment of Sex Offenders. *Fordham Urban Law Journal*, 44(3), 867–917.

Watson, J. B. (1919). *Psychology: From the Standpoint of a Behaviorist*. Lippincott.
Waxman, O. B. (2019). "It Just Goes On and On": How the Race Riots of 1919's "Red Summer" Helped Shape a Century of American History. *Time*, July 29. https://time.com/5636454/what-is-red-summer/ (accessed December 12, 2022).
Weber, M. (2012 [1905]). *The Protestant Ethic and the Spirit of Capitalism*. Dover.
Wechsler, I. S. (1930). The Legend of the Prevention of Mental Disease. *Journal of the American Medical Association*, 95(1), 24–26.
Weisman, R. (2008). Remorse and Psychopathy at the Penalty Phase of the Capital Trial: How Psychiatry's View of "Moral Insanity" Helps Build the Case for Death. *Studies in Law, Politics, and Society*, special issue "Law and Society Reconsidered," 41, 187–217.
Weissman, A. (1889). The Supposed Transmission of Mutilations. In E. B. Poulton, S. Shönland, and A. E. Shipley (eds.), *Essays upon Heredity and Kindred Biological Problems*, 1: 419–48. Clarendon Press.
Werlinder, H. (1978). *Psychopathy: A History of the Concepts—Analysis of the Origin and Development of a Family of Concepts in Psychopathology*. Almqvist & Wiksell.
Whyte, W. H. (2013 [1957]). *The Organization Man*. University of Pennsylvania Press.
Widom, C. S. (1989a). Child Abuse, Neglect, and Adult Behavior. *American Journal of Orthopsychiatry*, 59(3), 355–67.
Widom, C. S. (1989b). Does Violence Beget Violence? A Critical Examination of the Literature. *Psychological Bulletin*, 106(1), 3–28.
Widom, C. S. (1992). *The Cycle of Violence*. Washington, DC: National Institute of Justice.
Wiebusch, R. G., Baird, C., Krisberg, B., and Onek, D. (1995). Risk Assessment and Classification for Serious, Violent, and Chronic Offenders. In J. C. Howell, B. Krisberg, J. D. Hawkins, and J. J. Wilson (eds.), *Sourcebook on Serious, Violent, and Chronic Juvenile Offenders*, 429–68. University of Chicago Press.
Wiener, M. J. (1994). *Reconstructing the Criminal: Culture, Law, and Policy in England, 1830–1914*. Cambridge University Press.
Williams, K. (2004). Texas: Tough on Murderers or on Fairness. *Drake Law Review*, 53(3), 631–50.
Winick, B. J. (2009). Supreme Court's Evolving Death Penalty Jurisprudence: Severe Mental Illness as the Next Frontier. *Boston College Law Review*, 50(3), 785–858.
Wolberg, L. R. (1954). *The Technique of Psychotherapy*. Grune & Stratton.
Wuthnow, R. (2014). *Rough Country: How Texas Became America's Most Powerful Bible-Belt State*. Princeton University Press.
Wylie, P. (1942). *Generation of Vipers*. Farrar & Rinehart.
Young, J. (1999). *The Exclusive Society: Social Exclusion, Crime, and Difference in Late Modernity*. Sage.
Zaretsky, E. (2005). *Secrets of the Soul: A Social and Cultural History of Psychoanalysis*. Vintage Books.
Zedner, L. (1991). *Women, Crime, and Custody in Victorian England*. Clarendon Press.

Zilboorg, G. (1943). *Mind, Medicine, and Man.* Harcourt, Brace.

Zimring, F. E. (2004). *The Contradictions of American Capital Punishment.* Oxford University Press.

Zippia. (2022). Psychiatrist Demographics and Statistics in the U.S. https://www.zippia.com/psychiatrist-jobs/demographics/ (accessed December 16, 2022).

Index

THE CULTURAL LIVES OF LAW
Austin Sarat, Editor

The Cultural Lives of Law series brings insights and approaches from cultural studies to law and tries to secure for law a place in cultural analysis. Books in the series focus on the production, interpretation, consumption, and circulation of legal meanings. They take up the challenges posed as boundaries collapse between as well as within cultures, and as the circulation of legal meanings becomes more fluid. They also attend to the ways law's power in cultural production is renewed and resisted.

Daniel LaChance and Paul Kaplan, *Crimesploitation: Crime, Punishment, and Pleasure on Reality Television*
2022

Nesam McMillan, *Imagining the International: Crime, Justice, and the Promise of Community*
2020

Jeffrey R. Dudas, *Raised Right: Fatherhood in Modern American Conservatism*
2017

Renée Ann Cramer, *Pregnant with the Stars: Watching and Wanting the Celebrity Baby Bump*
2015

Sora Y. Han, *Letters of the Law: Race and the Fantasy of Colorblindness*
2015

Marianne Constable, *Our Word Is Our Bond: How Legal Speech Acts*
2014

Joshua C. Wilson, *The Street Politics of Abortion: Speech, Violence, and America's Culture Wars*
2013

Irus Braverman, *Zooland: The Institution of Captivity*
2012

Nora Gilbert, *Better Left Unsaid: Victorian Novels, Hays Code Films, and the Benefits of Censorship*
2012

Edited by Winnifred Fallers Sullivan, Robert A. Yelle, and Mateo Taussig-Rubbo, *After Secular Law*
2011

Keith J. Bybee, *All Judges Are Political—Except When They Are Not: Acceptable Hypocrisies and the Rule of Law*
2010

Susan Sage Heinzelman, *Riding the Black Ram: Law, Literature, and Gender*
2010

David M. Engel and Jaruwan S. Engel, *Tort, Custom, and Karma: Globalization and Legal Consciousness in Thailand*
2010

Ruth A. Miller, *Law in Crisis: The Ecstatic Subject of Natural Disaster*
2009

Ravit Reichman, *The Affective Life of Law: Legal Modernism and the Literary Imagination*
2009

Edited by David M. Engel and Michael McCann, *Fault Lines: Tort Law as Cultural Practice*
2008

William P. MacNeil, *Lex Populi: The Jurisprudence of Popular Culture*
2007

Edited by Austin Sarat and Christian Boulanger, *The Cultural Lives of Capital Punishment: Comparative Perspectives*
2005

Printed in the USA
CPSIA information can be obtained
at www.ICGtesting.com
JSHW081106170923
48585JS00001B/2

9 781503 630321